Corporations

BY JESSE H. CHOPER
University of California, Berkeley

MELVIN A. EISENBERG
University of California, Berkeley

Fifteenth Edition

THOMSON
WEST

EDITORIAL OFFICES: 1 North Dearborn St., Suite 650, Chicago, IL 60602
REGIONAL OFFICES: Chicago, Dallas, Los Angeles, New York, Washington, D.C.

PROJECT EDITOR
Steven J. Levin, B.A., J.D.
Attorney At Law

SERIES EDITOR
Elizabeth L. Snyder, B.A., J.D.
Attorney At Law

QUALITY CONTROL EDITOR
Sanetta M. Hister

Summary of Contents

Text Correlation Chart

Gilbert Law Summary CORPORATIONS	Choper, Coffee, Gilson *Corporations* 2004 (6th ed.)	Eisenberg *Corporations and Other Business Organizations* 2000 (8th ed.— Unabridged), 2004 Supp.	Eisenberg *Corporations and Other Business Organizations* 2000 (8th ed.— Concise), 2004 Supp.	Hamilton, Macey *Corporations Including Partnerships and Limited Liability Companies* 2003 (8th ed.)	Klein, Ramseyer, Bainbridge *Business Associations* 2003 (5th ed.)	O'Kelley, Thompson *Corporations and Other Business Associations* 2003 (4th ed.)
I. CHARACTERISTICS OF THE CORPORATION AND OTHER BUSINESS ORGANIZATIONS						
A. Corporations	Page 1-15	Page 100, 166-203, 219-262, 480	Page 67, 162-163	Page 16-29	Page 101, 287	Page 135, 136
B. General Partnerships	719-738	29-99; Supp. 1-2, 8-9	23-66; Supp. 1-10	10, 11, 30-159	92-196	47, 48, 68-77, 80-134
C. Joint Ventures	722-727	65-79	45-50	34	112	47, 48, 78, 79
D. Limited Partnerships	820-832	480-497; Supp. 2-8	342-354	11, 14, 161-198	196-198	50, 64
E. Limited Liability Partnerships ("LLPs")	844-845	518-519; Supp. 66, 67	371, 372	11, 60-66	287, 295	52, 548
F. Limited Liability Companies ("LLCs")	832-844	498-518	354-370	15, 16, 199-221	287-315	51, 466-485
G. Taxation of Noncorporate Entities	210, 717-719, 832	496-498; Supp. 45	342, 353, 354	2, 15, 161-175, 189	228, 287	
II. ORGANIZING THE CORPORATION						
A. Formalities in Organizing a Corporation	15-25, 237-244	101-114	68-75, 107-114	259-275	199-231	135-187
B. Defects in Formation Process— "De Jure" and "De Facto" Corporations	245-255	117-126	78-85	297-314	199-204, 716-726	554, 600-609, 644, 645
C. Disregard of Corporate Entity	255-285	219-257, 262, 263	173-185	315-366	206-231	501-547
D. Subordination of Shareholder Debts—"Deep Rock" Doctrine	285	258-261	186, 187	367-381	860-861	517
III. LIABILITIES FOR TRANSACTIONS BEFORE INCORPORATION						
A. Promoters	293	114-116	76	285-288	199	551-553
B. Contracts Made by Promoters on Corporation's Behalf	293-306		76-78	288-294	199-205	549-559
C. Obligations of Predecessor Business	286-293		44, 45, 883-885	375-381	206-231	488-500
IV. POWERS OF THE CORPORATION						
A. Corporate Powers	35-39, 79, 82, 242	127, 139-147	98-107	275-285	270-286	221-230
B. Ultra Vires Transactions	67-74	126-129	85-91	275-285	270	576-578

Gilbert Law Summary CORPORATIONS	Choper, Coffee, Gilson *Corporations* 2004 (6th ed.)	Eisenberg *Corporations and Other Business Organizations* 2000 (8th ed.— Unabridged), 2004 Supp.	Eisenberg *Corporations and Other Business Organizations* 2000 (8th ed.— Concise), 2004 Supp.	Hamilton, Macey *Corporations Including Partnerships and Limited Liability Companies* 2003 (8th ed.)	Klein, Ramseyer, Bainbridge *Business Associations* 2003 (5th ed.)	O'Kelley, Thompson *Corporations and Other Business Associations* 2003 (4th ed.)
V. MANAGEMENT AND CONTROL						
A. Allocation of Powers Between Directors and Shareholders	55-57, 553-591, 738-781	166-203, 338-400; Supp. 10-34, 43	123-146, 267-279; Supp. 10-34	499-592, 659-683	539, 606-671	276-318, 381-407
B. Directors	55-59, 74-112, 139-164, 617-621, 642-657, 740, 772-781	169, 181, 203-210, 220, 371-383, 520-597, 637-669; Supp. 10-34, 70-83, 92-112	126, 149-152, 321, 322, 373-433, 464-478, Supp. 80-83	274, 275, 499-528, 608-621, 659-713, 800-907	316-377, 395-403	136, 137, 150-174, 221-323
C. Officers	59-67, 114-130	210-214, 520-597; Supp. 70-83	152-157, 373-433; Supp. 80-83	608-620	316-377	156, 165, 550-576
D. Conflicts of Interest in Corporate Transactions	114-183	334-337, 622-736; Supp. 92-112	434-495; Supp. 112-118	908-973	368-403	276-369, 407-411, 609-630
VI. INSIDER TRADING						
A. Introduction	307-314	768-774	544-548	974	377	
B. Section 10(b) and Rule 10b-5	358-443, 457-517	774-875; Supp. 150-217	549-619; Supp. 150-217	975-1076, 1091-1133	443-510	872-936, 986-1004
C. Section 16 of the 1934 Act	517-541	876-912; Supp. 209-217	620-634	1084-1090	512-523	1037
D. Section 16(b) Compared to Rule 10b-5						
E. Common Law Liability for Insider Trading	541-553	912-927	635-650	976		983-985
VII. RIGHTS OF SHAREHOLDERS						
A. Voting Rights	553-710, 763-772	159, 181, 188, 189, 207, 215-219, 285-337, 354-371; Supp. 40-42	208-242, 256-283; Supp. 40-42	383, 529-607, 723-798	539-637	146-174, 197-220, 835-866
B. Restrictions on Transfer of Shares	742-751	422-440, 737	307-319	573-578	644-671	452-465
C. Shareholders' Informational Rights	642-658	264-285; Supp. 35-40	189-208; Supp. 35-40	1254-1275	579-591	216-220, 829-866
D. Fiduciary Obligations of Controlling Shareholders	782-790, 1084-1104	388-403, 697-767; Supp. 43-45, 112-149	284-295, 481-543; Supp. 43, 44, 118-133	621-642, 908-973	300-303, 377-395, 638, 695-714	276-295, 311-317, 413-437, 680-704
E. Shareholder Suits	847-962	928-1060; Supp. 218-241	651-747; Supp. 218-241	800-907	232-269, 525-538	324-369, 427-429, 841-848
VIII. CAPITALIZATION OF THE CORPORATION						
A. Shares—In General	13-15, 204, 215-220, 600	108	70-75, 138, 266, 908, 909	383, 384	199, 404, 405, 594, 595	11, 137, 182
B. Classes of Shares—Preferences	205, 206	109-113, 188, 189, 347-349, 369-371, 663	70, 72-75	384-389	393, 700-702	144
C. Authorization and Issuance of Shares	224-227, 230, 242-244	1332, 1333, 1336-1342	924-940	392-400	403-405, 417	176-179

Gilbert Law Summary CORPORATIONS	Choper, Coffee, Gilson *Corporations* 2004 (6th ed.)	Eisenberg *Corporations and Other Business Organizations* 2000 (8th ed.— Unabridged), 2004 Supp.	Eisenberg *Corporations and Other Business Organizations* 2000 (8th ed.— Concise), 2004 Supp.	Hamilton, Macey *Corporations Including Partnerships and Limited Liability Companies* 2003 (8th ed.)	Klein, Ramseyer, Bainbridge *Business Associations* 2003 (5th ed.)	O'Kelley, Thompson *Corporations and Other Business Associations* 2003 (4th ed.)
D. Stock Subscriptions	286-295	113, 114, 1284	75-78	391		178
E. Consideration Required to Be Paid for Shares	23, 224-227, 925-929	1281-1284	883-887	392-407	206-211	490, 491
F. Fiduciary Duties of Promoters	232-235, 293-306	114-116	76-84	285-297	199-204	221, 551-553
G. Preemptive Rights	151, 152, 242	108, 109, 939, 945	69, 70	443-458	385-395, 443-445, 592-638	144
H. Underwriting	344-346	1289-1292, 1332-1336	905-908	421	403-415	
I. Statutes Regulating Issuance of Shares	23-27, 307-433	1308-1394; Supp 283-287	901-960; Supp. 283-287	418-442	416-443	175-188

IX. DISTRIBUTIONS TO SHAREHOLDERS

A. Dividends	35, 74-76, 136, 224-227	1234-1264	878-899	459-498	276-281, 316, 336, 386,475, 655-660, 678	408-412, 491-492
B. Redemption and Repurchase of Shares	230, 971, 1122, 1166	1267-1280	899-900	470-472, 495	389-402, 763-772, 891-898	452-466

X. FUNDAMENTAL CHANGES IN CORPORATE STRUCTURE

A. Introduction	963, 964	1161-1163	748-749		716-718	579
B. Appraisal Rights	965-977, 1135-1137	403-477, 1069-1073	315, 752-754, 778, 779	593-599, 940-956, 1250-1252	336, 337, 716-718, 738, 739	632-680
C. Statutory Mergers	1162-1185	1073-1076	754-757, 874-877; Supp. 247-282	952-956	716-718	582-595
D. De Facto Mergers	225, 578, 579	1080-1094	760-771	1168-1170, 1250-1252	716-726, 738, 739	600-699
E. Triangular Mergers	968, 969, 1123-1126, 1135-1137	1094-1099	771-777	1169-1170, 1247	724, 738, 739	599
F. Sale of Substantially All Assets	1084-1111	1064-1068	748-752	1248	862-867	598, 599, 606, 607
G. Amendment of Articles	614-617	171-199, 214-216	280, 755	260-265, 1248	714	607, 613
H. Dissolution and Liquidation	805-820	444-477	319-341	584-607	311-315, 673-715	438-452
I. Limitations on Power of Controlling Shareholders to Effect Fundamental Changes in Corporate Structure	135, 1123-1162	1101-1132	523-543, 748-754, 779-798; Supp. 242-246	911-973	727-752	310-318, 598-704
J. Tender Offers	968-1084, 1116-1123, 1162-1183	1132-1233	798-877; Supp. 242-282	1165-1262	763-859	937-981

XI. CONFLICT OF LAW PRINCIPLES

A. General Rule	237	101-107	68, 69, 874-877, 959	258	221, 222	140
B. Limitations	244, 245		68, 69	352, 353	201, 320	141-143

Capsule Summary

I. CHARACTERISTICS OF THE CORPORATION AND OTHER BUSINESS ORGANIZATIONS

A. CORPORATIONS

1. Entity Status §1
A corporation is a legal entity created under the authority of the legislature.

2. Limited Liability §2
As a legal entity, a corporation is responsible for its own debts; its shareholders' liability is limited to their investment.

3. Free Transferability of Interests §3
Shares, representing ownership interests, are freely transferable.

4. Centralized Management and Control §4
A corporation's management is centralized in a board of directors and officers. Shareholders generally have no direct control over the board's activities.

5. Duration—Continuity of Existence §5
A corporation is capable of perpetual existence.

6. Taxation §6
As a general rule, a corporation is taxed on its income and its shareholders pay taxes on their dividends (*firm taxation*). Under *flow-through taxation,* a firm is not subject to taxation. Rather, all of the firm's income, expenses, losses, etc., are taxable directly to its owners.

    a. Subchapter S corporations §8
    The owners of a qualifying Subchapter S corporation (*e.g.,* no more than 100 shareholders) can elect a special tax status under which the corporation and its shareholders receive flow-through taxation similar to partnership taxation.

B. GENERAL PARTNERSHIPS §9
Corporation characteristics may be understood by contrasting them to other forms of business associations, beginning with general partnerships. The Revised Uniform Partnership Act ("RUPA") governs general partnerships in about two-thirds of the states, while the remaining states follow the Uniform Partnership Act ("UPA").

1. Definition §10
A partnership is an association of two or more persons to carry on as co-owners a business for profit.

2. Formation
General partnerships can be organized with no formalities and no filing, in contrast to corporations.

3. Legal Status—Entity vs. Aggregate
Under the UPA, a partnership is an aggregation of two or more persons. The RUPA expressly confers entity status on a partnership, which means that it is a separate legal entity, allowing a partnership to hold property in its name, sue or be sued in its name, etc.

4. Personal Liability
In contrast to corporations, partners in a general partnership have unlimited personal liability for the firm's debts and obligations. However, the RUPA has an *exhaustion rule*, under which partnership assets must be exhausted before a partner's individual assets can be reached, subject to certain exceptions (*e.g.*, partnership bankruptcy).

5. Transferability of interests
A partner cannot make a transferee a *member* of the partnership. She can, however, *assign* her interest in the partnership, thus permitting the assignee to receive distributions of profits. Because the assignee does *not* become a member of the partnership, he is not entitled to participate in partnership business or management.

6. Dissolution, Dissociation, Winding-Up, and Termination
A partnership does not have perpetual existence and may be terminated for many reasons.

a. UPA
Under the UPA, dissolution refers to a change in the *legal status* of the partners and the partnership (*e.g.*, death of partner); winding-up describes the *economic event* of liquidation, and termination is the *endpoint of winding-up.*

(1) Rightful dissolution
A partnership is terminable at will unless a definite term is specified or can be implied.

(2) Wrongful dissolution
Dissolution can also occur by the express will of a partner in contravention of the partnership agreement, or by a court when a partner's conduct is wrongful.

(3) Consequences of wrongful dissolution
A partnership is *dissolved* under wrongful dissolution although the remaining partners can *continue the business as a new partnership if* they either (i) pay the breaching partner her partnership interest (minus dissolution damages), or (ii) put up a bond to secure the payment and indemnify her against present and future partnership liabilities. Note that dissolution may also affect *third parties* (*e.g.*, transfer of leases, licenses, or franchises to a *new* partnership may be required).

b. RUPA §30

Under the RUPA, a partner can dissociate any time at will. *Wrongful dissociation* occurs when a partner (i) *breaches an express condition* of the partnership agreement; (ii) *withdraws before expiration* of the partnership term; (iii) engages in *wrongful conduct* that materially affects the business; or (iv) willfully commits a *material breach* of the agreement or of a duty of care, loyalty, good faith, or fair dealing owed to the partnership. Generally any other dissociation is rightful.

(1) Consequences of dissociation—winding up §33

Dissociation of a partner does not necessarily cause dissolution, which results only upon the occurrence of certain events (*e.g.*, notice from a partner that she wishes to *withdraw* from a *partnership at will; expiration of the partnership term* in a partnership for a definite term or undertaking; a *judicial determination* that the economic purpose of the partnership is likely to be unreasonably frustrated). In such cases, the partnership is dissolved and *winding up* is commenced.

(2) Consequences of dissociation—buyout §36

If winding up is not required, dissociation results in a *mandatory buyout* of the dissociated partner. A *wrongfully* dissociating partner is *not* entitled to payment *until* the expiration of the term or completion of the undertaking, unless she demonstrates that earlier payment will not cause undue hardship to the partnership. The buyout price is *reduced by damages* for a wrongful dissociation.

7. Management and Control §38

Absent a contrary agreement, every partner has a right to participate equally in the partnership management.

8. Authority §39

Every partner is an agent of the partnership for purposes of its business.

a. UPA §40

Under the UPA, a partner has apparent authority for carrying on in the usual way the business of the partnership unless she has no actual authority and the third party has *knowledge* of the lack of authority.

b. RUPA §41

RUPA makes clear that a partnership is bound by a partner's act for carrying on in the usual way either the *actual* partnership business or a *business of the kind* carried on by the partnership. Further, RUPA provides for the filing of a *Statement of Partnership Authority*, which is conclusive in favor of third persons even if they are unaware of the statement. However, *limitations* on a partner's authority contained in such a statement, other than those regarding *real estate transfers*, are ineffective unless the third party *knows of them* or a *statement was delivered to him*.

9. Ownership of Property §44

Under the *UPA*, title to property may be held in the name of the partnership, but the property is *owned* by the individual partners as tenants in partnership.

There is no tenancy in partnership under the **RUPA**, which provides that property acquired by the partnership is owned by the partnership, not by individual partners.

10. Capacity to Sue and Be Sued §46

Under the **UPA**, a lawsuit must be brought by or against individual partners, rather than the partnership. Partners are **jointly and severally** liable for wrongful acts and breaches of trust; they are only jointly liable for debts and obligations of the partnership.

a. Statutory reforms §48

Many state statutes specifically allow a UPA partnership to be sued in its own name. Other states make all partnership liabilities joint and several. Other reforms provide that not all joint obligors need be joined in a suit.

b. RUPA §49

Under RUPA, a partnership **may sue and be sued** in its own name, and partners are **jointly and severally liable for all** partnership obligations. However, a claim against the partnership cannot be satisfied from a partner's personal assets unless partnership assets have been exhausted.

C. JOINT VENTURE §50

A joint venture is essentially a partnership formed for some **limited** investment or operation, as opposed to a continuing business enterprise. Joint ventures are governed by most, if not all, of the rules applicable to partnerships.

D. LIMITED PARTNERSHIP §52

This is a partnership consisting of two classes of partners—general partners (with rights and obligations as in an ordinary partnership) and limited partners (with no control and limited liability). There are four versions of the Uniform Limited Partnership Act, each with different provisions regarding a limited partner's liability to third parties. The RUPA provides that a limited partner is **not** personally liable for obligations **even if** the partner **participates in management and control** of the limited partnership.

1. Fiduciary Duties §59

Some state statutes provide that a limited partnership agreement can vary, or even eliminate, a general partner's fiduciary duties, but the duty of good faith normally cannot be eliminated.

E. LIMITED LIABILITY PARTNERSHIPS ("LLPs") §60

In a limited liability partnership ("LLP"), a general partner is **not** personally liable for **all** partnership obligations, but rather is liable only for obligations arising **from his own** activities. Some LLP statutes declare a partner to also be liable for the conduct of persons under his supervision, for contractual obligations, or for both. Note that LLPs must be registered with the appropriate state office.

F. LIMITED LIABILITY COMPANIES ("LLCs") §63

A limited liability company ("LLC") is a non-corporate business entity created under highly variable statutes that combine elements of corporation and partnership law. An LLC's owners (**members**) have limited liability and can participate actively in its management.

1. **Formation** §64

   An LLC is formed by filing *articles of organization*, containing specific information, with the state. Most statutes provide either that an LLC has all *powers* necessary to its purposes or contain a specific list of LLC powers.

2. **Operating Agreement; Management** §65

   The LLC operating agreement provides operation details such as governance methods, capitalization, distributions, etc. Management may be by members or by managers, who may or may not be members.

3. **Voting** §67

   Absent a contrary agreement, voting may be per capita (one vote per member) or pro rata, by financial interests, depending on the statute. Majority vote is usually the rule, although some statutes require a unanimous vote for certain actions.

4. **Agency Powers** §68

   Generally, the apparent authority of members in a *member-managed LLC* is comparable to that of a partner (*i.e.,* each member has power to bind the LLC for acts done in carrying on business in the usual way). *Manager-managed* LLCs generally have authority rules comparable to corporate rules (*i.e.,* only the LLC managers have apparent authority to bind the firm). Also note that, like shareholders of a corporation, LLC members usually have a *right to inspect* the LLC's books and records.

5. **Fiduciary Duties** §71

   Fiduciary duties within an LLC are largely unspecified by statute, and courts are expected to greatly rely on corporate and partnership case law. Some LLC statutes permit the operating agreement to *waive all fiduciary duties.* Most statutes allow members to bring *derivative actions* on an LLC's behalf based on a breach of fiduciary duty.

6. **Distributions** §73

   Absent a contrary agreement, most LLC statutes provide that distributions are pro rata, according to each member's contribution. Some statutes, however, provide for per capita distributions, absent a contrary agreement.

7. **Members' Interests** §74

   A member's interests include *financial* rights (*i.e.,* interests in distributions) and *governance* rights (*e.g.,* right to participate in management). Generally, an LLC member can freely *transfer* (*e.g.,* assign) her financial rights. Governance rights are transferable, depending on the statute, only with unanimous member consent, with approval of a majority of the members, or without the members' consent if the articles or operating agreement so provide.

   a. **Consequences of assignment** §76

      A member who assigns her financial interest normally *cannot assign* her *governance* rights, but it is not always clear whether the assigning member *retains* her governance rights.

8. **Personal Liability** §77

   All LLC statutes provide that members and managers are not personally liable for the firm's debts, obligations, and other liabilities, although courts are developing a form of piercing the veil for LLCs.

9. Dissociation §78

Statutes vary greatly as to dissociation. A typical statute allows dissociation upon the death, bankruptcy, or lawful expulsion of a member.

G. TAXATION OF NONCORPORATE ENTITIES §79

A general partnership, limited partnership, limited liability partnership, or an LLC can elect either firm taxation or flow-through taxation. Note that a limited partnership with publicly traded interests (*master limited partnership*) is usually taxed as a corporation and cannot elect partnership taxation.

II. ORGANIZING THE CORPORATION

A. FORMALITIES IN ORGANIZING A CORPORATION

1. General Corporation Laws §80

Generally, corporations are created under and according to statutory provisions of the state in which formation is sought.

2. Certificate or Articles of Incorporation §81

State law governs the content of the articles, which are filed with the secretary of state. Under the Model Business Corporation Act ("Model Act"), the articles *must* specify the corporate name, number of shares authorized, address of the corporation's initial registered office and name of initial registered agent, and the name and address of each incorporator. Optional provisions may include provisions concerning the purpose, management and powers of the corporation, par value of shares, shareholder liability for corporate debt, and any provision that is required or permitted in the bylaws.

a. Purpose clause §84

Under most statutes, no elaborate purpose clause is needed. It is sufficient to state that the purpose of the corporation is to engage in any lawful business activity.

3. Organizational Meeting §85

Filing the certificate or articles in proper form creates the corporation, after which an organizational meeting is held by either the incorporators or the initial board of directors named in the articles.

a. Matters determined at meeting §86

If no directors are named in the articles, directors are elected and bylaws are adopted at the meeting of the incorporators. Matters determined at the meeting of the initial directors include adoption of bylaws (if necessary), election of officers, adoption of corporate seal and form of stock certificate, authorization of share issuance at designated prices, and designation of corporate bank.

B. DEFECTS IN FORMATION PROCESS—"DE JURE" AND "DE FACTO" CORPORATIONS

1. **In General**
   When there is a defect or irregularity in formation, the question is whether the corporation exists "de jure," "de facto," "by estoppel," or not at all. This issue usually arises when a third party seeks to impose personal liability on would-be shareholders. Another method for challenging corporate status, used only by the state, is a *quo warranto proceeding*.

2. **De Jure Corporation**
   This exists when the corporation is organized *in compliance with the statute*. Its status cannot be attacked by anyone—not even the state. Most courts require only "*substantial compliance*"; others require exact compliance with the *mandatory requirements*.

3. **De Facto Corporation**
   This exists when there is insufficient compliance as to the *state* (*i.e.*, state can attack in quo warranto proceeding), but the steps taken are sufficient to treat the enterprise as a corporation with respect to its *dealings with third parties*. A *colorable attempt to incorporate* and some *actual use* of the corporate existence is required.

4. **Corporation by Estoppel**
   Certain parties are estopped from asserting defective incorporation when they have dealt with the corporation as though properly formed. For example, shareholders who claimed corporate status in an earlier transaction are estopped to deny that status in a suit brought against the corporation. The estoppel theory normally does *not* apply to bar suit against would-be shareholders by tort claimants or other involuntary creditors.

5. **Who May Be Held Liable**
   When a would-be corporation is not a de jure or de facto corporation or a corporation by estoppel, the modern trend imposes personal liability against only those owners who *actively participated* in management of the enterprise.

6. **Effect of Statutes**

   a. **On de facto doctrine**
      States following the prior version of the Model Act have abolished the de facto doctrine, thus making all purported "shareholders" jointly and severally liable for all liabilities incurred as a result of the purported "corporation." However, statutes based on the current Model Business Corporation Act require a person acting on behalf of the enterprise to *know* that there was no incorporation before liability attaches.

   b. **On estoppel doctrine**
      The effect of both Acts is an unsettled issue.

   c. **On liability**
      Under the prior Model Act, liability extends to investors who also exercise control or actively participate in policy and operational decisions. It is expected that the current Model Act will be interpreted in the same manner.

C. DISREGARD OF CORPORATE ENTITY

1. **In General** §110

   Because a corporation is a distinct legal entity, shareholders are normally shielded from corporate obligations. In certain instances, however, the corporate entity will be disregarded.

2. **Suits by Corporate Creditors Against Shareholders** §111

   This is the most common situation for disregarding the corporate entity, and it is called "piercing the corporate veil." For the doctrine to apply, there usually must be such *unity of interest and ownership* that the corporation and shareholders are effectively one personality, so that treating the entity as a corporation would *sanction a fraud or promote injustice.*

   a. **Commingling of assets** §112

      Commingling of corporate assets and personal assets of shareholders (*e.g.*, paying private debts with corporate funds) may lead to piercing of the corporate veil.

   b. **Lack of corporate formalities** §113

      Whether basic corporate formalities (*e.g.*, regular meetings, corporate records maintained, issuance of stock) were followed is also relevant. Note that *statutory close corporations* are permitted more flexibility regarding corporate formalities.

   c. **Undercapitalization** §115

      If the corporation was organized without sufficient capital or liability insurance to meet obligations reasonably expected to arise, the corporate veil may be pierced.

   d. **Domination and control by shareholder** §116

      The corporate veil is often pierced when an individual or other corporation owns most or all of the stock so that it completely dominates policy or business decisions.

   e. **"Alter ego"; "instrumentality"; "unity of interest"** §117

      When no separate entity exists and the corporation is merely the alter ego or instrumentality of its shareholders, or when there is a unity of interest between the corporation and its shareholders, the corporate veil is often pierced. Note that these terms are usually applied only if other grounds (*see* above) are present.

   f. **Fraud, wrong, dishonesty, or injustice** §118

      Generally, the veil will be pierced only if one of these elements is available, *e.g.*, no piercing of veil if there is a lack of corporate formalities without resultant injustice. Piercing the veil usually involves corporations with a small number of shareholders.

3. **Piercing the Wall Between Affiliated Corporations** §120

   This occurs when a plaintiff with a claim against one corporation attempts to satisfy the claim against the assets of an affiliated corporation under common ownership. This type of aggregation is permitted only when each affiliated corporation is not a free-standing enterprise but is merely a fragment of an entity composed of affiliated corporations.

4. Use of Corporate Form to Evade Statutory or Contract Obligations §122
The corporate form may be ignored when it is used to evade a statutory or contractual obligation. The issue is whether the contract or statute was intended to apply to the shareholders as well as the corporation.

5. Disregard of Corporate Entity in Favor of Corporation or Its Shareholders §123
Only *third parties*, not the corporation or its shareholders, are generally allowed to disregard the corporate entity.

D. SUBORDINATION OF SHAREHOLDER DEBTS—"DEEP ROCK" DOCTRINE §124
If a corporation goes into bankruptcy, debts to its *controlling* shareholders *may* be subordinated to claims of other creditors. When subordination occurs, shareholder loans are treated as if they were *invested capital* (stock).

1. Grounds §127
Major factors in determining whether to subordinate include fraud, mismanagement, undercapitalization, commingling, excessive control, and other equitable reasons.

III. LIABILITIES FOR TRANSACTIONS BEFORE INCORPORATION

A. PROMOTERS

1. Definition §128
A promoter participates in the formation of the corporation, usually arranging compliance with the legal requirements of formation, securing initial capital, and entering into necessary contracts on behalf of the corporation during the time it is being formed.

2. Fiduciary Duties to Each Other §129
Full disclosure and *fair dealing* are required between the promoters and the corporation and among the promoters themselves.

B. CONTRACTS MADE BY PROMOTERS ON CORPORATION'S BEHALF

1. Rights and Liabilities of Corporation

a. English rule §131
Under the English rule, the corporation is *not directly liable* on preincorporation contracts even if later ratified. *Rationale:* The corporation was not yet in existence at the time the promoter was acting. However, courts may allow recovery based on quasi-contract.

b. American rule §134
Under the American rule, the corporation is *liable if it later ratifies or adopts* such contracts. The ratification may be *express or implied.* A promoter has a right to *reimbursement* by the corporation to the extent of any *benefits* that the corporation received under the promoter's contracts. Recovery in *quasi-contract* may also be available.

that charitable contributions were ultra vires; the modern view permits *reasonable* donations for public welfare, humanitarian, educational, or philanthropic purposes without showing the probability of a direct benefit to the corporation.

B. ULTRA VIRES TRANSACTIONS

1. In General §164

Ultra vires transactions are those beyond the purposes and powers, express *and* implied, of the corporation. Under common law, *shareholder ratification* of an ultra vires transaction nullified the use of an ultra vires defense by the corporation.

2. Tort Actions §167

Ultra vires is *no defense to tort liability*.

3. Criminal Actions §168

Claims that a corporate act was beyond the corporation's authorized powers are *no defense* to criminal liability.

4. Contract Actions §169

At common law, a purely *executory* ultra vires contract was not enforceable against *either party*; *fully performed contracts* could not be rescinded by either party; and, under the majority rule, *partially performed contracts* were generally enforceable by the performing party because the nonperforming party was estopped to assert an ultra vires defense.

5. Statutes §175

Most states now have statutes that preclude the use of ultra vires as a defense in a suit between the contracting parties, but permit ultra vires to be raised in certain other contexts.

a. Suit against officers or directors §177

If performance of an ultra vires contract results in a loss to the corporation, it can sue the officers or directors for *damages* for exceeding their authority.

b. Suit by state §178

These limiting statutes do not bar the state from suing to *enjoin* a corporation from transacting unauthorized business.

c. Suit by shareholders §179

Shareholders can sue to *enjoin performance* of an ultra vires contract. In a suit by shareholders, the court may also award *damages, exclusive of lost profits.*

d. Broad certificate provisions §182

When the certificate of incorporation states that the purpose is to engage in any lawful act or activity for which corporations may be organized, ultra vires issues are unlikely to arise.

V. MANAGEMENT AND CONTROL

A. ALLOCATION OF POWERS BETWEEN DIRECTORS AND SHAREHOLDERS

(1) Functioning as a close corporation §198

Once qualified as a statutory close corporation, a corporation has great flexibility in its management methods. (However, nearly the same flexibility now can be utilized without close corporation status under the modern trend.) There may be shareholder agreements relating to any phase of the corporation's affairs (some statutes require *all* shareholders to join in such agreements). Under some statutes, the shareholders, rather than the directors, directly manage the corporation's affairs and thereby become personally liable for managerial acts or omissions to the same extent as managing directors.

(2) Rights and liabilities of transferees §202

Restrictions (*e.g.*, number of shareholders, transfer restrictions) are often required to be conspicuously noted on the stock certificates. Statutes vary as to the problem of transfers to ineligible or unknowing transferees. For example, Delaware law provides that if a transferee has actual notice or is conclusively presumed to have notice that (i) he is ineligible to be a shareholder, (ii) the transfer will cause the number of shareholders to exceed that permitted in the certificate of incorporation, or (iii) the transfer violates a valid restriction, the corporation may refuse to register the transfer.

B. DIRECTORS

1. Appointment of Directors §207

Initial directors are either designated in the articles of incorporation or elected at a meeting of the incorporators. Subsequent elections are by the shareholders at their annual meetings. The board may fill vacancies occurring between shareholders' meetings. The *number* of directors is usually set by the articles or bylaws.

a. Qualifications §209

Absent a contrary provision in the articles or bylaws, directors need not be shareholders of the corporation or residents of the state of incorporation.

b. Vacancies §210

Statutes vary, but under the Model Act, a vacancy may be filled by either the shareholders *or* the directors.

(1) Distinguish—removal §211

Some statutes require that vacancies created by removal of a director be filled by the shareholders unless the articles or bylaws provide otherwise.

2. Tenure of Office

a. Term of appointment §212

Under most statutes, office is held until the next annual meeting, although on a classified board, directors may serve staggered multiyear terms.

transaction is **effective**, as is a matter receiving the explicit approval by a majority of directors without a meeting, plus acquiescence by the remaining directors.

c. Delegation of authority §228

The board has the power to appoint committees of its own members to act for it either in particular matters or to handle day-to-day management between board meetings. Typically, these committees **cannot** amend the articles or bylaws, adopt or recommend major corporate changes (*e.g.*, merger), recommend dissolution, or declare a dividend or authorize issuance of stock unless permitted by the articles or bylaws. Note that while the board may delegate operation of the business to an officer or management company, the ultimate control must be retained by the board.

d. Provisional directors §232

A growing number of statutes (some apply only to close corporations) provide for provisional directors to be appointed by court if the board is deadlocked and corporate business is endangered. A provisional director serves until the deadlock is broken or until removed by a court order or the majority of shareholders.

e. Voting agreements §235

An agreement in advance among **directors** as to how they will vote as directors is void as contrary to public policy. There are certain exceptions for statutory close corporations; *e.g.*, the Model Act allows directors to enter into a voting agreement if the corporation's shares are not publicly traded and the agreement is in the articles, bylaws, or a separate writing; it is approved by all shareholders; and its existence is conspicuously noted on outstanding shares.

4. Compensation §236

Directors are **not** entitled to compensation unless they render **extraordinary services** or compensation is otherwise provided for (*e.g.,* in the articles) **before** the services are rendered. Officers are entitled to reasonable compensation for services.

5. Directors' Rights, Duties, and Liabilities

a. Right to inspect corporate records §241

If done in **good faith** for purposes germane to his position as director, this right is absolute.

b. Duty of care §244

As fiduciaries of the corporation directors must exercise the care of an **ordinarily prudent and diligent person** in a like position under similar circumstances. There is no liability (absent a conflict of interest, bad faith, illegality, fraud, or gross negligence and, in some cases, ordinary negligence) for errors of judgment (**"business judgment rule"**), but the director must have been **reasonably diligent** before the rule can be invoked.

(1) Extent of liability §251

A director is personally liable for corporate losses that are the **direct and proximate cause** of her breach of duty. She is liable for the wrongful **acts of others** only if she **participated** in the acts, was **negligent in failing to discover** the misconduct, **or** was **negligent in appointing** the wrongdoer. A director may seek to avoid being held personally liable for acts of the board by recording her **dissent**.

(a) Note §255

Many statutes permit the articles to **abolish or limit** directors' liability for breach of the duty of care absent bad faith, intentional misconduct, or knowing violation of law.

(2) Defenses to liability §256

These include good faith reliance on management or experts' reports. It is usually no defense that a director was serving gratuitously or had a disability.

c. Duty of loyalty §261

Directors have a duty of loyalty in all dealings with the corporation (discussed *infra*).

d. Statutory duties and liabilities §262

In addition to the general duty of care, federal and state laws also impose certain duties and liabilities, *e.g.*, registration requirements under the Securities Act of 1933, liability for rule 10b-5 violations, liability for illegal dividends. Some statutes also impose **criminal liability** on corporate managers for unlawful corporate actions.

C. OFFICERS

1. Election §267

Officers are generally elected by the board of directors, or as determined by the certificate, bylaws, or board resolution, and hold office at its pleasure.

2. Authority of Corporate Officers—Liability of Corporation to Outsiders §268

Only authorized officers can bind the corporation. Authority may be: **actual** (expressed in bylaws or by valid board resolution), **apparent** (corporation gives third parties reason to believe authority exists), or **power of position** (inherent to position). If **ratified** by the board, even unauthorized acts may bind the corporation.

a. Authority of president §273

The majority rule is that the president has power to bind the corporation in transactions arising in the **ordinary and regular course of business**.

3. Duties of Corporate Officers §278

The duty of care owed by an officer is similar to that owed by directors (and sometimes higher).

D. CONFLICTS OF INTEREST IN CORPORATE TRANSACTIONS

6. Compensation for Services to the Corporation §336
The compensation plan must be *duly authorized* by the board and its terms *reasonable*. Good faith and the business judgment rule ordinarily protect disinterested directors from liability to the corporation for approving compensation.

a. Publicly held corporations §342
The SEC has increased the type and amount of information about executive compensation that must be disclosed by large corporations, and has authorized shareholders to make proposals about executive pay in management's proxy materials. Further, the tax code limits expense deductions for executive pay over $1 million unless it is tied to the corporation's performance.

(1) Distinguish—close corporations §344
Executive compensation in a close corporation is more often held to be unreasonable because it is usually not approved by either disinterested directors or disinterested shareholders.

b. Past and future services §350
Compensation for *past services* is generally invalid; compensation for *future services* is proper if there is reasonable assurance that the corporation will receive the benefit of the services. There must be a *reasonable relationship* between the amount paid and the services rendered.

VI. INSIDER TRADING

A. INTRODUCTION §359
The purchase and sale of corporate stock by a director, officer, or other insider raises issues of fiduciary responsibility.

1. Common Law Approaches §360
At common law, under the majority rule, there was *no* duty to disclose to the shareholders inside information affecting the value of shares (the minority rule imposed a duty to disclose).

2. Securities Exchange Act of 1934—In General §364
The common law rules governing insider trading have been largely superseded by the Securities Exchange Act. Section 12 of the Act requires *registration* of any security *traded on a national exchange*, or any equity security held by *500 or more persons* of a corporation with *assets exceeding $10 million.*

B. SECTION 10(b) AND RULE 10b-5 §365
Section 10(b) prohibits any manipulation or deception in the purchase or sale of any security, whether or not registered; rule 10b-5 prohibits the use of the mails or other instrumentality of interstate commerce to defraud, misrepresent, or omit a material fact in connection with a purchase or sale of *any* security.

1. Covered Conduct and Persons §366
Rule 10b-5 applies to *nondisclosure* by directors or officers, as well as to *misrepresentations*. It applies not only to insider trading, but also to *any*

person who makes a misrepresentation *in connection with* a purchase or sale of stock. Since courts read "in connection with" very broadly; the test is usually satisfied whenever a transaction involves some kind of securities and some kind of fraud.

2. Covered Securities §369

Rule 10b-5 applies to the purchase or sale of *any* security, registered or unregistered. A jurisdictional limitation requires that the violation must involve the use of some *instrumentality of interstate commerce*.

3. Who Can Bring Suit Under Rule 10b-5 §370

Suits for violation of rule 10b-5 can be brought by the SEC and by private plaintiffs. However, private plaintiffs must be either purchasers or sellers of securities.

4. Materiality §372

For rule 10b-5 to apply, the information misrepresented or omitted must be material (*i.e.*, a reasonable shareholder would consider it important in deciding whether to buy or sell).

5. Fault Required—Scienter §373

A defendant is not liable under rule 10b-5 for a misrepresentation or omission if he was without fault or merely negligent. The scienter requirement is satisfied by *recklessness* or an intent to deceive, mislead, or convey a false impression. Scienter is also required for injunctive relief.

a. Forward-looking statements §376

Forward-looking statements are statements about the future (*e.g.,* projections of revenue, income, dividends, future economic performance, etc.).

(1) Safe harbor §377

The Securities Exchange Act provides a safe harbor against civil liability for forward-looking statements made by certain issuers or persons acting for them if either: (i) the statement is identified as a forward-looking statement and is accompanied by cautionary statements; or (ii) it is shown that the issuer had *no actual knowledge* that the statement was false or misleading.

(2) "Bespeaks caution" §378

Under the bespeaks caution doctrine, a misleading forward-looking statement does not result in liability if the document containing the statement includes sufficient cautionary language.

b. Effect of Private Securities Litigation Reform Act ("PSLRA") §379

Under the PSLRA, a plaintiff alleging a fraudulent *forward-looking statement* must establish "actual knowledge" of the statement's falsity, thus eliminating recklessness as sufficient scienter in these cases. However, recklessness still may be considered sufficient in cases involving historical or existing facts.

6. Causation and Reliance §387

The requirements of causation and reliance have been considerably watered down.

a. Causation
§388

The causal connection between a rule 10b-5 violation and the plaintiff's purchase or sale of a security is **transaction causation,** *i.e.*, the defendant's fraudulent statement or omission **must have caused the plaintiff to engage in the transaction** (**but for** test). This is generally called "**reliance.**" **Loss causation** is also required. This requires proof that a violation **caused plaintiff's economic harm**, and is often described as proximate cause (*i.e.*, a foreseeable result of the misrepresentation or material omission).

(1) Omissions
§392

Positive proof of reliance is not required in omission cases; in such cases there is a rebuttable **presumption of reliance** once materiality is established.

b. "Fraud on the market"
§394

If securities are traded on a well-developed market (rather than in a face-to-face transaction), reliance on a **misrepresentation** may be shown by alleging reliance on the integrity of the market, thus creating a **presumption** of reliance.

c. Face-to-face misrepresentations
§395

A plaintiff can show actual reliance in face-to-face misrepresentation cases by showing that the misrepresentation was material, testifying that she relied upon it, and showing that she traded soon after the misrepresentation.

7. When Nondisclosure Constitutes a Violation

a. Mere informational imbalance
§397

Generally, nondisclosure of material, nonpublic information by one party to a transaction violates rule 10b-5 **only** if there is a duty, independent of rule 10b-5, to disclose. A plaintiff need show only that the person making the purchase or sale was **aware** of the material nonpublic information at the time of the transaction, not that he actually used it.

(1) Affirmative defense
§401

An affirmative defense exists for a person possessing the inside information if he had either entered into a binding contract to purchase or sell the security, provided instructions to another to trade for his account, or adopted a written plan for trading **before** he was **aware of the relevant information.**

b. Trading by insiders
§402

Insiders (directors, officers, controlling shareholders, and corporate employees) violate rule 10b-5 by trading on the basis of material, nonpublic information obtained through their positions. They have a duty to disclose before trading.

c. Misappropriation
§403

When a noninsider misappropriates confidential information in breach of a **duty she owes to the source of the information,** she commits fraud "in connection with" a securities transaction. In contrast to conventional insider trading, misappropriation liability is based on the deception of a person, other than the issuer, who entrusted the defendant with access to material confidential information (*e.g.,* a corporation's lawyer).

(1) United States v. O'Hagan §405
In **United States v. O'Hagan**, the Supreme Court held that an unlawful misappropriation can be proved if the defendant used for his own benefit information that he acquired in the course of a *relationship of trust and confidence.* A defendant, however, apparently will not be liable if he *discloses* his use of the information to whom he owes the duty of trust and confidence (*i.e.,* deception is necessary for misappropriation).

d. Liability to contemporaneous traders §408
A person who violates rule 10b-5 while possessing material nonpublic information is liable to *any persons* who, contemporaneously with the defendant's purchase or sale, purchased or sold securities of the same class. However, defendant's total liability is limited to his profit (or the loss he avoided).

e. Mail fraud §409
The federal mail fraud act makes it a criminal offense to use the mail or wire to transmit false or fraudulent pretenses, representations, or promises to further a scheme to defraud.

f. Special rule for tender offers §410
Once substantial steps toward making a tender offer have begun, it is a fraudulent, deceptive, or manipulative act for a person possessing material information about the tender offer to purchase or sell any of the target's stock if that person knows that the information is nonpublic and has been acquired from the bidder, the target, or someone acting on the bidder's or target's behalf.

g. "Disclose or abstain" §411
Nondisclosure by a person with a duty to disclose violates rule 10b-5 *only* if she trades.

8. Liability of Nontrading Persons for Misrepresentations §412
A nontrading corporation or person who makes a misrepresentation that could cause reasonable investors to rely on the statement in the purchase or sale of securities is liable under rule 10b-5, provided the scienter requirement is satisfied.

a. Liability of nontrading corporation for nondisclosure §414
The basic principle is "*disclose or abstain*." Thus, a nontrading corporation is generally not liable under rule 10b-5 for nondisclosure of material facts.

(1) Exceptions §415
A corporation has a duty to: (i) *correct* misleading statements (even if unintentional); (ii) *update* statements that have become

materially misleading by subsequent events; (iii) **correct** material errors in **statements by others** (e.g., analyst's reports) about the corporation—if the corporation was involved in the preparation of the statements; and (iv) **correct inaccurate rumors** resulting from leaks by the corporation or its agents.

9. **Tippee and Tipper Liability**

A person, not an insider, who trades on information received from an insider is a tippee and may be liable under rule 10b-5 if (i) she received information through an insider who breached a fiduciary duty in giving the information, and (ii) the tippee knew or should have known of the breach.

a. **Breach of insider's fiduciary duty**

Whether an insider's fiduciary duty was breached depends largely on whether the insider communicated the information to realize a gain or advantage. Accordingly, tips to friends or relatives and tips that are a quid pro quo for a past or future benefit from the tippee result in a fiduciary breach. Note that if a tippee is liable, so too is the tipper.

b. **Outsiders**

Outsiders who trade on the basis of information received from the corporation as a result of a **special confidential relationship** (e.g., the corporation's lawyer or accountant) may be liable as "temporary insiders."

10. **Selective Disclosure—Regulation FD**

Selective, rather than general, disclosure by a corporation involves disclosure of material nonpublic information to favored persons (e.g., specific securities analysts, institutional investors), thus giving them a trading advantage over the general public. In 2000, the SEC adopted Regulation FD, which provides that intentional selective disclosure must be simultaneously accompanied with public disclosure of the information. If the disclosure is not intentional, the information must be promptly disclosed.

11. **Aiders and Abettors**

These are people who aid and abet **another person** who acts improperly. Liability **cannot** be imposed solely because that person aided and abetted a violation of the rule (i.e., a lawyer, accountant, bank, etc., who somehow furthers a primary violator's course of conduct cannot be sued on an aiding-and-abetting theory).

12. **Application of Rule 10b-5 to Breach of Fiduciary Duties by Directors, Officers, or Controlling Shareholders**

a. **"Ordinary mismanagement"**

A breach of fiduciary duty not involving misrepresentation, nondisclosure, or manipulation **does not violate rule 10b-5**.

b. **Misrepresentation or nondisclosure**

If misrepresentation or nondisclosure is the basis of a purchase from or sale to the corporation by a director or officer, the corporation can sue the fiduciary under rule 10b-5 **and** also for breach of fiduciary duty. If the corporation does not sue, a minority shareholder can maintain a **derivative** suit on the corporation's behalf.

a. **Note**

Trading in **all** of a corporation's equity securities is subject to section 16 if **any class** of its securities is registered under section 12.

2. **Disclosure Requirement** §484

Section 16(a) requires every **beneficial owner** of **more than 10%** of registered stock **and directors and officers** of the issuing corporation to file periodic reports with the SEC showing their holdings and any changes in their holdings.

3. **Liability** §487

To prevent the unfair use of information, section 16(b) allows a corporation to recover profits made by an officer, director, or more-than-10% beneficial owner on the purchase and sale **or** sale and purchase of its securities within less than six months.

a. **Coverage** §488

Section 16(b) does not cover all insider trading and is not limited to trades based on inside information. The critical element is short-swing trading by officers, directors, and more-than-10% beneficial owners.

b. **Calculation of short-swing profit** §489

The profit recoverable is the difference between the price of the stock sold and the price of the stock purchased within six months **before or after** the sale.

(1) **Multiple transactions** §490

If there is more than one purchase or sale transaction within the less-than-six-month period, the transactions are paired by matching the highest sale price with the lowest purchase price, the next highest sale price with the next lowest purchase price, etc. A court can look six months forward or backward from any sale (to find a purchase) or from any purchase (to find a sale). **Any pair** of transactions within that period must be accounted for.

c. **Who may recover** §492

The profit belongs to the corporation alone. Although not a typical derivative action, if the corporation fails to sue after a demand by a shareholder, the shareholder may sue on the corporation's behalf. The cause of action is federal, so there is no posting of security requirement and no contemporaneous shareholder requirement.

d. **"Insiders"** §495

Insiders are officers (named officers and those persons who function as officers), directors, and beneficial owners of more than 10% of the shares. **Control** over stock determines who is more than a 10% owner for purposes of short-swing profits. (*Compare:* **Pecuniary interest** in the relevant securities determines whether a shareholder owns a sufficient amount of stock to trigger reporting obligations.) Insider status for officers and directors is determined at the time they made a purchase **or** sale. Transactions made before taking office are not within section 16(b), but those made after leaving office are subject to the statute if they can be matched with a transaction made while in office. Liability is imposed on a beneficial owner only if she owned more than 10% of the shares at the time of **both** the purchase and sale.

amend the articles or bylaws, and on *major corporate action* or *fundamental changes*.

2. **Shareholders' Meetings** §537
Generally, shareholders can act only at meetings duly called and noticed at which a quorum is present. Written notice generally must be given not less than 10 or more than 60 days before the meeting.

3. **Shareholder Voting**

4. **Voting by Proxy** §558
A proxy authorizes another person to vote a shareholder's shares. The proxy usually must be ***in writing***, and its effective period is statutorily limited (*e.g.*, 11 months) unless it is validly irrevocable.

corporation). Absent written notice to the corporation, the death or incapacity of a shareholder does **not** revoke a proxy. A shareholder may revoke a proxy by notifying the proxy holder, giving a new proxy to someone else, or by personally attending the meeting and voting.

b. Proxy solicitation §566

Almost all shareholders of publicly held corporations vote by proxy. Solicitations of proxies are regulated by the Securities Exchange Act of 1934 (section 14(a)), federal proxy rules, and, in some cases, state law. Federal proxy rules apply to the solicitation of all proxies of registered securities, but not to nonmanagement solicitation of 10 or fewer shareholders. The term "solicitation" is broadly interpreted by the SEC to include any part of a plan leading to a formal solicitation, *e.g.*, inspection of shareholder list.

(1) Communications between shareholders §573

The proxy rules include a **safe harbor** for communications between shareholders that do not involve solicitation of voting authority. Requirements also are more relaxed for **broadcast or published communications**; and **preliminary filings** for solicitations.

c. Disclosure §578

The proxy rules require full disclosure of all pertinent facts relating to transactions for which approval is sought (**transactional disclosure**) and relevant information contained in certain forms of **annual disclosure** (*e.g.*, annual reports).

(1) Proxy statement §581

In addition, the proxy statement must contain certain nontransactional information, such as **compensation** of the CEO and the four most highly paid executives, significant **conflicts of interest**, and various facts relating to the corporation's auditor, compensation, and nominating **committees.**

(2) Inclusion of shareholder proposal §593

Shareholder proposals must be included in corporate proxy materials if the proponent is a record or beneficial owner, for at least one year, of **at least 1% or $2,000** worth of securities entitled to vote on the matter, subject to a number of exceptions. The proposal must not exceed 500 words.

(a) Exceptions §594

A proposal need **not** be included if it: is **not a proper subject** for shareholder action, would be **illegal**, is **false or misleading**, seeks **redress of a personal claim**, relates to **operations** accounting for **less than 5% of the corporation's total assets** and is not otherwise significantly related to the corporation's business, concerns a matter **beyond the corporation's power** to effectuate, relates to **ordinary business operations**, relates to an **election to office**, conflicts with a proposal submitted by the corporation at the same meeting, is moot or **duplicative**, deals with the same subject matter as a very unsuccessful prior proposal, or relates to **specific amounts of cash or stock dividends**.

        (b)   Private right of action   **§601**
A private right of action is available to a shareholder whose proposal was rejected by the corporation on the ground that it falls within one of the proposal exceptions.

        (c)   Providing shareholder lists   **§602**
A shareholder has the right to obtain a list of shareholders or to have her communication included with the corporate proxy materials.

    (3)   Remedies for violation of proxy rules   **§603**
Remedies for violation of the proxy rules include suit by the SEC to enjoin violations or to set aside an election and individual suits, class actions, or derivative suits by the shareholders. (In a private suit, the plaintiff must show **materiality and causation**, but causation is normally presumed from materiality. Fairness to the corporation is not a defense to a violation of proxy rules.) The court may rescind corporate action resulting from a misleading proxy solicitation or award damages.

   d.   Expenses incurred in proxy contests   **§619**
Corporate funds may be used by management with respect to reasonable proxy solicitation expenses incurred in order to obtain a quorum for the annual meeting or regarding a controversy over **corporate policy** (as opposed to a personnel controversy). The corporation may, with shareholder approval, **voluntarily** pay the reasonable expenses of insurgents who win a proxy contest involving policy.

5.   Other Methods to Combine Votes for Control—Close Corporations   **§622**
Other methods to combine votes for control include shareholder **voting agreements** (e.g., pooling and self-executing agreements), which may be enforced by specific performance; agreements requiring **greater-than-majority approval**; shareholder agreements **binding the discretion** of the directors; and **voting trusts.**

B.   RESTRICTIONS ON TRANSFER OF SHARES

1.   Restrictions Imposed by Articles, Bylaws, or Shareholder Agreement   **§650**
Although most frequently used in close corporations, stock transfer restrictions may also be imposed by larger corporations (e.g., to restrict ownership to employees). The two most common types of restrictions are a **right of first refusal** and a **mandatory buy-sell provision**. Restrictions must be **reasonable** and will be strictly construed.

   a.   Notice requirements   **§670**
A lawful stock transfer restriction is of no effect unless **noted conspicuously** on the stock certificate or a third party who is unaware of the

restriction. If there is no such notice, an innocent transferee is entitled to have the shares transferred to him.

C. SHAREHOLDERS' INFORMATIONAL RIGHTS

1. Types of Books and Records §674

A corporation's books and records include shareholder lists, minutes, financial records, and business documents.

2. Common Law §675

At common law, a shareholder has a qualified right to inspect records for a **proper purpose**.

3. Statutes §676

Statutes govern inspection rights in most states. Some statutes apply only to certain shareholders (*e.g.*, those who own 5% or those who have been record holders for six months), but are usually interpreted to supplement the common law. Most statutes preserve the proper purpose test, but place the burden on the corporation to prove improper purpose.

4. Proper vs. Improper Purposes §678

The test for proper purpose is whether the shareholder is seeking **to protect his shareholder interest**. Multiple purposes that include a proper one usually will not preclude inspection. Generally, a shareholder can inspect the shareholder list because it is often necessary to the exercise of other rights, *e.g.*, proxy fights, shareholder litigation. Inspection of shareholder lists for a proxy contest is a proper purpose. However, it has been held that corporate records cannot be examined solely for the purpose of advancing political or social views or to aid a shareholder as a litigant on a personal, nonshareholder claim.

5. Mandatory Disclosure of Information §685

A shareholder's inspection right is separate and distinct from the statutory requirements governing the affirmative disclosure of certain information by corporations (*e.g.*, section 12 of Securities Exchange Act of 1934, proxy rules, state statutes).

D. FIDUCIARY OBLIGATIONS OF CONTROLLING SHAREHOLDERS

1. Introduction §693

A controlling shareholder owes a fiduciary duty in his **business dealings with the corporation**, in taking advantage of **corporate opportunities** (rules more lenient than those applied to officers and directors), and in **causing fundamental changes**.

2. Transactions in Corporate Control §704

In a transaction where control of the corporation is material, the controlling shareholder must act with good faith and inherent fairness toward the minority shareholders.

3. Obligations of Shareholders in Close Corporations §705

In close corporations, both majority and minority shareholders owe each other an even stricter duty (utmost good faith and loyalty) than is owed by controlling shareholders in publicly held corporations. This duty has been interpreted to mean that there must be **equal treatment** of all shareholders, *i.e.*, they must be afforded equal opportunities.

4. Disclosure
$§711$
A controlling shareholder must make full disclosure when dealing with minority shareholders.

5. Sale of Control
$§712$
In most jurisdictions, a controlling shareholder is permitted to sell his stock at a premium, *i.e.*, a price not available to other shareholders. Exceptions to this rule include a bare sale of office (invalid), the corporate action theory, sales involving fraud or nondisclosure, and knowing sales to transferees who plan to loot or deal unfairly with the corporation.

E. SHAREHOLDER SUITS

1. Direct (Individual) Suits
$§733$
A direct suit may be brought by a shareholder **on her own behalf** for injuries to shareholder interests. If the injury affects a number of shareholders, the suit may be brought as a **class action**.

2. Derivative Suits
$§735$
If a duty owed to the corporation has been abridged, suit may be brought by a shareholder **on behalf of the corporation**.

a. Distinguish direct from derivative suits
$§738$
The test for distinguishing between a basis for a direct and derivative suit is whether the injury was suffered by the **corporation** directly or by the shareholder, and to whom the defendant's **duty** was owed.

(1) Close corporations
$§744$
In some cases, minority shareholders have been allowed to bring a direct action against controlling shareholders for breach of fiduciary duty.

b. Prerequisite to suit—exhaustion of corporate remedies
$§746$
The plaintiff-shareholder must specifically **plead and prove** that she exhausted her remedies within the corporate structure.

(1) Demand on directors
$§747$
The plaintiff-shareholder must make a demand on the directors to remedy the wrong, unless such demand would have been futile. Note that in the absence of negligence, self-interest, or bias, the fact that a majority of directors approved the transaction does not itself excuse the demand.

(a) Model statutes
$§750$
Under both model statutes, demand should be excused only if it is shown that irreparable injury to the corporation would result.

(b) Effect of rejection of demand
$§752$
If the matter complained of does not involve wrongdoing by

the directors, the board's good faith refusal to sue bars the action, unless the plaintiff-shareholders can raise a reasonable doubt that the board exercised *reasonable business judgment* in declining to sue. If the suit alleges wrongdoing by a majority of the directors, the board's decision not to sue will not prevent the derivative suit.

(2) Demand on shareholders §768
In a number of states, the plaintiff-shareholder must also make a demand on shareholders unless excused (*e.g.*, the alleged wrongdoing is beyond the power of the shareholders to ratify). Where demand on shareholders is required, a good faith refusal to sue by the majority of disinterested shareholders will preclude the suit.

c. Qualifications of plaintiff §778
A few states require the plaintiff to be a registered shareholder; most states also allow a beneficial owner of shares to bring suit. (Also, a shareholder of a parent corporation can bring a derivative suit on a subsidiary's cause of action.) Shareholders cannot complain of wrongs committed before they purchased their shares except: (i) where the plaintiff acquires the shares by operation of law, (ii) in section 16(b) violations, (iii) where serious injustice will result, or (iv) where the wrong is continuing in nature. The plaintiff must *fairly and adequately represent* the interests of the shareholders.

d. Security for expenses §798
In a few states, the plaintiff, under certain circumstances, must post a bond to indemnify the corporation against certain of its litigation expenses, including attorneys' fees, in the event the plaintiff loses the suit. A plaintiff-shareholder who loses may also be liable for the court costs incurred by the parties.

e. Defenses §811
Defenses to a derivative suit include the statute of limitations and equitable defenses (*e.g.*, laches, unclean hands, etc.).

f. Settlement and recovery §814
Any settlement or judgment belongs to the corporation, absent special circumstances. Settlement or dismissal of the suit is generally subject to *court approval* after notice to all shareholders. Judgment on the merits or a court-approved settlement is *res judicata* as to the asserted claims.

g. Reimbursement to plaintiff §823
A victorious plaintiff may be entitled to reimbursement from the corporation for litigation expenses. Even absent a monetary recovery, many courts order reimbursement if the suit resulted in a *substantial benefit* to the corporation.

h. Indemnification of officers and directors §829
Indemnification issues arise when officers and directors are sued for

conduct undertaken in their official capacity. If the officer or director wins on the merits, she **may** be indemnified; indeed, in many states indemnification is **mandatory** if a director or officer wins on the merits. Most statutes also authorize the corporation to **advance** (not pay) expenses in defending against the claim. Statutes vary when the officer or director settles or loses; they are more liberal concerning indemnification in a third-party suit as opposed to a derivative suit.

i. **Liability insurance** §846

In most states, a corporation can obtain liability insurance for its indemnification costs and for any liability incurred by its officers and directors in serving the corporation.

VIII. CAPITALIZATION OF THE CORPORATION

A. SHARES—IN GENERAL §849

A "share" represents the shareholder's proprietary interest in a corporation; specifically, it represents a right to declared dividends, a right to share in corporate assets upon liquidation, and if voting shares, the right to vote.

B. CLASSES OF SHARES—PREFERENCES

1. **Common Stock** §852

Common shares generally entitle the owner to pro rata dividends, voting rights, and rights to liquidated assets—without any preferences. There may be more than one class of common stock with each class having differing rights.

2. **Preferred Stock** §854

Preferred stock is a class of stock having some preference over other classes of stock—generally as to dividends or liquidation rights. Preferred stock may also have several classes or series. Preferred shares may be given redemption rights (right to compel the corporation to repurchase shares).

a. **Particular preferences**

(1) **Preference in receipt of dividends** §858

Preferred shares may be entitled to a specified rate before dividends are paid to other classes. The dividend rights may be cumulative or noncumulative.

(2) **Participation rights** §861

The preferred shares may be entitled to participate with common shares in the funds available for distribution **after the preferred dividend** is paid.

b. **Convertibles** §862

Preferred stockholders may have a right, under specified circumstances, to convert their shares into common stock.

3. **Derivatives** §863

Newer types of securities are "derived" from stock (*e.g.*, a **warrant** is issued by a corporation giving the owner an option to purchase stock on certain terms).

C. AUTHORIZATION AND ISSUANCE OF SHARES §864

Subject to detailed regulations, shares must be authorized by the articles and issued by the board of directors; share certificates are issued for consideration. Under certain circumstances, a corporation may have authority to *repurchase* its shares.

D. STOCK SUBSCRIPTIONS

1. Definition §871

Stock subscriptions are agreements by subscribers to purchase stock to be issued.

2. Offer and Acceptance Problems §872

If the agreement is post-incorporation, both parties are bound. *If the agreement is pre-incorporation*, at common law, it was *not* enforceable because the corporation did not yet exist; the subscription is merely a continuing offer to purchase shares and can be revoked prior to acceptance by the corporation. By statute in most states today, pre-incorporation subscriptions are *irrevocable for a designated period*, absent contrary agreement.

E. CONSIDERATION REQUIRED TO BE PAID FOR SHARES

1. Form of Consideration §878

In states following the traditional approach, consideration is limited to "money paid, labor done, or property acquired."

    a. Executory promises §879

    Unless adequately secured, executory promises are not legal consideration under the traditional approach. However, more modern statutes consider promises of future payment or services to be adequate consideration. The Model Act permits issuance of shares for *any tangible or intangible property or benefit to the corporation.*

2. Amount of Consideration §882

The price the corporation must receive for shares depends on whether shares have a par value.

    a. Par value shares §883

    In states following the traditional approach, shares with a par value must be sold at least at par (with some exceptions—*e.g.*, to remedy impairment of capital).

        (1) "Watered stock" §885

        If par value shares are sold for less than par, the stock is "watered."

            (a) Remedies for creditors §886

            If the corporation becomes insolvent, creditors may recover from the shareholders the amount by which their shares were watered.

1) Which creditors may sue §887

Under the majority view, only those extending credit *after* watered stock is issued can recover. Some courts require creditor reliance on the corporation's having received par value for its shares. Under the minority view, all creditors can recover; the capital stock of the corporation constitutes a trust fund for all of its creditors.

2) Extent of liability §891

Under the majority view, watered stock liability exists only where there is *intentional overvaluation* of the assets being received by the corporation.

b. No-par value shares §892

All states allow the issuance of no par shares. Indeed, the Model Act generally has eliminated the concept of par value. Shares without a par value may be sold at any price deemed *reasonable* by the directors. Most states require that assets of the corporation be actually worth the "stated value."

F. FIDUCIARY DUTIES OF PROMOTERS

1. Duty to Corporation §896

A promoter owes the corporation fiduciary duties. Typical problems occur when a promoter sells property he owns to the corporation.

a. Duty of disclosure §897

A promoter owes the corporation a duty of *full disclosure* as to dealings with it in which the promoter has a personal interest. This requires a full revelation of *all material facts* that might affect the corporation's decision.

b. Effect of no plan to issue additional shares §898

If the promoters are the *sole* shareholders of the corporation and there is no plan to issue additional shares, a failure to disclose their adverse financial interest does *not* violate their fiduciary duty to the corporation. (*But note:* The *corporation* may have a cause of action under rule 10b-5 for nondisclosure.)

c. Effect of plan to issue additional shares §899

Under the majority ("Massachusetts") rule, the corporation can maintain an action for nondisclosure against promoters who were the only original shareholders if a further issue to innocent subscribers was contemplated as part of the original capitalization.

2. Effect of Securities Laws §902

Promoters' fiduciary duties are now governed by comprehensive state and federal laws mandating disclosure (*e.g.*, Securities Act of 1933), violations of which may result in penal sanctions and/or civil damages.

G. PREEMPTIVE RIGHTS

(*i.e.*, all securities traded on approved stock exchanges) from **substantive** blue sky regulation, although states may continue to enforce fraud provisions and some administrative procedures.

2. Federal Regulations §934

The 1933 Securities Act requires registration (**full disclosure**) of certain securities when using interstate facilities to "offer to sell" (this includes any type of solicitation or stirring of interest) a "security" (stocks, bonds, some promissory notes, etc.). No **written** offer to sell may be made unless it satisfies the requirements for a **statutory prospectus** (*i.e.*, a document disclosing key information from the registration materials).

a. Integrated disclosure §938

Corporations with actively traded shares may incorporate by reference their 1934 Act filings into their 1933 Act registration statements. Under these circumstances, a corporation may also offer securities over a two-year period after a registration statement's effective date (*i.e.*, **shelf registration**).

b. Exempt securities §949

The 1933 Act lists a number of securities exempted from registration requirements. If a security is exempt, it can be sold and resold without registration. However, such securities are still subject to the Act's anti-fraud rules.

c. Exempt transactions §950

A transaction exemption means that the securities being sold in this type of transaction do not have to be registered, but if they are resold in a different type of transaction they may then have to be registered. These include the following types of transactions:

(1) **Ordinary trading transactions** between individual investors **not** underwriters, issuers, or dealers;

(2) **Dealer transactions**, unless the dealer is acting as an underwriter or during the initial distribution of the securities;

(3) **Private placements**—*i.e.*, offerings to a small number of private subscribers who are **sufficiently experienced or informed** that disclosure requirements are unnecessary and who are acquiring the shares **as an investment** rather than for resale to the public;

(4) **Intrastate offerings** where the offering and sale is made entirely to residents of the same state in which the issuer resides and does business; and

(5) **Other exemptions**—for a public offering **not exceeding $5 million** in any 12-month period, the SEC permits an abbreviated offering circular (**Regulation A**); limited registration is available for securities issued pursuant to certain shareholder approved transactions, *e.g.*, mergers; and a simplified system of offerings by small business issuers (under $25 million in revenue in last fiscal year and no more than $25 million of outstanding public securities) is permitted.

IX. DISTRIBUTIONS TO SHAREHOLDERS

A. DIVIDENDS

1. Definition
§1012

A dividend is any distribution of **cash or property** paid to shareholders on account of share ownership.

2. Right to Dividends
§1013

Payment of dividends is within the **business judgment of the board**, unless bad faith or abuse of discretion is shown.

3. Source of Lawful Dividends

a. Traditional par value approach
§1018

Under traditional statutes, money received upon issuing par value stock is placed into the stated capital account. Dividends can be paid only when the corporation's net assets exceed the stated capital (subject to the **wasting asset**, e.g., oil wells, exception). Dividends cannot be paid from the stated capital account, and generally must be paid from surplus.

(1) Nimble dividends
§1022

Some states permit payment of dividends out of **current net profits** regardless of impairment of the capital account.

(2) Type of surplus account from which dividends may be paid
§1025

In traditional states earned surplus (all states), paid-in surplus (most states), and capital reduction surplus (most states) are proper sources of dividends. (The two latter sources may be subject to restrictions.) In most states, reappraisal surplus is not a proper source.

b. Model Act
§1039

The Revised Model Act authorizes dividends as long as the corporation's total assets are at least equal to its total liabilities. Dividends in such states are not limited to surplus.

4. Other Restrictions

a. Insolvency or endangerment of liquidation preference
§1040

If a corporation is insolvent or a dividend would render it insolvent, it may not legally pay a dividend. Similarly, a corporation cannot pay a dividend that would endanger the liquidation preference of preferred shares.

b. Contractual restrictions
§1043

Some lending institutions may insert a provision in a loan agreement with a corporation limiting payment of dividends until the loan is repaid.

5. Remedies for Illegal Dividends
§1044

Directors who declare an illegal dividend are jointly and severally liable to the corporation. Most states limit recovery to the amount of injury suffered by the creditors and preferred shareholders. Directors held liable may compel *contributions* from other directors who could be held liable and from shareholders who received the unlawful dividend with knowledge of the illegality. *Shareholder* liability is absolute when illegal dividends are declared and the corporation is insolvent.

B. REDEMPTION AND REPURCHASE OF SHARES

1. Redemption   §1052
Redemption is a corporation's acquisition of some or all of its outstanding shares at a stipulated price. Redeemed shares are usually canceled.

a. Source of funds   §1053
In most states (even those following the traditional par value approach), a corporation is permitted to redeem out of *any available funds* unless it would prejudice the rights of creditors.

2. Repurchase of Shares   §1054
"Repurchase" is generally authorized by statute. In traditional states, usually repurchased shares are not canceled but remain issued and are held by the corporation as *treasury stock* until resold. Generally, any accounts available for payment of dividends may be used to repurchase outstanding shares. In states following the modern approach, repurchased shares generally revert to authorized but unissued shares.

3. Further Limitations on Repurchase and Redemption   §1061
No redemption or repurchase is permitted if the corporation is *insolvent* or would be rendered insolvent. A corporation's solvency is determined at the time of payment on the redemption or when repurchase is made.

a. Note   §1067
Any discretionary redemption or repurchase must serve some bona fide *corporate purpose* rather than the personal interests of the directors or insiders.

4. Remedies   §1071
The same remedies available for illegal dividends are available against directors and shareholders for unlawful redemptions or repurchase of shares.

X. FUNDAMENTAL CHANGES IN CORPORATE STRUCTURE

A. INTRODUCTION   §1072
Fundamental changes in a corporation's structure (*i.e.*, mergers, sales of substantially all assets, article amendments, and dissolution) are subject to special statutory requirements. Special rules also apply to tender offers.

B. APPRAISAL RIGHTS

1. In General   §1073
Usually, shareholders who *dissent* from certain fundamental corporate changes are entitled to have the corporation purchase their shares at *"fair value"* (determined by either the Delaware block method or a modern financial method) or "fair market value."

2. **Procedure**   §1088

The procedural requirements for exercising appraisal rights vary widely. Under the Model Act, before a vote is taken, a shareholder must give **written notice** of her intent to demand payment for her shares **and** must not vote for the proposed action. If the action is approved, the corporation must deliver **notice to the dissenters** within 10 days of the approval vote after which the shareholder must **demand payment**. The corporation must then pay each dissenter who followed the proper procedure and must include certain information with payment (*e.g.*, financial statements, corporation's estimate of fair value, etc.).

   a. **Appraisal proceedings**   §1093

   Under the Model Act, a dissenting shareholder is unwilling to accept the corporation's fair value estimate she must give the corporation written notice with an estimate of the fair value and a demand for payment. If the corporation is not willing to pay the estimated value, it must, within 60 days, petition the court to determine fair value. The corporation is liable for costs unless the dissenters acted arbitrarily, vexatiously, or in bad faith.

C. STATUTORY MERGERS

1. **In General**   §1095

A statutory merger occurs when one corporation is legally absorbed into another. Shares of the disappearing corporation are converted into shares or other securities (or cash or other interests) of the surviving corporation.

   a. **Consolidation**   §1096

   A consolidation occurs when two or more corporations combine to form a wholly new corporation. Requirements are virtually identical to those for mergers.

2. **Effect of Merger**   §1097

The surviving corporation, by operation of law, succeeds to all of the disappearing corporation's rights, assets, and liabilities, including its contracts.

3. **Board Approval**   §1099

The board of each corporation must adopt a plan of merger.

4. **Notice**   §1100

If shareholders must approve the plan of merger, the corporation must notify each shareholder of the meeting and its purpose. After receiving this notice, a shareholder must give notice to the corporation that she intends to seek appraisal rights.

5. **Shareholder Approval**   §1102

After board approval, the plan of merger must be approved by that majority of shareholders (of each corporation) as is required by statute (usually a majority of the **outstanding stock**; some statutes require only a majority vote). Furthermore, some statutes require approval by each class. Dissenting shareholders normally have **appraisal rights** which, under some statutes, is an **exclusive remedy**.

6. Mergers Not Requiring Shareholder Approval

a. Short-form mergers §1107

Mergers between a parent (owning 90% or more of the stock of a subsidiary) and its subsidiary usually require only the approval of the two boards (or of the parent board alone). However, the *subsidiary's shareholders* do have *appraisal rights*.

b. Small-scale mergers §1110

Some statutes do not require approval by the shareholders of the *survivor* corporation if: (i) the voting stock of the survivor issued to effect the merger does not constitute more than a certain percentage (usually one-sixth) of the outstanding shares after the merger, *and* (ii) the merger does not make any change in the survivor's articles. *Note:* Approval by shareholders of the disappearing corporation *is* still necessary and these shareholders (unlike those of the survivor) have appraisal rights.

7. Mergers with No Appraisal Rights §1113

Appraisal rights are denied under certain circumstances based on (i) the *nature of the merger* (e.g., survivor's shareholders in a short-form merger), or (ii) the *nature of the stock* (e.g., listed on a national stock exchange, stock held by more than 2,000 shareholders). These exceptions vary according to statutes.

8. Articles of Merger Must Be Filed §1118

After approval of the plan of merger, articles of merger must be filed with the state and generally must include the parties' names and the changes, if any, made to the survivor's articles of incorporation.

D. DE FACTO MERGERS §1119

Many courts hold that transactions having the effect of a merger are subject to the procedural requirements of merger (e.g., rules for voting and appraisal rights). Examples of a de facto merger are sale of substantially all assets in exchange for stock and sale of a majority of stock for the stock of the acquiring corporation. The issue turns on whether the transaction has the *"indicia"* or *"all the characteristics and consequences"* of a merger. Some courts reject the de facto doctrine, applying instead the *equal dignity rule*—various combination forms have equal dignity— and the label used by management is determinative. Several jurisdictions have *statutes* that treat each corporate combination on the basis of *substance* rather than form.

E. TRIANGULAR MERGERS

1. Conventional Triangular Merger §1134

In a conventional triangular merger A and X plan to merge but instead of A (the survivor corporation) issuing its shares to X's shareholders, A creates a subsidiary (B) and transfers a certain number of shares to B in exchange for all of B's stock. X is then merged into B, whereupon B issues its shares of A stock to X's shareholders. Thus, A now owns X indirectly, through its wholly owned subsidiary. The major purpose for this procedure is to avoid assuming X's liabilities.

2. Reverse Triangular Merger §1135

In a reverse triangular merger, the same procedure as above is followed except that B is merged into X. B disappears and X becomes a wholly owned subsidiary of A. This form of merger may insulate A from X's liabilities, and X's legal status as a corporation is preserved, allowing it to retain valuable rights (*e.g.*, leases, licenses, franchises, etc.) that may have been lost in a conventional merger.

3. Voting and Appraisal Rights in Triangular Mergers §1136

Triangular mergers may be used to erode voting and appraisal rights. However, at least one court has refused to apply the de facto merger doctrine to such a transaction.

F. SALE OF SUBSTANTIALLY ALL ASSETS

1. Shareholder Approval §1137

Approval by a certain percentage (usually, a majority of the outstanding shares) is normally required for sale of substantially all of the assets of the corporation.

a. Exception—sales in ordinary course of business §1138

If the sale is made in the ordinary course of business of the corporation, shareholder approval is generally not required.

b. Other exceptions §1139

Other exceptions to shareholder approval may include sales when the corporation is in failing circumstances and execution of mortgage. The Model Act also excludes transfers of a corporation's assets to a wholly owned subsidiary and a pro rata distribution of assets to the corporation's shareholders.

2. Appraisal Rights §1142

Most statutes provide dissenting shareholders with appraisal rights.

3. What Constitutes "Substantially All Assets" §1143

The percentage of assets sold is not determinative. The issue is whether the assets constitute substantially all of the corporation's operating assets, account for most of the corporation's revenues, or are vital to the operation of the business. Under the Model Act, retention of a business activity comprising at least 25% of the corporation's total assets and 25% of either income (before taxes), or revenues for that fiscal year from continuing operations constitutes retention of a significant portion of the corporation's assets and removes the requirement of a shareholder vote.

G. AMENDMENT OF ARTICLES

1. Vote Required §1146

An amendment of the articles of incorporation must normally be approved by the board and approval by a stated percentage (usually a majority) of the outstanding shares.

Amendments affecting a certain class, *e.g.*, change of preference, may require approval by all shareholders and by the class voting separately.

The articles (or shareholder agreement) may require a higher (but not lower) percentage of shareholder approval for any proposed amendment than would otherwise be required by statute. By statute, other changes may require special procedures, *e.g.*, reducing the number of directors.

Many states give appraisal rights in connection with certain kinds of article amendments, *e.g.*, abolishment of a preferential right.

Because a certificate of incorporation is a contract—between the state and corporation **and** also among the shareholders—the Contract Clause limits the state's power to regulate corporations and also limits shareholders' power, absent unanimity, to amend the articles or make fundamental changes. Thus, today most statutes contain **reserved power clauses** permitting a state to alter, amend, or repeal its corporation laws; statutes were also amended to allow fundamental changes or amendments with a **less than unanimous shareholder** vote. These clauses are given effect because they are deemed to be part of every contract (*i.e.*, certificate of incorporation).

A **state** today may enact laws restricting or prohibiting certain business activities that were proper when organized. However, under the Due Process Clause, it cannot eliminate vested property rights or impair the obligations of contracts with third persons. **Shareholders** are limited in amending the articles of incorporation by the **fairness** requirement.

H. DISSOLUTION AND LIQUIDATION

Dissolution is the termination of a corporation's status as a **legal entity**. Liquidation is the termination of the corporation's business.

Voluntary dissolution generally requires board approval and approval by a stated percentage of the outstanding shares, although some statutes require only a simple majority vote.

Most statutes give directors or shareholders the right to petition a court for dissolution on various grounds: **deadlock** among management or shareholders, **oppressive or fraudulent** management, and **waste** of assets. In practice, involuntary dissolution is rarely ordered for any corporation other than a **close corporation**.

Agreements among shareholders (usually of a close corporation) to dissolve upon the occurrence of a specified event are valid even if not statutorily authorized.

5. Action by Directors §1173
Some statutes permit directors to petition for involuntary dissolution on specified grounds.

6. Action by State §1174
The state may bring a dissolution action in *quo warranto* when a particular requirement in which the state has an important interest is not met (*e.g.,* nonpayment of taxes).

7. Liquidation §1175
After dissolution, the corporate business continues only to wind up its affairs, *e.g.,* pay debts, distribute assets, etc. The winding up period must be reasonable or the directors may be personally liable for corporate debts.

a. Rights of shareholders §1177
If only one class of shares is outstanding, each shareholder receives a pro rata share of the assets after the creditors are satisfied. If there are several classes, preferred shareholders are paid off before a pro rata distribution among common stock.

b. Rights of creditors §1180
A corporation remains liable on its debts after dissolution. Statutes govern the manner in which creditors must be given *notice* of the dissolution and the time within which they must file their claims.

I. LIMITATIONS ON POWER OF CONTROLLING SHAREHOLDERS TO EFFECT FUNDAMENTAL CHANGES IN CORPORATE STRUCTURE

1. Fiduciary Duty to Minority Shareholders §1184
The fiduciary duty owed by controlling shareholders to the minority exists when any fundamental change in which the controlling shareholder is interested occurs.

2. Freeze-Outs

a. Sale of substantially all assets §1185
A controlling shareholder normally may not freeze out the minority by a sale of substantially all of the corporation's assets to a corporation that he controls.

b. Merger §1187
A freeze-out occurs in a merger if a surviving corporation issues cash, rather than stock, in exchange for the stock of the disappearing corporation. The minority shareholders end up with stock in a corporation that holds only cash, while the survivor owns all of the corporate business.

c. Reverse stock splits §1188
Most statutes allow the corporation to adopt a reverse stock split and eliminate fractional (less than one full share) shares.

d. When permissible §1191
A freeze-out may be permissible *if* effected for a *legitimate business*

purpose, e.g., operating efficiency. This requirement does not apply in Delaware, but Delaware does require "entire fairness."

3. **Effect of Securities Acts** §1195

In addition to rights under state law (*e.g.*, appraisal rights), a shareholder dissenting from a fundamental change may sue under rule 10b-5 or the federal proxy rules if the controlling shareholders engaged in deceptive conduct.

4. **Self-Tender** §1196

A corporation may make a tender offer for its minority shares. This is *not* technically a freeze-out because shareholders are not legally required to accept the offer, although it may be the only economically feasible alternative.

5. **Going-Private Transactions** §1197

Transactions eliminating public ownership are governed by rule 13e-3 of the Securities Exchange Act, which defines such transactions to include: (i) *a purchase* of any equity security by the issuer; (ii) *a tender offer* for any equity security by the corporation; and (iii) *a solicitation of proxies* in connection with a fundamental corporate change under defined circumstances that tend to devalue the remaining securities.

a. **Other factors** §1199

In going-private actions, the issuer is required to *file and disseminate* certain information. The transaction is also subject to an *anti-fraud rule* similar to that of rule 10b-5 (minus the "purchase and sale" requirement).

6. **Effect of Appraisal Rights** §1201

Even under statutes making appraisal an exclusive remedy, usually a dissenting shareholder can attack the transaction on the basis of lack of authorization, improper procedures, and fraudulent misrepresentation. Under statutes not making appraisal an exclusive remedy, shareholders can generally request injunctive relief or rescission, but not money damages.

J. TENDER OFFERS

1. **Terminology**

a. **Raider** §1207

A raider (more accurately called a *bidder*) is a person or corporation that makes a tender offer for the shares of a corporation (*target*) that the bidder is seeking to acquire.

b. **White knight** §1209

To prevent a takeover by a certain corporation, the target management may solicit competing offers from more friendly corporations (white knights).

c. **Lock-up; crown jewels** §1210

A "lock-up" is a device that gives a friendly bidder an option to acquire certain assets or shares to defeat less friendly bidders. "Crown jewels" refers to the target's most desirable business, which the target may give or sell to a white knight.

statutes. Under a control share acquisition statute, if a designated stock-ownership level (*e.g.,* 20% of the outstanding shares) is crossed by a person purchasing shares, he cannot vote the acquired shares unless the persons holding a majority of the other shares approve. A control share acquisition statute has been ruled constitutional. Some statutes ("third-generation statutes") regulating takeovers do not fall into either category, *e.g.,* five-year delay required between tender offer and merger with bidder absent target board's prior approval. **Constituency statutes** allow a board to consider interests of nonshareholder groups in making decisions to resist takeovers.

XI. CONFLICT OF LAWS PRINCIPLES §1289

As a general rule, all questions concerning the organization or internal affairs of a corporation are decided according to the law of the state in which it was incorporated. A few states have statutes subjecting foreign corporations having substantial local contacts to local regulations intended to protect shareholders and creditors. Corporations listed on a national securities exchange may be exempt from the statutes.

Approach to Exams

Corporations problems may require a determination either of the rights and liabilities of parties within the corporate structure (shareholders, officers, directors); parties outside the corporate structure (creditors, underwriters, promoters, etc.); and/or of the corporation itself.

Such rights and liabilities may arise under three separate bodies of law: First, the traditional *common law* rules governing corporations; second, *state statutes*, as most states today have enacted comprehensive codes that have altered or displaced the common law rules; and third, *federal securities laws* which, in various areas, have engrafted totally new doctrines into the law of corporations.

Analysis of corporations problems may be facilitated by considering the following factors:

A. Has the Status of a Corporation Been Attained?

1. Has the entity been organized in *sufficient compliance* with statutory requirements governing the formation of a corporation?

2. If not, should the case be decided *as if* a corporation has been validly formed?

    a. Has the entity attained at least a *"de facto"* status?

    b. Or, are the facts such that a particular party may be *estopped* from challenging the corporate status?

3. If there is still no basis for treating the entity as a corporation, what are the *liabilities of the members*? Are the members *individually liable* for the debts incurred in the entity's name?

4. Assuming that a corporation has been formed, are the circumstances such that the *corporate entity should be disregarded*? That is, should the case be decided *as if there were no corporation*?

5. Is there any issue as to *consequence of the corporate status*? The fact that a valid corporation has been formed may in itself be determinative of various issues involved (*e.g.*, the corporation's right to hold title to property, or to sue in the corporate name). More frequently, however, the fact that the entity has attained corporate status is merely a stepping stone to a determination of some issue as to the validity of a corporate act or the rights and liabilities of individuals involved with the corporation.

B. Is There Any Issue as to the Validity of a Corporate Act?

Examine each act undertaken by the corporation, and each act for which the corporation is sought to be held liable (*e.g.*, each contract, conveyance, distribution to shareholders), with the following in mind:

1. Was the act within the *express or implied powers* of the corporation?

    a. *What is the source of the power*? Remember that a corporation, by its very nature, has only the powers conferred upon it by its articles, bylaws, or applicable statutes or case law.

    b. *Are any limitations or prohibitions* applicable?

        (1) Consider whether the act would violate any *statutory or certificate restriction* (*e.g.*, unlawful dividend; unlawful redemption or purchase of shares).

        (2) Of at least equal importance, consider whether the act would violate any *equitable limitation* on corporate powers—*i.e.*, limitations implied by courts for the protection of minority shareholders, creditors, or the public (*e.g.*, interested director transactions; inadequate capitalization).

2. Was there a *valid exercise* of such power by the corporation?

    a. If the corporation is sought to be held liable for the act of some *individual* (promoter, officer, director, etc.), the issue is basically one of authority—was the individual the authorized agent of the corporation with respect to the particular act?

    b. As to corporate resolutions or other direct acts by the entity, the issue is whether the necessary *internal procedures* specified in the articles, bylaws, statutes, etc., have been complied with:

        (1) Was there a valid *adoption or ratification by the board* of directors?

        (2) Was *shareholder approval* required, and if so, was it obtained?

        (3) Did the *personal interest* of directors or shareholders disqualify their vote?

3. *Who may challenge* the validity of the corporate act?

    a. Are the parties to the transaction (including the corporation) *estopped* to challenge it?

    b. Will a shareholders' *derivative suit* lie?

    c. What about *quo warranto* proceedings by the state?

C. What Are the Rights and Liabilities of the Particular Individuals Involved?

1. Characterization

The first step in analyzing the rights and liabilities of the various individuals involved in a corporations problem is to determine their status—*e.g.*, shareholders, officers, directors, creditors, contracting parties, etc.

a. This may require a determination of the *validity of some prior corporate act or other event* (*supra*) upon which their status depends. For example, as to a claimed shareholder, were the shares validly issued in the first place? Were the shares validly transferred to this individual? What is the effect of any restriction on the transfer of the shares? Of failure to deliver the certificate to the transferee, etc.?

    (1) In characterizing corporate acts or events, remember that *de facto doctrines* may be employed to avoid injustice (*e.g.*, a sale of corporate assets that has the effect of a merger may be treated as such, with appropriate requirements for shareholder approval, etc.).

b. It may not be enough merely to categorize an individual as "shareholder," "creditor," etc. *Distinctions* may have to be drawn between the rights and liabilities of *persons in the same category*, *e.g.*, as a shareholder (controlling vs. minority); as a creditor (prior vs. subsequent); as a director (dissenting vs. approving, present vs. absent, interested vs. noninterested).

c. Keep in mind that *the same person may play multiple roles* in the problem—the person may be both a director and a shareholder, or both an officer and creditor of the corporation, etc. In such cases, consider whether that person owes any duties to the corporation in one capacity (*e.g.*, as officer or director) that might impair or limit her rights in the other capacity (*e.g.*, as creditor or shareholder).

2. Rights

Once the status of each individual is ascertained, the next step is to determine the nature and extent of his rights with respect to whatever issues are raised in the problem. For example, as to a shareholder, the problem may require an analysis of the "right" to dividends, voting rights, the right to protection against majority action, etc.

3. Liabilities

The determination of liability usually flows from the determination of status; *e.g.*, a person who is shown to be a promoter, director, or controlling shareholder may owe various duties to the corporation, to the shareholders, to creditors, or to others.

a. Consider first what duties are prescribed by the *articles or bylaws* of the corporation itself.

b. Next consider what duties are prescribed by statute—with attention both to state corporations statutes and *federal securities laws*.

c. If there are no statutory duties, consider whether any *common law fiduciary duty* is owed by such person *to the corporation* (full disclosure regarding transactions in which she has an interest, right of first refusal as to corporation opportunities, etc.) and/or to *any other aggrieved party* (minority shareholders, creditors, etc.).

d. The rules may vary somewhat where *close corporations* are involved. By statute or case law, fewer formalities are required in the corporate structure, but stricter fiduciary duties are usually imposed among the shareholders.

4. Remedies

Consider what remedies should be made available to each possible plaintiff (including the corporation), as against each possible defendant (including the corporation):

a. Form of action

Federal or state court? Law or equity? Individual suit or class action? Suit by corporation or derivative action by shareholder?

b. Form of relief

Appraisal, injunction, rescission, constructive trust, specific performance, or damages? What is the measure of damages (secret profits measure, penalty measure, restitutionary measure)?

Chapter One: Characteristics of the Corporation and Other Business Organizations

CONTENTS

Chapter Approach

This chapter describes the principal characteristics of corporations and compares those characteristics with the characteristics of other business organizations. You may find a question on your exam asking you to determine which form of business organization would best meet particular clients' needs. In such a case, you would need to consider the advantages and disadvantages of the various forms. Or you may find a question dealing with issues concerning one of these forms. In such a case, you would need to know the most important rules that govern these business business forms.

A. Corporations

1. **Entity Status [§1]**

    A corporation is a legal entity created under the authority of the legislature.

2. **Limited Liability [§2]**

    As a legal entity, a corporation is responsible for its own debts. A corporation's shareholders normally are not responsible for its debts. Their liability—or more accurately, their risk—is *limited* to the amount of their investment.

3. **Free Transferability of Interests [§3]**

    Ownership interests in a corporation are represented by shares, which are freely transferable.

4. **Centralized Management and Control [§4]**

    The management and control of a corporation's affairs are centralized in a board of directors and in officers acting under the board's authority. Although the shareholders elect the board, they cannot directly control its activities. Shareholders, as such, generally have no power to either participate in management or to determine questions within the scope of the corporation's business. These matters are for the board. **[Charlestown Boot & Shoe Co. v. Dunsmore,** 60 N.H. 85 (1880)] Correspondingly, shareholders, as such, have no authority to act on the corporation's behalf.

5. **Duration—Continuity of Existence [§5]**

    As a legal entity, a corporation is capable of perpetual duration. The corporation's existence continues notwithstanding the death or incapacity of its shareholders or a transfer of its shares.

6. Taxation [§6]

Business entities generally are taxed under either the firm-taxation model or the flow-through taxation model. Under the *firm-taxation* model, a business firm is taxable on its income. Accordingly, if the firm has income or expenses, or gains or losses, those items go to the firm's taxable income, and not to the owners' taxable income. If the firm then makes distributions to its owners out of after-tax income, ordinarily the owners pay taxes on those distributions. This is sometimes referred to as "double taxation." Under the *flow-through* taxation model, a firm is not subject to taxation. Instead all of the firm's income and expenses, and gains and losses, are taxable directly to the firm's owners. Distributions are not taxed. Thus there is no "double taxation" effect. Correspondingly, if the firm has losses, the owners can use the losses to offset their income from other sources.

a. General rule [§7]

Generally speaking, corporations are taxed under the firm-taxation model.

b. Subchapter S corporations [§8]

There is an exception to the general rule for "Subchapter S" corporations. Under Subchapter S of the Internal Revenue Code, the owners of qualifying corporations can elect a special tax status under which the corporation and its shareholders receive flow-through taxation that is comparable (although not identical) to partnership taxation. Among the conditions for making and maintaining a Subchapter S election are the following:

(i)   The corporation may not have more than 100 shareholders;

(ii) The corporation may not have more than one class of stock;

(iii) All the shareholders must be individuals or qualified estates or trusts; and

(iv) No shareholder may be a nonresident alien.

The amount of the corporation's assets and income is immaterial under Subchapter S.

B. General Partnerships

1. Introduction [§9]

A useful way to understand the principal characteristics of the corporation is to contrast corporate characteristics with those of other forms of business organizations, such as general partnerships, limited partnerships, limited liability partnerships, and limited liability companies. The remainder of this chapter will concern those forms of business organization beginning here with a discussion of general partnerships. In about two-thirds of the states, general partnerships are governed by the Revised Uniform Partnership Act ("RUPA"). In the remaining one-third, general partnerships are governed by the Uniform Partnership Act ("UPA"). Where the two acts differ, both will be discussed.

2. Definition [§10]

A partnership is "an association of two or more persons to carry on as co-owners a business for profit." [UPA §6; RUPA §201]

3. Formation [§11]

Corporations can be organized (formed) only if certain formalities are complied with and a filing is made with the state. In contrast, general partnerships can be organized with no formalities and no filing. The absence of a filing requirement reflects, in part, a conception that partnership status depends on the factual characteristics of a relationship between two or more persons, not on whether the persons think of themselves as having entered into a partnership.

4. Legal Status—Entity vs. Aggregate [§12]

Individuals may associate in a wide variety of forms, and the issue often arises whether a given form of association is simply an aggregate of its members, or has a legal status separate from that of its members. Frequently, this issue is stated in terms of whether a particular form of association is—or is not—a "separate legal entity" or a "legal person" (as opposed to a natural person, *i.e.*, an individual). A variety of issues may turn on the answer to this question—*e.g.*, whether the association can sue and be sued in its own name, and whether it can hold property in its own right.

a. UPA [§13]

UPA section 6 provides that, "[a] partnership is an association of two or more persons to carry on as co-owners a business for profit." Although the language of this provision does not in itself render the issue free from doubt, it is fairly clear that the Act was intended to adopt the aggregate theory rather than the entity theory of partnership.

b. RUPA [§14]

In contrast to the UPA, the RUPA confers entity status on partnerships. RUPA section 101, like UPA section 6, defines a partnership as "an association of two or more persons to carry on as co-owners a business for profit." However, RUPA section 201 then specifically provides that, "[a] partnership is an entity."

5. Personal Liability [§15]

In contrast to corporations, in which the liability (or more accurately, risk) of the shareholders is limited to their investment, in a general partnership every partner is subject to unlimited personal liability for the debts and obligations of the partnership.

a. **Distinguish—limited liability partnerships [§16]**

Note that in limited liability partnerships (discussed below), the rule is different from the rule in general partnerships—partners are not subject to unlimited personal liability for partnership obligations.

b. **UPA [§17]**

Under the UPA, partners are individually liable for wrongful acts and omissions of the partnership (such as torts), breaches of trust, and "for all other debts and obligations of the partnership." [UPA §15]

c. **RUPA [§18]**

The RUPA also provides that partners are liable for all obligations of the partnership. [RUPA §306] However, the RUPA adds a new barrier to *collecting* against an individual partner. Under the RUPA, a judgment against a partner based on a claim against the partnership normally cannot be satisfied against the partner's individual assets unless and until: (i) a judgment on the same claim has been rendered against the partnership, and (ii) a writ of execution on the judgment has been returned unsatisfied. [RUPA §30] To put this differently, the RUPA adopts an *exhaustion* rule, under which partnership assets must be exhausted before a partner's individual assets can be reached. (The exhaustion rule is made subject to certain exceptions, one of which is that the rule does not apply if the partnership is in bankruptcy.) Thus, as the Comment to RUPA section 306 points out, "Joint and several liability under RUPA differs . . . from the classic model [of joint and several liability outside RUPA], which permits a judgment creditor to proceed immediately against any of the joint and several judgment debtors."

6. **Transferability of Interests [§19]**

In contrast to corporate stock, which is freely transferable unless transferability is limited by a valid certificate, bylaw, or contractual provision, unless otherwise agreed a partner *cannot* transfer his partnership interest in such a way as to make the transferee a *member* of the partnership, except with the consent of all remaining partners. [UPA §8; RUPA §401(i)]

a. **Distinguish—interest in partnership profits [§20]**

Although a partner cannot make a transferee a *member* of the partnership, a partner can assign his *interest* in the partnership. Such an assignment does not entitle the assignee, during the continuance of the partnership, to take part in the management or administration of the partnership business or affairs, to require any information or account of partnership transactions, or to inspect the partnership books. It merely entitles the assignee to receive, in accordance with his contract, the profits to which the assigning partner would otherwise be entitled. In case of a dissolution of the partnership, the assignee is entitled to receive his assignor's interest. [UPA §27; **Rapoport v. 55 Perry Co.**, 50 A.D.2d 54 (1975)]

7. Dissolution, Dissociation, Winding Up, and Termination [§21]

A corporation typically has perpetual existence; a partnership does not. The existence of a partnership may be terminated for a number of reasons, and different reasons for termination may result in different consequences.

a. In general [§22]

Assume that a partnership is to be terminated as a going concern. Typically, the termination process is divided into three phases.

(1) First phase

The first phase consists of an event—which may, among other things, be the decision of a partner or of a court—that sets the termination in motion.

(2) Second phase

The second phase consists of the process of actually terminating the partnership's business. Inevitably, some period of time must elapse between the moment at which the event that sets termination in motion occurs, and the time at which termination of the partnership's business is completed. For example, if the partnership is in the manufacturing business, to terminate the business the partnership will need to pay off its debts, settle its contracts with employees and suppliers, find a purchaser for the factory, and so forth.

(3) Third phase

The final phase consists of the completion of the second phase and an end to the partnership as a going concern.

b. UPA [§23]

Under the UPA, the first phase is referred to as "*dissolution*," the second phase is referred to as "*winding up*," and the third phase is referred to as "*termination*." The principal draftsman of the UPA explained as follows the manner in which that statute uses the term "dissolution":

> [Dissolution designates] a change in the relation of the partners caused by any partner ceasing to be associated in the carrying on of the business. As thus used "dissolution" does not terminate the partnership, it merely ends the carrying on of the business in that partnership. The partnership continues until the winding up of partnership affairs is completed.

[Lewis, *The Uniform Partnership Act*, 24 Yale L.J. 617, 626-27 (1915)] To put all of this somewhat differently, the term "dissolution" is used in the UPA to describe a change in the *legal status* of the partners and the partnership. "Winding up" is used to describe the *economic event* of liquidation that follows dissolution. "Termination" is used to describe the *end point of winding up*.

(1) Dissolution under the UPA [§24]

Under the UPA, any termination of a person's status as a partner effects a "dissolution" of the partnership. Because the UPA treats a partnership as an aggregation, the drafters believed that any change in the identity of the partners who make up the aggregation necessarily works a dissolution of the partnership. That is, if a partnership is conceptualized as an aggregation of the partners, and if the partners in Partnership P are A, B, C, and D, then the drafters of the UPA took the position that if D ceases to be a partner, there must be a dissolution of Partnership P, because there is no longer an aggregation of A, B, C, and D. Following this line, UPA section 29 defines dissolution as "the change in the relation of partners caused by any partner ceasing to be associated in the carrying on" of the partnership's business.

(a) Rightful dissolution [§25]

Under the UPA, a partnership is terminable at will unless a definite term is specified or can be implied. [UPA §31(1)(a); **Page v. Page,** 55 Cal. 2d 192 (1961)] Furthermore, because a partnership is not an entity, but only an aggregation of the individual partners, under the UPA a partnership is normally dissolved—even before the expiration of any stated term—by the death, incapacity, or withdrawal of any partner.

(b) Wrongful dissolution [§26]

Under the UPA, dissolution can also be caused, *in contravention of the agreement between the partners,* by the express will of any partner at any time, or by a court, where a partner has: (i) been guilty of conduct that tends to prejudicially affect the carrying on of the business, (ii) willfully or persistently committed a breach of the partnership agreement, or (iii) otherwise so conducted himself, in matters relating to the partnership business, that it is not reasonably practicable to carry on the business in partnership with him. [UPA §§31, 32]

1) Consequences of wrongful dissolution under the UPA [§27]

Broadly speaking, the law may attach consequences to dissolution (i) among the partners themselves, and (ii) between the partners as a group and third persons, such as individuals or firms with whom the partnership has contracted.

a) Consequences among the partners [§28]

Under the UPA, upon the occurrence of dissolution (which, under the UPA means simply that any partner ceases to be a partner) unless otherwise agreed, the partnership normally must sell its assets for cash and distribute the proceeds of the sale among all the partners. If, however, a partner,

A, wrongfully causes dissolution, the *partnership* is dissolved but the remaining partners can continue the partnership's *business*. To do so, the remaining partners must either: (i) pay A the value of her partnership interest, minus any damages caused by the dissolution; or (ii) put up a bond to secure such a payment, and indemnify A against present and future partnership liabilities. [UPA §38(2)(b)] Accordingly, a wrongfully dissolving partner is subject to two sanctions: (i) she must pay damages for any loss caused to the other partners by her wrongful dissolution; and (ii) the remaining partners do not have to pay her the full value of her partnership interest, but instead only the value of that interest without taking goodwill into account. Agreements that enable remaining partners to continue the business after dissolution are common. Such agreements are usually known as business-continuation agreements or, more simply, continuation agreements.

b) Effect on relationship with third parties [§29]

Dissolution may also affect the relationship between the partnership and third persons. For example, suppose that Partnership P consists of partners A, B, C, and D. The partnership is dissolved by the withdrawal of D, but the business of the partnership is continued by A, B, and C under a continuation agreement. Because Partnership P has been dissolved, the partnership of A, B, and C may be deemed a "new" partnership for legal purposes. Accordingly, P's assets and agreements, such as leases, licenses, or franchises, must be "transferred" to the new partnership. This can be a problem when an agreement is not transferable. In **Fairway Development Co. v. Title Insurance Co.**, 621 F. Supp. 120 (N.D. Ohio 1985), Fairway, a partnership, sued Title Insurance Co. under a title guarantee policy. The policy had been issued at a time when the partners in Fairway were B, S, and W. Subsequently, B and S transferred their partnership interests to W and a third party, V. W and V continued Fairway's business under the Fairway name. The court held that Title Insurance was not bound under its policy because the partnership to which Fairway issued the policy had been legally dissolved.

c. RUPA [§30]

The RUPA continues to use the terms "dissolution," "winding up," and "termination." However, the RUPA adds a new term, "dissociation," to describe the termination of a person's status as a partner.

(1) Rightful and wrongful dissociation under the RUPA [§31]

The RUPA distinguishes between events of dissociation that involve *rightful* conduct by the dissociated partner and events of dissociation that involve *wrongful* conduct. An event of dissociation is rightful unless it is specified as wrongful.

(a) Wrongful dissociation [§32]

Under the RUPA, a partner has the power to dissociate at any time by expressing a will to withdraw, even in contravention of the partnership agreement. [RUPA §602] However, there is a distinction between a partner's *power* to withdraw in contravention of the partnership agreement and a partner's *right* to do so. Although a partner cannot be enjoined from exercising the power to dissociate, the dissociation may be wrongful. The major significance of a wrongful dissociation is that it may give rise to damages. The major types of wrongful dissociation under the RUPA are:

(i) A *dissociation that is in breach of an express provision* of the partnership agreement;

(ii) A *withdrawal of a partner by the partner's express will before the expiration of the partnership term* or the completion of an undertaking for which the partnership was formed;

(iii) A partner's *engaging in wrongful conduct* that adversely and materially affected the partnership business; and

(iv) A partner's willfully or persistently *committing a material breach of the partnership agreement or of a duty* of care, loyalty, good faith, or fair dealing owed to the partnership or the other partners.

Generally speaking, under the RUPA any other dissociation is rightful.

(b) Consequences of dissociation under the RUPA [§33]

Recall that under the UPA, if the partnership status of one or more partners is terminated the partnership is dissolved, although the remaining partners might continue the business as a *new* partnership. In contrast, under the RUPA the dissociation of a partner does not necessarily cause dissolution.

1) Winding up and buyout [§34]

Under the RUPA, dissociation leads to two forks in the statutory road: *winding up* under Article 8, or mandatory *buyout* under Article 7. Which fork must be taken depends on the nature of the event of dissociation.

a) First fork—winding up [§35]

The basic rule under RUPA section 801 is that a partnership is dissolved, and its business must be wound up upon, but only upon, the occurrence of one of the following events:

1/ In a *partnership at will*, the partnership's having notice from a partner of that *partner's express will to withdraw* as a partner; and

2/ In a *partnership for a definite term or particular undertaking*:

    a/ The express *will of all of the partners* to wind up the partnership business;

    b/ The *expiration of the partnership term or the completion of the undertaking*;

    c/ An *event agreed to in the partnership agreement* as resulting in the winding up of the partnership business;

    d/ An event that makes it *unlawful for all or substantially all of the business* of the partnership to be continued (but a cure of the illegality within 90 days after notice to the partnership of the event is effective retroactively to the date of the event for purposes of this section);

    e/ A partner's *dissociation by death, incapacity, or bankruptcy, or the like,* or a partner's *wrongful dissociation*, if within 90 days at least half of the remaining partners decide to wind up the partnership business;

    f/ A *judicial determination*, on application by a partner, that either:

        1] The *economic purpose* of the partnership is likely to be *unreasonably frustrated*;

        2] Another partner has engaged in conduct relating to the partnership which makes it *not reasonably practicable to carry on the business* in partnership with that partner; or

        3] It is *not otherwise reasonably practicable to carry on the partnership business* in conformity with the partnership agreement;

g/ A *judicial determination*, on application by a transferee of a partner's transferable interest, that it is equitable to wind up the partnership business, either:

1] *After the expiration of the term of the partnership or completion of the undertaking* for which the partnership was formed, if the partnership was for a definite time or particular undertaking; or

2] At any time, if the *partnership was a partnership at will*.

b) Second fork—buyout [§36]

If, upon the dissociation of a partner, winding up is not required, then dissociation does not result in dissolution and winding up. Instead, dissociation results in a mandatory buyout of the dissociated partner's interest by the remaining partners and a continuation of the partnership entity and business by the remaining partners. However, a partner who *wrongfully dissociates* before the expiration of a definite term, or the completion of the undertaking for which the partnership was formed, is not entitled to payment of the buyout price *until the expiration of the term or the completion of the undertaking*, unless the dissociating partner establishes to the satisfaction of the court that earlier payment will not cause undue hardship to the business of the partnership.

1/ Buyout price [§37]

The buyout price of a dissociated partner's interest is the amount that would have been distributable to him on the date of the dissociation if the assets of the partnership were sold at a price equal to the *greater* of: (i) the partnership's liquidation value; or (ii) the partnership's value if the entire business was sold as a going concern. [RUPA §701] However, if the dissociation was wrongfully caused by the dissociated partner, the buyout price is *reduced by damages* for the wrongful dissociation. [RUPA §701(c)]

8. Management and Control [§38]

In contrast to shareholders, who have no right to participate in the corporation's business, *unless otherwise provided in the partnership agreement*:

(i) Every partner has a *right to participate* in the management of the partnership business.

(ii) Any *difference* arising as to ordinary matters connected with the partnership business may be decided by a *majority* of the partners, with each partner having one vote regardless of the relative amount of his capital contribution.

(iii) *Extraordinary* matters require approval by *all* the partners.

[UPA §18; **Summers v. Dooley,** 481 P.2d 318 (Idaho 1971); *and see* RUPA §401(f)]

a. Comment

The right of a partner to participate in the management of the partnership's business is one reason that partners have unlimited liability. In contrast, the fact that a shareholder has no right to participate in the management of a corporation's business is one reason that shareholders have limited liability.

9. Authority [§39]

In contrast to a corporate shareholder, who has no authority to bind the corporation, every partner is an *agent* of the partnership *for the purpose of its business*.

a. UPA [§40]

Under the UPA, a partner has apparent authority for carrying on in the usual way the business of the partnership—unless the partner so acting in fact has no actual authority to act for the partnership in the particular matter, and the person with whom he is dealing "has knowledge" that the partner has no such authority. The UPA defines "knowledge" broadly, to include both actual knowledge and "knowledge of such facts as in the circumstances shows bad faith." However, an act of a partner that is not for the carrying on of the business of the partnership in the usual way does not bind the partnership unless the act is actually authorized by the other partners. [UPA §9; **Owens v. Palos Verdes Monaco,** 142 Cal. App. 3d 855 (1983)]

b. RUPA [§41]

The RUPA takes the same general approach to a partner's authority as the UPA, but there are several differences in important details.

(1) Business of the same kind [§42]

Under the UPA, it was unclear whether a partner had apparent authority for carrying on business of the *kind* carried on by the partnership, or only for carrying on the *actual* business of the partnership. [*See* **Burns v. Gonzalez,** 439 S.W.2d 131 (Tex. 1969)] In contrast, under RUPA even if a general partner's actual authority is restricted by the terms of the partnership agreement, she has apparent authority to bind the partnership in either (i) the ordinary course of the partnership's actual business, or (ii) business of the *kind* carried on by the partnership, unless the third party *knew* or *had received a notification* that the partner lacked authority. **[RNR Investments Limited Partnership v. Peoples First Community Bank,** 812 So. 2d 561 (Fla. 2002)]

(2) Statement of authority [§43]

Also, the RUPA provides for the filing of a "Statement of Partnership Authority." A *grant* of authority set forth in such a statement is normally conclusive in favor of third persons, even if they have no actual knowledge of the statement, unless they have actual knowledge that the partner has *no* such authority. However, a *limitation* on a partner's authority that is contained in such a statement—other than a limitation on the partner's authority to transfer real property—will not be effective unless the third party *knows of the limitation* or the *statement has been delivered to him*. A limitation on a partner's authority to transfer *real property* will be effective if properly filed, even if the third party does not know of the statement and it has not been delivered to him. [RUPA §303]

10. Ownership of Property

a. UPA [§44]

Like a corporation, a partnership can hold and convey title to property in its own name. [UPA §8] But under the aggregate theory of the UPA, even though title to assets may be held in the name of the partnership, the property is said to be "owned" by the partners—in a unique form of ownership known as "tenancy in partnership." [UPA §25(1)] However, the partners' "ownership" interest in partnership property under the UPA's tenancy in partnership is largely theoretical, because UPA section 25(2) strips away from the partners all the usual incidents of ownership, such as the right to assign and the right to bequeath.

b. RUPA [§45]

The RUPA abolishes the tenancy-in-partnership apparatus of the UPA. Under the RUPA, a partnership is an entity, and property acquired by the partnership is owned by the partnership, not by the individual partners. [RUPA §203]

11. Capacity to Sue and Be Sued

a. UPA [§46]

Unlike a corporation, which as an entity can sue and be sued in its own name, under the UPA a partnership cannot sue or be sued in its own name, because it is an aggregation rather than an entity. Rather, under the UPA, suit on a partnership obligation must be brought by or against individual partners.

(1) Type of liability [§47]

Under general law, if an obligation is "joint and several," the obligors can be sued either jointly or separately. If, however, an obligation is only "joint," the obligee normally must join all the obligors. Under the UPA, partners are *jointly and severally* liable for wrongful acts and omissions (*e.g.*, torts) of the partnership and breaches of trust. [UPA §15(a)] However, partners are only *jointly* liable "for all other debts and obligations of the partnership." [UPA §15(b)] Therefore, under the UPA, a *contract creditor* of the partnership is not only barred from suing the partnership as such, but also must join *all* the individual partners in her suit.

(2) Statutory reforms [§48]

The inability of a partnership contract creditor to sue a partnership in its own name under the UPA is obviously undesirable, and many states have statutorily patched up the UPA rule by adopting "common name statutes," which explicitly allow a partnership to be sued in its own name. Also, some states address this issue by making *all* partnership liabilities joint and several, so that not all the partners need to be joined in a suit. Other states have adopted general "joint debtor statutes," which provide that a suit against joint obligors can proceed even if some of the obligors are not joined.

b. RUPA [§49]

Unlike the UPA, the RUPA specifically provides that a partnership may both *sue and be sued* in its own name [RUPA §307(a)], and that partners are *jointly and severally liable for all obligations* of the partnership [RUPA §306]. However, the RUPA adds a new barrier to *collecting* against an individual partner on such a liability. A judgment against a partner, based on a claim against the partnership, normally cannot be satisfied against the partner's individual assets unless and until a judgment on the same claim has been rendered against the partnership and a writ of execution on the judgment has been returned unsatisfied. [RUPA §307] To put this differently, the RUPA adopts an *exhaustion* rule, under which partnership assets must be exhausted before a partner's individual assets can be reached.

C. Joint Ventures

1. In General [§50]

A joint venture is essentially a species of partnership, except that a joint venture is formed for some *limited investment or operation*, such as the construction of a single building, while a partnership is generally formed as a continuing business enterprise.

2. Governing Law [§51]

There is a split of authority on the extent to which joint ventures are governed by partnership law. Some cases suggest that joint ventures are governed by all the rules applicable to partnerships, while other cases suggest that joint ventures are not entirely subject to partnership rules. Even under the concept that joint ventures are not subject to *all* the rules of partnership law, however, it is clear that they are subject to most of those rules.

D. Limited Partnerships

1. Introduction [§52]

In a limited partnership, the partners are divided into two classes: *general partners*, who essentially have the rights and obligations of partners in an ordinary partnership, and *limited partners*, who normally do not participate in the management of the partnership's business and are subject to only limited liability.

2. General Partners [§53]

A limited partnership must have one or more general partners. The general partners have unlimited liability for partnership obligations, as in an ordinary partnership. (However, a corporation can be a general partner. If a corporation is the sole general partner, as a practical matter no individual will have unlimited liability.)

3. Limited Partners [§54]

Generally, the liability of a limited partner for partnership debts is limited to the capital she contributes to the partnership. Under certain circumstances, however, a limited partner may have the liability of a general partner. There have been four versions of the Uniform Limited Partnership Act ("ULPA"). Each version has a different provision concerning the liability of limited partners to third parties, and each version is in force in at least some states.

a. Uniform Limited Partnership Act (1916) [§55]

Under the ULPA, a limited partner is not liable as a general partner unless, in addition to the exercise of her rights and powers as a limited partner, she takes part in the control of the business. [**Holzman v. de Escamilla,** 86 Cal. App. 2d 858 (1948)]

b. Revised Uniform Limited Partnership Act (1976) [§56]

Under the original (1976) version of the Revised Uniform Limited Partnership Act ("RULPA"), a limited partner is not liable for the obligations of a limited partnership unless either: (i) she is also a general partner, or (ii) in addition to the exercise of her rights and powers as a limited partner, she takes part in the control of the business. However, if the limited partner's participation in the control of the business is not *substantially the same as the exercise of the powers of a general partner*, she is liable only to persons who transact business with the limited partnership with actual knowledge of her participation in control.

c. **Revised Uniform Limited Partnership Act (1985) [§57]**

Under the 1985 version of the RULPA, a limited partner is not liable for the obligations of a limited partnership unless, in addition to the exercise of her rights and powers as a limited partner, she participates in the control of the business. However, even if the limited partner participates in the control of the business, she is liable only to persons who transact business with the limited partnership *reasonably believing, based upon the limited partner's conduct, that the limited partner is a general partner.* [RULPA §303]

d. **Fiduciary duties [§58]**

The limited partnership statutes of some states allow considerable freedom to contractually vary or even eliminate the general partner's fiduciary obligations by provisions in the limited partnership agreement. (This is also true of some limited liability company statutes as well.) For example, the Delaware Revised Uniform Limited Partnership Act provides that the general partner's duties and liabilities may be "expanded or restricted" by provisions in the partnership agreement. When the limited partnership agreement provides for fiduciary duties, the agreement sets the standard for determining whether the general partner has breached its fiduciary duty to the partnership. However, the Delaware Supreme Court has stated that this language does not allow a limited partnership agreement to *eliminate* the duty of good faith. [**Gotham Partners, L.P. v. Hollywood Realty Partners, L.P.,** 817 A.2d 160 (Del. 2002)]

4. **Revised Uniform Partnership Act (2001) [§59]**

The Revised Uniform Partnership Act 2001 provides that an obligation of a limited partnership, whether arising in contract, tort, or otherwise, is not the obligation of a limited partner. A limited partner is not personally liable, directly or indirectly, by way of contribution or otherwise, for an obligation of the limited partnership solely by reason of being a limited partner, *even if the partner participates in the management and control of the limited partnership.*

E. Limited Liability Partnerships ("LLPs")

1. **In General [§60]**

Limited liability partnerships ("LLPs") essentially are general partnerships with one core difference and several ancillary differences. The core difference is that, as the name indicates, the liability of general partners of a limited liability partnership is less extensive than the liability of a general partner. Although the statutes vary, generally speaking a partner in an LLP is not personally liable for *all* partnership obligations, but rather only for obligations arising *from her own activities*—with the exception that under some LLP statutes a partner is also liable for activities closely related to her, for contractual obligations, or both. This core idea is articulated differently under different statutes, and the precise liability of a partner in an LLP will depend on the statute.

2. Some Liability Unlimited [§61]

As indicated above, a partner in an LLP is personally liable for certain obligations, and as to those obligations a partner's liability is unlimited—*i.e.,* a partner is personally liable for those obligations to the entire extent of her wealth.

3. Other Distinguishing Features [§62]

An ancillary difference between ordinary general partnerships and LLPs is that under some LLP statutes there is a tradeoff for limited liability, in the form of a requirement of a minimum amount of liability insurance or segregated funds. Another ancillary difference between LLPs and ordinary general partnerships is that LLPs must be registered with the appropriate state office.

F. Limited Liability Companies ("LLCs")

1. In General [§63]

Limited liability companies ("LLCs") are noncorporate entities that are created under special statutes that combine elements of corporation and partnership law. As under corporation law, the owners (called *"members"*) of LLCs have limited liability. As under partnership law, an LLC has great freedom to structure its internal governance by agreement. Like a corporation, an LLC is an entity, so that it can, *e.g.,* hold property and sue and be sued in its own name. LLCs come in two flavors: member-managed LLCs, which are managed by their members, and manager-managed LLCs, which are managed by managers who may or may not be members. The LLC is a relatively new form. As a result, the LLC statutes are still evolving and the case law is still sparse. Moreover, the LLC statutes are highly variable. The central characteristics of LLCs will be described below in terms of prevailing statutory patterns. However, bear in mind that as to any given characteristic there will usually be some LLC statutes that fall outside the major patterns described.

2. Formation; Articles of Organization; Powers [§64]

An LLC is formed by filing articles of organization in a designated state office—usually, the office of the secretary of the state. (Some statutes use the term *certificate of organization* rather than the term *articles of organization.*) Most statutes allow LLCs to be formed by a single person. The articles must include the name of the LLC, the address of its principal place of business or registered office in the state, and the name and address of its agent for service of process. Many or most statutes also require the articles to state: (i) the purpose of the LLC; (ii) if the LLC is to be manager-managed, the names of the initial managers or, if the LLC is to be member-managed, the names of its initial members; and (iii) the duration of the LLC or the latest date on which it is to dissolve. Many statutes also require the articles to include other information, the nature of which varies considerably. Most statutes either provide that LLCs have all powers necessary to effectuate their purposes or contain an exhaustive laundry list of an LLC's powers.

3. Operating Agreements [§65]

An LLC's articles of organization are usually very sketchy. In most LLCs, most operational details are set forth in the *operating agreement*. This is an agreement among the members concerning the LLC's affairs. (Some statutes use the term *limited liability agreement* rather than the term *operating agreement*.) The operating agreement typically provides for the governance of the LLC, its capitalization, the admission and withdrawal of members, and distributions. The statutes vary as to whether an operating agreement must be in writing.

4. Management [§66]

Almost all of the LLC statutes provide as a default rule—which prevails unless agreed otherwise—that an LLC is to be managed by its members. A few statutes provide as a default rule that an LLC is to be managed by managers, who may or may not be members, unless otherwise agreed. Most of the statutes provide that the statutory default rule can be varied only by a provision in the LLC's articles of organization, but some provide that the statutory default rule can be varied in the operating agreement. One way to vary the statutory rule is to completely reverse it—either by providing for manager-management in a state where the default rule is member-management, or by providing for member-management in a state where the default rule is manager-management. Another way to vary the statutory default rule is to distribute management functions between members and managers.

5. Voting by Members [§67]

About half the statutes provide as a default rule that members vote per capita—*i.e.*, one vote per member—unless otherwise agreed. The other half provide that members vote pro rata, by financial interests, unless otherwise agreed. Normally, members act by a majority vote, per capita or pro rata as the case may be. However, some of the statutes require a unanimous vote for certain designated actions.

6. Agency Powers

a. Member-managed LLCs [§68]

Under a majority of the statutes, the apparent authority of a member of a member-managed LLC is comparable to the apparent authority of a partner—*i.e.*, each member has the power to bind the LLC for any act that is for apparently carrying on the business of the LLC in the usual or ordinary way. Even if an action is not in the usual or ordinary way, the remaining members may confer on a given member actual authority to bind the LLC to an action or a type of action. Conversely, the remaining members may withdraw the actual authority of a member to take a certain kind of action that is in the ordinary or usual way. In that case, if the member takes such an action, the LLC will be bound by virtue of the member's apparent authority, but the member may be obliged to indemnify the LLC for any loss that results from her contravention of the other members' decision.

b. Manager-managed LLCs [§69]

In manager-managed firms, the rules concerning authority are comparable to those in corporations—*i.e.*, typically only the managers have apparent authority to bind the firm. Members of a manager-managed LLC have no apparent authority to bind the LLC, just as shareholders have no apparent authority to bind a corporation. Most of the statutes provide that a manager in a manager-managed LLC has partner-like apparent authority.

7. Inspection of Books and Records [§70]

The statutes generally provide that members are entitled to access to the LLC's books and records, or to specified books and records. Some statutes include an explicit provision that the inspection must be for a proper purpose. Such a limitation might or might not be read into other statutes.

8. Fiduciary Duties [§71]

The fiduciary duties of managers and members of LLCs are largely unspecified by the LLC statutes, just as the fiduciary duties of directors, officers, and shareholders are largely unspecified by corporations statutes. Presumably, in deciding LLC cases involving fiduciary duties the courts will borrow very heavily from the corporate and partnership case law. It should be noted that the LLC statutes do include some important provisions concerning particular issues of fiduciary duty; *e.g.*, most statutes specify the elements of the duty of care. Some statutes also provide that a manager will be liable only for gross negligence, bad faith, recklessness, or equivalent conduct. Others require a manager to act as would a prudent person in similar circumstances. Many of the LLC statutes, like most corporate statutes, also provide mechanisms for the authorization or ratification of self-interested transactions.

a. Waiver of fiduciary duties

The most striking divergence between the LLC statutes and the corporate and partnership statutes is that some of the LLC statutes, at least on their face, permit the operating agreement to waive all fiduciary duties. It is unclear how the courts will interpret these provisions, particularly because usually the duty of good faith cannot be restricted, and that duty can encompass elements of fiduciary duties. In general, it can be predicted that courts will read these statutes restrictively. (*See supra*, §58.)

9. Derivative Actions [§72]

Most of the statutes explicitly permit members of LLCs to bring derivative actions on the LLC's behalf based on a breach of fiduciary duties. Even where the statute does not explicitly permit such actions, courts are highly likely to permit them, both on analogy to corporation and limited partnership law, and because a failure to do so might allow fiduciaries who were in control of an LLC to violate their fiduciary duties without any sanction.

10. Distributions [§73]

Most LLC statutes provide that in the absence of an agreement to the contrary, distributions to members are to be made pro rata, according to the members' contributions, on analogy to corporate law, rather than per capita—the default rule in partnership law. Some of the statutes, however, provide that in the absence of agreement, distributions are to be on a per capita basis.

11. Members' Interests [§74]

A member of an LLC has financial rights, and may also have governance rights as a member (*i.e.,* apart from any governance rights she may have as a manager in a manager-managed LLC). A member's *financial* rights include her right to receive distributions. A member's *governance* rights include her right, if any, to participate in management, to vote on certain issues, and to be supplied with information. Some but not all statutes provide a list of actions that require member approval, in the absence of a contrary provision in the organic documents. Most statutes define a member's interest in an LLC to consist of the member's financial rights. A few define a member's interest to include her governance rights.

a. Transferability [§75]

Generally speaking, a member of an LLC can freely transfer her financial rights by assigning her interest in the LLC. Governance rights are treated differently. A number of statutes provide that a member can transfer her governance rights only with the unanimous consent of the other members. Some statutes provide that in the absence of an agreement to the contrary, a member can transfer her governance rights with the approval of a majority of the other members or a majority of other members' financial interests, depending on the statute. Some statutes provide that a member can transfer governance rights, even without the unanimous or majority consent of the other members, if the articles of organization or operating agreement so provides.

(1) Consequences of assignment [§76]

It is clear that a member of an LLC who assigns her interest normally cannot *assign* her governance rights, but it is not always clear whether an assigning member *retains* her governance rights. Some statutes provide that a member who assigns her membership interest loses her membership status. Some statutes provide that a member who assigns her membership interest loses her membership status if and when the assignee becomes a member. Some statutes provide that if a member assigns her membership interest, the remaining members can remove the assignor as a member. Some statutes do not speak to the issue.

12. Personal Liability [§77]

All of the LLC statutes provide that the members and managers of an LLC are not liable for the LLC's debts, obligations, and other liabilities. However, the courts have begun to develop a form of piercing-the-veil doctrine applicable to LLCs. [**Bastan v. RJM & Associates, LLC,** 29 Conn. L. Rptr. 646 (2001)]

COMPARISON OF KEY BUSINESS ENTITY ATTRIBUTES

gilbert

	CORPORATION	GENERAL PARTNERSHIP	LIMITED PARTNERSHIP	LIMITED LIABILITY PARTNERSHIP	LIMITED LIABILITY COMPANY
LIABILITY OF OWNERS	Shareholders generally *not personally liable* for corporate obligations	Partners *personally liable* for obligations of the partnership; the RUPA requires exhaustion of partnership assets first	*General partners personally liable* for all partnership obligations; limited partners generally are not	Partners *generally liable for own acts* but not for acts of others; under some statutes may be liable for partnership contracts too	Members *not personally liable* for LLC's obligations
MANAGEMENT	Generally managed by *officers* who are controlled by *directors;* shareholders generally have no management rights	*Partners* manage	Generally managed by *general partner(s);* limited partners may have certain voting rights	*Partners* manage	*Members* may manage or appoint managers
TAXATION	*Firm-taxation* (firm is taxable on its income)	May choose *firm-taxation or flow-through taxation* (firm's income or losses are not attributed to firm, but instead flow through to firm owners)	May choose *firm-taxation or flow-through taxation*	May choose *firm-taxation or flow-through taxation*	May choose *firm-taxation or flow-through taxation*
FORMATION REQUIREMENTS	Must *file articles* of incorporation with state	Can be formed by *oral or written agreement* or through conduct	Must *file certificate* of limited partnership with state	Must *file articles* of limited liability partnership with state	Must *file articles* of organization with state
TRANSFERABILITY OF OWNERSHIP	Shareholders generally *free to transfer their ownership interests at will*	Partners cannot transfer their full ownership interest without *unanimous consent*	Partners (whether general or limited) cannot transfer their full ownership interest without *unanimous consent*	Partners generally cannot transfer their full ownership interest without *unanimous consent*	Members generally *can freely transfer their financial rights, but cannot transfer their management rights without unanimous consent*

13. Dissociation [§78]

The LLC statutes vary considerably in their treatment of dissociation (*i.e.*, termination of a member's interest in an LLC other than by the member's voluntary transfer of her interest). The statutes typically provide that the death, bankruptcy, or lawful expulsion of a member results in her dissociation, and a number of statutes provide that a member either has: (i) the right to withdraw (or resign) at any time; (ii) the power, although not necessarily the right, to withdraw at any time; or (iii) the right to withdraw at any time unless otherwise provided in the operating agreement.

G. Taxation of Noncorporate Entities

1. In General [§79]

Under the Internal Revenue Service's "check-the-box" regulations, an unincorporated *"eligible entity,"* such as a general partnership, a limited partnership, an LLP, or an LLC, can elect either firm-taxation (the basic corporate form of taxation) or flow-through taxation (in which income and expenses and gains and losses are taxable directly to the firm's owners). Generally speaking, an eligible entity is any business entity other than a corporation or a business entity that is specifically made taxable as a corporation under the Internal Revenue Code. The most important entity in the latter category is the *master limited partnership*. Essentially, a master limited partnership is a limited partnership whose limited partnership interests are publicly traded—*i.e.*, traded on an established securities market or readily tradeable on a secondary market. With certain exceptions, under the Internal Revenue Code publicly traded limited partnerships are taxed as corporations and cannot elect partnership taxation.

Chapter Two: Organizing the Corporation

CONTENTS

Chapter Approach

This chapter details the formation (or "organization") of a corporation and disregard of the corporate entity. If you see a question concerning the incorporation of a business, keep in mind that various formalities are required to perfect incorporation—*i.e.,* to perfect the formation of a corporation. Most exam questions in this area will probably concern defects in the formation process, which may subject would-be shareholders of a would-be corporation to personal liability. In analyzing such a question, ask yourself the following:

1. Was there *substantial compliance* with statutory requirements? If so, the would-be corporation may be a *de jure* corporation, which cannot be attacked by anyone.

2. Was there a *good faith and colorable attempt* to incorporate and *good faith actual use* of the corporate existence? If so, then even if the statutory compliance was insufficient to constitute a de jure corporation, it may be sufficient to create a *de facto* corporation. A de facto corporation has corporate status with respect to dealings with third parties, but not with respect to the state. However, statutes in many jurisdictions have abrogated or modified the de facto doctrine.

3. Even if there is no de jure or de facto corporation, do the circumstances suggest a *corporation by estoppel*? Persons who have claimed corporate status will generally be estopped to deny that status if suit is brought against the corporation. Likewise, a party who has dealt with a business as a corporation may be estopped from claiming that the business lacks corporate status.

4. If there is not a de jure nor de facto corporation, nor a corporation by estoppel, who may be held liable? Under the traditional view, all the would-be shareholders are subject to liability for the would-be corporation's debts and other obligations. However, the modern trend is to impose liability only on those owners who *participated* in management.

Another fairly common exam question involves the disregard of the corporate entity (*i.e.,* piercing the corporate veil). For suits seeking to impose liability on *shareholders*, you should determine whether elements such as undercapitalization or commingling of funds were present. In suits to pierce the wall between *affiliated corporations*, you should determine whether each affiliated corporation is a freestanding enterprise. Remember too that the corporate entity may also be disregarded when it is used to evade statutory or contractual obligations. Finally, in questions involving an insolvent corporation, keep in mind that a shareholder-creditor's claim may be subordinated to other creditors' claims on equitable grounds.

A. Formalities in Organizing a Corporation

1. **General Corporation Laws [§80]**

   Under early English and American law, corporations were created by a "special charter" granted by the King or the legislature. Today, with only a few exceptions, corporations are created by compliance with a "general corporation law" or "business corporation law" of the state in which formation is sought.

2. **Certificate or Articles of Incorporation [§81]**

   Typically, a corporation is organized by the execution and filing of a "certificate" or "articles" of incorporation. (The nomenclature varies from state to state.) The articles of incorporation are executed by one or more "incorporators." What must and what may go into the articles of incorporation depends on state law. The Revised Model Business Corporation Act ("Model Act") is fairly typical.

   a. **Required provisions [§82]**

      Under the Model Act, the articles of incorporation *must* set forth the corporate name, the number of shares the corporation is authorized to issue, the street address of the corporation's initial registered office and the name of its initial registered agent at that office, and the name and address of each incorporator. [Revised Model Business Corporation Act ("RMBCA") §2.02(a)]

CHECKLIST OF PROVISIONS TYPICALLY REQUIRED IN ARTICLES OF INCORPORATION

THE FOLLOWING ARE TYPICAL OF PROVISIONS THAT MUST BE INCLUDED IN A CORPORATION'S ARTICLES OF INCORPORATION:

☑ The corporation's *name*;

☑ The *number of shares* that the corporation is authorized to issue;

☑ The street *address* of the corporation's initial registered office and the *name* of the registered agent at that office; and

☑ The *name and address* of each incorporator.

---

   b. **Optional provisions [§83]**

      In addition, the articles of incorporation *may* set forth the names and addresses of the individuals who are to serve as the initial directors, and provisions, not inconsistent with law, regarding:

      (i) *The purpose* or purposes for which the corporation is organized;

      (ii) *Managing the business and regulating the powers* of the corporation, its board of directors, and its shareholders;

      (iii) *The definition, limitation, and regulation* of the powers of the corporation, its board of directors, and its shareholders;

      (iv) *A par value,* if any, for authorized shares or classes of shares;

(v) *The imposition of personal liability* on shareholders for the debts of the corporation to a specified extent and upon specified conditions;

(vi) *Eliminating or limiting the liability* of a director to the corporation or its shareholders for money damages for any action taken, or any failure to take any action, as a director (except liability for the amount of a financial benefit received by a director to which he is not entitled, for an intentional infliction of harm on the corporation or the shareholders, for a violation of the rules governing the payment of dividends, or for an intentional violation of criminal law); and

(vii) *Any provision that is required or permitted* to be set forth in the *bylaws*.

[RMBCA §2.02(b)]

c. Purpose clause [§84]

Before the adoption of modern statutes, the clauses in the articles of incorporation that stated the purpose for which the corporation was formed tended to be extremely elaborate, to avoid the problem of ultra vires (*see infra*, §164). Under modern statutes, elaborate purpose clauses are no longer necessary. For example, under the Model Act, every corporation has "the purpose of engaging in any lawful business unless a more limited purpose is set forth in the articles of incorporation." [RMBCA §3.01(a)] Similarly, under the Delaware statute it is sufficient to state, either alone or with other business purposes, that the purpose of the corporation is to engage in any lawful activity for which corporations may be organized. All lawful acts and activities are thus within the purposes of the corporation, except for express limitations, if any. [Del. Gen. Corp. Law §102(e)]

3. Organizational Meeting [§85]

Filing the certificate of incorporation in proper form creates the corporation. However, several steps are required to complete the corporation's structure. These steps are taken at organizational meetings of either (i) the incorporators or (ii) the initial board of directors named in the articles, if the statute provides for naming the initial board this way. [*See, e.g.*, Del. Gen. Corp. Law §§107, 108]

a. Matters determined at organizational meeting of incorporators [§86]

If initial directors are *not named* in the articles of incorporation, the incorporators, at their organizational meeting, will typically adopt bylaws, fix the number of directors (if the certificate of incorporation or bylaws do not fix that number), and elect directors to serve until the first shareholders' meeting. The directors so elected will then typically adopt a corporate seal and form of stock certificate, authorize the issuance of stock to designated persons at designated prices, elect officers, and designate the corporation's bank.

b. Matters determined at organizational meeting of initial directors [§87]

If initial directors are *named* in the certificate of incorporation, at their organizational meeting they will typically adopt bylaws, elect officers, adopt a form of corporate seal and a form of stock certificate, authorize the issuance of shares to designated persons at designated prices, elect officers, and designate the corporation's bank.

B. Defects in Formation Process—"De Jure" and "De Facto" Corporations

1. In General [§88]

Sometimes there is a defect or irregularity in the process of forming a corporation. For example, fewer than the required number of incorporators may have signed the certificate of incorporation, the certificate may fail to include a required provision in proper form, or the certificate may not have been properly filed. The issue is then the effect of such a defect on corporate status. This issue is usually put in terms of whether the corporation exists "de jure," "de facto," "by estoppel," or not at all.

a. Liability actions [§89]

This issue arises most commonly (but not exclusively) in cases in which a third party seeks to impose personal liability on would-be shareholders on the ground that corporate status was not attained and, therefore, neither was limited liability.

b. Quo warranto actions [§90]

The issue of corporate status may also arise in a quo warranto proceeding brought by the state to challenge the legal status of the corporation. Most states provide by statute for such proceedings, often without using the term "quo warranto." [*See, e.g.*, N.Y. Bus. Corp. Law §109; Cal. Corp. Code §180(a)]

2. De Jure Corporation [§91]

A de jure corporation is a corporation organized in compliance with the requirements of the state of incorporation. Its status as a corporation *cannot be attacked by anyone*, not even by the state in a quo warranto proceeding. [**People v. Ford**, 128 N.E. 479 (Ill. 1920)]

a. "Substantial compliance" sufficient [§92]

Most courts hold that perfect compliance with statutory requirements is not required for de jure status. Instead, "substantial compliance" will suffice. Therefore, an enterprise that fails to meet all the requirements for incorporation may nevertheless be a de jure corporation if the noncompliance is insubstantial. What constitutes substantial compliance is determined on a case-by-case basis, according to the nature of the unsatisfied requirement and the extent to which compliance has been attempted. [**People v. Montecito Water Co.**, 97 Cal. 276 (1893)]

Is there a **de jure corporation** (*i.e.,* have substantially all statutory formalities been met)?

NO

YES

Is the **de facto corporation** doctrine available (*i.e.,* was there a **colorable attempt** to incorporate coupled with some actual use or **exercise of corporate privileges**)? Note that some statutes have abolished this doctrine, and under the RMBCA the shareholder must not have known of the lack of incorporation.

YES

NO

Is there a **corporation by estoppel** (in particular, in a **contractual** situation, have the parties acted as if there were a corporation)?

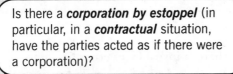

NO

YES

The shareholder **can** be held personally liable for corporate obligations.*

The shareholder **cannot** be held personally liable for corporate obligations.

Can the **corporate veil be pierced** because fraud or injustice otherwise would arise because:

(i) There has been a **commingling** of the corporation's assets and the shareholder's personal assets;

(ii) Basic corporate **formalities were not followed** (*e.g.,* no stock was issued, no records were kept, no meetings were held, etc.);

(iii) The corporation was **undercapitalized** (*i.e.,* the shareholders did not put up sufficient unencumbered capital to meet the corporation's prospective liabilities);

(iv) The corporation's policies and practices were so **dominated and controlled** by an individual or other corporation that it cannot be said to have a separate mind or will;

(v) The corporation is an **alter ego** or instrumentality of the shareholders (which generally means that one of the other factors above is present); or

(vi) The corporate form was **used to commit fraud or wrong**, violate a legal duty, or commit a dishonest or unjust act in contravention of a creditor's right.

NO

YES

The shareholder **cannot** be held personally liable for corporate obligations.

The shareholder **can** be held personally liable for corporate obligations.*

*Modern courts will hold only **active shareholders** liable; a passive investor generally will not be held liable.

> **Example:** If the articles were properly filed except that the address for the corporation's principal place of business inadvertently states the wrong street number, there would undoubtedly be substantial compliance.

b. Distinction between mandatory and directory requirements [§93]

Some courts hold that for a corporation to attain de jure status, there must be exact compliance with all *mandatory* statutory requirements, but that failure to comply with requirements that are only *directory* will not preclude de jure status. [**J.W. Butler Paper Co. v. Cleveland**, 77 N.E. 99 (Ill. 1906)] Whether a particular requirement is mandatory or directory is a matter of statutory interpretation. Factors to be considered include the wording of the statute (*e.g.,* "must," "shall," or "may") and the relative importance of the provision.

> **Example:** The attorney general filed a proceeding in the nature of a quo warranto against three incorporators who had failed to comply with a statutory requirement that the certificate of incorporation be sealed. The incorporators had used the secretary of state's forms, which neither contained nor mentioned a seal. The court concluded that de jure status had been attained. The provision for a seal was only directory, it said, because the purpose of the statute was to make a public record, and a seal did not further that purpose. [**People v. Ford,** *supra,* §91]

3. De Facto Corporation [§94]

A de facto corporation is said to exist when there is insufficient compliance to constitute a de jure corporation vis-a-vis the *state*, but the steps taken toward formation are sufficient to treat the enterprise as a corporation with respect to its *dealings with third parties.* In such cases, the corporate status can be invalidated by the state through quo warranto proceedings, but not by creditors or other persons who have had dealings with the enterprise.

a. Requirements [§95]

A de facto corporation requires a *colorable attempt to incorporate* and *some actual use or exercise of corporate privileges.*

> **Example:** On November 21, the corporate name of Sunshine Greenery, Inc. was reserved for B by the secretary of state. On December 3, B and C executed a certificate of incorporation for that corporation. The certificate was sent by mail to the secretary of state on that same date, with a check for the filing fee, but for some unexplained reason the certificate was not officially filed until December 18, two days after the execution of a lease by Sunshine Greenery. *Held:* Sunshine Greenery was a de facto corporation prior to December 18, and therefore, B and C were not personally liable to the lessor. [**Cantor v. Sunshine Greenery, Inc.,** 398 A.2d 571 (N.J. 1979)]

b. **Quo warranto [§96]**

A quo warranto proceeding can be maintained by the state to challenge the legal status of the corporation even against a de facto corporation, because the de facto theory is a defense only against a collateral attack on corporate status—in effect, only against a challenge raised by private parties—not against a challenge by the state itself.

4. Corporation by Estoppel [§97]

In appropriate cases, even though the enterprise has not achieved de jure or de facto status, a party may be estopped from challenging the corporate status of an enterprise. The estoppel principle is not a single theory, but rather is a cluster of different rules.

EXAM TIP **gilbert**

Defective formation is a somewhat common exam topic. Be sure to remember the basics. If investors attempted to set up a corporation but failed, they might be able to avoid personal liability under the de facto corporation doctrine or the estoppel doctrine. The **de facto corporation doctrine** will apply if the investors made a **colorable attempt** to incorporate **and exercised corporate privileges**, such as where the investors mail a certificate of incorporation to the secretary of state, open a corporate bank account, enter into a lease in the corporate name, and then discover that the certificate has not been filed because of a minor defect. A court likely will treat the business as a corporation under the de facto corporation doctrine. Similarly, if the parties to a transaction treat a business entity as if it were a corporation, they may be **estopped** from later denying the corporation's existence, even if there was no good faith attempt to incorporate.

---

a. **Shareholders estopped to deny corporate status [§98]**

The shareholders of a would-be corporation, having claimed corporate status in an earlier transaction with a third party, are estopped to deny that status in a suit brought by the third party against the corporation.

b. **Technical defenses [§99]**

Sometimes the question of corporate status is raised in a technical procedural context. For example, in a suit brought against a third party by a would-be corporation, the third party may seek to raise the defense that the would-be corporation is not really a corporation and, therefore, cannot sue in a corporate name. The courts tend to regard such a defense as nonmeritorious, and hold that the third party is estopped from raising the defense, on the ground that the defense is technical and would defeat the interests of justice.

c. **Personal liability of would-be shareholders [§100]**

A third party who has dealt with an enterprise as a corporation may seek to impose personal liability on would-be shareholders, who in turn raise estoppel as a defense. Here, the issue is whether, as a matter of equity, the third party, having dealt with the enterprise as if it were a corporation, should be prevented (*i.e.*, estopped) from treating it as anything else. Less must be shown to establish a corporation by estoppel than to establish a de facto corporation.

> **Example:** Without the knowledge of the would-be shareholders, their attorney negligently failed to file the certificate of incorporation before the business entered into a transaction with a third party. A third party who dealt with the business as if it were a corporation was held to be estopped from suing the would-be shareholders. [**Cranson v. IBM Corp.,** 200 A.2d 33 (Md. 1964)]

(1) Tort claims [§101]

The basis of estoppel theory in cases in which a third party seeks to impose liability on would-be shareholders is that the third party has *dealt with the business as if it were a corporation.* Therefore, the theory does not apply to bar suit against would-be shareholders by tort claimants or other involuntary creditors. [*See* **Kardo Co. v. Adams,** 231 F. 950 (6th Cir. 1916)] *Rationale:* A tort victim does not allow himself to be injured in reliance on the fact that the defendant was acting as a corporation.

5. Who May Be Held Liable [§102]

If a would-be corporation is neither a de jure nor de facto corporation, nor a corporation by estoppel, the courts have split on whether *all* of the would-be shareholders may be held personally liable for debts incurred in the corporation's name.

a. Traditional view [§103]

Older decisions imposed personal liability against all of the would-be shareholders, on the theory that if the enterprise is not a corporation, it is a partnership, and therefore the would-be shareholders are general partners. [**Hamill v. Davis,** 168 F. 187 (8th Cir. 1909)]

b. Modern trend [§104]

The modern trend, however, imposes personal liability against only those owners who actively participated in the management of the business. Owners who actively participated are held personally liable as if they were partners, but passive investors are not. [**Baker v. Bates-Street Shirt Co.,** 6 F.2d 854 (1st Cir. 1925)]

CORPORATE STATUS—A SUMMARY — **gilbert**

	DE JURE	DE FACTO	ESTOPPEL
METHOD OF FORMATION	Substantially follow *all* statutory provisions	Colorable compliance with statutory provisions and exercise of corporate privileges	Parties act as if there is a corporation; no requirement of following statutory provisions
EFFECT ON PERSONAL LIABILITY	Insulates against personal liability of shareholders	Insulates against personal liability of shareholders, but corporation subject to quo warranto proceeding by state	Insulates against personal liability in contract, but not in tort

6. Effect of Statutes [§105]

A number of statutes directly or indirectly address the de facto and estoppel doctrines.

a. Effect of statutes on de facto doctrine [§106]

Under the prior version of the Model Act, persons who act as a corporation without the authority of a properly issued certificate of incorporation are jointly and severally liable for all debts and liabilities incurred as a result of that action. [Model Business Corporations Act ("MBCA") §146 (1979)] This section was designed "to prohibit the application of any theory of de facto incorporation." [MBCA §146, comment] Accordingly, in those states with statutes based on this provision, the de facto doctrine was abolished. [**Timberline Equipment Co. v. Davenport**, 514 P.2d 1109 (Or. 1973); **Robertson v. Levy**, 197 A.2d 443 (D.C. 1964); *but see* **Vincent Drug Co. v. Utah State Tax Commission**, 407 P.2d 683 (Utah 1965)]

(1) Revised Model Business Corporation Act [§107]

The Revised Model Business Corporation Act (section 2.04) makes a significant change in the prior Model Act language. Under the Revised Model Act, only persons acting as or on behalf of a corporation who *know* that there was no incorporation are jointly and severally liable for all liabilities created while so acting. The requirement that a defendant *knew* there was no incorporation protects would-be shareholders of defectively formed corporations against liability under a variety of circumstances. For example, this requirement affords protection in cases where the would-be shareholders honestly and reasonably, but erroneously, believe that a certificate of incorporation has been filed [**Cranson v. IBM Corp.**, *supra*, §100], or in cases where an incorporator mails a certificate of incorporation to be filed, but either the letter is delayed in the mails or the secretary of state's office does not file the certificate immediately after receiving it [**Cantor v. Sunshine Greenery, Inc.**, *supra*, §95].

b. Effect of statutes on estoppel doctrine [§108]

The effect of section 146 of the prior Model Act and section 2.04 of the Revised Model Act on estoppel doctrine is an unsettled point. [*See* **Robertson v. Levy**, *supra*—section 146 abrogates the estoppel doctrine; **Thompson & Green Machinery Co. v. Music City Lumber Co.**, 683 S.W.2d 340 (Tenn. 1984)—same; *but see* **Namerdy v. Generalcar**, 217 A.2d 109 (D.C. 1966)—contra; **Timberline Equipment Co. v. Davenport**, *supra*—raises but does not resolve the issue]

c. Effect of statutes on issue of liability of passive investors [§109]

Even section 146 of the prior version of the Model Act, which imposes liability on all persons who act as a corporation without a properly issued certificate of incorporation, has been held not to include persons whose only connection with the enterprise is as an investor. Instead, the provision is interpreted to reach only those persons who not only have an investment in the enterprise, but who also exercise control or actively participate in policy and operational decisions. [**Timberline Equipment Co. v. Davenport**, *supra*; **Flanagan v. Jackson Wholesale Building Supply Co.**, 461 So. 2d 761 (Miss. 1984)] Presumably, section 2.04 of the Revised Model Act will be interpreted in much the same way.

C. Disregard of Corporate Entity

1. In General [§110]

Because a corporation is a legal entity distinct from its shareholders, the rights and obligations of a corporation are normally separate from those of the shareholders. Under the corporate statutes, a shareholder normally has no liability for corporate debts or other obligations. Instead, her liability—more accurately, her risk—is limited to the loss of her investment.

2. Suits by Corporate Creditors Against Shareholders [§111]

Under certain circumstances, shareholders can be found liable to corporate creditors. In such cases, it is said, the courts "pierce the corporate veil." The tests for whether the corporate veil will be pierced are generally vague. Often, courts put the issue in terms of whether the corporation was the "alter ego" or "instrumentality" of its shareholders. One common formulation is that a corporate entity will be disregarded, and the veil of limited liability pierced, when two requirements are met. First, there must be such *unity of interest and ownership* that the separate personalities of the corporation and its shareholder or shareholders no longer exist. Second, circumstances must be such that adherence to the fiction of separate corporate existence would *sanction a fraud or promote injustice*. [**Van Dorn Co. v. Future Chemical and Oil Corp.**, 753 F.2d 565 (7th Cir. 1985)] In determining whether a corporation is so controlled by another to justify disregarding their separate identities, the cases focus on four factors: (i) the commingling of funds or assets, (ii) the failure to maintain adequate corporate records or to comply with corporate formalities, (iii) undercapitalization, and (iv) domination and control.

a. Commingling of assets [§112]

A commingling of the corporation's assets and the shareholders' personal assets occurs when the shareholders have dealt with the assets of the corporation as if those assets were their own, *e.g.*, by using corporate funds to pay private debts, or by using corporate assets for other private purposes.

Example: The sole shareholder of several corporations was found to have commingled corporate assets when he used his various corporate bank accounts to pay all kinds of personal expenses, including: alimony to his ex-wife, child support and education expenses for his children, maintenance expenses for his personal automobiles, health care charges for his pet, and even $460 for a picture of himself with President Bush. [**Sea-Land Services Inc. v. Pepper Source**, 941 F.2d 519 (7th Cir. 1991)]

b. Lack of corporate formalities [§113]

Also relevant to piercing the corporate veil is whether basic corporate formalities were followed (*e.g.*, whether stock was issued, corporate records maintained, directors or officers elected, and regular meetings of directors and shareholders held).

(1) Statutory close corporations [§114]

Many states today have special provisions for "statutory close corporations," which among other things permit less formal management of these corporations' affairs. (*See infra,* §§191-206.) Some of these statutes provide that the failure to hold formal meetings of the board of directors or shareholders, pursuant to shareholder agreement, is not to be considered a factor in determining whether the shareholders of a statutory close corporation should be held liable for the corporation's debts. [*See, e.g.,* Cal. Corp. Code §300(e)]

c. Undercapitalization [§115]

An extremely important factor in deciding whether the corporate veil should be pierced is whether the corporation was organized with sufficient resources, by way of capital, liability insurance, or both, to meet the obligations that reasonably could be expected to arise in its business. [**Minton v. Cavaney,** 56 Cal. 2d 576 (1961)] The issue here is not whether the shareholders have respected and maintained the corporation as a separate entity; rather, the issue is whether the shareholders should reasonably have anticipated that the corporation would be unable to pay the debts it would be likely to incur. The rationale of piercing the veil on the basis of undercapitalization is that the legislature, in conferring limited liability, assumed that shareholders would in good faith put up *unencumbered capital* (or insurance) *reasonably adequate for its prospective liabilities.*

Example: Cavaney, an attorney, helped form Seminole Corp., a company that operated a public swimming pool. He was an officer and director of the corporation. The corporation had applied to the California Commissioner of Corporations to issue three shares of stock, one of which would be issued to Cavaney. It was not clear whether Cavaney was to be a beneficial owner, or whether the share would be issued to him only as an accommodation. In any event, the Commissioner denied permission to issue the shares, and none were ever issued. The corporation carried no insurance and its sole asset was a lease of the swimming pool. Minton's daughter drowned in the pool and Minton obtained a judgment against Seminole Corp. for $10,000, which Seminole could not pay. Minton attempted to collect the judgment from Cavaney's estate (because Cavaney by then was dead). The court held that an attorney who participates in the affairs of an undercapitalized corporation as a director, officer, or shareholder can be personally liable for the corporation's obligations. (It should be noted, however, that the case was remanded to determine liability, because

Cavaney was not joined as a defendant in the underlying case and so did not have an opportunity to litigate.) [**Minton v. Cavaney,** *supra*]

---

cf. **Compare:** Carlton was a principal shareholder and organizer of several corporations, each of which owned two taxicabs in New York. Each cab carried the minimum liability insurance ($10,000) mandated by state law. The only assets of each corporation were the cabs, which were subject to mortgages. Walkovszky was run over by one of the cabs and he sued Carlton, claiming, among other things, that Carlton should be personally liable for Walkovszky's injuries because the cab company was undercapitalized. Carlton moved to dismiss the complaint against him for failure to state a claim upon which relief could be granted. The court dismissed the complaint, holding that there was nothing wrong with Carlton's forming several corporations to insulate his assets. The state has set the minimum insurance requirements for cabs and Carlton's corporation met those requirements. Therefore, the corporate veil cannot be pierced here for inadequate capitalization. [**Walkovszky v. Carlton,** 18 N.Y.2d 414 (1966)] The court implied, however, that a valid complaint would be stated if the plaintiff alleged that the defendant shareholders were conducting the business of the taxicab fleet "in their personal capacities for purely personal rather than corporate ends." Subsequently, the plaintiff filed an amended complaint, and the New York Appellate Division held that "the amended complaint sufficiently sets forth a cause of action . . . , *i.e.,* that [the] individual defendants were conducting the business of the taxicab fleet in their individual capacities." [*See* **Walkovszky v. Carlton,** 29 A.D.2d 763 (1968)]

EXAM TIP	gilbert

As you can see from the above case, courts may be reluctant to pierce the corporate veil based on inadequate capitalization. You should note that even among courts that are willing to pierce for inadequate capitalization, the focus is on the *initial capitalization of the corporation*. If the shareholders invested sufficient capital when they formed their corporation, the fact that the business never really succeeded, and the corporation is now bankrupt and does not have enough money to pay current creditors, is not grounds for piercing for inadequate capitalization.

d. **Domination and control by shareholder [§116]**

Courts will often pierce the corporate veil of one corporation, C, when a shareholder who owns most or all of C's stock so completely dominates C's policy and business practices that C can be said to have no separate mind, will, or existence of its own. The prime example occurs when a parent corporation directly determines the business policy of a subsidiary, rather than allowing that policy to be determined by the subsidiary's board. In contrast, the court is less likely to pierce a subsidiary's veil if the subsidiary's business policies are determined by its own board, even though the directors are elected by the parent, and even though they are also officers or employees of the parent.

> **e.g.** **Example:** Defendant Flemming was the president of an indebted corporation that shipped fruit from growers. When the trucking company that he hired to haul the fruit asked about unpaid bills, Flemming assured them that he would pay the hauling charges if the corporation failed to pay. When the bills remained unpaid, the trucking company sued. The court determined that because Flemming was the sole beneficiary of the corporation's operations and the one who totally dominated it, his assurance to pay was sufficient to pierce the corporate veil and hold him responsible personally. [**DeWitt Truck Brokers v. W. Ray Flemming Fruit Co.**, 540 F.2d 681 (4th Cir. 1976)]

e. **"Alter ego"; "instrumentality"; "unity of interest" [§117]**

Courts that pierce the corporate veil often do so on the ground that no separate entity has been maintained and the corporation is only the "alter ego" or "instrumentality" of its shareholders, or there is a "unity of interest" between the corporation and its shareholders. Although the terms "alter ego," "instrumentality," and "unity of interest" are often treated as if they were grounds for piercing the corporate veil, more typically these terms are conclusory in nature, and applied only if other grounds (like those listed in §§112-116, *supra*) are present.

> **e.g.** **Example:** Polan formed two corporations, A and B. Corporation A subleased space from plaintiff Kinney. Corporation A then subleased to Corporation B. Neither A nor B paid rent to Kinney. Kinney filed suit for unpaid rent and obtained a judgment against Corporation A. Because Corporation A had no assets, Kinney wanted to pierce the corporate veil and hold Polan personally responsible. The court held that because Polan set up his corporation without putting in any capital and the corporation had no assets, no income, no bank accounts, observed no corporate formalities, had no stock, kept no minutes, and had no officers, the corporation was a transparent shell which provided Polan with no protection from liability to his corporation's creditors. [**Kinney Shoe Corp. v. Polan,** 939 F.2d 209 (4th Cir. 1991)]

f. **Requirement of fraud, wrong, dishonesty, or injustice [§118]**

It is often said that the corporate veil will be pierced only if it was used to commit fraud or wrong, perpetuate the violation of a statutory or other positive legal duty, or commit a dishonest or unjust act in contravention of the creditor's legal right. [**Zaist v. Olson,** 227 A.2d 552 (Conn. 1967)] As a practical matter, this means that certain elements that can lead to piercing, like the failure to follow corporate formalities, may not lead to piercing unless the court also concludes that an injustice of some sort would be done to the plaintiff if the veil is not pierced.

> **e.g.** **Example:** Olson formed East Haven Corp. and contracted with plaintiff Zaist to clear and grade land for a shopping center. Olson also formed another corporation, Olson Inc. After some juggling about, ownership of the land being developed came to rest in Olson individually and in Olson Inc.

When East Haven failed to pay Zaist for its work and materials, Zaist sought to hold both Olson and Olson Inc. liable for the debt. Because Olson left East Haven financially unable to pay its creditor, East Haven reaped no benefit from Zaist's work, and Olson planned East Haven's undertakings and carried out these plans for his own and Olson Inc.'s enrichment, the corporate entity of East Haven could be disregarded and Olson and Olson Inc. were held responsible for the services and material furnished by the plaintiff. [**Zaist v. Olson,** *supra*]

EXAM TIP   **gilbert**

Your professor will likely spend some time on the issue of disregarding a corporate entity, so you should be prepared for exam questions raising this issue. A court will consider factors showing a *unity of interest* between the shareholders and the corporation (*e.g.,* a commingling of assets, domination of control by a shareholder, the corporation is the shareholder's alter ego, etc.) or that the corporate form is being used to *perpetrate a fraud or to promote an injustice*. Don't be too quick to pierce the corporate veil absent these factors—sloppy administration alone is rarely a sufficient ground for piercing.

---

g. **Usually limited to corporations with few shareholders [§119]**

Cases in which the courts pierce the corporate veil to impose personal liability on shareholders are almost always limited to corporations with only a small number of shareholders (including corporations that are wholly owned subsidiaries of other corporations).

3. **Piercing the Wall Between Affiliated Corporations [§120]**

A related but somewhat different problem arises where a plaintiff with a claim against one corporation, C, seeks to satisfy the claim against the assets of an affiliated corporation, D, under common ownership with C. Here, the plaintiff is not seeking to impose individual liability on C's *shareholders*, but rather to *aggregate* brother-sister corporations (C and D) as if they were one corporation. [38 A.L.R. 3d 1102]

a. **Enterprise liability [§121]**

Some opinions suggest that this kind of aggregation may be permitted where each affiliated corporate entity is not a free-standing business enterprise, but only a fragment of an enterprise that is composed of all the affiliated corporations. [**Walkovszky v. Carlton,** *supra*, §115] *Rationale:* In permitting incorporation and limited liability, the legislature contemplated the incorporation of business enterprises. Separate incorporation of enterprise fragments was not within the legislative intent in granting limited liability. [Berle, *The Theory of Enterprise Entity*, 47 Colum. L. Rev. 343 (1947); Landers, *A Unified Approach to Parent, Subsidiary and Affiliate Questions in Bankruptcy*, 42 U. Chi. L. Rev. 589 (1975)]

Example: Where a parent corporation operated through three wholly owned subsidiaries, each of which actively implemented the activities of the other as part of a single business enterprise, tort liabilities incurred by any one of the subsidiaries could be imposed upon any of the other subsidiaries. [**Sisco-Hamilton Co. v. Lennon**, 240 F.2d 68 (7th Cir. 1957)]

4. Use of Corporate Form to Evade Statutory or Contract Obligations [§122]

The courts may ignore the corporate form when it is used to evade a statutory or contractual obligation. Typically, the question in these cases is not whether the shareholders are personally liable for the debts of the corporation. Rather, the question is one of statutory or contract interpretation: was a statute or contract that nominally applies only to the corporation intended to also apply to the corporation's shareholders?

e.g. Example: A statute prohibited railroads from giving rebates to shippers. The statute was held to apply to rebates given to a corporation that was not itself a shipper, but had been formed by a shipper's officers and principal shareholders for the purpose of obtaining what were in substance, although not in form, rebates to a shipper. [**United States v. Milwaukee Refrigerated Transit Co.**, 142 F. 247 (E.D. Wis. 1905)]

e.g. Example: A consent decree was entered against S Corporation, a subsidiary of P Corporation. P was controlled by a single family. The decree prohibited S from violating the Fair Labor Standards Act. Later, S was merged into T, another subsidiary of P. T had the same officers as S, and few assets. The court held that the consent decree was binding on T, and moreover that it applied not only to the employees at S's old operation, but also to a new operation T began after the merger. [**Wirtz v. Ocala Gas Co.**, 336 F.2d 236 (5th Cir. 1964)]

5. Disregard of Corporate Entity in Favor of Corporation or Its Shareholders [§123]

Only *third parties*, and not the corporation or its shareholders, are generally allowed to disregard the corporate entity. So, for example, in an action by P against Corporation C, C normally could not assert, as a set-off to P's claim against C, an obligation running from P to C's shareholders.

D. Subordination of Shareholder Debts—"Deep Rock" Doctrine

1. In General [§124]

If a corporation goes into bankruptcy, any debts owed by the corporation to *controlling* shareholders *may*, under certain circumstances, be subordinated to the claims of other creditors under the doctrine of equitable subordination. This means that the shareholders' debt claims against the corporation will not be paid unless and until all other corporate creditors are paid—even if the controlling shareholders' claims are secured and all other creditor claims are unsecured. [**Taylor v. Standard Gas & Electric Co.,** 306 U.S. 307 (1939)]

---

e.g. **Example:** Standard Gas had complete control of Deep Rock Oil Corp. through ownership of common stock. Deep Rock's officers were officers or directors of Standard Gas or its management corporation. Standard Gas wholly controlled all fiscal affairs of Deep Rock. Among other things, Standard Gas charged Deep Rock management and supervision fees, interest on open account balances, and rental on oil leases—even when the lease arrangements were detrimental to Deep Rock. Following several years of such operation, Deep Rock went bankrupt. Standard Gas filed a claim in the bankruptcy proceedings to recover unpaid debts from Deep Rock. Deep Rock's preferred shareholders brought suit. The Court held that the transactions were accomplished through the complete control and domination of Standard Gas and without the participation of the original preferred shareholders, who had no voice or vote in Deep Rock's management. Deep Rock was bankrupt not only because of the enormous sums owed to Standard Gas, but also because of the abuses in management due to Standard Gas's paramount interest in the interlocking officers and directors. Therefore, the preferred stockholders were given priority over Standard Gas's claims. [**Taylor v. Standard Gas & Electric Co.,** *supra*]

---

2. **Effect of Subordination [§125]**

When shareholders' claims are subordinated in bankruptcy, "loans" from the shareholders to the corporation are treated as if they were not loans but rather *invested capital* (stock), at least vis-a-vis the claims of creditors who are not shareholders. In practice, this usually means that the shareholders' "loans" to the corporation will not be repaid, because if the corporation has gone into bankruptcy, typically there will not even be enough money to pay off the outside creditors' claims.

   a. **Distinguish—piercing [§126]**

   Subordination differs in a crucial way from piercing the corporate veil. When the corporate veil is pierced, the shareholder is ordered to *pay* the corporation's debts. In subordination, the shareholder's claims merely get placed behind the claims of nonshareholder debtors. The shareholder may lose his "loans" but he is not liable for corporate debts.

3. **Grounds [§127]**

The doctrine of equitable subordination is often referred to as the "Deep Rock" doctrine, named after one of the corporations involved in the seminal case of **Taylor v. Standard Gas & Electric Co.,** *supra*. Under the Deep Rock doctrine, when a corporation is in bankruptcy, the claim of a controlling shareholder (which can be either an individual or a parent of a bankrupt subsidiary) may be subordinated to other claims, including the claims of preferred shareholders, on equitable grounds. [**Costello v. Fazio,** 256 F.2d 903 (9th Cir. 1958)] Among the factors that a court may regard as inequitable conduct that will justify subordination are:

(i)   *Fraud* or other wrongdoing;

(ii) *Mismanagement* in excess of simple negligence;

(iii) *Undercapitalization*;

(iv) *Commingling of funds and properties*;

(v)   *Failure to develop the corporation* into an independently profitable business, overdependence of the corporation's business upon that of the shareholder, or both;

(vi) *Excessive control*, indicated by a failure to observe the formalities of separate corporations; and

(vii) Whether the transaction that gave rise to the shareholder's debt claim carries the earmarks of an *arm's length bargain*.

[**Arnold v. Phillips,** 117 F.2d 497 (5th Cir. 1941)]

Chapter Three: Liabilities for Transactions Before Incorporation

Chapter Approach

Promoters participate in the formation of the corporation. Most exam questions about promoters concern the rights and liabilities of the promoter and the corporation with respect to contracts entered into by the promoter on the corporation's behalf prior to formation of the corporation. Unless the question specifically asks about the liability of one or the other, your approach to this type of question should be as follows:

1. The first issue to consider is whether the corporation is liable. Under the American rule, the corporation is liable if it *ratifies or adopts* the contract.

2. The second issue to consider is the *rights and liabilities of the promoter*. Recall that a promoter is not personally liable on these contracts if he has made it explicit that he is contracting solely on behalf of the proposed corporation. But if this is not explicit, the promoter is liable. If the corporation is never formed, the promoter may be permitted to enforce the contract himself; but if a corporation is formed and it adopts or ratifies the contract, only the corporation may enforce it.

A. Promoters

1. Definition [§128]

A promoter is one who participates in the formation of a corporation. The promoter usually arranges compliance with the legal requirements to form a corporation, secures initial capitalization, and enters into necessary contracts on behalf of the corporation before it is formed. Often the promoter remains active in the corporation after it comes into existence.

2. Fiduciary Duties to Each Other [§129]

Prior to formation of the corporation, the promoters are regarded as joint venturers (similar to partners) and for that reason owe to each other a duty of *full disclosure* and *fair dealing* as to all matters pertaining to the corporation.

B. Contracts Made by Promoters on Corporation's Behalf

1. Introduction [§130]

Litigation frequently arises from contracts entered into by promoters on the corporation's behalf prior to formation of the corporation. For example, if the promoter negotiates a lease in the name of the proposed corporation on property to be used as its principal office, what are the rights and liabilities of the corporation and the promoters on this lease?

2. Rights and Liabilities of Corporation

a. English rule [§131]

Under the English rule, the corporation cannot be held liable on contracts made on its behalf prior to incorporation—even if the corporation has adopted or ratified the contract. The corporation may become a party only by entering into a new contract or by formal novation. *Rationale:* Under agency law, the promoter cannot be said to be acting as an agent of the corporation, because the corporation was not yet in existence and therefore could not have authorized the acts. Nor can a subsequent ratification by the corporation make it a party to the contract, because ratification relates back to the time the contract was made and the corporation was not then in existence. [**Kelner v. Baxter,** 2 L.R.-C.P. 174 (1866)]

(1) Quasi-contractual liability [§132]

However, courts following this view recognize recovery in quasi-contract against the corporation for the value of any goods or services that it chose to accept after it came into being. If the corporation had a choice to accept or reject the services offered under a contract negotiated by the promoters, and chose to accept them, it would constitute unjust enrichment if the corporation were not required to pay the reasonable value thereof.

(2) Massachusetts rule [§133]

Massachusetts has been thought to follow the English rule [**Abbott v. Hapgood,** 22 N.E. 907 (Mass. 1899)], but a more recent decision suggests that the corporation can be held liable on a promoter's contract if the other party performs and the corporation knowingly accepts the benefits of the contract [**Framingham Savings Bank v. Szabo,** 617 F.2d 897 (1st Cir. 1980)].

b. American rule [§134]

Under the American rule, a corporation can be held liable on contracts negotiated on its behalf by its promoters prior to incorporation, but only if the corporation *ratifies or adopts* the contract. The ratification may be *express* or may be *implied.*

(1) Supporting rationale [§135]

Some courts treat the promoter's contract as a continuing offer to the corporation, which it is free to accept or reject. Basically, however, the courts have developed a rule in response to commercial needs surrounding the formation of corporations.

(2) What constitutes ratification or adoption by corporation [§136]

Corporations may *expressly* ratify or adopt promoters' contracts by a resolution by the board of directors. The more difficult problem is to determine the sufficiency of the acts constituting *implied* ratification or adoption of promoters' contracts. Usually, some affirmative act by the corporation is required, *e.g.*, accepting benefits or making use of services or materials obtained under the contract with knowledge of the contract. [**D.A. McArthur v. Times Printing Co.,** 51 N.W. 216 (Minn. 1892)]

Example: The corporation is clearly charged with knowledge of the promoters' contracts if the board of directors is wholly composed of promoters with such knowledge. And it *may* be deemed to have knowledge if the promoter who made the contract has become a director of the corporation or is a controlling shareholder. [**Chartrand v. Barney's Club, Inc.,** 380 F.2d 97 (9th Cir. 1967)]

(a) Note

There is a split of authority on whether mere use of the corporate charter is sufficient "acceptance" of benefits to hold the corporation liable on pre-incorporation contracts for the services essential to its formation (attorneys' fees to incorporate, etc.). [**Kridelbaugh v. Aldrehn Theatres Co.,** 191 N.W. 503 (Iowa 1923)]

(3) Quasi-contractual liability [§137]

Even where the corporation expressly disavows its promoters' contracts, it cannot with impunity keep the benefits obtained thereby. Quasi-contractual liability can be imposed to the extent of the fair value of the services or materials obtained, although some courts do not impose quasi-contractual liability for pre-incorporation services that it had no real option to reject (*e.g.*, attorneys' fees, filing costs, etc.). [**David v. Southern Import Wine Co.,** 171 So. 180 (La. 1936)]

c. Corporation's right to enforce contract [§138]

Under both the English and American rules, the corporation may enforce the contract against the party with whom the promoter contracted, if it chooses to do so.

(1) *Under the English rule* (no contract with corporation), the corporation must sue as an *assignee* of the promoters.

(2) *Under the American rule*, the corporation's adoption of the contract makes it a party to the contract so that it can maintain the action directly. [**Builders' Duntile Co. v. W.E. Dunn Manufacturing,** 17 S.W.2d 715 (Ky. 1929)]

3. Rights and Liabilities of Promoters

a. Liability on pre-incorporation contract [§139]

Where the corporation either never comes into existence or rejects the preformation contracts negotiated for it by its promoters, or *ratifies preformation contracts but never performs or pays* as agreed, the other party to the contract frequently attempts to hold the promoters personally liable.

(1) No liability [§140]

If the contracting party *clearly intended* to contract with the proposed corporation and *not* with the promoters individually, it must rely solely on the credit of the proposed corporation and has no claim against the promoters individually. [**Quaker Hill, Inc. v. Parr**, 364 P.2d 1056 (Colo. 1961)] *Rationale:* Where this is so, there really is *no contract* at all prior to the corporation's becoming a party—only a continuing offer to be communicated to the corporation after its formation, which it can then accept (expressly or impliedly) or reject.

Example: In May, Quaker Hill Corp. ("Quaker Hill") sold over $14,000 in nursery stock to the Denver Memorial Nursery, Inc. ("Denver Memorial"), a corporation to be formed to operate a cemetery. Quaker Hill knew that Denver Memorial was not yet formed, but urged that the contract be made immediately, so that the stock could be planted during the spring. The contract noted that Denver Memorial was not yet formed and was signed "Denver Memorial Nursery, Inc., E.D. Parr, Pres." The contract was accompanied by a promissory note, signed similarly, but that also included the signature, "James P. Presba, Sc'y-Treas." A $1,000 down, payment was made, and the stock was shipped and planted. Under the contract, the balance owed was not due until the end of the year. Denver Memorial was never formed, instead a corporation called "Mountain View Nurseries, Inc." ("Mountain View") was formed. A new contract and note were executed for the sale under that name. The plants died before the balance owed was due, and Mountain View never functioned as a going concern. Quaker Hill then sought to recover the balance from Parr and Presba, claiming that they were liable as promoters. *Held:* Because Quaker Hill knew that Denver Memorial was not yet formed and there is little evidence that Quaker Hill ever intended Parr and Presba to be personally liable, they cannot be held liable as promoters. [**Quaker Hill, Inc. v. Parr**, *supra*]

---

(2) Liability [§141]

However, where the promoters have *not* made it explicit that they are contracting solely on behalf of the proposed corporation, courts tend to hold the promoters *personally liable* on preformation contracts. This is particularly true where such contracts require the other party to render *performance prior* to formation of the corporation. [**Stanley J. How & Associates v. Boss,** 222 F. Supp. 936 (S.D. Iowa 1963)]

---

e.g. **Example:** Boss entered into a contract with How, who agreed to provide architectural services. Boss signed the contract "Edwin A. Boss, agent for a Minnesota corporation to be formed, who will be the obligor." Under the contract, monthly payments were to be made to How. How performed but was only partially paid the money promised. The corporation was never formed, and How sued Boss to recover from him personally. Boss argued that he should not be liable because the contract clearly shows that the parties did not intend him to be personally liable. However, the words "who will be the obligor" say nothing about who is the present obligor. Because the contract called for monthly payments for services that How was to provide and the corporation was not yet formed, the parties must have contemplated that someone (Boss) would be liable. [**Stanley J. How & Associates v. Boss,** *supra*] The court also noted that the signature was ambiguous as to its intent, that Boss drafted that part of the contract, and that as a matter of contract construction, ambiguities are construed against the drafter.

LIABILITY ON PROMOTERS' PREINCORPORATION CONTRACTS—A SUMMARY **gilbert**	
CORPORATION	*English rule:* Corporation is liable only if it enters into a *new contract* or a *novation* *American rule:* Corporation is liable if it *expressly* or *impliedly adopts or ratifies* the contract
PROMOTERS	Promoters are *personally liable* unless parties clearly intended that only the corporation was to be liable, even if the corporation adopts or ratifies the contract but does not pay

---

EXAM TIP **gilbert**

It is important to note that where the parties do not clearly intend to hold only the corporation liable, the promoters are liable *and remain liable* even if the corporation adopts or ratifies the contract after it is formed. The promoters can be released from such liability only if there is a specific release or a novation.

(a) Supporting rationale [§142]

Various theories for holding promoters liable have been advanced. Some courts talk about the promoters having impliedly warranted their authority, or having impliedly warranted that the corporation would be formed and, once formed, would adopt the preformation contract. Other courts talk about the promoter remaining personally liable as surety or guarantor of the corporation's performance.

(b) Right to reimbursement [§143]

Where the promoters have been held personally liable on preformation contracts, they have a right to be *reimbursed* or indemnified by the corporation for their expenses or losses, at minimum to the extent of any *benefits* received by the corporation under the contracts.

b. Right to enforce against other party [§144]

Only a few cases have dealt with an attempt by a promoter to enforce a contract made by him for a corporation to be formed. At least where the corporation was *never formed,* the promoter may be permitted to enforce the contract on the theory that because the promoter could have been held liable in the event of a breach (*see* above), there was sufficient "mutuality" to allow him to enforce it against the other party. Unless the contract was expressly limited to the proposed corporation, the failure to incorporate is not deemed an essential condition to the other party's duty to perform. [**Erskine v. Chevrolet Motors Co.,** 117 S.E. 706 (N.C. 1923)]

(1) Distinguish

On the other hand, if the corporation is formed and adopts or ratifies the contract, it alone has the right to enforce the contract; thus, the promoter cannot sue. [**Speedway Realty Co. v. Grasshoff Realty Corp.,** 216 N.E.2d 845 (Ind. 1966)]

C. Obligations of Predecessor Business

1. Introduction [§145]

Although corporations may be created to undertake an entirely new venture, they are often formed to take over an existing business that is already being conducted by a sole proprietorship, a partnership, or a different corporation. The newly formed corporation frequently acquires all of the assets of the predecessor business. The owners of the predecessor business (*i.e.*, the sole proprietor, the partners, or the earlier corporation) continue to be liable for its debts. But the newly formed corporation that takes over the predecessor business may also be liable to its creditors under certain circumstances.

2. General Rule [§146]

A corporation that acquires all of the assets of a predecessor business *does not ordinarily succeed to the predecessor's liabilities*. There are, however, a series of exceptions to this general rule. [**Tift v. Forage King Industries, Inc.,** 322 N.W.2d 14 (Wis. 1982)]

a. **Third-party beneficiary [§147]**

If the newly formed corporation expressly or impliedly assumes the obligations of its predecessor, then the creditors of the old business may hold the new corporation liable as third-party beneficiaries.

b. **Fraud [§148]**

The successor corporation will be held liable for the debts of the predecessor business if the sale of its assets was an attempt to defraud the predecessor's creditors.

(1) **Inadequate consideration [§149]**

This may arise if the successor corporation gives inadequate consideration for the assets received, thus rendering the predecessor business unable to pay its existing debts. [**Ortiz v. South Bend Lathe**, 46 Cal. App. 3d 842 (1975)]

Example: The Bergstrom Manufacturing Company ("Company") owed debts of about $244,000. Its assets had a book value of about $242,000, but Company's fair market value as a going concern was much higher. Company sold all of its assets to the Bergstrom Manufacturing Corporation ("Corporation"), including a checking account containing over $2,500, for $1,148. Neither Company nor Corporation paid Village $131.98 that Company owed to Village as property tax, and Village sought to recover from Corporation. *Held:* Corporation is liable for Company's debts because Corporation did not pay fair value for Company's assets. [**Village of West Milwaukee v. Bergstrom Manufacturing Co.**, 7 N.W.2d 587 (Wis. 1943)]

c. **Merger [§150]**

The successor corporation will be held liable for the debts of the predecessor business if it is merged into, or absorbed by, the successor. This reorganization ends the predecessor's existence and transforms it into a different enterprise. [**McCarthy v. Litton Industries, Inc.**, 570 N.E.2d 1008 (Mass. 1991)]

d. **Continuation [§151]**

The successor corporation *may* be held liable for the debts of the predecessor business on the theory that the successor is merely a continuation of the predecessor. Some decisions (involving strict liability product defect claims) have found such a continuation simply because the successor corporation conducts the same business as the predecessor, using the same name and management. [**Tift v. Forage King Industries, Inc.**, *supra*, §146] But most courts require a more formal "reorganization" of the predecessor business (as described *supra*). [**J.F. Anderson Lumber Co. v. Myers**, 206 N.W.2d 365 (Minn. 1973)—successor not liable even though predecessor corporation was insolvent; **Pendergrass v. Card Care, Inc.**, 424 S.E.2d 391 (N.C. 1993)—successor corporation not liable, partners of predecessor partnership remain liable]

Chapter Four: Powers of the Corporation

CONTENTS

Chapter Approach

Generally, corporations have those powers expressly set forth in their certificate of incorporation or conferred by statute, and those implied powers necessary to carry out the express powers. Transactions beyond the purposes and powers of the corporation are ultra vires.

Although exam questions often raise the issue of ultra vires transactions, under modern statutes ultra vires is not usually a viable defense. For example, it is not a defense to tort or criminal actions, and even in contract actions, there are very few situations where ultra vires may be allowed:

(1) At common law, if a contract is *purely executory*, either party can raise ultra vires as a defense. However, most states now have *statutes* that prohibit the use of ultra vires as a defense in an action between the contracting parties.

(2) Most statutes do allow the corporation to *sue directors or officers* for damages for their ultra vires acts.

(3) Most statutes also allow shareholders to *enjoin performance* of an ultra vires contract.

A. Corporate Powers

1. Express and Implied Powers [§152]

At one time, a corporation's purposes and powers were generally limited to those purposes and powers set forth in the corporation's certificate of incorporation ("express powers") and those powers reasonably necessary to accomplish the purposes set forth in its certificate of incorporation ("implied powers"). This approach gave rise to various ultra vires problems and verbose certificates of incorporation intended to minimize such problems. (*Note:* An "ultra vires" transaction is a transaction that is outside the scope of the purposes or powers of the corporation.)

2. Modern Statutes [§153]

Modern statutes minimize these problems in two ways. First, modern statutes dispense with the need for setting out a long list of corporate purposes, by simply providing that a corporation can engage in any lawful business. Second, modern statutes set out a long list of powers conferred on every corporation, whether or not those powers are stated in the certificate of incorporation. Under the Delaware statute, which is typical, a corporation is granted the following express powers, among others:

    (i)   To have *perpetual succession* (*i.e*, perpetual existence);

    (ii)   To *sue and be sued;*

    (iii) To have a *corporate seal;*

    (iv) To *acquire, hold, and dispose of personal and real property;*

    (v)   To *appoint officers;*

    (vi) To *adopt and amend bylaws;*

    (vii) To *conduct business* inside and outside the state;

    (viii)To establish *pension and other incentive and compensation plans;*

    (ix) To *acquire, hold, vote, and dispose of securities* in other corporations;

    (x)   To make *contracts of guaranty and suretyship;*

    (xi) To *participate with others in any corporation, partnership, or other association* of any kind that it would have power to conduct by itself, whether or not such participation involves sharing or delegating control with others; and

    (xii) To *make donations* for the public welfare or for charitable, scientific, or educational purposes, and in time of war or other national emergency, in aid thereof.

[Del. Gen. Corp. Law §122] The Delaware statute also provides that a certificate of incorporation can simply state that the purpose of the corporation is to engage in any lawful act or activity for which corporations may be organized under Delaware law. [Del. Gen. Corp. Law §102(a)(3)] As more and more corporations use this kind of sweeping purpose clause, the problem of corporate powers becomes less and less significant, because a corporation has implied powers to accomplish the purposes set forth in its certificate of incorporation.

EXAM TIP   **gilbert**

Under modern corporations statutes, a corporation is given the power to do all things necessary or convenient to effect its purposes. Most modern statutes also provide that a corporation may be formed for any lawful purpose. Combined, these provisions provide authority for a corporation to do *almost anything that is rationally related to a business purpose*. Thus, unless an exam question restricts a corporation's purposes, you should usually find corporate acts to be *within* the corporation's powers.

---

3. Traditional Problem Areas [§154]

The last three of the above listed powers are the most significant, in the sense that the existence of these powers was deemed questionable under the older statutes, which did not specifically confer them.

a. **Guaranties [§155]**

The older statutes typically did not explicitly confer upon corporations the power to guarantee the debts of others. Cases under these statutes held that the exercise of such a power was normally ultra vires. Modern statutes explicitly permit a corporation to make contracts of guaranty and suretyship. Like other corporate powers, however, this power can be exercised only in furtherance of the corporate business (*e.g.*, by guaranteeing a loan to a customer to enable the customer to buy the corporation's product).

b. **Participation in a partnership [§156]**

The older statutes did not explicitly confer upon corporations the power to be a partner. Cases under those statutes held that a corporation had no implied power to enter into a partnership (although a corporation could enter into a joint venture, which is usually temporary in nature and for a limited purpose). The rationale was that in a partnership the corporation would be bound by the acts of its partners, who are not its duly appointed agents and officers, and that such responsibility cannot be delegated by the board. [60 A.L.R.2d 920] Modern statutes make these cases moot by explicitly conferring upon corporations the power to be a partner.

c. **Donations [§157]**

The law concerning donations and other uses of the corporation's resources for public welfare, charitable, educational, or like purposes, in the absence of an explicit statutory power, has never been completely well-defined, partly because it is in a process of continual growth.

(1) **General rule [§158]**

The general rule is that the objective of the business corporation is to conduct business activity with a view to corporate profit and shareholder gain. [**Dodge v. Ford Motor Co.**, 170 N.W. 668 (Mich. 1919)]

(2) **Traditional view [§159]**

Some cases, mostly arising at or before the turn of the century, built either on the general rule or on a strict notion of ultra vires (or on both) to preclude use of corporate resources, by donation or otherwise, for humanitarian, educational, philanthropic, or other public activities. [*See, e.g.,* **Brinson Railway v. Exchange Bank**, 85 S.E. 634 (Ga. 1915); **McCrory v. Chambers**, 48 Ill. App. 445 (1892)] Normally, however, use of corporate resources for public welfare, humanitarian, philanthropic, or educational purposes can be justified on traditional profit grounds (*e.g.*, on the ground that it increases goodwill). Accordingly, this strict position was modified by cases holding that a corporation *could* use its resources for such purposes if the use was likely to produce a ***direct benefit*** to the corporation. [**Whetstone v. Ottawa University**, 10 Kan. 240 (1874); **Corning Glass Works v. Lucase**, 37 F.2d 798 (D.C. Cir. 1929), *cert. denied*, 281 U.S. 742 (1930)]

(3) Modern view [§160]

Modern cases have in effect dropped this direct-benefit test and permit the use of corporate resources for public welfare, humanitarian, educational, or philanthropic purposes without requiring a showing that a direct benefit is likely. Some cases reach this result by treating such uses as *profit-maximizing* and within the board's business judgment even where the evidence indicates that the motive behind the conduct was not a profit motive. [**Shlensky v. Wrigley,** 237 N.E.2d 776 (Ill. 1968); **Union Pacific Railroad v. Trustees, Inc.,** 329 P.2d 398 (Utah 1958); **Kelly v. Bell,** 266 A.2d 878 (Del. 1970)] Other cases take the more direct approach that the use of corporate resources for such purposes is a *legitimate end* in itself, on the ground that (i) activity that maintains a healthy social system necessarily serves a long-run corporate purpose; or (ii) there is an independent social policy to maintain diversified centers of charitable, educational, etc., activity, and full effectuation of that policy depends upon, and therefore justifies, corporate support. [*See, e.g.,* **A.P. Smith Manufacturing Co. v. Barlow,** 98 A.2d 581 (N.J. 1953); **Union Pacific Railroad v. Trustees, Inc.,** *supra*]

(a) Limitation—reasonableness test [§161]

The corporation's ability to make donations is not unlimited. The modern cases have invoked a limit of *reasonableness* on the use of corporate resources for public welfare, humanitarian, educational, or philanthropic purposes.

(4) Statutes [§162]

Many statutes, like Delaware's, explicitly confer upon corporations the power to make donations for charitable and like purposes. This power is also subject to an implied limit of reasonableness. Thus, even under such a statute, it would still be improper to give away most of the corporation's assets.

(5) Restatement view [§163]

According to the American Law Institute's Principles of Corporate Governance, the "objective of the business corporation is to conduct business activities with a view to corporate profit and shareholder gain, except that, even if corporate profit and shareholder gain are not thereby enhanced, the corporation, in the conduct of its business . . . may devote resources, within reasonable limits, to public welfare, humanitarian, educational, and philanthropic purposes." [A.L.I. Prin. Corp. Gov. §2.01]

B. Ultra Vires Transactions

1. In General [§164]

An "ultra vires" transaction is one that is *beyond the purposes and powers* of the corporation. In principle, a corporation is not bound by an ultra vires transaction.

However, that principle has been so heavily eroded that there is almost nothing left of it. Even at an early period, two exceptions were made to the principle:

a. Implied powers [§165]

It was established even in early cases that corporate powers could be implied as well as explicit. [*See* **Sutton's Hospital Case,** 10 Coke 23a (1613)] The courts eventually became very liberal in finding implied powers, including implied powers to enter into business activities not specified in the articles. Thus, in **Jacksonville, Mayport, Pablo Railway & Navigation Co. v. Hooper,** 160 U.S. 514 (1896), the Supreme Court held that a Florida company whose purpose was to operate a railroad could also engage in leasing and running a resort hotel, on the ground that the latter activity was auxiliary or incidental to the former.

b. Effect of shareholder ratification [§166]

Even where an ultra vires defense would otherwise be allowed, under American common law a corporation was not permitted to assert the defense if all shareholders had given their consent to or acquiesced in the contract.

2. Tort Actions [§167]

Under modern law, ultra vires is *no defense to tort liability.* A corporation cannot escape civil damages by claiming that it had no legal power to commit the wrongful act. [**Nims v. Mt. Herman Boys' School,** 35 N.E. 776 (Mass. 1893)] *Rationale:* The fact that a wrongful act exceeded the powers conferred upon the corporation by statute or its articles should not result in the loss falling on the innocent injured party, assuming that the act was one for which the corporation would otherwise be civilly liable.

3. Criminal Actions [§168]

Similarly, it is *no defense to criminal liability* that a corporate act was beyond the corporation's authorized powers.

4. Contract Actions—Common Law [§169]

The most substantial questions at common law arose when a corporation entered into a contract that was not explicitly or impliedly authorized under its articles of incorporation or the relevant statute. The extent to which a plea of ultra vires was allowed in contract actions depended largely on the extent to which the contract had been performed.

a. Contract purely executory [§170]

Where there had been no performance on either side, the defense of ultra vires could be raised by either the corporation or the party with whom it had contracted. The rationale was that because the contract was beyond the corporation's powers, it was unenforceable *against* the corporation; and under the doctrine of mutuality of obligation (*i.e.,* a contract that cannot be enforced against one party should not be enforceable against the other), the contract was therefore unenforceable *by* the corporation. [**Ashbury Railway Carriage & Iron Co. v. Riche,** 7 L.R.-E. & I. App. 653 (1875)]

b. Contract fully performed on both sides [§171]

At the opposite end of the spectrum, if the contract was fully performed by both parties, neither party could rescind on the ground that the contract had been ultra vires. The courts left the parties where they were. [**Long v. Georgia Pacific Railway,** 8 So. 706 (Ala. 1891)]

c. Contract partly performed [§172]

The difficult case occurred where the contract had been fully or partly performed on one side, and the nonperforming party then sought to assert ultra vires as a defense to enforcement of its side of the contract.

(1) Majority view—no defense [§173]

Under the majority view, the nonperforming party, having received a benefit, was estopped to assert a defense of ultra vires. [**Joseph Schlitz Brewing Co. v. Missouri Poultry & Game Co.,** 229 S.W. 813 (Mo. 1921)]

(2) Minority view (federal rule) [§174]

Some cases held that the nonperforming party could assert the defense of ultra vires on the ground that the contract was void ab initio (from the outset) and could not be enforced. (This rule was sometimes referred to as "the federal rule.") However, even cases that adopted this minority rule recognized that a party who had received a benefit from the part performance would be liable in *quasi-contract* for the *value* of the benefit, as opposed to the contract price. [**Central Transportation Co. v. Pullman's Palace Car Co.,** 139 U.S. 24 (1891)]

5. Statutes [§175]

Most states now have statutes that severely curtail the doctrine of ultra vires. The most common type of statutory provision prohibits the use of ultra vires as a defense in a suit between the contracting parties, although it permits ultra vires to be raised in certain other contexts. [RMBCA §3.04; Del. Gen. Corp. Law §124]

a. Corporation and third party [§176]

Under this type of statute, neither the corporation nor the third party with whom it contracts can assert ultra vires as a *defense* to the other's suit to enforce the contract; and this is true regardless of whether the contract is still executory or has been performed in whole or in part.

b. Suit against officers or directors [§177]

However, if the contract has been performed and has resulted in a loss to the corporation, the corporation can sue the officers or directors for damages for exceeding their authority. And if the corporation refuses to sue, a shareholder may bring a derivative suit (*see infra,* §735).

c. Suit by the state [§178]

These statutes do not prohibit the state from suing to enjoin the corporation from transacting unauthorized business.

d. Suit by shareholders for injunctive relief [§179]

These statutes also permit a shareholder of the corporation to sue to *enjoin performance* of an ultra vires contract, provided that all parties to the contract are made parties to the action and the court finds that injunctive relief would be equitable.

WHEN ULTRA VIRES DOCTRINE CAN BE RAISED   **gilbert**

UNDER MODERN STATUTES, THE ULTRA VIRES DOCTRINE CAN BE RAISED IN ONLY THREE SITUATIONS:

☑ The *corporation* may sue an officer or director for damages arising from the commission of an ultra vires act authorized by the officer or director;

☑ The *state* can sue a corporation to enjoin it from transacting unauthorized business; and

☑ A *shareholder* can sue to enjoin performance of an ultra vires act if all parties to the contract are made parties to the suit and injunctive relief would be equitable.

---

(1) Damages [§180]

If an injunction is granted, the court may allow compensation to the injured party for any damages resulting from noncompletion of the contract, *exclusive of lost profits*.

(2) Interpretation [§181]

These statutes do not provide that the court *must* enjoin an ultra vires contract upon the suit of a shareholder, but only that the court may do so if an injunction would be equitable. A shareholder who actively participated in authorizing an ultra vires contract, or who purchased shares in a corporation knowing that it had made such a contract, would probably be unable to enjoin performance of the contract, because an injunction in favor of such a shareholder would normally be inequitable. [**Goodman v. Ladd Estate Co.,** 427 P.2d 102 (Or. 1967)]

Example: Liles owned all of the voting shares of Westover. Wheatley, a Westover director, borrowed $10,000 from a bank in exchange for a promissory note. Wheatley had Ladd Estate Co. guarantee payment of the note to the bank and induced Liles to have Westover guarantee payment of the note to Ladd. Wheatley defaulted. Ladd paid the bank and sought payment from Westover under the guarantee. Westover refused to pay, and Ladd filed suit against Westover and Liles (who had also personally guaranteed the note). The court ordered a receiver to sell Liles's shares in Westover. The Goodmans purchased the shares with knowledge of the guarantees and then brought suit to enjoin payment by the corporation, claiming that the guarantee was ultra vires because it was solely for the personal benefit of a Westover director. The court held that the Goodmans could not invoke the ultra vires doctrine. Liles actively participated in the ultra vires act and so is not in a position to invoke the doctrine. The Goodmans purchased their shares knowing of the ultra vires guarantee and Liles's participation in it. Thus, they stand in his shoes and cannot raise the doctrine either. [**Goodman v. Ladd Estate Co.,** *supra*]

e. **Broad certificate provisions [§182]**

Finally, if a corporation is incorporated under a statute like the Delaware statute, which provides that a certificate of incorporation can state that the purpose of the corporation is to engage in any lawful act or activity for which corporations may be organized [Del. Gen. Corp. Law §102(a)(3)], and the corporation's certificate of incorporation contains such a statement, ultra vires issues are extremely unlikely to arise.

Chapter Five: Management and Control

CONTENTS

Chapter Approach

Chapter Approach

This chapter covers a great deal of material, so to help you study, the most likely topics for exam questions are discussed below.

1. **Allocation of Powers Between Directors and Shareholders**

    Remember that generally the power to manage the business of the corporation belongs to the board of directors, not the shareholders. However, in exam questions, look for indications of a *close corporation* (*e.g.,* small number of shareholders, no general market for stock, limitations on admission of shareholders, etc.), which may mean that shareholder participation in management is acceptable.

2. **Directors**

    A likely topic for an exam question concerning directors is whether the directors have acted properly and effectively. Ask yourself the following questions: Was there proper *notice* of the meeting? Was a *quorum* present? Was the action *approved by the necessary majority*? If there was an *agreement* affecting board decisions, was it valid?

    A question concerning directors may also test your knowledge of the rights, duties, and liabilities of directors. Keep in mind that although directors owe the corporation the duty to exercise the care of *ordinarily prudent and diligent persons* in like positions under similar circumstances, they are *not* liable for mere bad business judgment. If a director fails to exercise the proper measure of care, he is personally liable for the losses resulting from the breach. A director is not liable for the wrongful acts of other directors or officers, unless he participated in the act, was negligent in discovering the misconduct, or was negligent in appointing the wrongdoer.

3. **Officers**

    Any question concerning officers (other than one dealing with a conflict or "insider" status, *see* below) will probably center on the officer's authority to act on behalf of the corporation. Note that an officer may have *actual or apparent authority*. Even an unauthorized act may bind the corporation, if the act is *ratified* by the board. Remember that officers owe a duty of care and loyalty to the corporation similar to that owed by directors.

4. **Conflicts of Interest in Corporate Transactions**

    This is a popular exam topic. Consider the five basic conflicts of interest situations:

    a. **Business dealings with corporations**

        Whenever you see a question where a corporation contracts either directly with a director or officer, or with a company in which the director or officer is financially interested, you should analyze it as follows:

(1) May the director *participate* in the meeting authorizing the transaction? Most statutes permit an interested director to be counted in a quorum and vote.

(2) Was there *full disclosure* to an *independent* board, *and* is the transaction *fair*? Most courts hold that an interested director transaction is voidable by the corporation only if it is unfair. For the transaction to be fair, the director must make a full disclosure to an independent board, and the transaction must be fair in price, terms, or other conditions. The burden of proof is on the interested director.

(3) Was there *shareholder ratification*, and if so, by how many shareholders? Unanimous shareholder ratification after full disclosure estops the corporation from challenging the transaction. Ratification by a majority of shareholders carries less weight, particularly when the interested director owns most of the shares.

(4) What is the appropriate *remedy*? If the interested director did not act in bad faith or profit personally, rescission may be the corporation's only remedy. Otherwise, the corporation may seek damages from the director.

b. Interlocking directorates

If the question concerns a contract between corporations having common directors, remember that most jurisdictions permit these transactions, subject to the same general requirements as *interested director transactions*.

c. Corporate opportunity doctrine

A director's fiduciary duty of loyalty bars her from personally taking any business opportunity that properly belongs to the corporation. To determine whether an opportunity properly belongs to the corporation, ask: Does the corporation have a *specific need* for it? Has the corporation *actively considered* acquiring it? Did the director discover the opportunity *while acting as a director*, and were any *corporate funds involved* in the discovery? Remember, if the director fully informs the board, and an independent board declines the opportunity, the director may usually pursue it. Similarly, if the corporation is financially unable to take advantage of the opportunity, or if doing so would be an ultra vires act, some courts allow the director to take advantage of it. However, if a director usurps a corporate opportunity, the corporation may seek a constructive trust of the property and profits, or if the property has been resold, damages in the amount of the director's profit.

d. Competing with corporation

Recall too that if a director or officer obtains an interest in a *business that competes* with the corporation, it is a conflict of interest and a possible breach of her fiduciary duty.

[§§183-186]

e. Compensation for services to corporation

Excessive compensation for services as a director, officer, or employee may be challenged as waste of corporate assets and thus a breach of the directors' duty of care. If this issue arises, discuss the following major issues: Was the compensation *duly authorized* by the board? Does the compensation bear a *reasonable relationship* to the value of services rendered?

A. Allocation of Powers Between Directors and Shareholders

1. Management of Corporation's Business [§183]

Virtually all the corporate statutes provide that the business of a corporation shall be managed by or under the direction of a board of directors, at least unless otherwise provided in the certficate of incorporation. Accordingly, except as provided by a valid agreement in a close corporation (*see infra,* §191) or a valid provision set forth in the bylaws or articles, or in a separate writing, the power to manage the business of the corporation is vested in its **board of directors**, not in the shareholders. At least in publicly held corporations, the shareholders have no power over the management of corporate affairs and cannot order the board of directors to take a particular course of action in managing the corporation's business. [**Charlestown Boot & Shoe Co. v. Dunsmore**, 60 N.H. 85 (1880)]

a. Limits on power—proper purpose [§184]

The board may validly exercise its powers only for a proper purpose. For example, the board may not exercise its powers for the primary purpose of perpetuating itself in office by interfering in a shareholder vote. [*See, e.g.,* **Schnell v. Chris-Craft Industries, Inc.,** 285 A.2d 437 (Del. 1971)—managers could not exercise a power to change the date of the annual shareholders' meeting for the purpose of obtaining an advantage in a proxy contest]

2. Shareholder Approval of Fundamental Changes [§185]

Shareholder approval is required for certain fundamental changes in the corporation—in particular, amendment of the articles of incorporation, merger, sale of substantially all assets, and dissolution. (*See infra,* §§1072 *et seq.*)

3. Power to Elect Directors [§186]

Shareholders have the power to elect directors, although if the board is staggered (*i.e.,* if directors serve overlapping, multi-year terms) it can take two or more years before a new majority of directors can be elected.

4. Power to Remove Directors [§187]

At common law, shareholders have the power to remove directors for cause. Statutes in many states also give shareholders the power to remove directors without cause. The board of directors generally does not have the power to remove one of its members even for cause. For further discussion, *see infra*, §§215-220.

5. Power to Ratify [§188]

Shareholders have power to ratify certain kinds of management transactions, and thereby either (i) insulate the transactions against a claim that the managers lacked authority, or (ii) shift the burden of proof or change the standard of proof that governs litigation concerning the transaction.

6. Power to Adopt Precatory Resolutions [§189]

Shareholders have power to adopt precatory (advisory but nonbinding) resolutions on proper subjects of shareholder concern.

> **Example:** In **Auer v. Dressel**, 306 N.Y. 427 (1954), the court held that the shareholders were entitled to vote on a resolution endorsing the administration of the former president of the corporation, who had been ousted from office, and demanding his reinstatement: "The stockholders, by expressing their approval of Mr. Auer's conduct as president and their demand that he be put back in that office, will not be able, directly, to effect that change in officers, but there is nothing invalid in their so expressing themselves and thus putting on notice the directors who will stand for election at the annual meeting."

7. Bylaws [§190]

Shareholders normally have the power to adopt and amend bylaws. Under some statutes, however, the board may have concurrent power to adopt and amend bylaws.

8. Close or Nonpublicly Held Corporations [§191]

Special problems are raised when shareholders of a close or nonpublicly held corporation attempt to vary the normal rule that the power to manage the corporation's business is vested exclusively in the directors.

a. Definition [§192]

Traditionally, a "close corporation" is generally regarded as having these attributes:

(1) *Ownership by a small number of shareholders*, most or all of whom are active in management of the corporation;

(2) *No general market* for the corporation's stock; and, often,

(3) *Some limitation upon the transferability* of stock.

b. Traditional view—shareholder agreements to control board discretion invalid [§193]

In the past, close corporations often were treated the same as any other corporation. Thus, courts tended to invalidate agreements among the shareholders of a close corporation that curtailed the powers of the board. [**Long Park, Inc. v. Trenton-New Brunswick Theatres Co.,** 297 N.Y. 174 (1948); **McQuade v. Stoneham & McGraw,** 263 N.Y. 323 (1934)] However, agreements among *all* of the shareholders of a close corporation that involved only a *slight* impingement on the statutory norms were generally upheld. [**Clark v. Dodge,** 269 N.Y. 410 (1936)]

c. Modern trend—special governance rules allowed [§194]

More recently, courts and legislatures have increasingly allowed contractual flexibility in the structure of corporations with a limited number of shareholders.

(i) *Court cases* have begun to hold that a corporation with a small number of shareholders, most of whom are involved in management, is similar to a partnership, and should be allowed to have contractual flexibility in its structure and governance, just as partnerships do. [**Galler v. Galler,** 203 N.E.2d 577 (Ill. 1964)]

(ii) *Legislatures* have taken a variety of approaches, which often turn on whether a corporation is publicly held, rather than on whether the corporation has only a small number of shareholders, most of whom are involved in management.

(1) Illustrations—New York and Model Acts

Under the New York statute, if a corporation's stock is not publicly traded, a certificate provision that would otherwise be prohibited by law as improperly restrictive of the board's discretion is valid if authorized by all shareholders. [N.Y. Bus. Corp. Law §620] Similarly, RMBCA section 7.32 provides that if a corporation's shares are not publicly traded and certain other criteria are satisfied, an agreement among the shareholders may, among other things: eliminate the board of directors or restrict the discretion or powers of the board of directors; govern distributions; establish who shall be directors or officers of the corporation, or their terms of office or manner of selection or removal; and govern the exercise or division of voting power by or between the shareholders and directors or by or among any of them. For an agreement to be effective under section 7.32, the corporation's shares must not be publicly traded, and the agreement must be set forth in the corporation's articles, in its bylaws, or in a written agreement signed by all persons who are shareholders at the time of the agreement. In addition, the existence of the agreement must be noted conspicuously on the front or back of each share certificate. (The failure to note the agreement on the share certificates does not affect the validity of the agreement, but a purchaser of shares who did not have notice of the agreement is entitled to rescission.)

d. Statutory close corporation status

Some statutes make special provisions for statutory close corporations.

(1) Definition [§195]

To qualify as a statutory close corporation under the typical statute, the corporation must: (i) identify itself as such in its articles of incorporation (and also, under some statutes, in its share certificates); (ii) include certain limitations in its articles of incorporation as to number of shareholders, transferability of shares; or (iii) both. However, the precise requirements vary considerably in different jurisdictions.

(a) Delaware statute [§196]

The Delaware statute defines a statutory close corporation as one whose articles of incorporation contain:

(i) A provision that all of the stock shall be held by *not more than 30 persons*;

(ii) A provision making all of the stock *subject to a restriction on transferability*;

(iii) A provision that the corporation shall make *no public offering* of its stock; and

(iv) A *statement* that the corporation is a close corporation.

[Del. Gen. Corp. Law §§342, 343] There must also be "conspicuous notice," on the share certificate, of any qualifications that must be met by persons in order to be entitled to be holders of the corporation's shares and any provision in the articles of incorporation that confers management powers on the shareholders, rather than the directors (*see* below). [Del. Gen. Corp. Law §351]

(b) California statute [§197]

The California statute defines a statutory close corporation as one whose articles provide that its stock shall not be held by more than 35 record shareholders and contain an express statement that "this corporation is a close corporation." [Cal. Corp. Code §158(a)] Share certificates for the corporation must also contain a conspicuous legend to the following effect: "This corporation is a close corporation. The number of holders of record cannot exceed _____ [a number not in excess of 35]. Any attempted voluntary inter vivos transfer that would violate this requirement is void. Refer to the articles, by-laws, and shareholder agreements on file with the secretary of the corporation for further restrictions." [Cal. Corp. Code §418(c)] If such a statement is *not* placed on the share certificate and there is a transfer resulting in the corporation having more than the maximum number of shareholders specified in its articles of incorporation, the corporation's status as a close corporation automatically terminates. [Cal. Corp. Code §158(e)]

(2) Functioning as a statutory close corporation [§198]

A corporation that qualifies as a statutory close corporation has great flexibility concerning management. (However, virtually the same flexibility can be achieved even without statutory close corporation status, either under statutes like Model Act section 7.32; the greatly increased tolerance of the courts for special contractual arrangements in close corporations; or simply by using the flexibility most statutes provide to vary the normal corporate governance rules by appropriate provisions in the corporation's certificate of incorporation.)

(a) Shareholder agreements concerning management [§199]

Typically, the statutory close corporation statutes provide that an agreement among the shareholders of a statutory close corporation relating to any phase of the corporation's affairs (*e.g.*, election of officers, payment of salaries, or distribution of dividends) is not subject to attack on the grounds that it interferes with the discretion of the directors or treats the corporation as if it were a partnership. [Del. Gen. Corp. Law §§350, 354; Cal. Corp. Code §§186, 300(b)] Some statutes provide that such agreements are valid only if entered into by *all* shareholders. [Cal. Corp. Code §§186, 300(b)] Others appear to permit a majority of the shareholders to enter into such agreements. [Del. Gen. Corp. Law §350]

(b) Management by shareholders [§200]

Under some statutes, the business of a statutory close corporation may be managed directly by the shareholders, rather than by directors. [Del. Gen. Corp. Law §351]

1) Liabilities for management [§201]

To the extent that the shareholders of a statutory close corporation are authorized to, and do, manage the affairs of the corporation, they become personally liable for managerial acts or omissions for which directors would be liable. [Del. Gen. Corp. Law §350; Cal. Corp. Code §300(d)]

EXAM TIP   **gilbert**

Most of the corporations that you encounter in a law school exam fact pattern will have few shareholders. Keep in mind that formalities may be relaxed in such corporations. The ordinary paradigm of a publicly held corporation—in which the power to run the corporation is vested in the board of directors and their discretion cannot be restricted—might not apply if the corporation qualifies for *close corporation status*, either because the courts in the jurisdiction will recognize it as such, or because a statute like the RMBCA applies that allows any nonpublicly traded corporation to be treated like a close corporation, or because the corporation has fulfilled the requirements to become a statutory close corporation. If the corporation is treated as a close corporation and all of the shareholders consent, they may enter into an agreement restricting director discretion—such as an agreement requiring directors to issue dividends under certain conditions, to appoint certain people officers, or, under some statutes, to dispense with the board altogether and run the corporation as if it were a partnership. Such agreements are *valid and enforceable* and are not, in and of themselves, grounds for piercing the corporate veil.

(c) Rights and liabilities of transferees [§202]

Close corporation statutes frequently provide that the share certificates of a statutory close corporation must contain a conspicuous notation of the corporation's status and the existence of shareholder agreements that impose special rules for the management of the corporation or other matters. The statutes address the problem of transfers to ineligible or unknowing transferees in a variety of ways:

1) Delaware statute [§203]

Under the Delaware statute, whenever any transferee has actual notice, or is conclusively presumed to have notice, that either (i) she is ineligible to be a shareholder of the corporation, (ii) the transfer would cause the corporation's stock to be held by more than the number of persons permitted by its articles of incorporation, or (iii) the transfer is in violation of a valid restriction on transfer, the corporation may refuse to register the transfer. [Del. Gen. Corp. Law §347]

a) Transfer to a person not entitled to be a holder [§204]

If stock of a Delaware statutory close corporation is issued or transferred to any person who is not entitled, under a valid provision of the articles of incorporation, to be a holder of the corporation's stock, and if the stock certificate conspicuously notes the qualifications of the persons entitled to be holders of the corporation's stock, the transferee is conclusively presumed to have notice of her ineligibility to be a stockholder.

b) **Transfer that will cause number of holders to exceed permitted number [§205]**

If the articles of incorporation of a Delaware statutory close corporation state the number of persons (not in excess of 30) who are entitled to be holders of record of its stock, the stock certificate conspicuously states that number, and the issuance or transfer of stock to any person would cause the corporation's stock to be held by more than that number of persons, the transferee is conclusively presumed to have notice of this fact.

c) **Transfer that violates a valid restriction on transfer [§206]**

If the stock certificate of a Delaware statutory close corporation conspicuously notes a valid restriction on the transfer of stock of the corporation, a transferee who acquires stock in violation of the restriction is conclusively presumed to have notice of that fact as well.

B. Directors

1. Appointment of Directors [§207]

The initial directors of the corporation are either designated in the articles of incorporation or elected at a meeting of the incorporators. Thereafter, the board is elected by the shareholders at their annual meetings, except that the board members themselves may fill vacancies on the board that occur between shareholders' meetings.

a. Number [§208]

The number of directors is usually prescribed in the articles or the bylaws. At one time, the statutes required a minimum of three directors, but none now do so. For example, both Delaware and the Model Act require only that the board consist of one or more members. [Del. Gen. Corp. Law §141; RMBCA §8.03(a)]

b. Qualifications [§209]

Unless otherwise provided in the articles of incorporation or bylaws, persons may be elected or appointed as directors even though they are not shareholders of the corporation or residents of the state of incorporation. [RMBCA §8.02]

c. Vacancies [§210]

Statutes vary somewhat in their treatment of vacancies. Under the Model Act, unless the articles of incorporation provide otherwise, if a vacancy occurs on a board of directors, including a vacancy resulting from an increase in the number of directors: (i) the shareholders may fill the vacancy; (ii) the board of directors may fill the vacancy; or (iii) if the directors remaining in office constitute fewer than a quorum (so board action is not possible), they may fill the vacancy by the affirmative vote of a majority of all the directors remaining in office. [RMBCA §8.10]

WHO MAY FILL BOARD VACANCIES?   **gilbert**

UNDER TYPICAL STATUTES, THE FOLLOWING PERSONS MAY FILL BOARD VACANCIES REGARDLESS OF HOW THEY ARISE:

☑ The *shareholders*

☑ The *board of directors*

☑ A *majority of the directors* remaining in office although less than a quorum

---

(1) Distinguish—removal of directors [§211]

Under some statutes, vacancies on the board caused by *removal* of a director (*see* below) must be filled by the *shareholders*, unless the articles or bylaws give the directors that authority. [Cal. Corp. Code §305(a); N.Y. Bus. Corp. Law §705(b)]

2. Tenure of Office

a. Term of appointment [§212]

Statutes generally provide that directors of a corporation hold office until the next annual meeting, unless the board is "classified." [RMBCA §8.05(b)]

(1) "Classified" boards [§213]

A number of statutes permit the board to be divided into some maximum number of classes, usually three to five. [*See, e.g.,* Del. Gen. Corp. Law §141 *and* RMBCA §8.06—up to three classes] The directors in each class are then elected for a multiyear term whose length corresponds to the number of classes into which the board is divided. For example, in a board consisting of nine directors divided into three classes, three new directors will be elected each year for three-year terms.

b. Power to bind corporation beyond term [§214]

Unless limited by the articles of incorporation, the board has power to make contracts that bind the corporation beyond the directors' terms of office.

c. Removal of director during term

(1) Removal by shareholders [§215]

Under the common law, the shareholders can remove a director during his term of office only for *cause* (*e.g.,* fraud, incompetence, dishonesty); the shareholders cannot remove a director without cause unless there is specific authority in the articles of incorporation or bylaws. [**Frank v. Anthony,** 107 So. 2d 136 (Fla. 1958)] However, an article or bylaw provision can permit the removal, without cause, of directors elected after the provision has been adopted. [**Everett v. Transnational Development Corp.,** 267 A.2d 627 (Del. 1970)]

(a) Hearing [§216]

When a director is to be removed for cause, he is entitled to a hearing by the shareholders before a vote to remove. [**Auer v. Dressel,** *supra,* §189; **Campbell v. Loew's, Inc.,** 134 A.2d 852 (Del. 1957)]

(b) Distinguish—statutes [§217]

In contrast to the common law, many statutes permit the shareholders to remove a director *without cause*, unless otherwise provided in the articles of incorporation. [Del. Gen. Corp. Law §141(k); RMBCA §8.08]

(2) Removal by board [§218]

Under common law, the board cannot remove a director, with or without cause. [**Bruch v. National Guarantee Credit Corp.,** 116 A. 738 (Del. 1922)] However, some statutes permit the board to remove a director for cause [Mass. Gen. L. ch. 156B, §51(c)] or for specified reasons, such as conviction of a felony [Cal. Corp. Code §302].

(3) Removal by court [§219]

The cases are split on whether a court can remove directors for cause. [**Webber v. Webber Oil Co.,** 495 A.2d 1215 (Me. 1985)—courts do not have power to remove directors; **Brown v. North Ventura Road Development Co.,** 216 Cal. App. 227 (1963)—courts have power to remove directors, at least for fraud or the like]

(a) Statutes [§220]

Some statutes permit the courts to remove a director for specified reasons, such as fraudulent or dishonest acts. These statutes usually provide that a petition for such removal can be brought only by a designated percentage of the shareholders (most commonly 10%), by the attorney general, or in some cases, by either. [Cal. Corp. Code §304; N.Y. Bus. Corp. Law §706(d); RMBCA §8.09]

WHO MAY REMOVE DIRECTORS? **gilbert**

	For Cause	Without Cause
SHAREHOLDERS	☑	☑*
DIRECTORS	☑*	☐
COURTS	☑**	☐

* Removal is allowed here only if a state statute provides for such removal.
** Cases are split on whether a court can remove a director for cause.

---

3. Functioning of Board

a. Meetings [§221]

Absent a statute, directors can act only at a duly convened meeting at which a quorum is present. However, most statutes provide that a meeting of the board can be conducted by conference telephone or any other means of communication through which all participating directors can simultaneously hear each other. [RMBCA §8.20] Most statutes also permit the board to act by *unanimous written consent*, without a meeting of any kind. [RMBCA §8.21]

(1) Notice [§222]

Formal notice is not required for a regular board meeting. In the case of a special meeting, however, notice of the date, time, and place must be given to every director. The notice need not state the purpose of a meeting unless the articles of incorporation or the bylaws otherwise provide. [*See, e.g.,* RMBCA §8.22] Most statutes provide that notice can be waived in writing before or after a meeting, and that attendance at a meeting constitutes a waiver unless the director attends only to protest the holding of the meeting. [*See, e.g.,* RMBCA §8.23]

(2) Quorum [§223]

A quorum consists of a majority of the *authorized number of directors*—not a majority of the directors then in office. Many statutes permit the articles of incorporation or bylaws to require a greater number for a quorum than a majority of the full board. A substantial number of the statutes, including the Delaware statute and the Model Act, permit the articles or bylaws to set a lower number, but usually no less than one-third of the full board.

(3) Voting [§224]

Assuming that a quorum is present when a vote is taken, the affirmative vote of a *majority of those present* (not simply a majority of those voting) is required. Most statutes provide that the articles or bylaws can require a greater-than-majority vote for board action. [*See, e.g.,* RMBCA §8.24(c)]

b. Effect of noncompliance with formalities

(1) Unanimous but informal approval [§225]

Some older cases hold that informal approval by directors is ineffective even if the approval is explicit and unanimous. [**Baldwin v. Canfield,** 1 N.W. 261 (Minn. 1879)] However, most modern courts would hold that informal but *explicit approval* by *all* the directors is effective, particularly where all the shareholders are directors or have acquiesced in the transaction or in a past practice of informal board action. [**Gerard v. Empire Square Realty Co.,** 195 A.D. 244 (1921); **Anderson v. K.G. Moore, Inc.,** 376 N.E.2d 1238 (Mass. 1978), *cert. denied,* 439 U.S. 1116 (1979)]

(2) Unanimous acquiescence [§226]

Most modern courts will also treat as effective the *explicit approval by a majority* of the directors without a meeting together with *acquiescence by the remaining directors*. [**Winchell v. Plywood Corp.**, 85 N.E.2d 313 (Mass. 1949)]

(3) Majority acquiescence [§227]

Where a majority of the directors approve a transaction explicitly or by acquiescence, without a meeting, but the remaining directors lack knowledge of the transaction, some courts hold the corporation is not liable [**Hurley v. Ornsteen**, 42 N.E.2d 273 (Mass. 1942)], while other courts hold that it is liable, at least if the *shareholders* acquiesced in the transaction, or the shareholders or the remaining directors acquiesced in a practice of informal action by the directors [**Holy Cross Gold Mining & Milling Co. v. Goodwin**, 223 P. 58 (Colo. 1924)].

EXAM TIP   **gilbert**

Your professor could ask you about the formalities of a directors' meeting by setting up facts where there is *no meeting*. That is, the facts tell you that a director has entered into an extraordinary contract with another entity on the corporation's behalf, either on his own accord or with the approval of some of the directors. You must recognize that a director does not have power to bind the corporation here unless: (i) proper *notice* was given for a director's *meeting*, a *quorum* was present, and *a majority* of the directors approved the transaction; *or* (ii) there was *unanimous consent or acquiescence* (although some courts might find majority acquiescence sufficient in certain circumstances).

---

c. Delegation of authority [§228]

It is within the power of the board, and is in fact a common practice, to appoint *committees of its own members* to act for the board, either in particular kinds of matters (*e.g.*, a nominating committee, an audit committee, a compensation committee) or to handle day-to-day management in the intervals between board meetings.

(1) Executive committees [§229]

Statutes in many states authorize the board to appoint a committee of its members (frequently called "executive committees") to exercise the authority of the board within certain limits. [Del. Gen. Corp. Law §141]

(a) Limitations [§230]

Typically, the statutes carve out certain powers that *cannot* be delegated to a board committee. For example, the Delaware statute prohibits delegating to a committee the power or authority to:

(i)   *Amend the articles of incorporation;*

(ii) *Adopt an agreement of merger or consolidation;*

(iii) *Recommend* to the shareholders the *sale, lease, or exchange* of all or substantially all of the corporation's property and assets;

(iv) *Recommend* to the shareholders a *dissolution* of the corporation;

(v) *Recommend* to the shareholders an *amendment of the by-laws*; or

(vi) *Declare a dividend or authorize the issuance of stock,* unless a board resolution, the bylaws, or the articles of incorporation expressly so provide.

[Del. Gen. Corp. Law §141; *and see* RMBCA §8.25(e)]

(2) General qualification [§231]

Although the board may delegate general operation of the corporation's business to an officer or to a management company, this authority must be exercised under the ultimate control of the board. [Cal. Corp. Code §300(a)] While what constitutes "undue delegation" has not been precisely defined, it is clear that the board may not assign to others its complete function to govern. [**Kennerson v. Burbank Amusement Co.,** 120 Cal. App. 2d 157 (1953)]

d. Provisional directors [§232]

A growing number of statutes provide that where the board is deadlocked and the business of the corporation is endangered, a court may appoint an impartial person as a "custodian" or "provisional director," to prevent impairment of business resulting from the deadlock. Such a provisional director serves with all the rights and powers of a director until the deadlock is broken, or until she is removed from office by court order or by vote or written consent of a majority of the shareholders. [Cal. Corp. Code §308]

(1) Close corporations [§233]

Some of these statutes apply only to close corporations, as statutorily defined. [Del. Gen. Corp. Law §353]

(2) Criteria for appointment [§234]

Pursuant to these statutes, a provisional director (or custodian) may be appointed when the board is deadlocked even though there may be no showing of special or irreparable injury to the corporation. [**Giuricich v. Emtrol Corp.,** 449 A.2d 232 (Del. 1982)]

e. Voting agreements among directors [§235]

Although the laws allow shareholders to make binding agreements as to how they will vote their shares (*see infra,* §§623-633), traditionally, an agreement in advance among shareholder-directors as to how they will vote *as directors* was void as contrary to public policy. [**McQuade v. Stoneham & McGraw**, *supra,* §193] *Rationale:* Directors are fiduciaries of the corporation and must have unfettered discretion in voting on corporate affairs. However, courts have become more liberal in permitting special rules of governance in close corporations, and thus, modern courts will usually permit such an agreement, at least when all of the shareholders agree, and particularly if the agreement covers only certain matters. [**Galler v. Galler**, *supra,* §194] Some statutes specifically validate such agreements in the case of statutory close corporations. For example, the Delaware statute provides that a written agreement among a majority of stockholders of a statutory close corporation is not invalid on the ground that it restricts or interferes with the discretion or powers of the board of directors. [Del. Gen. Corp. Law §350; *and see* N.Y. Bus. Corp. Law §620] The RMBCA goes even further and allows such agreements in any corporation whose shares are not publicly traded, as long as (i) the agreement is in the articles, bylaws, or a separate writing; (ii) the agreement is approved by all of the shareholders; and (iii) the existence of the agreement is noted conspicuously on outstanding shares.

4. Compensation

a. Compensation for services as director [§236]

The traditional rule is that a director is ***not*** entitled to compensation for services ***as director,*** unless the services are extraordinary (*see* below) or compensation is provided for in the articles or by a resolution of the board passed ***before*** the services are rendered.

(1) Extraordinary services [§237]

Where the services rendered are ***beyond the scope*** of normal duties of a director, and where properly authorized corporate officials either request the services or accept the benefits for the corporation, recovery in quasi-contract may be allowed for their reasonable value even without a specific agreement (*e.g.,* a member of the board travels cross-country to investigate possible corporate business opportunity).

b. Compensation for services as officer or employee [§238]

A director who also serves as an officer or employee of the corporation is entitled to compensation for such services—even if the rate of compensation is ***not*** set in advance.

(1) Limitation—conflict of interest problem [§239]

A director-officer has a conflict of interest in connection with any action by the board adopting or approving a contract fixing compensation for his services as an officer or employee of the corporation. (As to the effect of such conflict of interest on his right to participate in the board action, *see* discussion *infra,* §§336-358.)

(2) Limitation—waste [§240]

Executive compensation is also subject to the test of waste. Even if approved by a disinterested board, an agreement to pay executive compensation that is unreasonable or excessive may be held unenforceable against the corporation (*see infra,* §§347-358).

5. Directors' Rights, Duties, and Liabilities

a. Right to inspect corporate records [§241]

A director is ordinarily entitled to inspect corporate records or properties first-hand to enable him to discharge his fiduciary duties.

(1) Limitation [§242]

This right of inspection is often said to be "absolute." [**Cohen v. Cocoline Products, Inc.,** 309 N.Y. 119 (1955)] However, some cases have held that the inspection must be in *good faith* and for some purpose germane to the director's position. Thus, a court *might* not order the corporation to permit inspection if it appeared that the director was attempting to obtain information for a purpose that would deliberately hurt the corporation (*e.g.,* to obtain lists of its customers to hand over to a competitor). [**Henshaw v. American Cement Corp.,** 252 A.2d 125 (Del. 1969)]

(2) Basis of right [§243]

The director's right to inspect corporate records is usually governed by common law principles. However, a few states have *statutes* recognizing such right. Where the statute provides that the director's right is "absolute" [*see, e.g.,* Cal. Corp. Code §1602; Del. Gen. Corp. Law §220(d)], courts may be less inclined to read in any exceptions.

b. Duty of care [§244]

Directors occupy a fiduciary relationship to the corporation and must exercise the care of *ordinarily prudent and diligent persons* in like positions under similar circumstances. [**Francis v. United Jersey Bank,** 432 A.2d 814 (N.J. 1981)] In many states this duty is codified by statute. For example, California requires that a director perform his duties "in good faith, in a manner such director believes to be in the best interests of the corporation, and with such care, including reasonable inquiry, as an ordinarily prudent person in a like position would use under similar circumstances." [Cal. Corp. Code §309(a)] Most other state statutes are basically similar. [RMBCA §8.30(a); N.Y. Bus. Corp. Law §717; A.L.I. Principles of Corporate Governance ("Prin. Corp. Gov.") §4.01(a)]

(1) Amount of care required [§245]

The standard of "reasonable care and prudence" is often difficult to apply to the judgmental decisions on "business risks," which directors are often called upon to make. Courts recognize that (i) since potential profit often corresponds to the potential risk, shareholders often assume the risk of bad business judgment; (ii) after-the-fact judgment is a most imperfect device to evaluate business decisions; and (iii) if liability were imposed too readily, it might deter many persons from serving as directors. [**Joy v. North**, 692 F.2d 880 (2d Cir. 1982)]

(a) "Business judgment rule" [§246]

For these reasons, some courts have adopted the rule that where the act or omission involves no fraud, illegality, or conflict of interest but is a question of policy or business judgment, a director who acts in good faith is not personally liable for mere errors of judgment or want of prudence, short of *clear and gross negligence*. [**Shlensky v. Wrigley**, *supra*, §160] The Delaware Chancery Court put it this way: "[C]ompliance with a director's duty of care can never appropriately be judicially determined by reference to the *content of the board decision* that leads to a corporate loss, apart from consideration of the good faith or rationality of the process employed. That is, whether a judge or jury, considering the matter after the fact, believes a decision substantively wrong, or degrees of wrong extending through 'stupid' to 'egregious' or 'irrational,' provides no ground for director liability, so long as the court determines that the process employed was either rational or employed in a *good faith* effort to advance corporate interests." [*In re* **Caremark International Inc. Derivative Litigation**, 689 A.2d 959 (Del. 1996)]

> **Example:** The board of directors of Wrigley Inc., which owned Wrigley Field and the Chicago Cubs baseball team, refused to install lights and schedule night games to increase revenue as other teams in professional baseball had done. Shlensky, a minority shareholder in Wrigley, brought suit against the directors, claiming that they breached their duty of care in making this decision. The court held that absent an allegation of fraud, illegality, or a conflict of interest, the court would not disturb the business judgment of a majority of the directors. There was no conclusive proof that scheduling night games would increase net revenues and the directors are not obliged to follow the direction taken by other, similar corporations. Moreover, there appeared to be valid reasons for refusing to install lights (*e.g.,* the detrimental effect on the surrounding neighborhood). [**Shlensky v. Wrigley**, *supra*]

1) Majority view [§247]

Most courts conclude that a director cannot invoke the business judgment rule if he has not been "*reasonably diligent,*" as where he knew or should have known that he did not have sufficient facts to make a judgment, yet failed to make *reasonable efforts to inform* himself. [**Francis v. United Jersey Bank,** *supra*] Some courts have stated that "*gross* negligence is the standard for determining whether a business judgment reached by the board of directors was an informed one." [**Smith v. Van Gorkom,** 488 A.2d 858 (Del. 1985)] But some decisions have adopted a standard of "ordinary negligence." [**Brane v. Roth,** 590 N.E.2d 587 (Ind. 1992)]

2) Illegality [§248]

A director cannot invoke the business judgment rule if he causes the corporation to engage in acts that are illegal or contrary to public policy. A director is liable for any loss sustained by the corporation because of such acts, even for acts undertaken for the benefit of the corporation. [**Miller v. American Telephone & Telegraph Co.,** 507 F.2d 759 (3d Cir. 1974)—directors could be personally liable for failing to collect a $1.5 million bill that the Democratic Party owed for communications services at its national convention if failure to collect the bill constituted an illegal campaign contribution that caused damage to the corporation]

3) Profit maximization and "other constituencies" [§249]

A director may invoke the business judgment rule even though he causes the corporation to undertake action that is not profit-maximizing, but instead considers the interests of employees, creditors, local communities, or other constituencies. [N.Y. Bus. Corp. Law §717(b)] It would seem that a limit of *reasonableness* would apply here, as it does in respect to other uses of corporate resources for public welfare, humanitarian, educational, or philanthropic purposes. (*See supra,* §160.)

(b) Directors of banks and other financial institutions [§250]

Many early cases impose a higher duty of care on directors of banks and other financial institutions, particularly in overseeing the activities of officers and management. Such directors may be found negligent for deviation from generally accepted banking principles. *Rationale:* Public interest in the safety of financial institutions requires a higher fiduciary duty of care by bank directors. [**Bates v. Dresser,** 251 U.S. 524 (1920)]

(2) Extent of liability

(a) Injury and causation [§251]

Even where a director has not exercised the proper measure of care, he will be held personally liable only for corporate losses suffered as the ***direct and proximate result*** of his breach of duty—*i.e.,* injury to the corporation and causation must still be shown. [**Barnes v. Andrews,**

298 F. 614 (S.D.N.Y. 1924); *and see* RMBCA §8.31(b)(1) *and* A.L.I. Prin. Corp. Gov. §401(d)]

1) Delaware rejected proximate cause test [§252]

The Delaware Supreme Court has rejected the tort principle of proximate cause. Under that ruling, when there has been a breach of the duty of care, the burden of proof shifts to the directors to demonstrate that the transaction was entirely fair. [**Cede & Co. v. Technicolor, Inc.,** 634 A.2d 345 (Del. 1993); *and see infra,* §290]

(b) Acts of others [§253]

A director is liable for the wrongful acts of other officers and directors only if he *participated* in the wrongful acts, was *negligent in failing to discover* the misconduct (he has the duty to inquire under the general standard of care above), *or* was *negligent in appointing* the wrongdoer. [**Graham v. Allis-Chalmers Manufacturing Co.,** 188 A.2d 125 (Del. 1963)]

1) Dissent defense [§254]

A director may seek to avoid being held liable for acts of the board by recording his *dissent.* However, in some circumstances, he may have to pursue other means, such as threatening suit. [**Francis v. United Jersey Bank,** *supra,* §244]

(c) Abolishing liability [§255]

Many state statutes permit the articles of incorporation to *limit or eliminate* the directors' liability for breach of the duty of care—apart from action in bad faith, intentional misconduct, or knowing violation of law. [*See, e.g.,* Del. Gen. Corp. Law §102(b)(7)] A few statutes either impose a maximum amount of liability [Va. Stock Corp. Act §692.1—greater of $100,000 or cash compensation during preceding 12 months], or authorize the shareholders to do so [A.L.I. Prin. Corp. Gov. §7.19]. Others have directly modified the standard of liability. [*See, e.g.,* Va. Stock Corp. Act §690A—"good faith business judgment of the best interests of the corporation"]

(3) Defenses to liability

(a) Nominal directors [§256]

It is usually no defense that the director was serving gratuitously or merely as a figurehead. [**Francis v. United Jersey Bank,** *supra*; *but see* **Harman v. Willbern,** 520 F.2d 1333 (10th Cir. 1975)—contra]

(b) Disabilities [§257]

Ill health, old age, and lack of experience have been held not to constitute defenses, on the theory that a person subject to one of these disabilities should not have accepted (or should have resigned from) the directorship. [**McDonell v. American Leduc Petroleums, Ltd.,** 491 F.2d 380 (2d Cir. 1974)]

(c) Reliance on reports of management [§258]

Directors are not required to make firsthand investigations of every detail of corporate business, at least in the absence of suspicious circumstances. As long as the director acts in good faith, he is entitled to rely on statements and reports made to him by corporate officers or employees and on reports by any committee of the board of which he is not a member, as to matters within their authority that appear to merit confidence. [RMBCA §8.30(b); A.L.I. Prin. Corp. Gov. §4.02]

1) Distinguish

This may not be a defense to a federal securities act violation (*see infra,* §§988-993).

(d) Reliance on expert opinion [§259]

A director is also entitled to rely on the advice given by attorneys, accountants, engineers, or other persons as to matters the director reasonably believes to be within that person's expertise. As long as the director's reliance was reasonable and in good faith, it is a defense to liability even if the opinion proves to be erroneous. [RMBCA §8.30(b); A.L.I. Prin. Corp. Gov. §4.02(b)]

(e) Shareholder ratification of directors' failure to exercise due care [§260]

This issue is discussed *infra,* §§768-776.

EXAM TIP   **gilbert**

When a shareholder is unhappy with director action, breach of fiduciary duty is an easy charge to make but a difficult charge to prove. If such a charge is made on your exam, you should first set out the business judgment rule—*a director who exercises the care of an ordinarily prudent person in a like position under similar circumstances cannot be held liable for the outcome of business decisions absent fraud, illegality, or conflict of interest*. Next, you should look to see whether the director **sufficiently informed himself** before making a decision. Remember that a director is entitled to rely on opinions of others within their areas of competency. Finally, be sure to check for a **provision in the corporation's articles** relieving the director of liability; such a provision is valid unless the director acted in bad faith, intentionally, or in violation of law.

---

c. Duty of loyalty [§261]

Directors have a duty of loyalty in all dealings with the corporation. (*See infra,* §§279 *et seq.*)

d. Statutory duties and liabilities regarding management [§262]

In addition to the general duty of care (above), various duties and liabilities are imposed on directors by federal and state statutes. These provisions seek to protect a broad range of public interests in addition to those of corporate shareholders and creditors.

(1) Securities Act of 1933 [§263]

The Securities Act of 1933 makes directors liable for misstatements or omissions of material fact in a registration statement required to be filed when a corporation issues securities, unless they exercise *due diligence*. (*See infra*, §§976-995.)

(2) Rule 10b-5 [§264]

Directors are liable for fraudulent misstatements or omissions of material fact by the corporation if they *participated* in or had *knowledge* of the fraud, or if their lack of knowledge resulted from *willful or reckless disregard of the truth*. (*See infra*, §§365 *et seq.*)

(3) Illegal dividends [§265]

Directors who participate in declaring a dividend from an unlawful source, or under other circumstances making a dividend illegal, are jointly and severally liable to the extent of the injury to creditors and preferred shareholders. (*See infra*, §§1044-1048.)

(4) Criminal liability [§266]

A wide variety of state and federal statutes impose criminal liability on corporate managers for unlawful corporate action. This liability may arise if the managers personally engage in or cause the unlawful act [*see, e.g.,* N.Y. Penal Law §20.25], or if they have control over the corporate employees who commit the unlawful act, even if they have no knowledge of the unlawful act [**United States v. Park,** 421 U.S. 658 (1975)—president of national retail food chain criminally liable for violation of Federal Food, Drug, and Cosmetic Act because of unsanitary conditions in a corporate warehouse. The Act "imposes not only a positive duty to seek out and remedy violations when they occur, but also, and primarily, a duty to implement measures that will insure that violations will not occur"; these responsibilities are "perhaps onerous, but they are no more stringent than the public has a right to expect of those who voluntarily assume positions of authority in business enterprises whose services and products affect the health and well-being of the public"].

C. Officers

1. Election [§267]

Officers are normally chosen by the board, or as determined by the certificate of incorporation, the bylaws, or board resolutions. Often, the board appoints the most senior officers, such as the chief executive officer, and one or more of those officers appoints the lesser officers. Officers hold their office at the pleasure of the board. Even if they have contracts, they can be discharged, subject to their right to damages for breach of contract.

2. Authority of Corporate Officers—Liability of Corporation to Outsiders

a. Types of authority [§268]

A corporate officer may have any of the following types of authority:

(1) Actual authority [§269]

Actual authority is the authority that a reasonable person in the officer's position would believe had been conferred upon him by the corporation. Actual authority may be *expressly* conferred on the officer by the bylaws, resolutions of the board of directors, a valid delegation from a superior, or acquiescence by the board or superior officers in a past pattern of conduct. An officer also has *implied* actual authority to do what can reasonably be implied from a grant of express authority.

(2) Apparent authority [§270]

Apparent authority is authority that the corporation allows third parties to reasonably believe an officer possesses. Apparent authority can arise from intentional or negligent representations by the corporation to the third party, or through permitting an officer or employee to assume certain powers and functions on a continuing basis with the third party's knowledge.

(3) Power of position [§271]

This is a special type of apparent authority, which arises by reason of the officer holding a particular position in the corporation that normally carries certain authority. For example, a vice president of sales would probably have power of position to hire a salesperson.

(4) Ratification [§272]

Even an unauthorized act by a corporate officer may bind the corporation, if the officer purports to act on the corporation's behalf and the act is later ratified by the board.

b. Authority of president [§273]

A common authority issue is the scope of authority possessed by a corporation's president by virtue of that title. There are three competing views:

(1) Only the power of a director [§274]

Under one view, the president has only those powers possessed by a director, except for the power of presiding at corporate meetings. This is obviously unrealistic and probably not good law today.

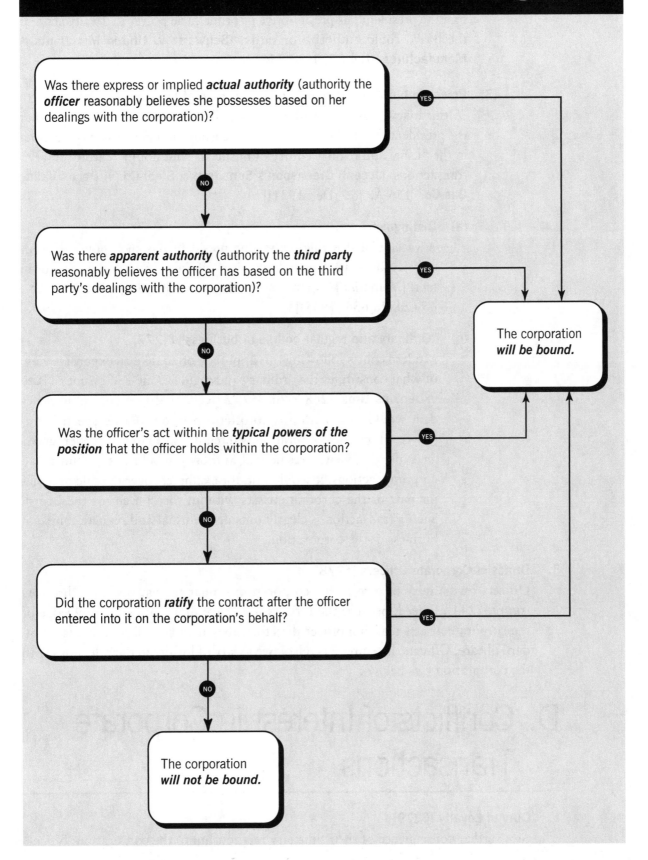

Was there express or implied ***actual authority*** (authority the ***officer*** reasonably believes she possesses based on her dealings with the corporation)?

NO

Was there ***apparent authority*** (authority the ***third party*** reasonably believes the officer has based on the third party's dealings with the corporation)?

NO

Was the officer's act within the ***typical powers of the position*** that the officer holds within the corporation?

NO

Did the corporation ***ratify*** the contract after the officer entered into it on the corporation's behalf?

NO

YES

YES

YES

YES

The corporation
will be bound.

The corporation
will not be bound.

    (2) Broad power to act [§275]

A second view, known as the "New York rule" (although it is not clear whether New York courts or any other courts still subscribe to it), holds that the president has presumptive or prima facie power to do any act that the board could authorize or ratify. [**Schwartz v. United Merchants & Manufacturers, Inc.,** 72 F.2d 256 (2d Cir. 1934)]

    (3) Power to bind corporation in regular course of business [§276]

A third view, which is the law in virtually all jurisdictions today, is that the president has the power to bind the corporation in transactions arising in the "usual and regular course of business," but not in "extraordinary" transactions. [**Joseph Greenspon's Sons Iron & Steel Co. v. Pecos Valley Gas Co.,** 156 A. 350 (Del. 1931)]

        (a) Distinguish

A variant of this rule is that the president has such power if—but only if—he is the "general manager" of the corporation by title or in fact. [**Memorial Hospital Association v. Pacific Grape Products Co.,** 45 Cal. 2d 634 (1955)]

        (b) "Ordinary and regular course of business" [§277]

Modern courts following this approach often take an expansive view of what constitutes the ordinary and regular course of business. [**Lee v. Jenkins Bros.,** 268 F.2d 357 (2d Cir. 1959)—a corporate president would have authority to offer a pension to a prospective employee whom the corporation wanted to hire] However, even under an expansive view, presidential authority would not extend to all corporate actions. It would not, for example, cover the sale of a major part of the corporate assets without the consent of the board. Such a transaction is clearly outside the usual and regular course of business of the corporation.

3. Duties of Corporate Officers [§278]

Officers owe a duty of care to the corporation similar to that owed by directors (*supra*, §244). Indeed, because the officers may have more intimate knowledge of the corporate affairs than nonofficer directors, they may be held to a higher standard of care. Officers, like directors, also owe a duty of loyalty in their dealings with the corporation (*see* below).

D. Conflicts of Interest in Corporate Transactions

1. Duty of Loyalty [§279]

As a further consequence of their fiduciary relationship to the corporation, officers and directors are held to a duty of *loyalty* in all dealings with the corporation—*i.e.*, the duty to promote the interests of the corporation without regard for personal gain.

2. Business Dealings with Corporations [§280]

Conflict of interest issues arise whenever a corporation contracts directly with one of its officers or directors, or with a company in which the officer or director is financially interested. For example, if Corporation contracts to purchase property in which Director has a financial interest, or to sell corporate assets to an entity in which Director has a financial interest, does Director's adverse interest disqualify her from voting on the contract? Does it render the contract voidable by the corporation, even where her adverse interest was disclosed at the meeting?

a. Effect of director's self-interest on right to participate in meeting authorizing transaction

(1) Common law [§281]

At common law, directors who had interests adverse to the corporation could not be counted for purposes of making up a quorum, or for purposes of making up a majority vote at the meeting in which the transaction was approved. [**Weiss Medical Complex, Ltd. v. Kim,** 408 N.E.2d 959 (Ill. 1980)]

(2) Statutes [§282]

Today, most statutes permit an "interested" director to be counted in determining the presence of a quorum, and further provide that interested director transactions are *not automatically voidable* by the corporation simply because the interested director's vote was necessary for approval. [Cal. Corp. Code §310(a); N.Y. Bus. Corp. Law §713; Del. Gen. Corp. Law §144] Under these statutes, such transactions may still be valid if other conditions are met. (*See infra,* §301.)

b. Effect of director's self-interest in rendering transaction voidable by corporation [§283]

The effect of a director's self-interest in a corporate transaction has evolved over time. The original common law view was that such transactions were automatically voidable at the option of the corporation. Most courts subsequently softened the original common law view and made such transactions voidable only if they were unfair. Today in most states the issue is governed by statutes based in large part on the more modern common law approach.

(1) Strict common law view [§284]

The historic common law rule was that any contract in which a director is financially interested is *voidable* at the option of the corporation—without regard to fairness or whether the director's adverse interest was disclosed in advance to the directors who then approved the transaction.

(2) Modern common law view [§285]

Most courts abandoned the strict common law rule in favor of the more liberal position that contracts and dealings in which a director has a personal financial interest are voidable by the corporation only where the contract is found to be *unfair* to the corporation considering all the relevant circumstances.

(a) Disclosure requirement [§286]

Following this view, it has been held that failure of an interested director to make *full disclosure* to an *independent* board respecting the transaction is in itself "unfair" to the corporation. [**State ex rel. Hayes Oyster Co. v. Keypoint Oyster Co.,** 391 P.2d 979 (Wash. 1964)] The Principles of Corporate Governance adopt this rule. [A.L.I. Prin. Corp. Gov. §5.02]

1) "Full disclosure" [§287]

"Full disclosure" requires that the director inform the board as to all matters affecting the *value* of the property involved and perhaps also the *amount of the director's profit*.

2) "Independent board" [§288]

An "independent board" is one where a majority of the directors are not under the control of the interested director (directly or indirectly).

(b) Fairness requirement [§289]

Under the modern common law view, even if there was a full disclosure to an independent board, courts generally held that the transaction was still voidable by the corporation (*e.g.,* where the board later changes its mind, new directors take office and reevaluate the transaction, a trustee in bankruptcy takes over, or a shareholder brings a derivative suit challenging the transaction) if it was unfair to the corporation in price, terms, or other conditions. [**Globe Woolen Co. v. Utica Gas & Electric Co.,** 224 N.Y. 483 (1918)—sale of valuable corporate asset to director who is otherwise insolvent, for a token down payment, with balance of purchase payable over many years and without adequate security, is voidable by corporation]

1) Burden of proof [§290]

The courts usually placed the burden of establishing the fairness of the transaction on the interested director. In effect, there was a *presumption of unfairness* that must be rebutted. [**Des Moines Bank & Trust Co. v. Betchtel,** 51 N.W.2d 174 (Iowa 1952)]; *but see* **Durfee v. Durfee & Canning, Inc.,** 80 N.E.2d 522 (Mass. 1948)—"Massachusetts rule"]

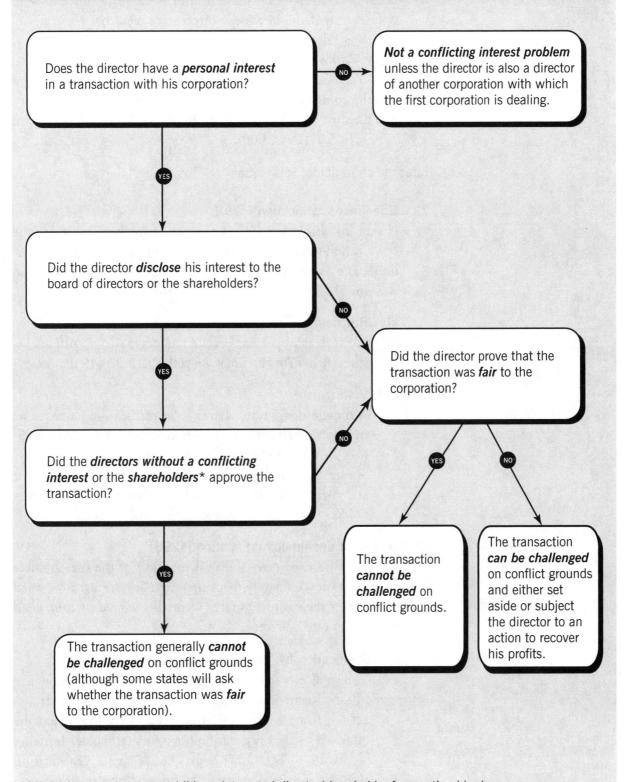

Does the director have a **personal interest** in a transaction with his corporation?

NO → **Not a conflicting interest problem** unless the director is also a director of another corporation with which the first corporation is dealing.

YES ↓

Did the director **disclose** his interest to the board of directors or the shareholders?

NO → Did the director prove that the transaction was **fair** to the corporation?

YES ↓

Did the **directors without a conflicting interest** or the **shareholders*** approve the transaction?

NO → Did the director prove that the transaction was **fair** to the corporation?

YES (to fair): The transaction **cannot be challenged** on conflict grounds.

NO (to fair): The transaction **can be challenged** on conflict grounds and either set aside or subject the director to an action to recover his profits.

YES ↓

The transaction generally **cannot be challenged** on conflict grounds (although some states will ask whether the transaction was **fair** to the corporation).

*Note that some states prohibit an interested director/shareholder from voting his shares.

2) Fairness where no ability to disclose [§291]

Where disclosure to an independent board was not possible (as where the interested director controlled a majority of the board), dealings between the corporation and an interested director were upheld only if the interested director proved that the transaction was fair and reasonable to the corporation. [**Shlensky v. South Parkway Building Corp.,** 159 N.E.2d 31 (Ill. 1959)] The same rule seems to apply to dealings between the corporation and the *controlling* shareholder, even though he does not serve as a director. [*See* **T. Rowe Price Recovery Fund, L.P. v. Rubin,** 770 A.2d 536 (Del. 2000)]

(c) Effect of shareholder ratification

1) Unanimous ratification [§292]

If after *full disclosure* the shareholders *unanimously* ratified the corporation's dealings with the interested director, the corporation was estopped from later challenging the transaction (and so was any shareholder bringing a derivative suit).

a) But note

No such estoppel was invoked unless there was *full* disclosure. [**Rivoli Theatre Co. v. Allison,** 152 A.2d 449 (Pa. 1959)]

b) Distinguish

Although unanimous shareholder ratification barred suits by or on behalf of the corporation, it did not preclude *creditors' suits* if the effect of the transaction was to deplete corporate assets and thereby render the corporation *insolvent* and unable to pay its debts—at least where the ratifying shareholders were also interested in the transaction.

2) Less-than-unanimous ratification [§293]

The effect of a *majority* (but less than all) of the shareholders voting to ratify dealings with an interested director usually turned on whether the majority shares were also *owned or controlled* by the interested director.

a) Ratification by "disinterested" majority [§294]

If the majority shareholders approving the transaction have full disclosure and have no financial interest in the transaction, some courts hold that the transaction cannot be attacked by the corporation (or by a shareholder bringing a derivative suit). Other courts hold that such ratification *shifts the burden of proving "unfairness"* to the corporation (or derivative suit plaintiff) challenging the transaction. [**Eliasberg v. Standard Oil Co.,** 92 A.2d 862 (N.J. 1952)]

1/ Waste [§295]

Even if a disinterested majority of the shareholders ratifies the transaction, if the interested director is charged with "waste," some cases have held that the court itself must examine the facts to determine whether they fall within the realm of business judgment. [**Cohen v. Ayers,** 596 F.2d 733 (7th Cir. 1979)]

b) Ratification by "interested" majority [§296]

Less weight is generally given to shareholder ratification where the majority shares are owned or controlled (directly or indirectly) by the interested director.

1/ Corporation can later rescind [§297]

Some courts hold an interested majority's ratification makes no difference even when most of the *disinterested* shareholders also approved the transaction. If even a single shareholder disapproved, the corporation (or derivative suit plaintiff) can later sue to rescind for unfairness, and the burden of proving fairness remains on the interested director. [**Pappas v. Moss,** 393 F.2d 865 (3d Cir. 1968)]

2/ Subsequent attack precluded or burden shifted [§298]

Other courts, however, are more lenient in holding that ratification by a majority of the disinterested shareholders (even though they are a minority in the corporation) precludes subsequent attack by the corporation, or at least shifts the burden of proving "unfairness" to the corporation (or derivative suit plaintiff). [**Harbor Finance Partners v. Huizenga,** 751 A.2d 879 (Del. 1999)]

3/ Older cases—corporation estopped even without disinterested majority [§299]

Some older cases go further and estop the corporation even where the shares of the interested director(s) were necessary to make up the majority shareholder vote ratifying the transaction. [**Kirwan v. Parkway Distillery, Inc.,** 148 S.W.2d 720 (Ky. 1941)]

c) Estoppel against shareholder [§300]

In any event, a shareholder who received full disclosure

and voted to approve the corporation's dealings with the interested director(s) would probably be estopped from later bringing a derivative suit charging "unfairness."

(3) Statutes [§301]

Most states have adopted statutes regulating interested director transactions. The Delaware law is illustrative. It provides that such transactions are not voidable by the corporation for conflict of interest if (i) the material facts as to the director's interest and the transaction were disclosed or known to the board and the transaction was nonetheless approved in good faith by a disinterested majority of the board; or (ii) the same information was disclosed or known to the shareholders, and a *majority of the shareholders* approved; or (iii) the transaction is fair to the corporation. [Del. Gen. Corp. Law §144]

---

e.g. **Example:** Cookies Food Products ("Cookies") was an Iowa corporation specializing in barbecue sauce. It was in dire financial straits and so entered into an exclusive distribution agreement with Herrig, one of its minority shareholders who owned a food distribution company. Through Herrig's efforts, business boomed, and Herrig eventually became Cookies's majority shareholder. Herrig then replaced four of the five board members. The new board extended the term of the exclusive dealing contract with Herrig as the previous board had done in the past. It also started paying Herrig a royalty for a taco sauce that he developed. The royalty plan was similar to the royalty plan that Cookies had with the developer of its barbecue sauce. Because Herrig was putting more time into managing Cookies and his distribution business due to increased sales volume, the board also increased Herrig's compensation. Minority shareholders (the directors who Herrig ousted) were unhappy. They received no dividends (Cookies was prohibited from paying dividends until a government business loan was repaid) and there was no market for their shares. They brought suit against the corporation, claiming that Herrig was paid too much and that he breached his fiduciary duty by negotiating for royalties, consulting fees, and warehousing fees without disclosing what benefits he would gain. Iowa had a conflict of interest statute similar to the Delaware statute above. The Iowa Supreme Court held that there was no improper self-dealing here. The directors knew of Herrig's interests when they approved the transactions. No one could expect Herrig to render services to the corporation without a profit, and he satisfied his burden of proof that the amount that he charged for his services was fair and not inconsistent with Cookies's corporate interests. [**Cookies Food Products v. Lakes Warehouse Distributing Inc.**, 430 N.W.2d 447 (Iowa 1988)]

(a) Fairness required notwithstanding disclosure [§302]

Although "fairness" and "approval after disclosure" seem to be alternatives under these statutes, some courts have interpreted the statutes as requiring fairness in any event. Thus, an interested director transaction may be set aside if unfair to the corporation, notwithstanding that there was full disclosure to, and approval by, the majority of the directors or shareholders. [**Remillard Brick Co. v. Remillard-Dandini Co.**, 109 Cal. App. 2d 405 (1952); **Flieger v. Lawrence**, 361 A.2d 218 (Del. 1976); *but see* **Marciano v. Nakash**, 535 A.2d 400 (Del. 1987)—contra (dictum)] Indeed, this is now expressly required under the California statute. Transactions between a corporation and one of its directors must be "just and reasonable as to the corporation" notwithstanding full disclosure and approval by the directors. [Cal. Corp. Code §310(a)(2)] This provision is *not applicable*, however, where there has been disclosure to, and approval by, the *shareholders*. [Cal. Corp. Code §310(a)(1)]

1) Model statutes [§303]

The Principles of Corporate Governance and Model Business Corporation Act take differing approaches. The Principles of Corporate Governance require that, notwithstanding full disclosure and approval, it is also required that disinterested directors "could reasonably have concluded that the transaction was fair to the corporation." [A.L.I. Prin. Corp. Gov. §5.02(a)(2)(B)] On the other hand, the Model Act appears to eliminate the fairness requirement if there has been compliance with the other statutory procedures. [RMBCA §§8.61, 8.62]

(b) Director approval [§304]

Under a number of statutes, a director who has a personal interest in a transaction can attend the meeting at which directors vote on the transaction and can be counted for purposes of determining whether a quorum is present. Other statutes provide that a quorum consists of a majority of the directors without a personal interest in the transaction. The interested director's vote is not counted for purposes of determining whether the transaction is approved; however, the transaction only need be approved by a majority of the directors without a personal interest in the transaction.

(c) Shareholder approval [§305]

Some statutes provide that the requisite shareholder approval must occur *without* counting the shares owned by interested directors. [Cal. Corp. Code §310(a)(1)] Others are less clear on whether such shares may be counted. [*See* Del. Gen. Corp. Law §144; N.Y. Bus. Corp. Law §713]

(d) Burden of proof [§306]

Some statutes are silent on whether the interested director has the burden of proving compliance with the statute. [Del. Gen. Corp. Law §144] Other statutes provide that if an interested director transaction is defended on grounds of "fairness," the interested director has the burden of proof. [N.Y. Bus. Corp. Law §713(b); Cal. Corp. Code §310(a)(3)]

(e) "Interested" [§307]

Although only a few state statutes define what is meant by an "interested" director, the model statutes provide greater detail: "A director or officer is 'interested' in a transaction . . . [if the] director or officer has a business, financial, or familial relationship with a party to the transaction or conduct, and that relationship would reasonably be expected to affect the director's or officer's judgment with respect to the transaction or conduct in a manner adverse to the corporation . . . ." [A.L.I. Prin. Corp. Gov. §1.23(a); *and see* RMBCA §8.60]

c. Remedy [§308]

If the transaction is voidable under any of the views above, the corporation is entitled to *rescind* (unwind the transaction). Alternatively, it may affirm the contract and hold the interested director liable for damages.

(1) Measure of damages [§309]

Where damages are granted, the usual measure is the amount of the *unfair profit* made on the transaction, *i.e.,* the difference between fair value and the price at which the transaction was consummated. Thus, where the interested director sold personal assets to the corporation at an inflated value, the corporation can recover the excess over the fair value. Or where the interested director purchased corporate assets at an inadequate price, the corporation can recover the *additional amounts* that it should have received. [**Shlensky v. South Parkway Building Corp.**, *supra*, §291]

(a) Loss of salary [§310]

In addition to damages, some courts have held that the interested director must repay any salary earned during the period of fiduciary breach. [**American Timber & Trading Co. v. Niedermeyer,** 558 P.2d 1211 (Or. 1976)]

(b) Punitive damages [§311]

Some courts have awarded punitive damages against directors who have breached their fiduciary duty. [**Rowen v. LeMars Mutual Insurance Co. of Iowa,** 282 N.W.2d 639 (Iowa 1979)]

(2) Alternate measure of damages [§312]

Alternatively (particularly in cases of *trickery* or *fraud,* or where the director acquired assets for the purpose of reselling to the corporation at an excessive price), some courts penalize the director by awarding damages based on the difference between the price paid by the corporation and the interested director's acquisition cost. This effectively *deprives the director of the profit* she could have made on a sale of the assets to any third party.

---

e.g. **Example:** Director buys assets for $5,000 for the purpose of resale to Corporation at $20,000, although fair value is only $12,000. Under the normal measure, Corporation could recover $8,000. Under the "penal" measure, it can recover $15,000. Director is thus deprived of the $7,000 she could have made had she sold to a third party.

---

(3) Rescission as sole remedy [§313]

If the interested director did not act in *bad faith* or *profit personally* from the transaction (as where her corporation sells property to another corporation in which she is a director but owns no shares, *see* below), courts may decide not to hold her personally liable for damages. In such cases, the corporation's *only remedy is to rescind.* [**Chelrob, Inc. v. Barrett,** 293 N.Y. 442 (1944)]

3. Interlocking Directorates [§314]

Conflicts of interest may also arise when the same individual sits as a director of two corporations that contract with each other. The conflict stems from the fact that the director owes each corporation the duty to make the best possible deal for it. The problem is even more acute when the boards of both corporations are comprised entirely of the same individuals (which is frequently the case with parent and subsidiary corporations).

a. Strict view [§315]

The historic common law rule held that contracts between corporations having common directors may be avoided by either corporation because of the conflict of interest—regardless of the fairness of the transaction.

b. Modern view [§316]

However, such intercorporate transactions are now permitted, subject to the same general requirements as for interested director transactions (*i.e.,* full disclosure and fairness).

(1) Statutes [§317]

Some statutes suggest that intercorporate dealings are not voidable for conflict of interest if the director who sits on both boards of the contracting corporations owns stock in neither. For example, the California statute provides that "a mere common directorship does not constitute a material financial interest" that should be disclosed. [Cal. Corp. Code §310(a)(3)]

(2) Parent-subsidiary transactions [§318]

There is no conflict of interest where one corporation is a wholly owned subsidiary of another. But conflicts frequently arise where the parent owns only a majority of the subsidiary's shares, and there are other (minority) shareholders who may be affected by parent-subsidiary dealings. The basic question in each case is whether the transaction was *fair* to the subsidiary.

(a) Burden of proof on parent [§319]

As in interested director cases generally, the burden of proof is usually on the parent corporation to demonstrate that it has not taken unfair advantage of the subsidiary through control of its board. [**Sterling v. Mayflower Hotel Corp.,** 93 A.2d 107 (Del. 1952)] The Principles of Corporate Governance adopt this position—except for transactions in the ordinary course of business, in which case the burden of coming forward with evidence of unfairness is on the person challenging. [A.L.I. Prin. Corp. Gov. §5.10]

(b) Limitation [§320]

However, some courts place this burden on the parent only where, by virtue of its domination, it has received something from the subsidiary to the *exclusion* of the minority shareholders of the subsidiary. For example, it has been held that minority shareholders of a subsidiary corporation cannot complain that the majority shareholder (parent) caused the subsidiary to pay "excessive" dividends (draining too much capital out of the subsidiary and injuring its operations) because the minority shareholders had received their proportionate share of the dividends. [**Sinclair Oil Corp. v. Levien,** 280 A.2d 717 (Del. 1971)]

4. Corporate Opportunity Doctrine [§321]

The fiduciary duty of loyalty, discussed above, bars a director from taking for herself any advantage or business opportunity that properly belongs to the corporation. As to any such opportunity, a director must first offer it to the corporation. [A.L.I. Prin. Corp. Gov. §5.05(a)] The director owes the corporation at least a *right of first refusal, i.e.,* the right to acquire it on the same terms offered to her.

a. What constitutes a corporate opportunity [§322]

There is no clear-cut definition of what constitutes a corporate opportunity.

Rather, it depends upon whether, under all the circumstances, it would be *unfair* for the director to exploit the opportunity. [**Johnston v. Greene,** 121 A.2d 919 (Del. 1956)] The following factors are those most frequently relied upon by courts in holding that an opportunity is "corporate" and hence may not legitimately be taken advantage of by the directors personally:

(1) Corporate plans and expectations [§323]

If the corporation has a present interest or "tangible expectancy" in the opportunity in the sense that it has a specific need for it, has resolved to acquire it, or has *actively considered* its acquisition, it may not be taken advantage of by a director.

(a) Note—"useful" not enough [§324]

The mere fact that the property or opportunity would be "useful" to the corporation is ordinarily not in itself enough to render it a corporate opportunity. [**Burg v. Horn,** 380 F.2d 897 (2d Cir. 1967)]

(2) Director's capacity in dealing [§325]

If the opportunity was discovered by the director in her *capacity as director* of the corporation (*e.g.,* offer delivered to the director intended for the corporation), it is a corporate opportunity. [*See* **Johnston v. Greene,** *supra*]

(a) Note

The fact that an opportunity relates to the corporation's "line of business" does *not* necessarily mean that the director must deal with it on behalf of the corporation—particularly where it also falls within the director's personal business interests that are outside the capacity of director of the corporation. [**Burg v. Horn,** *supra*]

---

e.g. **Example:** George and Max Horn owned low rent buildings in Brooklyn and encouraged their friends, Mr. and Mrs. Burg, to "get their feet wet" in real estate too. Mrs. Burg and the Horns formed Darand Realty Corp. ("Darand"), and each became a Darand director. The Horns managed Darand's properties and Mr. Burg handled the corporation's accounting and tax planning. While managing Darand, the Horns continued to buy and sell other low rent buildings for their own account, and sometimes borrowed money from Darand or Mr. Burg to finance their purchases. Mrs. Burg brought suit against the Horns, claiming that the Horns usurped Darand's corporate opportunities by purchasing the buildings on their own account. *Held:* The mere fact that a director has purchased something that is within his corporation's line of business does not automatically mean that he has usurped a corporate opportunity. A court must consider the relationship of the director to the corporation. Here, Mrs. Burg knew that the Horns already owned similar low rent buildings when they formed Darand and that the Horns would not be employed by Darand full-time because they had other business ventures. Under these circumstances, it would be unreasonable for Mrs. Burg to expect the Horns to turn over to the corporation every low rent property coming to their attention. [**Burg v. Horn,** *supra; and see* **Northeast Harbor Golf Club, Inc. v. Harris,** 661 A.2d 1146 (Me. 1995)—court rejected line of business test where director of golf course purchased lots surrounding the course and a number of years later subdivided the lots for development against the wishes of the corporation's board; court adopted test requiring the director to either disclose the opportunity to the board and give them a fair opportunity to accept or reject or prove that taking the opportunity was fair]

(3) Funds used [§326]

If the corporation's property, information, or funds were involved in the director's discovering or acquiring the opportunity, or if the corporation's *facilities or employees* were used in developing it, the opportunity may not be personally taken advantage of by a director. [**Guth v. Loft, Inc.,** 5 A.2d 503 (Del. 1939)]

b. Where corporation unable to take advantage [§327]

Although much depends on the particular facts of the case, it is frequently stated that directors *may* take advantage of corporate business opportunities of which the corporation is unable to take advantage. Thus, if the corporation is *insolvent or financially unable* to make the investment required, it has been held that the director is free to do so. [**Miller v. Miller,** 222 N.W.2d 71 (Minn. 1974)]

(1) Disclosure [§328]

Some courts have held that the director must promptly disclose all known material facts to the disinterested directors (or, if there are no such directors, then to the disinterested shareholders). The rationale is that if the investment is sufficiently attractive, the corporation might itself be able to raise the necessary funds. After full disclosure, the director may take advantage of the business opportunity if it is rejected by the corporation, or if the director proves that the corporation unreasonably failed to reject it and it would be otherwise fair for the director to personally take the opportunity. [**Klinicki v. Lundgren,** 695 P.2d 906 (Or. 1985)]

(a) Distinguish

A few courts have held that the director's fiduciary duty *precludes* her taking advantage of such opportunities, reasoning that to permit her to do so might discourage her making her best efforts *to obtain* the needed money for the corporation. [**Irving Trust Co. v. Deutsch,** 73 F.2d 121 (2d Cir. 1934)]

(2) Ultra vires transaction [§329]

If the acquisition would be ultra vires by the corporation (*e.g.*, the corporation was not authorized to enter the particular business), a number of cases hold that the director may make use of the opportunity. [**Alexander & Alexander of New York, Inc. v. Fritzen**, 147 A.D.2d 241 (1989)] *But note:* There is a strong contrary argument on the rationale that the corporation should at least have the right to consider the investment. It might be sufficiently advantageous as to justify amending the articles or taking other action to enable the corporation to engage in the business.

c. Where corporation unwilling to take advantage [§330]

If the director *fully* informs the board of the opportunity, and an independent board declines to take it, the director generally may pursue it for herself. [*See* **Kerrigan v. Unity Savings Association**, 317 N.E.2d 39 (Ill. 1974)]

d. Remedies [§331]

If a director usurps a corporate opportunity, the corporation may invoke any of the following remedies:

(1) Constructive trust [§332]

Courts may declare that the director holds the opportunity as constructive trustee for the corporation, forcing a *conveyance* of the business or property to the corporation at the cost to the director and an accounting to the corporation for any *rents, income, or profits derived* through ownership thereof. [**Irving Trust Co. v. Deutsch**, *supra*]

(2) Damages [§333]

If the director has already *resold* the business or property, a suit will lie for damages for breach of fiduciary duty—forcing the director to disgorge all profits made on the transaction.

EXAM TIP   **gilbert**

Usurpation of a corporate opportunity is a very common Corporations exam issue. Whenever the facts of a question mention that a **director learns of a business opportunity**, be sure to consider whether her corporation would be interested. Especially if she learned of it in her capacity as director of this corporation, she probably must present the opportunity to the corporation, disclosing all material facts, and she can take advantage of the opportunity personally **only if the corporation decides not to pursue it**. If the corporation is not given a chance to take advantage of the opportunity, the director can be forced to turn over the opportunity and/or any profits derived from the opportunity to the corporation.

---

5. Competing with Corporation [§334]

A director (or officer) who obtains a financial interest in a business that competes with that of the corporation puts herself in a conflict of interest situation—even where the competing business is *not* a corporate opportunity. Depending on all the circumstances, competition by a director or officer may be held a breach of fiduciary duty, in which event she may be barred from such competition or held liable for damages. [**Lincoln Stores, Inc. v. Grant,** 34 N.E.2d 704 (Mass. 1941)]

---

e.g. **Example:** A breach of fiduciary duty will most likely be found where the director has used corporate funds, facilities, or employees (or corporate secrets) in starting up or acquiring the competing business. [**Guth v. Loft, Inc.,** *supra,* §326]

---

a. Distinguish—preparation [§335]

The mere fact that an officer or director makes *preparations* to compete with the corporation before resigning from office does not in itself establish a breach of fiduciary duty; nor does the failure to disclose to the board any plans to compete. [**Maryland Metals, Inc. v. Metzner,** 382 A.2d 564 (Md. 1978)] But if there are added circumstances (*e.g.*, concealment of material facts, use of corporate facilities or assets, or "raids" on key corporate personnel), this clearly constitutes a breach of fiduciary duty. [**Veco Corp. v. Babcock,** 611 N.E.2d 1054 (Ill. 1993)]

6. Compensation for Services to Corporation [§336]

Finally, a conflict of interest issue arises in dealings between the corporation and one of its directors relative to compensation for services as director, officer, or employee of the corporation. Such compensation may take various forms—*e.g.*, salary, bonuses, profit-sharing and pension plans, stock options, expense accounts, severance pay ("golden parachutes"), etc. Usually, the conflict of interest issue is raised by a dissident minority shareholder in a derivative suit charging excessive compensation to the director and resultant unfairness to the corporation.

a. Authorization [§337]

The first question is whether the compensation arrangement has been *duly authorized* by the board. This often turns on whether the interested director is entitled to participate in the meeting and to vote on her own compensation.

(1) Issues [§338]

Because this is simply another form of interested director transaction, the various common law and statutory rules (*supra,* §§279-313) govern (i) whether the director may be counted in determining the presence of a quorum at the meeting, (ii) whether her vote may be counted on her own compensation, and (iii) the effect of shareholder ratification and the like.

(2) Statutory resolution [§339]

Statutes in some states resolve the problem by expressly authorizing members of the board to establish reasonable compensation for directors notwithstanding their personal interest in such matters (provided there are no contrary provisions in the articles or bylaws). [*See* Ill. Bus. Corp. Act §8.05(c)]

b. "Reasonableness" [§340]

Assuming the compensation plan is duly authorized and adopted by the board, the next question is whether the terms of the plan are reasonable. If not, the plan may be challenged as a *waste* of corporate assets by the directors, and hence a violation of their duty of care to the corporation.

(1) Disinterested directors protected by business judgment rule [§341]

Good faith and the business judgment rule (*supra,* §246) will *ordinarily* protect disinterested directors from liability to the corporation for approving executive compensation plans to other directors, officers, or employees of the corporation. Courts are reluctant to second guess the directors' business decisions on the value of an employee's services.

(a) Publicly held corporations [§342]

Despite recent criticism of the large amounts of compensation paid to executives of America's biggest companies, the business judgment rule has resulted in virtually no modern judicial decisions finding excessive pay in this context.

Example: The Walt Disney Company hired Ovitz as its president, and the board approved a $1 million annual salary with bonus and stock options and a generous severance package. Business quickly soured under Ovitz and the board approved granting the contracted for severance package, which was valued at $140 million. Shareholders filed suit alleging that the directors breached their fiduciary duty in approving an excessive and wasteful severance and compensation package. The court disagreed. The directors acted reasonably in relying on a corporate compensation expert in creating Ovitz's compensation package. Although they failed to apprise themselves of the possible costs of the severance package, they were not required to inform themselves of every fact. Moreover, Ovitz had been sought after by other companies, and the board felt that the total compensation package that was offered was needed to attract Ovitz. The fact that Ovitz ultimately did not do a good job is not really relevant. [**Brehm v. Eisner,** 746 A.2d 244 (Del. 2000)]

1) Federal action [§343]

Nonetheless, the SEC has greatly increased the type and amount of information about executive compensation that must be disclosed by large corporations (*see infra,* §§582, 946), and has authorized shareholders to make proposals about executive pay in management's proxy materials. (*See infra,* §§593 *et seq.*) And the Internal Revenue Code now limits expense deductions from the federal income tax for executive pay over $1 million unless tied to the corporation's performance [I.R.C. §162(m)]. Also, the Sarbanes-Oxley Act of 2002 forbids public corporations from extending credit or personal loans to directors (or executive officers). [Securities Exchange Act §13(R)(1)]

2) Distinguish—close corporations [§344]

In contrast, courts often hold executive compensation to be unreasonable in the context of closely held corporations because ordinarily the compensation is not approved by either disinterested directors or disinterested shareholders. [**Crowley v. Communications for Hospitals, Inc.**, 573 N.E.2d 996 (Mass. 1991)]

(b) Recipients also protected [§345]

When compensation is authorized by disinterested directors, recipients of the compensation will usually be protected against a suit by the corporation (or a shareholder's derivative suit) for rescission or return of allegedly excessive compensation.

(c) Caution—"mutual back scratching" [§346]

Directors who vote for each other's compensation plans or for trade-offs in some other capacity (*e.g.*, retainer fee as attorney for the corporation) are *not* considered disinterested.

(2) Limitation—doctrine of waste [§347]

Even disinterested directors have no power to "give away" or "waste" corporate assets, absent unanimous shareholder approval. Nor may a mere majority of the shareholders condone a waste or "gift" of the corporate assets to the prejudice of the minority. Consequently, courts have placed limitations on executive compensation plans *notwithstanding approval* by disinterested directors and/or a majority of the disinterested shareholders.

(a) Legally sufficient consideration to corporation [§348]

Courts have held that it must appear that the compensation is paid for services that constituted legally sufficient consideration to the corporation for such payment.

1) Expressly or impliedly authorized [§349]

It must appear that the services rendered by the officer or director were expressly or impliedly authorized by the corporation. Normally, the fact that the services are reasonably related to the corporation's business is sufficient to satisfy this requirement.

2) Compensation for past services [§350]

Several courts have *invalidated* agreements by the corporation to pay an officer or director (or the surviving spouse of an officer or director) for past services (or to increase compensation retroactively), on the rationale that there is no legal consideration for the agreement. [**Adams v. Smith**, 153 So. 2d 221 (Ala. 1963)]

a) Future consulting fees [§351]

One way to avoid this rule is for the corporation to grant compensation to a departing employee in exchange for a promise to be available to "advise" or "consult" with the corporation in the *future* or for a promise not to compete with the corporation. [**Osborne v. Locke Steel Chain Co.,** 218 A.2d 526 (Conn. 1966)]

b) Bonuses [§352]

Some courts hold that reasonable bonuses (or the like) may be paid to officers and employees for recent past services, at least if approved by a majority of the shareholders. [**Chambers v. Beaver-Advance Corp.,** 14 A.2d 808 (Pa. 1958)]

c) Retirement benefits [§353]

A number of statutes now specifically authorize the board to provide pensions and retirement benefits in recognition of past services.

3) Compensation for future services [§354]

Compensation for services to be rendered in the future may be held improper if there is no reasonable assurance that the corporation will ultimately receive the benefit of the services for which it is paying.

a) Stock options [§355]

Some courts have invalidated the grant of stock options exercisable by officers and employees in future years when the options were *not conditioned* on the recipient's remaining in the corporation's employ for any designated period of time and when the option would be exercised even after the recipient left the corporation's employ. [**Kerbs v. California Eastern Airways,** 90 A.2d 652 (Del. 1952)] Other courts have upheld such plans (when adopted by a disinterested board) as an exercise of "reasonable business judgment." [**Beard v. Elster,** 160 A.2d 731 (Del. 1960)]

(b) Value of services rendered [§356]

There must be some *reasonable relationship* between the amount paid by the corporation and the value of the services rendered. [**Rogers v. Hill,** 289 U.S. 582 (1933)]

1) "Reasonable" [§357]

What constitutes "reasonable" (as opposed to "excessive" or "wasteful") compensation is determined by all the facts and circumstances, such as: the recipient's qualifications; time spent and responsibilities assumed; the size and complexity of the corporation's business; the amount of its income; and amounts paid to comparable persons performing similar services for other corporations. [**Ruetz v. Topping,** 453 S.W.2d 624 (Mo. 1970)]

2) **Percentage of profits [§358]**

The mere fact that the officer or employee is to receive a percentage of corporate profits is **not** ordinarily enough by itself to show the compensation "excessive," even though another individual could be found to do the same work on a straight salary basis. [*Compare* **Rogers v. Hill,** *supra*—bonus percentage, valid when established 18 years earlier, might amount to waste due to enormous increase in corporate profits]

Chapter Six:
Insider Trading

CONTENTS

Chapter Approach

This chapter considers securities trading by corporate insiders, such as officers, directors, and controlling shareholders. Most exam questions in this area concern the *federal* securities laws that regulate insider trading; thus, that is the primary focus of this chapter. Whenever you have a question involving trading by insiders, or by persons to whom insiders have given inside information (tippees), consider applying rule 10b-5 and section 16(b).

1. **Rule 10b-5**

    Analyze rule 10b-5 issues as follows:

    a. Look for a *material misrepresentation,* or an *omission* of material nonpublic information in connection with the sale or purchase of *any* security.

    b. In the case of an omission (as opposed to a misrepresentation), consider whether the person who trades is an *insider.*

    c. If, in an omission case, the person who trades is *not* an insider, consider whether she is a *tippee.* If so, analyze her liability by determining whether: (i) the insider-tipper breached her *fiduciary duty*, (ii) the insider-tipper communicated the information *for her own advantage*, and (iii) the *tippee knew of the breach.*

    d. If the facts of your question do not involve either an insider or a tippee, consider whether the person trading on the material, nonpublic information obtained the information by *misappropriation*. For example, did she obtain the information through a breach of duty to her employer?

    e. Remember that a suit can be brought under rule 10b-5 either by a private plaintiff who is a *purchaser or seller* or by the *Securities Exchange Commission*. Keep in mind that even nontrading parties (*e.g.*, a corporation that makes a material misrepresentation) may be liable under rule 10b-5.

    f. Consider the *defenses* to a rule 10b-5 action—such as *lack of scienter, lack of reliance, lack of causation, lack of due diligence*, or *in pari delicto*—and determine whether one of the defenses applies to the facts in question.

    g. Finally, discuss the *remedies*. Potential remedies for *private plaintiffs* are damages and restitutionary forms of relief. Remedies available to the *government* include injunctive relief, criminal sanctions, and civil penalties.

2. **Section 16(b)**

    Whenever you encounter a question concerning an acquisition or disposition of securities that were issued by a corporation that had a class of securities that must be *registered* under section 12 of the 1934 Act, consider the application of section

16(b). Under this section, a corporation can recover any profit made by certain insiders from any *purchase and sale* (or sale and purchase) of its securities made *within a six-month period*. Remember that, for this purpose, *officers, directors, and beneficial owners of more than 10% of the shares* are considered insiders, and that any transaction in which an acquisition or disposition of securities occurs (such as a merger) may involve a "purchase" or "sale" for purposes of section 16(b).

a. When analyzing a question under section 16(b), first determine whether the person is a statutory insider and, if so, *at what time* she became an insider. Then, try to *pair up* an acquisition and a disposition within a six-month period and calculate the short-swing profits.

3. Common Law

Remember that some courts now impose liability on insiders in favor of the corporation as a matter of common law.

A. Introduction

1. The Basic Problem [§359]

The purchase and sale of a corporation's stock by a director, officer, or other insider raises important and complex issues. The basic problem is the possibility that an insider has an unfair advantage because he knows facts about the corporation that are not known to those with whom he deals, and he knows those facts only because of his fiduciary position, not because he has exercised skill or diligence.

2. Common Law Approaches [§360]

It was clear at common law that a director or officer was liable if he made misrepresentations, or stated half-truths, in connection with the purchase or sale of the corporation's stock. However, the courts were divided concerning the liability of officers and directors who purchased or sold stock without making misrepresentations or stating half-truths, but failed to disclose material facts of which they had inside knowledge.

a. Majority rule [§361]

The majority rule at common law was that an officer or director had no duty of disclosure, when buying or selling the corporation's securities, regarding any inside information that might affect the value of the securities, on the rationale that officers and directors owed fiduciary duties only to the corporation, not to the shareholders. [**Goodwin v. Aggasiz,** 186 N.E. 659 (Mass. 1933)]

(1) "Special facts" exception [§362]

A number of jurisdictions that followed the majority rule nevertheless adopted an exception under which an insider did have a duty of disclosure if there were "special facts" that made nondisclosure unfair to the person with whom the insider dealt. [**Strong v. Repide,** 213 U.S. 419 (1909)] This exception was most typically applied where the parties dealt face-to-face, rather than over a stock exchange. However, "special facts" were found in so many cases that the exception sometimes overshadowed the rule. [**Taylor v. Wright,** 69 Cal. App. 2d 371 (1945)]

b. Minority rule [§363]

Under a minority rule, an insider was considered a fiduciary for the shareholders, as well as the corporation, and was required to disclose any material information she had obtained as an insider that might affect the value of the shares, even in the absence of special facts. [**King Manufacturing Co. v. Clay,** 118 S.E.2d 581 (Ga. 1961)]

3. Securities Exchange Act of 1934—In General [§364]

The common law rules governing insider trading have been largely superseded by the Securities Exchange Act of 1934. [15 U.S.C. §§78a *et seq.*] The principal focus of the 1934 Act is the regulation of trading in securities after their initial issuance. Most, but not all, of the Act's provisions are keyed to whether securities are required to be registered with the Securities Exchange Commission ("SEC") under section 12 of the Act. Generally speaking, section 12 and the rules thereunder require registration of (i) any security that is *traded on a national securities exchange*, and (ii) any security that is issued by a corporation that has *total assets* (not net worth) *exceeding $10 million* and is held by *500 or more persons*. [15 U.S.C. §78l; 17 C.F.R. 240.12g-1] However, *section 10(b)* of the Act is *not* keyed to whether securities are required to be registered; it applies to all securities, even shares in close corporations.

EXAM TIP   **gilbert**

On your exam, be sure to keep in mind that there are two categories of companies that must register under 1934 Act section 12: those with securities **listed on a national exchange** and those that have **at least $10 million in assets and a class** of securities held **by at least 500 shareholders**.

B. Section 10(b) and Rule 10b-5

1. The Rule—In General [§365]

Section 10(b) of the 1934 Act makes it unlawful "to use or employ . . . any manipulative or deceptive device" in contravention of SEC rules, in connection with the purchase or sale of any security. [16 U.S.C. §78j] To implement section 10(b), the SEC promulgated Securities Exchange Act ("Exchange Act") Rule 10b-5. Under rule 10b-5, it is unlawful, in connection with the purchase or sale of any security, by use of the mails or any means of interstate commerce to:

(i) Employ any *device, scheme, or artifice to defraud*;

(ii) Make any *untrue statement of a material fact* or *omit a material fact* necessary to make the statements made not misleading; or

(iii) Engage in any *act, practice, or course of business that operates as fraud or deceit* upon any person

in connection with a purchase or sale of securities.

2. Covered Conduct—Misrepresentation and Nondisclosure [§366]

Rule 10b-5 applies not only to misrepresentations, but also to nondisclosure by insiders and, in certain cases, by tippees and outsiders. [*In re* **Cady, Roberts & Co.,** 40 S.E.C. 907 (1961)]

3. "In Connection With" [§367]

Conduct will not violate rule 10b-5 unless it is "*in connection with* the purchase or sale of any security." However, the courts read the phrase "in connection with" very broadly, so that the test is normally satisfied as long as there has been some kind of transaction in securities and some kind of fraud. In **SEC v. Texas Gulf Sulphur Co.,** 401 F.2d 833 (2d Cir. 1968), *cert. denied,* 394 U.S. 976 (1969), the court said:

> [I]t seems clear . . . that Congress when it used the phrase "in connection with the purchase or sale of any security" intended only that the device employed, whatever it might be, be of a sort that would cause reasonable investors to rely thereon, and, in connection therewith, so relying, cause them to purchase or sell a corporation's securities. There is no indication that Congress intended that the corporations or persons responsible for the issuance of a misleading statement would not violate the section unless they engaged in related securities transactions or otherwise acted with wrongful motives; indeed, the obvious purposes of the Act to protect the investing public and to secure fair dealing in the securities markets would be seriously undermined by applying such a gloss onto the legislative language . . . . The mere fact that an insider did not engage in securities transactions does not negate the possibility of wrongful purpose; perhaps the market did not react to the misleading statement as much as was anticipated or perhaps the wrongful purpose was something other than the desire to buy at a low price or sell at a high price.

e.g. **Example:** In **SEC v. Zandford,** 536 U.S. 862 (2002), Zandford, a securities broker, persuaded Wood, an elderly man in poor health, to open a joint investment account for Wood and his mentally retarded daughter. According to the complaint, the stated investment objectives for the account were safety of principal and income. The Woods granted Zandford discretion to manage their account and a general power of attorney to engage in securities transactions for their benefit without prior approval. Relying on Zandford's promise to conservatively invest their money, the Woods entrusted Zandford with $419,255. Before Mr. Wood's death, all of the money was gone. On over 25 separate occasions, money had been transferred from the Woods account to accounts controlled by Zandford. In each case, Zandford sold securities in the Woods account and then made personal use of the proceeds. The Court held that Zandford had engaged in fraudulent conduct "in connection with" a purchase or sale of securities, even though Zandford had neither purchased securities from nor sold securities to the Woods. The Woods were injured as investors through Zandford's deceptions, which deprived them of any compensation for the sale of their securities.

---

e.g. **Example:** In **United States v. O'Hagan,** 521 U.S. 642 (1997), the Court held that the defendant had committed fraud "in connection with" a securities transaction when he used misappropriated confidential information for trading purposes. The Court said that this is so even though the person or entity defrauded is not the other party to the trade, but is, instead, the source of the nonpublic information.

---

4. Covered Persons [§368]

Rule 10b-5 is often referred to as an insider-trading rule, because its major significance is to prohibit insider trading. In fact, however, rule 10b-5 extends well beyond insider trading. For example, *any person* who makes a misrepresentation in connection with the purchase or sale of stock may be liable under rule 10b-5, whether or not he is an insider.

5. Covered Securities [§369]

Rule 10b-5 applies to the purchase or sale of *any security*, whether or not required to be registered under section 12. The rule applies whether the corporation is large or small, and whether its shares are widely or closely held. [**Hooper v. Mountain States Securities Corp.,** 282 F.2d 195 (5th Cir. 1960); **Kardon v. National Gypsum Co.,** 83 F. Supp. 613 (E.D. Pa. 1947)] The only limitation is jurisdictional: The violation must involve the use of some instrumentality of interstate commerce. However, this limitation is seldom a problem, because use of the telephone or mail, for example, satisfies the interstate-commerce requirement.

6. Who Can Bring Suit Under Rule 10b-5

a. Suit by SEC [§370]

A suit for violation of rule 10b-5 may be brought by the SEC. [**SEC v. Texas Gulf Sulphur Co.,** *supra*]

b. Suit by private plaintiff [§371]

Although neither section 10(b) nor rule 10b-5 expressly provides that a private person who is injured by a violation of the rule can bring suit, it is well established that section 10(b) and rule 10b-5 create an "implied" private right of action in favor of an injured private party. [**Superintendent of Insurance v. Bankers Life & Casualty Co.,** 404 U.S. 6 (1971); **Kardon v. National Gypsum Co.,** *supra*]

7. Materiality [§372]

Rule 10b-5 is applicable to misrepresentations and nondisclosures only if the misrepresented or omitted fact is *material*. An "omitted fact is material if there is a substantial likelihood that a reasonable shareholder would consider it important in deciding" on her course of action. There "must be a substantial likelihood that the disclosure of the omitted fact would have been viewed by the reasonable investor as having significantly altered the 'total mix' of information made available." [**Basic, Inc. v. Levinson,** 485 U.S. 224 (1988)] Materiality depends "at any given time upon a balancing of both the indicated probability that the event will occur and the anticipated magnitude of the event in light of the totality of the company activity." [**Basic, Inc. v. Levinson,** *supra—quoting* **SEC v. Texas Gulf Sulphur Co.,** *supra*]

EXAM TIP — gilbert

You should memorize the test of materiality for your exam: Information is material if there is a *substantial likelihood that a reasonable shareholder would consider it important in deciding on her course of action*.

Example: Where insiders knew that the corporation had done exploratory drilling that gave a promise of a gigantic mineral strike, the knowledge was deemed material even though it was possible that after thorough exploration it would turn out that the company did not have a minable body of ore. Knowledge of the possibility of a gigantic mine could affect the price of stock. If it turned out there was a minable body of ore, the market price of the stock would rise substantially when that news was disclosed. If it turned out there was no minable body of ore, the market price of the stock would not fall, assuming the information about the exploratory drilling was neither leaked nor acted upon by insiders. [**SEC v. Texas Gulf Sulphur Co.,** *supra*]

8. Fault Required—Scienter [§373]

In **Ernst & Ernst v. Hochfelder,** 425 U.S. 185 (1976), the Supreme Court held that a material misrepresentation or omission will not violate rule 10b-5 if the defendant was without fault or merely negligent. Liability can be imposed under rule 10b-5 only if the defendant had scienter.

a. Definition of scienter—recklessness [§374]

Under tort law, scienter is satisfied by an intent to deceive, to mislead, or to convey a false impression. Court of Appeals decisions since *Ernst & Ernst* have unanimously held that recklessness also satisfies the scienter requirement. [*See, e.g.,* **Rolf v. Blyth, Eastman Dillon & Co.,** 570 F.2d 38 (2d Cir. 1976), *cert. denied,* 439 U.S. 1039 (1978)] Many courts have adopted a definition under which "recklessness" is highly unreasonable conduct, "involving not merely simple or even inexcusable negligence, but an extreme departure from the standards of ordinary care, and which presents a danger of misleading buyers or sellers that is either known to the defendant or is so obvious that the actor must have been aware of it." [**Sundstrand Corp. v. Sun Chemical Corp.,** 553 F.2d 1033 (7th Cir.), *cert. denied,* 434 U.S. 875 (1977)]

b.   Injunctive relief [§375]

Scienter is also a requirement in an injunctive action by the SEC under rule 10b-5. [**Aaron v. SEC,** 446 U.S. 680 (1980)]

c.   Forward-looking statements

(1)   Defined [§376]

The securities acts provide special protection for "forward-looking statements"—*i.e.,* certain kinds of statements about the future, such as predictions of earnings. Securities Exchange Act section 21E(i), added by the Private Securities Litigation Reform Act ("PSLRA"), defines the term "forward-looking statement" to mean:

(a)   A statement containing a projection of revenues, income (including income loss), earnings (including earnings loss) per share, capital expenditures, dividends, capital structure, or other financial items;

(b)   A statement of the plans and objectives of management for future operations, including plans or objectives relating to the products or services of the issuer;

(c)   A statement of future economic performance, including any such statement contained in a discussion and analysis of financial condition by the management or in the results of operations included pursuant to the rules and regulations of the SEC;

(d)   Any statements of the assumptions underlying or relating to any statement described in subparagraph (a), (b), or (c), above;

(e)   Any report issued by an outside reviewer retained by an issuer, to the extent that the report assesses a forward-looking statement made by the issuer; or

(f)   A statement containing a projection or estimate of such other items as may be specified by rule or regulation of the SEC.

(2)   Safe harbor [§377]

Securities Exchange Act section 21E(c)(1) provides a safe harbor against civil liability for forward-looking statements (as defined above) that are made by (i) an issuer that either has a security registered under section 12 of the Act or has filed a registration statement as described in section 15(d), and (ii) certain persons acting on behalf of such an issuer. If a forward-looking statement is made by such an issuer or person, the issuer or person is protected from liability if either (i) the statement is identified as a forward-looking statement and is accompanied by cautionary statements identifying important factors that could cause actual results to differ materially from those in the statement, or (ii) the plaintiff fails to show that the statement was made with *actual knowledge* (not simply with recklessness) that the statement was false or misleading.

(3) "Bespeaks caution" [§378]

In addition to Securities Exchange Act section 21E, under a doctrine known as "bespeaks caution" a forward-looking statement does not give rise to liability, even though it is misleading, if the document in which the statement is contained includes sufficient cautionary language. [*See, e.g.,* **Saltzberg v. T.M. Sterling/Austin Associates, Ltd.,** 45 F.3d 399 (11th Cir. 1995)] This doctrine is of special relevance when a forward-looking statement is made by an issuer or person who is not within the safe harbor provided by Securities Exchange Act section 21E—*e.g.,* an issuer who neither has a class of stock registered under section 12 nor has filed a registration statement under section 15(d).

d. Effect of Private Securities Litigation Reform Act ("PSLRA") [§379]

As discussed below, liability under rule 10b-5 usually requires a showing that the defendant acted with "scienter"—the intent to mislead or recklessness as to truth. However, under the PSLRA, a plaintiff whose claim is based on an allegedly fraudulent forward-looking statement must establish that the misstatement was made with "actual knowledge." Accordingly, the PSLRA eliminates recklessness as sufficient scienter under rule 10b-5 for forward-looking statements, within the limits discussed above. However, the PSLRA does not, on its face, eliminate recklessness as sufficient scienter in the case of statements of historical or existing (rather than forward-looking) facts. Nevertheless, the PSLRA does bear on scienter even in those kinds of cases.

(1) Pleading standard prior to PSLRA [§380]

Prior to the PSLRA, the pleading requirements in a securities fraud case were governed only by Federal Rule of Civil Procedure 9(b), which requires that all types of fraud be pleaded with "particularity." The most stringent pleading *standard* in securities act fraud cases under the requirement of Rule 9(b) was a standard established by the Second Circuit. This standard required the plaintiff to state with particularity facts that gave rise to a "strong inference" of the defendant's intent, *i.e.,* of scienter. Under the Second Circuit test for applying that standard, the plaintiff could establish the required strong inference by detailed factual allegations that showed either direct evidence of scienter (conscious misbehavior or recklessness), circumstantial evidence of scienter, or that the defendant had the *motive and opportunity* to commit fraud.

(a) Motive

To satisfy the motive element of this test, a plaintiff could not merely allege that the defendant had motives of a kind possessed by virtually all corporate insiders, such as the desire to sustain the appearance of corporate profitability. Rather, the plaintiff had to allege that the defendant benefited in some concrete and personal way from his purported fraud. This requirement was normally satisfied when a corporate insider was alleged to have publicly misrepresented material facts about the corporation's performance or prospects in order to keep the stock price artificially high while he sold his own shares at a profit.

(2) PSLRA pleading standard [§381]

The PSLRA adopted the Second Circuit standard, but not necessarily the motive-and-opportunity test under that standard. Securities Exchange Act section 21D(b)(2) provides that a plaintiff who alleges securities fraud must "state with particularity *facts giving rise to a strong inference* that the defendant acted with the required state of mind,"—*i.e.*, scienter. There are two primary issues concerning the meaning of the PSLRA requirement. The first issue is what the standard entails, and in particular, whether a plaintiff can satisfy this standard solely by detailed factual allegations that the defendant had the motive and opportunity to commit fraud, as previously held by the Second Circuit. The second issue is whether the PSLRA was intended to change the rule that recklessness suffices to establish scienter.

(a) The pleading issue [§382]

A number of circuits have addressed the pleading issue. Three different views have been adopted:

1) Motive and opportunity suffice [§383]

Under one view, the PSLRA effectively adopted the Second Circuit's pleading standard for scienter wholesale. Accordingly, plaintiffs can state a claim by pleading either (i) strong circumstantial evidence of recklessness or conscious misbehavior, or (ii) motive and opportunity. [*See, e.g.,* **Press v. Chemical Investment Services Corp.**, 166 F.3d 529 (2d Cir. 1999); *and see* **In re Advanta Corp. Securities Litigation**, 180 F.3d 525 (3d Cir. 1999)]

2) Motive and opportunity are relevant but are never by themselves sufficient [§384]

Other circuits have concluded that motive and opportunity may be relevant when combined with other facts, but as a matter of law, they are never sufficient alone. [**In re Silicon Graphics Inc. Securities Litigation (Janas v. McCracken)**, 183 F.3d 970 (9th Cir. 1999); **Bryant v. Avado Brands, Inc.**, 187 F.3d 1271 (11th Cir. 1999)]

3) The facts of the case determine whether motive and opportunity suffice [§385]

Some circuits explicitly refuse to decide whether motive and opportunity are, as a matter of law, sufficient. Depending on the facts of the case, such pleadings might or might not be sufficient. [**Ottman v. Hanger Orthopedic Group, Inc.,** 353 F.3d 338 (4th Cir. 2003)—adopting a "flexible, case-specific analysis" because Congress ultimately chose not to specify particular types of facts that would or would not show a strong inference of scienter] This fact-sensitive view has been taken by most circuits. Even the Second Circuit now takes the view that "Congress's failure to include language about motive and opportunity suggests that we need not be wedded to these concepts in articulating the prevailing standard." [**Novak v. Kasaks,** 216 F.3d 300 (2d Cir. 2000)] The position of the cases taking the fact-sensitive view has been summarized as follows in *Ottman*:

> [Many courts have adopted] a case-specific approach that examines the particular allegations in their entirety to determine whether they provide the requisite strong inference, without regard to whether those allegations fall into defined, formalistic categories such as "motive and opportunity." . . . Still, these circuits generally agree that specific facts showing a motive and opportunity to commit fraud (or the absence of such facts) may be relevant in determining whether a plaintiff's complaint demonstrates a strong inference of scienter . . . .

> [A] flexible, case-specific analysis is appropriate in examining scienter pleadings . . . . We therefore conclude that courts should not restrict their scienter inquiry by focusing on specific categories of facts, such as those relating to motive and opportunity, but instead should examine all of the allegations in each case to determine whether they collectively establish a strong inference of scienter. And, while particular facts demonstrating a motive and opportunity to commit fraud (or lack of such facts) may be relevant to the scienter inquiry, the weight accorded to those facts should depend on the circumstances of each case.

(b) Recklessness [§386]

Most circuits have concluded that the PSLRA did not change the rule that recklessness suffices to establish scienter and have retained their pre-PSLRA definitions of recklessness. However, the Ninth Circuit has concluded that the PSLRA heightened the substantive requirement of scienter, and that circuit strengthened its definition of scienter from "recklessness" to "deliberate recklessness." [*In re* **Silicon Graphics Inc. Securities Litigation,** *supra*]

9. Causation and Reliance [§387]

In principle it is well established that causation and reliance are required elements of a *private action* under rule 10b-5. In practice, however, those requirements have been considerably watered down.

a. Causation [§388]

In the area of causation, the case law under rule 10b-5 has distinguished between "transaction causation" and "loss causation."

(1) Transaction causation [§389]

Transaction causation means that there must be a causal connection between the defendant's violation of rule 10b-5 and the plaintiff's purchase or sale of a security. To satisfy this requirement, a violation of rule 10b-5 must have *caused the plaintiff to engage in the transaction* in question. [**Schlick v. Penn-Dixie Cement Corp.,** 507 F.2d 374 (2d Cir. 1974)] The plaintiff must allege and show that *but for* the fraudulent statement or omission, she would not have entered into the transaction.

(2) Loss causation [§390]

In contrast to transaction causation, loss causation requires a showing that the violation of rule 10b-5 *caused the economic harm* of which the plaintiff complains. While transaction causation is generally understood as reliance, loss causation has often been described as proximate cause, meaning that the damages suffered by plaintiff must be a foreseeable consequence of any misrepresentation or material omission. An alternative formulation of loss causation is that it requires that "the misrepresentation touches upon the reasons for the investment's decline in value." [**Binder v. Gillespie,** 184 F.3d 1059 (9th Cir. 1998)] "The loss causation inquiry typically examines how directly the subject of the [violation] caused the loss, and whether the resulting loss was a foreseeable outcome of the [violation]," while also taking into account issues such as the presence of intervening causes and the lapse of time between the behavior complained of and the loss. [**Suez Equity Investors v. Toronto-Dominion Bank,** 250 F.3d 87 (2d Cir. 2001)] Essentially, "loss causation" is a fancy name for the concept that even if an investment is induced by a violation of rule 10b-5, the investor's loss may have been the result of an investment risk that was independent of the violation.

(a) Illustration

The Fifth Circuit court used the following example to explain loss causation:

[Assume that a vessel is described in a prospectus as having] a certain capacity when in fact it had less capacity than was represented in the prospectus. However, the prospectus does disclose truthfully that the vessel will not be insured. One week after the investment the vessel sinks as a result of a casualty and the stock becomes worthless. In such circumstances, a fact-finder might conclude that the misrepresentation was material and relied upon by the investor but that did not cause the loss.

[**Huddleston v. Herman & MacLean,** 640 F.2d 534 (5th Cir. 1981), *aff'd in part, rev'd in part on other grounds* 459 U.S. 375 (1983)]

b. Reliance [§391]

In theory, to show transaction causation (hereafter "causation") the plaintiff must prove that he relied on the defendant's wrongful misstatement or omission. At one time, it seemed that the plaintiff would be required to prove that he actually and specifically relied on the defendant's misstatement or omission. Later, however, the requirement of reliance became radically transformed. The reasons for the transformation differed somewhat as to (i) omissions and (ii) misstatements.

(1) Omissions [§392]

In **Affiliated Ute Citizens of Utah v. United States**, 406 U.S. 128 (1972), the Supreme Court held that in omissions cases, "positive proof of reliance is not a prerequisite to recovery. All that is necessary is that the facts withheld be material . . . ."

(a) Presumption of reliance [§393]

Subsequent court of appeals cases have held that *Ute* "merely established a presumption that made it possible for the plaintiffs to meet their burden." [*See, e.g.,* **Shores v. Sklar,** 647 F.2d 462 (5th Cir. 1981) (en banc), *cert. denied,* 459 U.S. 1102 (1983)] The defendant can rebut this presumption by showing that the plaintiff would have followed the same course of conduct even with full disclosure. For example, the defendant might show that the plaintiff learned the omitted fact from an independent source before making her investment, so that the investment could not have been caused by the defendant's nondisclosure.

(2) Misrepresentations

(a) "Fraud on the market" [§394]

Where securities are sold in a well-developed market (rather than in a face-to-face transaction), a plaintiff may be able to prove reliance on a misrepresentation by alleging that she relied on the integrity of the market. This is known as the "fraud on the market" theory. [**Basic, Inc. v. Levinson,** *supra*]

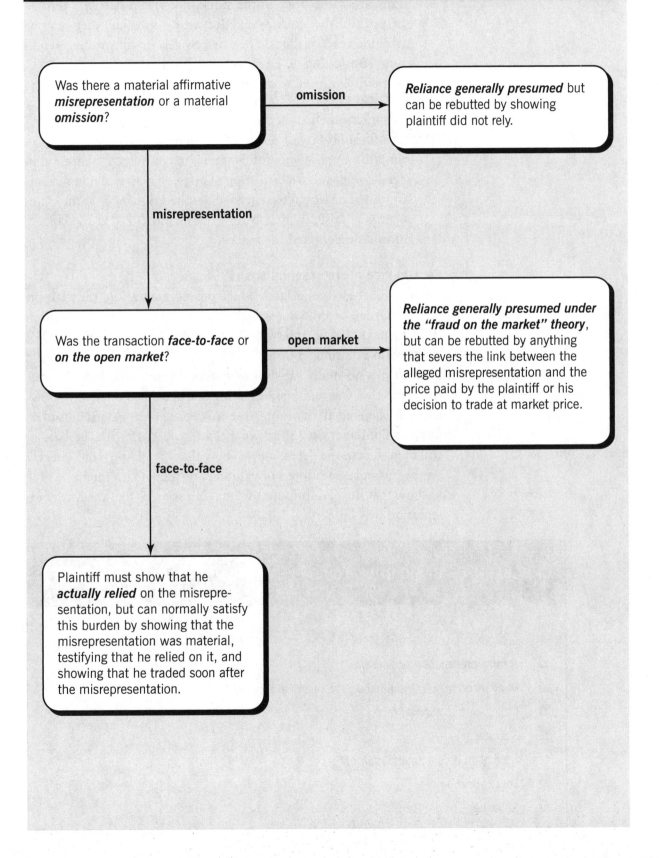

Was there a material affirmative **misrepresentation** or a material **omission**?

— omission → **Reliance generally presumed** but can be rebutted by showing plaintiff did not rely.

— misrepresentation ↓

Was the transaction **face-to-face** or **on the open market**?

— open market → **Reliance generally presumed under the "fraud on the market" theory**, but can be rebutted by anything that severs the link between the alleged misrepresentation and the price paid by the plaintiff or his decision to trade at market price.

— face-to-face ↓

Plaintiff must show that he **actually relied** on the misrepresentation, but can normally satisfy this burden by showing that the misrepresentation was material, testifying that he relied on it, and showing that he traded soon after the misrepresentation.

1) Rationale

In an open and well-developed securities market, material misrepresentations (or the withholding of material information) generally affect the price of the stock. Because purchasers rely on the price of the stock as a reflection of its value, they may be defrauded even if they do not directly rely on the misrepresentations. [**Basic, Inc. v. Levinson,** *supra*]

2) Practical effect

The practical effect of the fraud-on-the-market theory is to create a *presumption* of reliance. The defendant can rebut the presumption by showing, for example, that a misrepresentation in fact did not lead to a distortion of price, that an individual plaintiff traded or would have traded despite knowing that the statement was false, or that before the plaintiff traded the correct information entered the market.

(b) Face-to-face misrepresentations [§395]

In an action based on a face-to-face misrepresentation, the plaintiff has the burden of showing actual reliance on the misrepresentation. [**REA Express, Inc. v. Interway Corp.,** 538 F.2d 953 (2d Cir. 1976); **Holdsworth v. Strong,** 545 F.2d 687 (10th Cir. 1976)] However, the plaintiff can normally satisfy this burden by showing that the misrepresentation was material, testifying that she relied on it, and showing that she traded soon after the misrepresentation. [**Robinson v. Cupples Container Co.,** 513 F.2d 1274 (9th Cir. 1975)] The burden will then shift to the defendant to show that the plaintiff did not rely on the misrepresentation. For example, the defendant might be able to show that the plaintiff knew from other sources that the misrepresentation was false.

CHECKLIST OF BASIC RULE 10b-5 ELEMENTS — gilbert

TO PROVE A PRIMA FACIE VIOLATION OF RULE 10b-5, PLAINTIFF MUST GENERALLY SHOW:

- ☑ A *misrepresenation or omission*
- ☑ *In connection with* the purchase or sale of a security
- ☑ Concerning a *material fact*
- ☑ *Scienter*

And, if the plaintiff is a *private plaintiff*

- ☑ *Loss causation*
- ☑ *Reliance*

---

10. When Nondisclosure Constitutes a Violation [§396]

Assuming that materiality and scienter are established, rule 10b-5 is clearly violated when a person makes a misrepresentation or states a half-truth in connection with the purchase or sale of stock. Most such cases constituted common law fraud even before rule 10b-5 was adopted, at least if the misrepresentation or half-truth was made face-to-face. The primary advantages of rule 10b-5 in such cases are the ability to bring suit in federal court, the liberal venue and service-of-process provisions of the 1934 Act, and a relatively expansive view of what constitutes a misrepresentation or half-truth. More difficult issues are presented, however, if the defendant is claimed to have violated rule 10b-5 not by a misrepresentation or half-truth, but by failure to make disclosure.

a. Mere informational imbalance [§397]

Broadly speaking, nondisclosure of material nonpublic information violates rule 10b-5 *only* when there is a duty, *independent of rule 10b-5*, to disclose. A duty to disclose under rule 10b-5 does not arise merely from the fact that one party to a transaction has material information and the other does not. [**Chiarella v. United States,** 445 U.S. 222 (1980); **Dirks v. SEC,** 463 U.S. 646 (1983)] So, for example, a person who acquires material nonpublic information solely by skill and diligence in searching out the information, without using an insider position or any wrongful methods, does not violate rule 10b-5 if he trades on the basis of that information. Similarly, a person who innocently overhears material nonpublic information can make use of the information in trading without violating rule 10b-5.

(1) Possession vs. use [§398]

A related issue in an omission case is whether a plaintiff must show that the defendant actually *used* the material undisclosed information in making a decision to trade.

(a) Case law [§399]

Prior to the adoption of Securities Exchange Act Rule 10b5-1, *infra,* the Ninth and Eleventh Circuits held that rule 10b-5 is not violated unless the plaintiff showed both that: (i) the defendant *possessed* material inside information that she was not permitted to trade on without disclosure, and (ii) that she *actually used* the information in deciding to buy or sell. These decisions rested on the theory that having inside information in one's possession when trading does not wrongfully cause harm; only using such information wrongfully causes harm. [**SEC v. Adler,** 137 F.3d 1325 (11th Cir. 1998); **United States v. Smith,** 155 F.3d 1051 (9th Cir. 1998)] However, the distinction between possession versus use of inside information was rejected by the Second Circuit in **United States v. Teicher,** 987 F.2d 112 (1993), where the court held that if the plaintiff proved knowing possession of inside information by the defendant, it can be assumed that the information affected his trading decisions. The court said:

[A] "knowing possession" standard has the attribute of simplicity. It recognizes that one who trades while knowingly possessing material inside information has an informational advantage over other traders. Because the advantage is in the form of information, it exists in the mind of the trader. Unlike a loaded weapon, which may stand ready but unused, material information cannot lay idle in the human brain. The individual with such information may decide to trade upon that information, to alter a previously decided-upon transaction, to continue with a previously planned transaction even though publicly available information would now suggest otherwise, or simply to do nothing. In our increasingly sophisticated securities markets, where subtle shifts in strategy can produce dramatic results, it would be a mistake to think of such decisions as merely binary choices—to buy or to sell.

(b) Rule 10b5-1 [§400]

The SEC has now addressed this issue in rule 10b5-1, which provides that, subject to certain affirmative defenses (*infra*), the "manipulative and deceptive devices" that are prohibited by rule 10b-5 include the purchase or sale of a security *"on the basis of"* material nonpublic information about the security or its issuer, in breach of a *duty of trust or confidence* that is owed directly, indirectly, or derivatively, to the issuer, its shareholders, or *any other person who is the source of the information*. Under the rule, a purchase or sale is deemed to be "on the basis of" material nonpublic information if the person making the purchase or sale was *aware* of the material nonpublic information when he made the purchase or sale.

(c) Affirmative defense [§401]

Rule 10b5-1 creates an affirmative defense that allows purchases and sales by a person in possession of inside information if the purchase or sale is pursuant to a preexisting contract, instruction, or plan. To come within this defense, a person must show that *before becoming aware of the relevant information*, he had either entered into a binding contract to purchase or sell the security, provided instructions to another person to execute the trade for his account, or adopted a written plan for trading securities, and that the purchase or sale that occurred was pursuant to the prior contract, instruction, or plan.

b. Trading by insiders [§402]

At the other end of the spectrum, it is clear that insiders—directors, officers, controlling shareholders, and corporate employees—violate rule 10b-5 if they trade on the basis of material nonpublic information that they obtained through their positions ("inside information"). The duty of such persons to disclose such information before trading rests on the existence of a relationship giving them access to information intended to be available only for a corporate purpose, and the unfairness of allowing a corporate insider to take advantage of that information by trading without disclosure. [*In re* **Cady, Roberts & Co.**, *supra*, §366; **Chiarella v. United States**, *supra*] Trading by insiders on the basis of inside information is commonly referred to as "insider trading."

c. Misappropriation [§403]

Between the extremes of skillfully or innocently acquired nonpublic information on the one hand, and inside information on the other, is information that a noninsider *wrongfully* acquires, *i.e.*, "misappropriates." The "misappropriation theory" is most useful where the defendant had no independent fiduciary duty to the party with whom he traded. Under the misappropriation theory, when a person misappropriates, for securities-trading purposes, confidential information in breach of a *duty that he owes to the source of the information*, he commits fraud "in connection with" a securities transaction, and thereby violates section 10(b) and rule 10b-5. Under the classical theory of insider trading, rule 10b-5 liability is based on a fiduciary relationship between the *issuer* and the insider-defendant, and deception of a buyer or seller through the use of material information gained through that relationship. In contrast, under the misappropriation theory, rule 10b-5 liability is based on the defendant's deception of a person, *other than the issuer*, who entrusted the defendant with access to material confidential information that the defendant then used without permission to make personal gains by trading.

(1) Chiarella v. United States [§404]

In **Chiarella v. United States**, *supra*, Chiarella worked in the composing room of a financial printer and learned of prospective takeover bids before they were made public. In violation of his employer's rules, Chiarella acquired stock in the target of the takeover bids before the bids were made, and sold the target's stock at a profit after the bids were made. Chiarella was indicted for violation of section 10(b) and rule 10b-5. The trial court instructed the jury that Chiarella should be found guilty if he used material nonpublic information at a time when he knew that other people trading in the securities market did not have access to the same information. The jury convicted Chiarella. The United States Supreme Court reversed, holding that the trial court's instruction imposed too broad a duty, because under the instruction Chiarella would be guilty even if he had obtained material information rightfully. However, the Court reserved decision on whether Chiarella could have been convicted on the theory that he breached a duty to the acquiring corporation when he acted upon information that he obtained by virtue of his position as an employee of a printer employed by that corporation. Furthermore, at least four Justices explicitly embraced the theory that trading on the basis of improperly obtained nonpublic information violated rule 10b-5 (the "misappropriation theory").

(2) United States v. O'Hagan [§405]

In **United States v. O'Hagan** (*supra*, §367), the Supreme Court upheld the misappropriation theory. O'Hagan was a partner in a law firm that Grand Metropolitan ("Grand Met") retained to represent it regarding a potential tender offer for Pillsbury. Both Grand Met and the law firm took precautions to protect the confidentiality of Grand Met's tender-offer plans. Nevertheless, O'Hagan began purchasing options to purchase shares of Pillsbury stock. When Grand Met announced its tender offer, the price of Pillsbury stock rose dramatically. O'Hagan then sold his options and common stock, making a profit of more than $4.3 million. The Supreme Court upheld O'Hagan's criminal conviction under rule 10b-5. The Court stated that misappropriation of information satisfies the requirement of section 10(b) (*see supra*, §365) that conduct involve a deceptive device because a misappropriator deals in deception—he deceives the person or entity that is the source of the information. Misappropriation also satisfies the requirement that the deceptive device be used "in connection with the purchase or sale of a security," because the fraud is consummated not when the defendant *acquires* the confidential information, but rather when, without disclosure to his source, he *uses* the information to purchase or sell securities. That is so even though the person or entity that the misappropriator defrauds is not the party with whom the misappropriator trades, but is instead the source of the information.

(a) Effect of disclosure to source of information [§406]

Under *O'Hagan*, a defendant apparently will not be liable if he discloses his proposed use of the information to the person from whom he misappropriated the information, because deception through nondisclosure is central to the misappropriation theory.

(b) Relationship of trust and confidence [§407]

Under the misappropriation theory, the defendant must have made use of information that he acquired in the course of a *relationship of trust and confidence* that imposed upon him an obligation not to use the information for personal gain. In most cases, the relevant relationship is a business or professional relationship, such as employer-employee or firm-partner. This is not always the case, however. Therefore, under the misappropriation theory an issue can arise whether a family, personal, or other nonbusiness relationship can provide the duty of trust or confidence that is required under the theory. This issue is addressed by SEC rule 10b5-2. This rule sets out three nonexclusive situations in which a person has a duty of trust or confidence for purposes of the misappropriation theory. Under this rule, a duty of trust or confidence exists:

(i) When a persons *agrees to maintain information in confidence*;

(ii) When two persons have a *history, pattern, or practice of sharing confidences* such that the recipient of the information knows or reasonably should know that the person communicating the material nonpublic information expects that the recipient will maintain its confidentiality (this is a "facts and circumstances" test based on the expectation of the parties in light of the overall relationship); or

(iii) When a person receives or obtains material, nonpublic information *from spouses, parents, children, and siblings.*

Note: An affirmative defense exists for the third prong of the rule that permits the person who receives or obtains the information to demonstrate that under the facts and circumstances of the particular family relationship, no duty of trust or confidence existed.

d. Liability to contemporaneous traders [§408]

Under section 20A of the Securities Exchange Act, any person who violates rule 10b-5 by purchasing or selling a security while in the possession of material nonpublic information is liable to *any person* who, contemporaneously with the purchase or sale, purchased or sold (as the case may be) securities of the same class. However, the defendant's total liability under this provision is limited to the profit that the defendant gained or the loss he avoided as a result of the violation.

e. Mail fraud—United States v. Carpenter [§409]

The federal mail fraud act [18 U.S.C. §§1341, 1343] makes it a criminal offense to employ false or fraudulent pretenses, representations, or promises in furtherance of a scheme or artifice to defraud, if any matter is transmitted by mail or wire to execute the scheme or artifice. In **United States v. Carpenter,** 791 F.2d 1024, *aff'd*, 484 U.S. 19 (1987), a *Wall Street Journal* reporter who wrote a widely read and influential column, participated, in violation of the *Journal's* rules, in a scheme in which he provided two stockbrokers with securities-related information that was scheduled to appear in his column. Based on this advance information, the two brokers would buy or sell the securities before the column appeared, and sell or buy immediately thereafter. The reporter was convicted of criminal mail and wire fraud, and the conviction was unanimously affirmed by the Supreme Court. The Court held that the interest of the *Journal's* owner in the confidentiality of the *Journal's* contents was a property right, and that by using the information for his own purposes the reporter had obtained "money or property" from the *Journal* by fraud.

f. Special rule for tender offers [§410]

Exchange Act Rule 14e-3 provides that if any person has taken substantial steps to begin, or has begun, a tender offer (*i.e.*, a public offer to purchase shares from a target corporation's shareholders), it is a fraudulent, deceptive, or manipulative act or practice for any other person who is in possession of material information relating to the tender offer to purchase or sell any of the target's securities if the person knows (or has reason to know) that the information (i) is nonpublic and (ii) has been acquired directly or indirectly from the bidder, the target, or a director, officer, or other person acting on the bidder's or the target's behalf.

(1) Scope and validity of rule

Rule 14e-3 applies even when the relevant information is not disclosed to the trading person in violation of the insider's fiduciary duty. Therefore, in the case of information that concerns a tender offer, in effect rule 14e-3 partially reverses the rule in *Chiarella* that it is not in and of itself improper to trade on the basis of nonpublic information acquired from an insider. The Second Circuit has held rule 14e-3 valid, upholding the conviction of a defendant who had traded on basis of material information relating to tender offer, even though, in the court's view, under *Chiarella* the defendant had not violated rule 10b-5. [**United States v. Chestman**, 947 F.2d 551 (2d Cir. 1991), *cert. denied,* 503 U.S. 1004 (1992); *and see* **SEC v. Peters**, 978 F.2d 1162 (10th Cir. 1992)]. In *O'Hagan* (*supra*, §405), the Supreme Court held that rule 14e-3(a) was generally valid, although the Court left open whether the rule could properly be applied in cases where "a substantial step . . . to commence" a tender offer has been taken but the tender offer has not actually begun.

g. "Disclose or abstain" [§411]

Where a person has a duty to disclose material nonpublic information in his possession before he trades, the applicable rule is often expressed as "disclose or abstain." That is, nondisclosure *in itself* normally does not violate rule 10b-5. Nondisclosure by a person with a duty to disclose violates rule 10b-5 *only* if the person trades. Such a person has a choice: disclose and trade, or do not disclose and do not trade.

11. Liability of Nontrading Persons for Misrepresentations [§412]

Normally, a rule 10b-5 action is brought against a person who traded in stock. However, even persons who do not trade may be liable under rule 10b-5 in certain types of cases. [**Basic, Inc. v. Levinson**, *supra*, §394] In particular, a corporation or other person who makes a misrepresentation that would cause reasonable investors to rely on the misrepresentation in the purchase or sale of securities would be liable under rule 10b-5, even though the corporation or other person does not trade, provided that the other elements of rule 10b-5 liability, such as scienter, are satisfied. So, for example, a nontrading corporation may be liable under rule 10b-5 if it issues a misleading press release that would be likely to affect investment decisions, provided scienter is present. [**SEC v. Texas Gulf Sulphur Co.**, *supra*, §372]

a. Scienter required [§413]

A nontrading corporation or other person, like any other defendant, will be liable under rule 10b-5 only if it had scienter. [**Ernst & Ernst v. Hochfelder**, *supra*, §373] A misrepresentation that is without fault, or that results only from negligence, will not result in rule 10b-5 liability.

b. Liability of nontrading corporation for nondisclosure [§414]

In the case of nondisclosure (as opposed to misrepresentation), the basic principle of rule 10b-5 is "disclose or abstain." Accordingly, a nontrading corporation is unlikely to be liable under rule 10b-5 for nondisclosure of material facts even though persons who do trade would have made different investment decisions if they had known the undisclosed facts. The general rule is that the timing of disclosure of material facts by a corporation is "a matter for the business judgment of the corporate officers entrusted with the management of the corporation within the affirmative disclosure requirements promulgated by the exchanges and by the SEC." [**SEC v. Texas Gulf Sulphur Co.,** *supra*; **Financial Industrial Fund, Inc. v. McDonnell Douglas Corp.,** 474 F.2d 514 (10th Cir.), *cert. denied*, 414 U.S. 874 (1973); **Electronic Specialty Co. v. International Controls Corp.,** 409 F.2d 937 (2d Cir. 1969)] There are, however, several exceptions to this rule.

(1) Duty to correct statement [§415]

If the corporation makes a statement that is misleading (inaccurate) when made, even though not intentionally so, and the corporation later learns that the statement was misleading, it is under a duty to ***correct*** the statement if the statement is still "alive," rather than "stale"—*i.e.*, if the statement would still be likely to be material to investors. [*See, e.g.,* **Backman v. Polaroid Corp.,** 910 F.2d 10 (1st Cir. 1990)]

(2) Duty to update statement [§416]

Several courts have held that if a corporation makes a public statement that is correct when made, but that has become materially misleading in light of subsequent events, the corporation may have a duty to ***update*** the statement. [*See* **Backman v. Polaroid Corp.,** *supra*—court qualified this position by taking the view that the duty to update applies only to forward-looking statements; **Greenfield v. Heublein, Inc.,** 742 F.2d 751 (3d Cir. 1984), *cert. denied*, 469 U.S. 1215 (1985)]

(3) Assumption of duty to correct others' statements [§417]

A corporation may so involve itself in the preparation of statements about the corporation by outsiders—such as analysts' reports or earnings projections—that it assumes a duty to correct material errors in those statements. Such a duty "may occur when officials of the company have, by their activity, made an implied representation that the information they have reviewed is true or at least in accordance with the company's views." [**Elkind v. Liggett & Myers, Inc.,** 635 F.2d 156 (2d Cir. 1980)]

(4) Duty to correct rumors [§418]

A corporation may be under a duty to correct erroneous rumors resulting from leaks by the corporation or its agents. [*See* **State Teachers Retirement Board v. Fluor Corp.,** 654 F.2d 843 (2d Cir. 1981)]

12. Tippee and Tipper Liability—Dirks v. SEC [§419]

A *tippee* is a person who is not an insider, but who trades on information that she has received from an insider. The basic principles of tippee liability were laid down by the Supreme Court in **Dirks v. SEC** (*supra*, §397), subject to certain rules later adopted in Regulation FD (*see infra*, §427).

a. Broad rule rejected [§420]

In *Dirks,* the Court rejected the broad rule that a person would be liable, as a tippee, solely because she knowingly received material nonpublic information from an insider and traded on it. Such a broad rule would conflict with the conclusion in *Chiarella* (*supra*, §§397-404) that trading on the basis of an informational advantage is not in and of itself a violation of rule 10b-5. (That is, it matters how the information was obtained.) The Court was also concerned that a broad rule would inhibit the role of market analysts, who often, as part of their research into particular stocks, interview corporate executives and acquire information that may not have theretofore been public. However, the Court identified certain situations in which tippees would be liable.

b. Tippee liability [§421]

A person who receives information from an insider and trades on it is liable if (i) the insider breached a fiduciary duty in communicating the information, and (ii) the tippee knew or should have known of the breach, and therefore knew that she (the tippee) had received the information improperly. The primary test for determining whether the communication of information by an insider constitutes a breach of fiduciary duty is whether the insider will personally benefit, directly or indirectly, from his disclosure. [**Dirks v. SEC**, *supra*]

(1) Breach of insider's fiduciary duty [§422]

An insider's fiduciary relationship with his corporation prevents him not only from using undisclosed corporate information for personal gain, but also from giving such information to others for that purpose. An insider who tips in order to give the tippee information to use for personal gain breaches his fiduciary duty to the corporation. Correspondingly, a tippee who knows or should know that the tipper, in disclosing inside information to the tippee, has breached his fiduciary duty to the corporation by using corporate information for his own gain or advantage, will be liable as a knowing participant in a breach of fiduciary duty. On the surface, this test seems narrow. However, the Court in *Dirks* defined gain or advantage, in this connection, so broadly as to include most tipping activity. For example:

(a) Tips to friends or relatives [§423]

Dirks held that there is a gain or advantage to the insider when he makes a gift of confidential information to a trading relative or friend. The tip to the relative or friend, followed by a trade by the tippee, is like a trade by the insider followed by a gift of his profits from the trade. [**Dirks v. SEC**, *supra*]

(b) Quid pro quo for past or future benefits [§424]

Even if the tippee is not a friend or a relative, the insider breaches his fiduciary duty, and the tippee is therefore liable, if there is a relationship between the insider and the tippee that suggests that the tip is a quid pro quo for a past or future benefit from the tippee. [**Dirks v. SEC**, *supra*]

c. Tipper liability [§425]

Under *Dirks*, if a tippee will be liable, so will the tipper.

d. Outsiders in special confidential relationships [§426]

Outsiders who trade on the basis of information from the corporation as a result of a *special confidential relationship* could also be liable if they are temporary insiders. [**Dirks v. SEC**, *supra*] Where corporate information is legitimately revealed to an underwriter, accountant, lawyer, or other professional or consultant working for the corporation, that person may become a fiduciary of the corporation's shareholders regarding that information. [**Dirks v. SEC**, *supra*] The theory is that the person has entered into a special confidential relationship with the corporation and is given access to the information solely for corporate purposes. If such a person trades on the information, he will be just as liable as an ordinary insider (and he will be liable as a tipper if he improperly tips the information). Persons who acquire information in this way are sometimes referred to as "temporary insiders."

13. Selective Disclosure; Regulation FD [§427]

Tipping characteristically involves the transmission of nonpublic information by an insider, with the result that the tippee can trade on information that is not generally available to the public. Typically in such cases, the insider does not act on the corporation's behalf. However, an issue closely related to tipping is raised when the corporation itself makes selective (rather than general) disclosure of nonpublic information. Like tipping, selective disclosure gives the persons to whom the information is provided the chance to trade on the basis of information that is not generally available to the public. Prior to 2000, corporations often made selective disclosure by giving nonpublic information to favored persons, primarily favored securities analysts and institutional investors. In 2000, however, the SEC adopted Regulation FD, which is intended to prevent most selective disclosure. Regulation FD provides that if a corporation (or a person acting on a corporation's behalf) discloses material nonpublic information to certain enumerated kinds of persons—in general, securities-market professionals or shareholders who may trade on the basis of the information—the corporation must make public disclosure of the information simultaneously, if the corporation's disclosure is intentional, or promptly, if the disclosure is not intentional.

14. Aiders and Abettors [§428]

An aider and abettor is a person who knowingly aids or abets someone who acts improperly. For example, an accountant or lawyer may knowingly aid or abet a client's improper trading, or a banker may knowingly finance improper trading. In **Central Bank of Denver v. First Interstate Bank of Denver,** 511 U.S. 164 (1994), the Supreme Court held that *liability cannot be imposed* on a person under rule 10b-5 solely because that person aided and abetted a violation of the rule.

a.   **Note**

Prior to *Central Bank*, issues concerning aiding-and-abetting liability under rule 10b-5 usually arose in the context of a suit against a primary violator in which the plaintiff joined as defendants such secondary actors as lawyers, accountants, or banks who had somehow furthered the primary violator's course of conduct. The *Central Bank* opinion held that such secondary actors could not be sued on an aiding-and-abetting theory, but left open the possibility of suing such actors as primary violators in appropriate cases.

15. **Application of Rule 10b-5 to Breach of Fiduciary Duties by Directors, Officers, or Controlling Shareholders**

a.   **"Ordinary mismanagement" without misrepresentation, nondisclosure, or manipulation—the *Santa Fe* rule [§429]**

A breach of fiduciary duty by a corporate manager that does not involve a misrepresentation, nondisclosure, or manipulation *does not violate rule 10b-5* even if it involves the purchase or sale of stock. [**Santa Fe Industries, Inc. v. Green,** 430 U.S. 462 (1977)] This kind of rule 10b-5 case is often referred to as an "ordinary mismanagement" case.

Example: A Corp. and B Corp. are both incorporated in State X. A Corp. owns 90% of B Corp. Under the law of State X, a short-form merger can be used to cash out minority shareholders if the parent corporation owns at least 90% of the subsidiary. A minority shareholder who is dissatisfied with the price offered for his shares may demand appraisal (*i.e.*, a statutory procedure for determining the fair value of his shares), but this is his only state law remedy. A Corp. proposes to merge B Corp. into itself by a short-form merger for a cash price that is wholly inadequate, but A Corp. discloses all the relevant facts concerning the value of B Corp., from which the inadequacy of the price could be determined. B Corp.'s minority shareholders have no cause of action against A Corp. under rule 10b-5, even if the inadequacy of the price violates A Corp.'s fiduciary duties. [**Santa Fe Industries, Inc. v. Green,** *supra*]

b.   **Purchase or sale of stock by fiduciary on the basis of misrepresentation or nondisclosure [§430]**

Notwithstanding the general rule established in *Santa Fe*, if a director or officer purchases stock from or sells stock to the corporation on the basis of a misrepresentation or nondisclosure, the corporation can sue the fiduciary under rule 10b-5, even though it can *also* sue her for breach of fiduciary duty.

(1) Derivative suits

If the corporation does not sue in such a case, a minority shareholder can maintain a derivative suit on the corporation's behalf (*see infra*, §735). The *Blue Chip* rule (*infra*, §436), which prohibits a private action by a person other than a purchaser or seller of the securities, would not be a barrier to such an action because the corporation *is* a purchaser or seller, and the action is maintained on its behalf.

c. Purchase or sale of stock by controlling shareholder with approval of majority of directors [§431]

Suppose that a controlling shareholder causes a corporation to issue stock to him, or buy stock from him, at an unfair price, and the material facts are not disclosed to the minority shareholders. A derivative action can be brought against the controlling shareholder under rule 10b-5 in such a case if the nondisclosure caused a loss to the minority shareholders. [**Goldberg v. Meridor**, 567 F.2d 209 (2d Cir. 1977), *cert. denied*, 434 U.S. 1069 (1978)]

(1) Causation [§432]

To show that the nondisclosure caused a loss to the minority shareholders in such a case, the plaintiff must establish that *an effective state remedy was forgone* as a result of the nondisclosure to the minority shareholders. The plaintiff usually attempts to satisfy this requirement by arguing that if disclosure had been made to the minority shareholders, they could have sued for injunctive relief against the proposed transaction under state law. The courts are divided on the issue of what the plaintiff must show concerning the likelihood that the suit would have been successful.

(a) Actual success [§433]

Some courts hold that the plaintiff must show that the minority shareholders would actually have succeeded if they had brought the forgone suit. [**Kidwell ex rel. Penfield v. Meikle**, 597 F.2d 1273 (9th Cir. 1979)]

(b) Reasonable probability of success [§434]

Other courts hold that the plaintiff must show "there was a reasonable probability of ultimate success." [**Healey v. Catalyst Recovery**, 616 F.2d 641 (3d Cir. 1980)]

(c) Prima facie case for relief [§435]

Still other courts have adopted a requirement "that the facts shown make out a prima facie case for relief." [**Alabama Farm Bureau Mutual Casualty Co. v. American Fidelity Life Insurance Co.**, 606 F.2d 602 (5th Cir. 1979), *cert. denied*, 449 U.S. 820 (1980)]

16. *Blue Chip* Rule—Private Plaintiff Must Be Purchaser or Seller [§436]

A private cause of action can be maintained only by a person who actually purchased or sold the securities to which the violation of rule 10b-5 relates. It is not enough that the violation caused the plaintiff *not* to buy or *not* to sell. [**Blue Chip Stamps v. Manor Drug Stores,** 421 U.S. 723 (1975)] This "purchaser or seller" requirement is based largely on considerations of administrability. The Supreme Court was concerned that it would be too easy for a person to bring a contrived suit under rule 10b-5, based on an allegation, which might be supported only by the plaintiff's oral testimony and therefore would be difficult to disprove, that the plaintiff decided not to buy or sell because of the defendant's misrepresentation or omission. In contrast, when a plaintiff has actually bought or sold, there is an objective and documented action, not merely a claim of a subjective response.

EXAM TIP   gilbert

Be careful to not extend this "purchaser or seller" requirement beyond its limits. A *private plaintiff* must be a purchaser or seller. If the plaintiff is the *government*, there is no purchaser or seller requirement. (See *infra*, §442.) Similarly, the *defendant* does not have to be a purchaser or seller. (See *supra*, §412.)

---

a. **Meaning of "sale" [§437]**

Although *Blue Chip* allows private actions to be brought only by persons who have actually purchased or sold, the term "sale" has an expansive meaning under the securities acts.

(1) **Stock for property [§438]**

An exchange of stock for assets, property, or other stock is a "sale" within the meaning of rule 10b-5.

(2) **Mergers and liquidations [§439]**

A merger can be a sale under rule 10b-5. [**Vine v. Beneficial Finance Co.,** 374 F.2d 627 (2d Cir. 1967)]

(3) **Contracts to sell stock [§440]**

An executory contract to sell stock is a sale under rule 10b-5. [**A.T. Brod & Co. v. Perlow,** 375 F.2d 393 (2d Cir. 1967)]

(4) **Pledges [§441]**

A pledge can be a sale under rule 10b-5. [**Rubin v. United States,** 449 U.S. 424 (1981); **Chemical Bank v. Arthur Andersen & Co.,** 726 F.2d 930 (2d Cir. 1984)]

b. **Standing of SEC [§442]**

The *Blue Chip* rule bars only actions under rule 10b-5 by private persons who have neither purchased nor sold the securities. The *SEC* can bring an action against a violator of rule 10b-5 even though the SEC neither purchased nor sold the securities. By its nature, the SEC is never a purchaser or a seller. Furthermore, the SEC is unlikely to bring contrived suits.

17. **Defenses [§443]**

Two important defenses to a rule 10b-5 claim are the "due diligence" and "in pari delicto" defenses.

a. **Due diligence [§444]**

If the plaintiff was *at fault* in relying on the defendant's misrepresentation, or in failing to learn an omitted fact, in the sense that had the plaintiff used due diligence he would not have been misled, that fault may bar recovery. Mere negligence by the plaintiff will normally not constitute a lack of due diligence for rule 10b-5 purposes: Because a *defendant* is not liable for negligence under rule 10b-5 (*see supra*, §413), it would be anomalous to hold that the *plaintiff's* negligence bars the suit. [**Dupuy v. Dupuy**, 551 F.2d 1005 (5th Cir.), *cert. denied*, 434 U.S. 911 (1977); **Holdsworth v. Strong**, *supra*, §395] However, under the due diligence defense, the plaintiff will be barred from recovery by his own *intentional misconduct*, and may also be barred by his own *recklessness* if the defendant's conduct was merely reckless rather than intentional. It is not clear whether the plaintiff will be barred by his own recklessness if the defendant was guilty of intentional misconduct.

Example: Seller recklessly makes incorrect oral statements to Buyer, a sophisticated businessperson, about C stock. Subsequently, however, and before Buyer agrees to purchase C stock, Seller furnishes Buyer with documents that correctly state the facts about C. Buyer does not read the documents. In a suit by Buyer against Seller under rule 10b-5, Seller may prevail under the due diligence defense because Buyer was reckless in not reading the documents. [**Zobrist v. Coal-X, Inc.**, 708 F.2d 1511 (10th Cir. 1983)]

b. **In pari delicto—Bateman Eichler, Hill Richards, Inc. v. Berner [§445]**

In the law generally, "in pari delicto" is a shorthand phrase for the doctrine that in a case of equal fault, the position of the defendant is better. In a rule 10b-5 context, the doctrine refers to the fault of a plaintiff who sues for a violation of rule 10b-5 but who has *himself* violated rule 10b-5. (The doctrine is most commonly raised in suits by a tippee against a tipper for misrepresentation of alleged inside information. The tipper replies that the tippee was in pari delicto because he violated rule 10b-5 by trading on the tipped information.) In **Bateman Eichler, Hill Richards, Inc. v. Berner**, 472 U.S. 299 (1985), the Supreme Court held that a private action for damages under the securities laws may be barred under the principle of in pari delicto on the ground of the plaintiff's culpability, but only where (i) as a direct result of his own actions the plaintiff bears at least *substantially equal responsibility* with the defendant for the violation that the plaintiff seeks to redress, and (ii) preclusion of the plaintiff's suit would not *significantly interfere* with the effective enforcement of the securities laws and the protection of the investing public. Note that an investor who engages in insider trading as a tippee is not necessarily as blameworthy as a corporate insider who discloses the information for personal gain.

(1) **Effect**

Although *Bateman Eichler* severely limited the in pari delicto defense in rule 10b-5 cases, it did not foreclose that defense in situations "in which the relative culpabilities of the tippee and his insider source merit a different mix of deterrent incentives." [**Rothberg v. Rosenbloom**, 808 F.2d 252 (3d Cir. 1986)]

(2) Note

In **Pinter v. Dahl,** 486 U.S. 622 (1988), the Supreme Court elaborated on the first prong of the *Bateman Eichler* test, concerning when the plaintiff, as a direct result of his own actions, bears at least substantially equal responsibility for the underlying illegality. The Court held that the plaintiff must be an "active, voluntary participant in the unlawful activity that is the subject of the suit," *i.e.*, the plaintiff must himself have violated the law in cooperation with the defendant, in order to be in pari delicto. Thus, unless the degrees of fault are essentially indistinguishable or the plaintiff's responsibility is clearly greater, the in pari delicto defense should not be allowed, and the plaintiff should be compensated.

18. Remedies [§446]

A great variety of remedies are available for violations of rule 10b-5.

a. Potential remedies [§447]

Before examining exactly which remedies are available in which kinds of cases, it is helpful to understand the potential remedies that might be available under rule 10b-5.

(1) Out-of-pocket damages [§448]

Out-of-pocket damages are the difference between the price paid for stock and its actual value. This measure is designed to put the injured person back in the same financial position that he was in before the transaction occurred, but not to give him the benefit of the bargain.

(a) Distinguish—benefit-of-the-bargain damages [§449]

Benefit-of-the-bargain damages are measured by the difference between the value of stock as it really is and the value that the stock would have had if a misrepresentation had been true. The difference between out-of-pocket and benefit-of-the-bargain damages can be illustrated as follows: Buyer pays seller $20,000 for O Oil Company stock, based on Seller's misrepresentation that O had just struck a new well. O stock would have been worth $22,000 if the representation had been true. In fact, O had not just struck a new well, and the stock is worth only $19,000. Benefit-of-the-bargain damages would be $3,000—the difference between the actual value of the O stock ($19,000) and the value it would have had if O had struck a new well ($22,000). Out-of-pocket damages, however, are only $1,000—the difference between the amount Buyer paid ($20,000) and the value of the stock ($19,000).

(b) **Standard measure of conventional damages in rule 10b-5 cases [§450]**

In private actions under rule 10b-5 in which the plaintiff seeks conventional damages, *out-of-pocket damages* is the standard measure; benefit-of-the-bargain damages are generally not granted. [**Estate Counseling Service, Inc. v. Merrill Lynch, Pierce, Fenner & Smith, Inc.,** 303 F.2d 527 (10th Cir. 1962); **Green v. Occidental Petroleum Co.,** 541 F.2d 1335 (9th Cir. 1976)]

(2) Restitutionary relief [§451]

A plaintiff in a rule 10b-5 case may seek restitutionary relief rather than conventional damages.

(a) Rescission [§452]

The most common form of restitutionary relief is rescission. If a seller sues for rescission and succeeds, she returns the purchase price and gets back the stock she sold. If a buyer sues for rescission and succeeds, he returns the stock he bought and gets back his purchase price.

(b) Rescissionary or restitutionary damages [§453]

Another form of restitutionary relief is rescissionary or restitutionary damages. Such damages are the money equivalent of rescission. They are measured by the difference between the value of what the plaintiff gave up and the value of what the defendant received.

(c) Difference between conventional damages and restitutionary relief [§454]

The major difference between conventional damages and restitutionary relief (whether rescission or rescissionary damages) is that out-of-pocket damages are based on the *plaintiff's loss*, while restitutionary relief is based on the *defendant's wrongful gain*.

1) Comment

Rescission or rescissionary damages may be especially attractive remedies to a plaintiff when the value of the stock in question changed radically after the transaction. For example, suppose the facts of the O Oil Company hypothetical (*supra*, §449) are reversed: O Oil Company *has* struck a new well, but Buyer tells Seller that it has not. As a result, Seller sells Buyer O stock for $20,000, when it is really worth $22,000. By the time of the trial, however, the O stock is worth $40,000. Under the conventional out-of-pocket damages measure, Seller would be entitled to $2,000, the difference between the value of what she gave up (stock worth $22,000) and the value of what she got ($20,000 in cash). Seller is much better off if she can either get back the stock itself (which will give her $40,000 worth of O stock in return for repaying only $20,000 in cash) or rescissionary damages (which will be $20,000—the value of the stock minus the value of what she received for it).

b. Application of potential remedies [§455]

The next several sections show how these potential remedies are actually used to remedy violations of rule 10b-5. Which remedies are available in which cases depends to a considerable extent on whether the stock in question is closely or publicly held.

(1) Remedies where stock is closely held [§456]

Suppose that Seller owns stock in C, a closely held corporation. Buyer makes a material misrepresentation to Seller concerning C. If the representation were true, it would have a negative impact on the value of C stock. In fact, it is false. In reliance on the misrepresentation, Seller sells his C stock to Buyer. Later, Seller learns that he was deceived.

(a) Out-of-pocket damages [§457]

Seller can sue Buyer for conventional damages under rule 10b-5. In that case, his recovery will normally be based on the out-of-pocket measure; thus, he will be awarded the difference between the price he received for his stock and its actual higher value. (Similarly, a buyer can sue a seller for out-of-pocket damages based on a misrepresentation by the seller. And either a seller or a buyer can sue for out-of-pocket damages based on failure to disclose a material fact if disclosure is required.)

(b) Restitutionary relief [§458]

Alternatively, a seller or buyer of close corporation stock who sold or bought on the basis of a misrepresentation or a wrongful nondisclosure can sue for restitutionary relief.

1) When plaintiff is a seller [§459]

If the plaintiff is a seller who sold for too low a price based on the buyer's misrepresentation and sues for rescission, he would return the purchase price to the buyer and recover the stock. But what happens if the buyer has already resold the stock? In that case, the seller may be able to recover the *profit on resale*, *i.e.*, the difference between the price at which the seller sold the stock to the buyer, and the price at which the buyer resold the stock. The theory of such a recovery is that the buyer holds the profit in constructive trust for the seller. In effect, the money that the buyer received when he resold the stock replaced the stock to which the seller was entitled. The seller should get the equivalent of rescission, by recovering the difference between the price at which he sold to the buyer and the proceeds of the buyer's resale. [**Janigan v. Taylor**, 344 F.2d 781 (1st Cir.), *cert.*

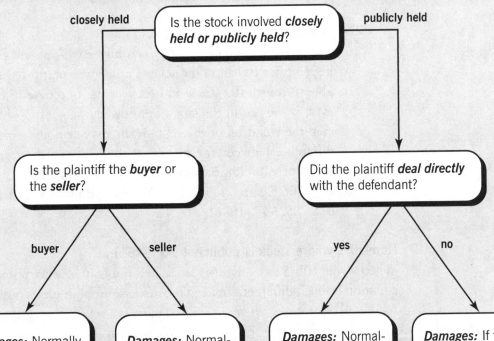

Is the stock involved *closely held or publicly held*?

closely held

publicly held

Is the plaintiff the *buyer* or the *seller*?

Did the plaintiff *deal directly* with the defendant?

buyer

seller

yes

no

Damages: Normally based on the difference between the price paid for the stock and its actual lower value

or

Restitution: Buyer may return the stock and recover the purchase price; or if she has since sold the stock, she should be able to recover the difference between the price she paid and the resale price.

Damages: Normally based on the difference between the price paid for the stock and its actual higher value

or

Restitution: Seller may return the purchase price and recover the stock or whatever the buyer received if he has since sold the stock.

Damages: Normally based on the difference between the price at which the stock was sold and the market price at the time corrective information is disclosed. ***Restitutionary relief generally is not available.***

Damages: If the plaintiff's harm arose from a ***misrepresentation***, the defendant probably is liable for all actual damages; if the plaintiff's harm arose from an omission, the defendant is liable for all actual damages up to the profit the defendant made or loss the defendant avoided.

denied, 382 U.S. 879 (1965); **Affiliated Ute Citizens of Utah v. United States**, *supra*, §392; **Harris v. American Investment Co.,** 523 F.2d 220 (8th Cir. 1975), *cert. denied*, 423 U.S. 1054 (1976)] This is a form of rescissionary damages.

2) When plaintiff is a buyer [§460]

Similarly, if the injured party is a buyer who purchased at too high a price based on the seller's misrepresentation, she may be able to return the stock and recover the purchase price. However, if she resold the stock at a lower price before she discovered the violation of rule 10b-5, she may be able to recover the difference between the price that she paid and the resale price. [**Chasins v. Smith, Barney & Co.**, 438 F.2d 1167 (2d Cir. 1970), *aff'g* 306 F. Supp. 177 (S.D.N.Y. 1969); **Randall v. Loftsgaarden**, 478 U.S. 647 (1986)]

(2) Remedies where stock is publicly held [§461]

When a rule 10b-5 case involves stock in a publicly held corporation, the situation is much different. To keep the discussion as simple as possible, the focus will be on cases where the injured party is a seller. The same principles generally apply where the injured party is a buyer.

(a) Plaintiff deals directly with defendant [§462]

Suppose that Seller owns stock in P, a publicly held corporation. Buyer publicly makes a material misrepresentation concerning P, which has a negative impact on the value of P stock. In reliance on the misrepresentation, Seller sells his stock to Buyer.

1) Damages [§463]

Assume first that Seller sues Buyer for conventional damages. Under the out-of-pocket measure, Seller would recover the difference between the price at which he sold P stock and the actual market value of the stock. There is a good reason, however, for measuring the actual value of the stock, not by its market price *at the time of the wrong*, but by its market price *at the time of disclosure of the correct information*. The market price of P stock at the time of the wrong is *not* a good indicator of the actual value of the stock at that time, because the market will have been affected by Buyer's misrepresentation. In contrast, the market price of P stock after the misrepresentation is corrected normally is a good indicator of the actual value of the stock at the time of the wrong, because that price will reflect the market's valuation of P stock in light of the new, correct information. [**Harris v. American Investment Co.**, *supra*] The use of market price at the time of disclosure to determine the actual value of the stock at the time of the wrong is sometimes referred to as the "modified" out-of-pocket measure.

a) Conversion measure [§464]

Some cases put a slight twist on this rule, and allow the seller to measure damages by the highest price within a reasonable time after disclosure. The theory is that if Buyer had not caused Seller to sell his P stock at an unfairly low price, Seller might have sold the stock at the highest price available in the market during a reasonable time after he learned the true facts. Of course, we cannot know exactly what price Seller would have obtained—he might have sold at less than the highest price—but the wrongdoer should bear the burden of this uncertainty, because she created it. [**Mitchell v. Texas Gulf Sulphur Co.**, 446 F.2d 90 (10th Cir.), *cert. denied*, 404 U.S. 1004 (1971)] This is sometimes known as the "conversion" measure.

2) Restitutionary relief [§465]

Restitutionary relief (rescission and rescissionary damages) is usually *unavailable* in the case of publicly held stock, because such relief is unnecessary to compensate the seller or prevent unjust enrichment of the buyer. Where publicly held stock is involved, once the misrepresentation is corrected, the seller can replace himself by purchasing the stock on the market.

Example: On January 10, Seller sells P stock to Buyer, who had made a material misrepresentation that P is badly off, when in fact it is not. The price is $30. On February 20, public disclosure is made of the true facts, and P stock goes up to $35, where it hovers until March 20. A year later, at the time of trial, P stock is at $60. Seller should not be entitled to restitution or rescissionary damages. Seller's failure to realize a gain from the further increase in the value of P stock from $35 to $60 after February 20 does not derive from Buyer's misrepresentation, but rather from Seller's fully informed decision not to buy P stock at $35. Similarly, Buyer's gain after February 20 reflects not her fraud, but her decision to retain the P stock, which she could have purchased at $35 on February 20 even without having made the misrepresentation. [**SEC v. MacDonald**, 699 F.2d 47 (1st Cir. 1983)]

---

a) Distinguish—close corporations [§466]

The rule that restitutionary relief is generally not available under rule 10b-5 in the case of stock in publicly held corporations is not inconsistent with the rule that restitutionary relief generally *is* available under rule 10b-5 in the case of close corporation stock. Where a close corporation is involved, disclosure normally does not put the plaintiff and defendant on an equal footing: Because stock in a close corporation cannot be purchased and sold on the market, the injured seller cannot replace himself by buying shares of the stock on the market after disclosure is made.

(b) Plaintiff does not deal directly with defendant [§467]

Suppose that although Buyer violates rule 10b-5 by a misrepresentation or wrongful omission, she does not deal directly with Seller. In other words, Seller did sell, and would not have sold but for the misrepresentation or omission, but Buyer did not buy from Seller.

1) Misrepresentation [§468]

If the defendant made a public misrepresentation that had the foreseeable effect of causing members of the public to buy or sell the stock, she will probably be liable for all the resulting damages. [**Mitchell v. Texas Gulf Sulphur Co.,** *supra*, §464; **Blackie v. Barrack,** 524 F.2d 891 (9th Cir. 1975), *cert. denied*, 429 U.S. 816 (1976)]

2) Omission [§469]

Suppose the defendant did not make a public misrepresentation, but traded on the basis of inside information without having made disclosure.

a) Case law [§470]

Two leading cases in the Second Circuit, **Shapiro v. Merrill Lynch, Pierce, Fenner & Smith, Inc.,** 495 F.2d 228 (2d Cir. 1974), and **Elkind v. Liggett & Myers, Inc.,** 635 F.2d 156 (2d Cir. 1980), imposed liability in such cases. However, *Elkind* limited damages to a "disgorgement" measure, in which the defendant is obliged only to surrender profits, not to compensate everyone who traded at the same time for the difference between the price they realized and the value of the stock. A Sixth Circuit case, **Fridrich v. Bradford,** 542 F.2d 307 (6th Cir. 1976) (decided after *Shapiro* but before *Elkind*), refused to impose liability, partly out of concern that to do so would "unduly" extend liability under rule 10b-5—a problem that is cured by using the disgorgement measure to limit damages.

b) Statutory solution [§471]

The Insider Trading and Securities Fraud Enforcement Act

of 1988 resolved the issue by adding section 20A to the Securities Exchange Act. Section 20A provides that any person who violates rule 10b-5 by purchasing or selling a security while in the possession of material nonpublic information is liable to any other person who, contemporaneously with the purchase or sale, sold or purchased securities of the same class. However, liability under this provision is limited to the profit the defendant gained or the loss the defendant avoided. The Act therefore adopts the approach taken in *Elkind*.

(3) Remedies available to the government [§472]

The SEC, as a government agency, rather than a buyer or a seller, cannot sue for damages in the normal sense because it suffers no loss. However, the SEC can seek several different remedies for violation of rule 10b-5, including special monetary remedies.

(a) Injunctive relief [§473]

The SEC can, and commonly does, seek injunctive relief. In seeking injunctive relief, the SEC often requests ancillary monetary relief in the form of disgorgement of profits, or other payments, that can be used as a fund for private parties injured by the defendant's violation. [**SEC v. Texas Gulf Sulphur**, *supra*, §414—insiders ordered to pay their profits from insider trading to corporation, corporation ordered to hold profits in escrow for five years for claimants, and at the end of the five-year period, balance to become property of corporation]

(b) Criminal sanctions [§474]

Violation of rule 10b-5 is a criminal act. The Justice Department often seeks fines and sometimes jail sentences for such violations.

(c) Civil penalties [§475]

Under the Insider Trading Sanctions Act, a person who purchases or sells securities while in the possession of material nonpublic information may be ordered, in an action by the SEC or the Attorney General, to pay a civil penalty to the Treasury of *up to three times the profit gained or loss avoided* as a result of the purchase or sale. [15 U.S.C. §§78c, 78o, 78t, 78u, 78ff] This penalty is *in addition* to liability for the profit gained or loss avoided.

19. Jurisdiction, Venue, and Service of Process

a. Jurisdiction [§476]

Suits under rule 10b-5 are based on the Securities Exchange Act. Under section 27 of that Act, the federal district courts have exclusive, federal question jurisdiction over suits based on violations of the Act or the rules promulgated under the Act.

(1) Preemption of state-law securities class actions [§477]

The Securities Litigation Uniform Standards Act of 1998 generally preempts (*i.e.,* precludes) state-law class actions relating to securities fraud in connection with the purchase or sale of securities listed on a national stock exchange. The Act is complex and includes a number of exceptions. Broadly speaking, however, the Act prohibits a class action from being brought under state law if: (i) the action is based on a misrepresentation or omission of a material fact in connection with the purchase or sale of a security that is listed on a national stock exchange; (ii) the defendant is alleged to have used or employed any manipulative or deceptive device or contrivance in connection with the purchase or sale of such a security; and (iii) either damages are sought on behalf of more than 50 persons or common questions of law or fact predominate.

b. Venue and service of process [§478]

Actions under rule 10b-5 are governed by the liberal venue provisions of the 1934 Act. Under those provisions, an action under rule 10b-5 can be filed wherever *any* act or transaction constituting a violation occurred, or in the district where the defendant is found or transacts business. Service of process is also governed by a liberal provision: Process can be served on the defendant in any district where the defendant can be found, or of which the defendant is an inhabitant, whether or not it is the district in which the action was brought. [15 U.S.C. §78aa]

20. Statute of Limitations [§479]

Until recently, no periods of limitation were statutorily provided for private rule 10b-5 actions. This state of affairs led to two developments: first, the Supreme Court's adoption of judicial periods of limitation for such actions in **Lampf, Pleva, Lipkind, Prupis & Petrogrow v. Gilbertson,** 501 U.S. 305 (1991), then, more recently, Congress's adoption of statutory periods of limitation for such actions, replacing the judicial periods adopted in *Lampf, Pleva.*

a. *Lampf, Pleva* [§480]

In 1991, at a time when there were no statutory periods of limitation for rule 10b-5 private actions, the Supreme Court held that under rule 10b-5 a private action cannot be brought more than one year after discovery of the facts constituting the cause of action or more than three years following accrual of the cause of action.

b. Sarbanes-Oxley [§481]

The Sarbanes-Oxley Act of 2002 enacted statutory periods of limitation for private rule 10b-5 actions. Under that Act, a private right of action that involves a claim of fraud, deceit, manipulation, or contrivance in contravention of a regulatory requirement concerning the securities laws must be brought not later than the earlier of (i) *two years* after the discovery of the facts constituting the violation, or (ii) *five years* after the violation.

C. Section 16 of the 1934 Act

1. Introduction [§482]

A second major provision of the 1934 Act governing insider trading is section 16, which relates to purchases followed by sales, or sales followed by purchases, by certain types of insiders, within a six-month period. Such trading is known as "short-swing trading." [15 U.S.C. §78p]

2. Securities Affected Under Section 16 [§483]

Section 16 applies only to trading in equity securities of those corporations that have a class of equity securities that must be registered under section 12 of the 1934 Act. Basically, this means a class of equity securities (i) *traded on a national securities exchange*, or (ii) held by at least *500 shareholders* and issued by a corporation having *total assets exceeding $10 million*. (*See supra*, §364.)

a. Note

It is enough to trigger section 16 that *any class* of the corporation's equity securities is registered under section 12. If so, trading in *all* of the corporation's equity securities is subject to section 16. For example, if a corporation has outstanding an issue of common stock registered under section 12, trading in the corporation's preferred stock is subject to section 16 even if that stock is not required to be registered (because, for example, it is not listed and is held by fewer than 500 persons).

3. Disclosure Requirement—Section 16(a) [§484]

Section 16(a) provides that every person who is directly or indirectly the *beneficial owner of more than 10%* of any class of equity securities registered under section 12, or who is a *director or officer* of a corporation that has issued such a class of securities, must file periodic reports showing the amount of the corporation's securities that he beneficially owns, and any changes in those holdings.

a. Place of filing [§485]

These reports must be filed electronically with the SEC and with any national securities exchange on which the stock is traded.

b. Time of filing [§486]

An initial statement of beneficial ownership (Form 3) must be filed within 10 days after the person has become a more-than-10% beneficial owner, officer, or director. A statement of change of beneficial ownership of securities (Form 4) must be filed before the end of the second business day following the day of

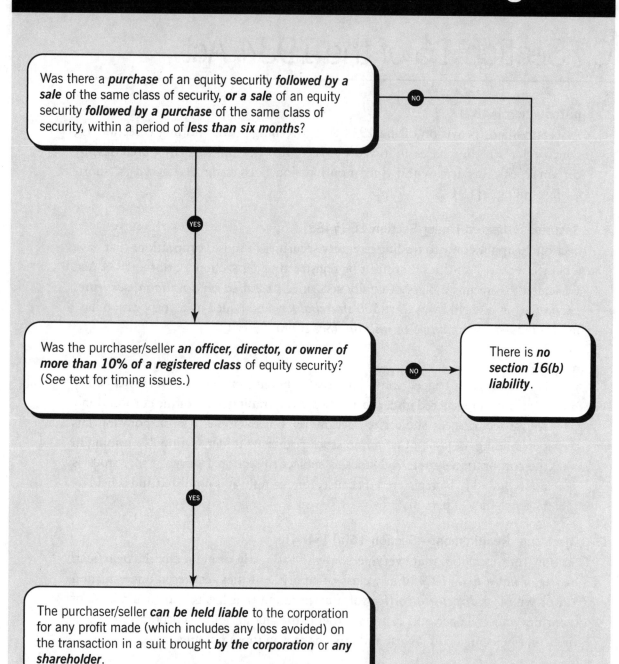

Was there a *purchase* of an equity security *followed by a sale* of the same class of security, *or a sale* of an equity security *followed by a purchase* of the same class of security, within a period of *less than six months*?

NO

YES

Was the purchaser/seller *an officer, director, or owner of more than 10% of a registered class* of equity security? (See text for timing issues.)

NO → There is *no section 16(b) liability*.

YES

The purchaser/seller *can be held liable* to the corporation for any profit made (which includes any loss avoided) on the transaction in a suit brought *by the corporation* or *any shareholder*.

the transaction resulting in a change in beneficial ownership. An annual statement of beneficial ownership of securities (Form 5) must be filed on or before the 45th day after the end of the corporation's fiscal year. A corporation that maintains a corporate website must post the report on that website by the end of the business day after it is filed.

4. Liability—Section 16(b) [§487]

To prevent the unfair use of information that may have been obtained by a more-than-10% beneficial owner, director, or officer by reason of his relationship to the issuer, a corporation can recover any profit realized by such a person from a *purchase and sale* (or *sale and purchase*), within *less than six months*, of equity securities of a corporation that has a class of equity securities registered under section 12.

EXAM TIP **gilbert**

Remember, if the matched purchase and sale transactions occur exactly six months apart, or extend beyond six months, there is no liabillity, because the purchase and sale are not *within six months*.

---

a. Coverage of section 16(b) [§488]

Although section 16(b) is popularly referred to as an insider-trading provision, it does not actually use the term "insider," does not cover all insider trading, and is not limited to trades based on inside information. On the one hand, section 16(b) covers short-swing trading by directors, officers, and more-than-10% beneficial owners, even if the trading is not based on inside information. On the other hand, a person who is not a director, officer, or more-than-10% beneficial owner does not fall within section 16(b) even if he does trade on the basis of inside information.

b. Calculation of short-swing profit [§489]

The profit recoverable under section 16(b) is calculated by subtracting, from the price of stock sold, the price of an equal amount of stock purchased within six months *before or after* the sale.

Example: On January 2, D, a director of C Corp. (whose common stock is registered under section 12 of the 1934 Act), sells 500 shares of C common stock at $40 per share. Four months later, on May 1, D purchases 400 shares of C common stock at $30 per share. D has realized a $4,000 profit within the meaning of section 16(b), *i.e.*, the excess of the $40 sale price over the $30 purchase price, multiplied by 400 shares.

---

(1) Multiple transactions [§490]

If there is more than one purchase or sale transaction within the six-month period, the court pairs off transactions by matching the highest sale price with the lowest purchase price, the next highest sale price with the next lowest purchase price, and so on. [**Gratz v. Claughton,** 187 F.2d 46 (2d Cir. 1951)] Of course, once any two transactions have been paired off with each other, neither can be paired off with a third transaction. The purpose of such matching is to squeeze all possible profits out of short-swing trading by insiders.

(2) Time computation [§491]

The court can look six months forward or backward from any sale to find a purchase, or from any purchase to find a sale. If there is *any pair* of transactions within a six-month period in which the sale price is higher than the purchase price, the officer, director, or more-than-10% beneficial owner must account for it even if there were other transactions during the period that involved losses.

---

e.g. **Example:** As a result of the governing formula, what looks to the untrained eye like a series of losses may be turned into a profit for purposes of section 16(b). For example, assume the following trading by Director D in C Corp.'s common stock:

Date	Purchases or Sells	Number of Shares	Price
6/1	Purchases	1,000	$60
7/1	Sells	1,000	$55
8/1	Purchases	1,000	$50
9/1	Sells	1,000	$45

D may believe that she has lost $10,000 on her trading ($60 - $55 × 1,000; and $50 - $45 × 1,000). However, for purposes of section 16(b), D has a $5,000 profit, because the purchase at $50 on August 1 can be matched with the sale at $55 on July 1.

EXAM TIP   gilbert

On your exam, be sure to remember that the term "profit" under section 16(b) is broader than what is commonly thought of as profit. As explained above, it includes *avoided losses as well as traditional gains*.

EXAM TIP   gilbert

When determining profit in a section 16(b) fact pattern, it is very important to remember that transactions will be matched "coldheartedly" to produce the *maximum profit*. Don't be fooled by facts designed to convince you to discard this rule based on sympathy for the purchaser/seller. For example, suppose Doug is a director of Bigco and has owned 10,000 Bigco shares for many years. He decides to buy his dream home and sells 5,000 of his Bigco shares to his friend Pete President for the then current market price of $70 per share. Doug uses the $350,000 proceeds of the sale as a down payment on his new home. Five months later, Doug inherits $250,000. Although Bigco is as profitable as ever, because of a downturn in the economy, Bigco shares are now selling for $25 per share. Doug has faith in Bigco and believes that Bigco shares will return to a $70 per share market value within the next three years. Therefore, he uses his $250,000 inheritance to purchase 10,000 shares of Bigco stock on the open market. Is Doug liable under section 16(b)? You bet. The sale of 5,000 shares for $350,000 will be matched with 5,000 of the 10,000 shares Doug subsequently purchased for $25 each, leaving a profit of $225,000 ($350,000 - (5,000 × $25)). Doug's motivation for each transaction, the different number of shares involved in each, and the cause of the price differences *all are irrelevant*.

c. **Who is entitled to recover [§492]**

The profit derived by the officer, director, or more-than-10% beneficial owner belongs to the corporation (rather than the shareholders with whom the insider dealt), and the corporation alone is entitled to recover that profit.

(1) **Shareholder action on corporation's behalf [§493]**

If the corporation fails to sue within 60 days after demand by a shareholder, the shareholder may bring an action on the corporation's behalf. However, this is not a typical derivative suit (*see infra*, §786). The cause of action is federal. Therefore, state security-for-expenses provisions (*see infra*, §§798-806) do not apply. Moreover, the "contemporaneous shareholder" requirement normally applicable to derivative suits (*see infra*, §783) does not apply; thus, the shareholder maintaining the action need not have been a holder at the time of the transactions in question. [**Dottenheim v. Murchison**, 227 F.2d 737 (5th Cir. 1955)]

(a) **"Security" ownership requirement [§494]**

Although plaintiffs seeking to sue under the statute must own a "security," section 16(b) places no significant restriction on the type of security adequate to confer standing. Any security suffices. The statutory definition is broad enough to include stock, notes, warrants, bonds, debentures, puts, calls, and a variety of other financial instruments. It expressly excludes only "currency or any note, draft, bill of exchange, or banker's acceptance which has a maturity at the time of issuance of not exceeding nine months . . . ." [**Gollust v. Mendel**, 501 U.S. 115 (1991)]

d. **"Insiders" under section 16(b) [§495]**

As mentioned, section 16(b) covers persons who are officers or directors at the time of either the purchase or the sale, and persons who are more-than-10% beneficial owners at the time of both the purchase and the sale. (*See infra*, §§499-510.)

(1) **"Officer" [§496]**

The term "officer" means an issuer's president; principal financial or accounting officer (or, if there is no such principal accounting officer, the controller); any vice-president of the issuer in charge of a principal business unit, division, or function (such as sales, administration or finance); any other officer who performs a significant policymaking function, or any other person who performs similar policymaking functions for the issuer. [Exchange Act Rule 16a-1(f)]

(a) Note

A person's functions, and not simply her title, determine the applicability of section 16. Therefore, "individuals with executive functions do not avoid liability under section 16 simply by forgoing a title, and conversely, persons with a title but no significant executive responsibilities are not subject to the automatic short-swing profit liability of section 16(b). Thus, for example, a vice-president of a bank who has no policymaking responsibility would not have to be concerned with possible liability under section 16(b), if, because of an unexpected family emergency, he needed to sell securities." [Barron, *Control and Restricted Securities*, 19 Sec. Reg. L.J. 292, 294-95 (1991)]

(2) "Director" [§497]

The term "director" clearly covers persons actually named as directors. In addition, it covers anyone who has *deputized* another to act as director for him. The person making such a deputization will himself be deemed a director.

Example: C Corp. deputizes one of its officers, D, to sit as C's representative on the board of X Corp., in which C holds less than 10% of the stock. D is a director of X Corp. for purposes of section 16(b), and so is C Corp.

(a) What constitutes "deputization" [§498]

Suppose that C Corp. holds stock in X Corp. and that D is both an officer of C Corp. and a director of X Corp. Deputization will be found if it was agreed that in serving as a director of X Corp., D would represent C's interests. Deputization will also be found if D regularly passes on inside information to C Corp., even in the absence of any agreement to do so. Short of these two situations, however, what constitutes "deputization" is unsettled.

Example: D was a partner in L Bros., a large investment-banking partnership. D was also a director of Oil Co. L Bros. traded in Oil Co. stock. Although D had succeeded another L Bros. partner on the Oil Co. board, L Bros. was found *not* to have deputized D to represent its interests in Oil Co. because (i) there was no express understanding that D was to represent L Bros.' interests; (ii) D had never discussed the operating details of Oil Co.'s affairs with any member of L Bros.; and (iii) L Bros.' purchase and sale of Oil Co. securities did not result from receipt of inside information from D. Thus, L Bros. was not a director of Oil Co. within the meaning of section 16(b). [**Blau v. Lehman,** 368 U.S. 403 (1962)]

---

cf. **Compare:** Martin Marietta owned Sperry Rand stock, and Martin Marietta's president, P, sat on Sperry Rand's board. Although there was no express understanding that P was to represent Martin Marietta's interests, and P had not passed any inside information to Martin Marietta, a number of facts showed deputization for section 16(b) purposes: P was ultimately responsible for the total operation of Martin Marietta and personally approved all of its financial investments—in particular, its purchase of the Sperry stock. P's control over Martin Marietta, coupled with his membership on Sperry's board, placed him in a position in which he could acquire inside information concerning Sperry and could use such information for Martin. Furthermore, P admitted discussing Sperry's affairs with two officials at Martin Marietta and participating in sessions when Martin Marietta's investment in Sperry was reviewed. P's ultimate letter of resignation stated that "When I became a member of the [Sperry] board . . . it appeared to your associates that the Martin Marietta ownership of a substantial number of shares of Sperry Rand should have representation on your Board." On these facts, the court held that P, in his capacity as a director of Sperry Rand, served as a deputy of Martin Marietta. Therefore, Martin Marietta was itself a director of Sperry Rand for purposes of section 16(b), and a purchase and sale by Martin Marietta of Sperry Rand stock within six months fell within that section. [**Feder v. Martin Marietta Corp.,** 406 F.2d 260 (2d Cir. 1969), *cert. denied,* 396 U.S. 1036 (1970)]

---

(3) Time at which insider status of officers and directors determined

(a) Office held at only one end of swing [§499]

A director or officer who purchases or sells stock while in office, and then sells or purchases after leaving office but within six months after the first end of the swing, is liable under section 16(b). [**Feder v. Martin Marietta Corp.,** *supra*] However, Exchange Act Rule 16a-2(a) exempts from the operation of section 16 a purchase or sale by a director or officer *before* she became a director or officer, even though the transaction could be matched with a sale or purchase that occurred after she became a director or officer and within six months of the transaction.

> **Example:** D, a director, purchases stock in her corporation, resigns her position, and makes a sale within six months after the purchase. D is liable under section 16(b). D would also be liable if she sells stock while a director, resigns, and then makes a purchase within six months after the sale. [**Feder v. Martin Marietta Corp.,** *supra*]

EXAM TIP   **gilbert**

Remember that transactions occurring *before* a person becomes an officer or director *are excluded* from section 16, but most other transactions by officers or directors *will trigger* section 16(a) reporting requirements and can trigger the section 16(b) liability provision if the transaction can be matched with another transaction occurring within six months.

(b) Office not held at either end of swing [§500]

Section 16(b) does not apply unless at least one end of the short-swing transaction occurred while the defendant was an officer or director. [**Lewis v. Varnes,** 505 F.2d 785 (2d Cir. 1974); **Lewis v. Mellon Bank,** 513 F.2d 921 (3d Cir. 1975)]

> **Example:** D is a director and officer of C Corp. On January 2, D purchases 5,000 shares of C stock. On February 1, D retires. On March 1, D purchases an additional 5,000 shares. On July 6, D sells 5,000 shares. D is not liable under section 16(b). Although the July 6 sale occurred within six months after the March 1 purchase, both ends of that purchase and sale occurred while she was no longer an officer or director. The July 6 sale cannot be matched with the January 2 purchase, because more than six months separated these two transactions.

(4) Beneficial ownership under section 16(b) [§501]

If a person is the record owner of an equity security and also has a pecuniary interest in the security, he is undoubtedly a beneficial owner for all purposes under section 16. Problems of interpretation arise, however, if a person is a record owner of shares but has no pecuniary interest; or if a person has a pecuniary interest but is not the record owner; or if a person is neither the record owner nor has a pecuniary interest, but there is nevertheless an important relationship between the person and the security, like the right to control the security. These problems are addressed by the rules under section 16. Those rules draw a distinction between (i) what constitutes beneficial ownership for purposes of determining *whether a person is a 10% owner* [Exchange Act Rule 16a-1(a)(1)], and (ii) what constitutes beneficial ownership for purposes of determining whether a person who *is* a 10% owner, or a director or officer, must *report* under section 16(a) and may *be liable* for short-swing profits under section 16(b) [Exchange Act Rule 16a-1(a)(2)].

(a) Determining more-than-10% ownership [§502]

For the purpose of determining whether a person *is* a beneficial owner of more than 10% of any class of equity securities, "beneficial owner" means "any person who, directly or indirectly, through any contract, arrangement, understanding, relationship, or otherwise" has or shares: (i) *voting power*, including the power to direct the voting of the security; and/or (ii) *investment power*, including the power to dispose of (or direct the disposition of) the security. [Exchange Act Rules 16a-1(a)(1), 13d-3] In short, in determining whether a person is a more-than-10% owner of stock, the emphasis under rule 16a-1 is on the person's *control* over the stock.

(b) "Beneficial ownership" for reporting and liability purposes [§503]

In contrast, for the purposes of reporting requirements and liability, a "beneficial owner" is "any person who, directly or indirectly, through any contract, arrangement, understanding, relationship or otherwise, has or shares a *direct or indirect pecuniary interest* in the equity securities . . . ." So, for example, if D is a director of C Corporation, and D has a direct or indirect pecuniary interest in shares of C stock that are owned by X, then X's trades in C stock are imputed to D for reporting and liability purposes under section 16. "Pecuniary interest" in any class of equity securities means "the opportunity, directly or indirectly, to profit or share in any profit derived from a transaction in the subject securities." [Exchange Act Rule 16a-1(a)(2)] In short, unlike rule 16a-1(a)(1), which emphasizes *control* for purposes of determining who *is* a more-than-10% owner, rule 16a-1(a)(2) emphasizes *pecuniary interest* for purposes of determining what transactions in equity securities may give rise to *reporting obligations and liability*. After stating the pecuniary-interest test as a general principle to govern the determination of beneficial ownership for reporting and liability purposes, rule 16a-1(a)(2) then goes on to deal with certain recurring cases:

1) Family members [§504]

The term "indirect pecuniary interest" is *presumed* to include securities held by members of a director's, officer's or more-than-10% shareholder's immediate family sharing the same household, but this presumption of beneficial ownership may be rebutted. [Exchange Act Rule 16a-1(a)(2)(ii)(A)] "Immediate family" means "any child, stepchild, grandchild, parent, stepparent, grandparent, spouse, sibling, mother-in-law, father-in-law, son-in-law, daughter-in-law, brother-in-law, or sister-in-law, and . . . adoptive relationships." [Exchange Act Rule 16a-1(e)]

EXAM TIP   **gilbert**

On your exam, be sure to remember that there are two tests for beneficial ownership under section 16. The test concerning ownership of more than 10% focuses on *voting* and/or *investment power*. The test for all other purposes focuses on *pecuniary interest* in the securities, and an officer or director will be assumed to have a pecuniary interest in securities of relatives who live with the officer or director unless the officer or director rebuts the presumption.

---

2) Partnerships [§505]

A director, officer, or more-than-10% shareholder who is a genral partner in a partnership has an indirect pecuniary interest in his proportionate interest in the portfolio securities held by the partnership. [Exchange Act Rule 16a-1(a)(2)(ii)(B)]

3) Corporations [§506]

A director, officer, or more-than-10% shareholder who is also a shareholder in another corporation or similar entity is not deemed to have a pecuniary interest in the portfolio securities held by the other corporation or similar entity if he is not a controlling shareholder of the entity and does not have or share investment control over the entity's portfolio. [Exchange Act Rule 16a-1(a)(2)(iii)] Note that this rule does not specify a general principle for determining when a corporation's portfolio securities will be attributed to shareholders in the corporation, but only provides a safe harbor against reporting and liability in the cases that the rule specifies.

4) Others [§507]

The rules under section 16 also contain elaborate provisions dealing with such matters as when a trustee is a beneficial owner for reporting and liability purposes, and when the ownership of a derivative security makes a person the beneficial owner of the derivative security.

(5) Time at which insider status of more-than-10% beneficial owner determined [§508]

Unlike the case of an officer or director, liability for short-swing profits is imposed on a more-than-10% beneficial owner only if the person owned more than 10% of the shares at the time of *both* the purchase and the sale.

(a) Purchase by stages [§509]

Section 16(b) does not cover any transaction where a more-than-10% beneficial owner was not such "both at the time of the purchase and sale, or the sale and purchase, of the security involved." [15 U.S.C. §78p] Furthermore, in **Foremost-McKesson, Inc. v. Provident Securities Co.,** 423 U.S. 232 (1976), the Supreme Court held that in the case of a short-swing purchase-sale sequence, a more-than-10% beneficial owner is not liable under section 16(b) unless he was a more-than-10% beneficial owner *before* he made the purchase in question. To put this differently, the purchase that first lifts a beneficial owner above 10% cannot be matched with a subsequent sale under section 16(b). One reason for this rule is that until a person is a more-than-10% beneficial owner, he does not presumptively have access to inside information.

e.g. **Example:** D purchases 6% of the outstanding shares of C Corp. on January 2, an additional 6% on February 1, and another 6% on March 1. D sells all of these shares at a substantial profit on April 1. The profit on the January 2 and February 1 purchases from the April 1 sale is not subject to section 16(b), because D was not a more-than-10% beneficial owner at the time he made either purchase. The profit on the March 1 purchase from the April 1 sale are subject to section 16(b), because D held a 12% interest at that time.

1) Sale followed by purchase [§510]

The *Foremost* case involved a purchase followed by a sale. However, a sale by a more-than-10% beneficial owner that reduces his interest to less than 10%, followed by a purchase within six months, presents greater potential for abuse. In such a case, the defendant would presumptively have had access to inside information prior to the first leg of the swing, and such information might well carry over to the second leg. Thus, the opinion in *Foremost* left open the question whether a short-swing sale-purchase sequence (as opposed to a purchase-sale sequence) by a person who was a more-than-10% beneficial owner at the time of the sale but had reduced his ownership to less than 10% prior to the later purchase might result in liability under section 16(b).

e. What constitutes a "purchase" or "sale" under section 16(b)

(1) Garden-variety transactions [§511]

Any "garden-variety" purchase or sale of stock—meaning, more or less, an exchange of shares for cash—is a purchase or sale for purposes of section 16(b). This is true regardless of motive, *i.e.*, whether or not the purchase or sale was based on inside information.

(2) Unorthodox transactions [§512]

The terms "purchase" and "sale" in section 16(b) are not limited to garden-variety purchases and sales. Rather, these terms potentially encompass *any* acquisition or disposition of stock. Acquisitions or dispositions other than garden-variety purchases or sales are sometimes referred to as "unorthodox transactions."

Example: A merger in which stock in C Corp. is exchanged for stock in D Corp. *may* be treated as a purchase or sale under section 16(b). Likewise, a conversion or redemption of stock, or the exercise of a stock option, *may* be treated as a purchase or sale under section 16(b). The SEC has adopted elaborate and complex rules under section 16(b) that exempt from the operation of section 16(b) certain transactions, like conversions and the exercise of options, if specified conditions are satisfied. However, these rules do not cover all types of unorthodox transactions, so that the courts must frequently determine whether an unorthodox transaction falls within section 16(b).

(a) Application of section 16(b)—theories of interpretation [§513]

Courts have relied on two conflicting theories in interpreting section 16(b) in cases involving unorthodox transactions.

1) "Objective" theory [§514]

Some decisions follow the theory that section 16(b) should be applied broadly to every transaction that it can be read to reach, regardless of whether the result is necessary to effectuate the stated purpose of section 16(b) (to prevent the unfair use of inside information). [*See* **Smolowe v. Delendo Corp.,** 136 F.2d 231 (2d Cir.), *cert. denied*, 320 U.S. 751 (1943)] This is known as the "objective" theory.

2) "Subjective" or "pragmatic" theory [§515]

Under an alternative approach, known as the "subjective" or "pragmatic" theory, section 16(b) is applied only to those unorthodox transactions that give rise to a potential for abuse. Under this theory, assuming that an unorthodox transaction *may* be deemed a purchase or sale, whether it *will* be deemed a purchase or sale depends in large part on whether the transaction is of *a type that has a potential for insider abuse.*

Example: Occidental Petroleum acquired more than 10% of the stock of Kern County Land as the result of a tender offer. To avoid a takeover by Occidental, Kern County entered into a merger with a subsidiary of Tenneco Corporation. The merger was consummated less than six months after the tender offer, and liability was sought against Occidental under section 16(b) on the theory that the share exchange pursuant to the merger constituted a sale by Occidental of its Kern stock within six months of its purchase. The Supreme Court held for Occidental on the ground that while a merger *could* constitute a sale of stock for purposes of section 16(b), under the circumstances of this case, in which the merger was involuntarily thrust upon Occidental by an antagonistic corporation, there was no real potential for speculative abuse by Occidental of the kind that section 16(b) was designed to prevent. [**Kern County Land Co. v. Occidental Petroleum Corp.**, 411 U.S. 582 (1973)]

3) Significance [§516]

Although the tension between the two approaches to the interpretation of section 16(b) is real and important, it is a tension only at the margins. The great bulk of potential cases involve garden-variety transactions that cannot be regarded as unorthodox. In these cases, the "pragmatic" approach is not applicable, and the application of section 16(b) is relatively straightforward. Furthermore, the pragmatic approach normally will be applied only to *involuntary* transactions, *i.e.*, to transactions over which the insider had no control. So, for example, if a section 16(b) insider has control over her corporation's decision to enter into a merger, the merger will almost certainly be treated as a sale for section 16(b) purposes. And even if the insider had no control over the transaction, she may be liable if she had access to inside information.

D. Section 16(b) Compared to Rule 10b-5

1. Introduction [§517]

Rule 10b-5 and section 16 both regulate insider trading, but their approach differs. It is useful to compare the approach of each provision.

2. Covered Securities [§518]

Section 16(b) applies only to securities of corporations that have a class of securities required to be registered under the 1934 Act. Rule 10b-5 applies to all securities.

3. Inside Information [§519]

Short-swing profits are recoverable under section 16(b) whether or not they are attributable to misrepresentations, inside information, or misappropriation. Recovery is available under rule 10b-5 only where the defendant has made a misrepresentation or has traded on the basis of inside or misappropriated information.

4. Plaintiff [§520]

Recovery under section 16(b) belongs to the corporation. Recovery under rule 10b-5 belongs to the injured purchaser or seller.

5. Overlapping Liability [§521]

It is conceivable that insiders who make short-swing profits by the use of inside information could end up subject to both a claim by the corporation suing under section 16(b) and a claim by the injured seller or buyer under rule 10b-5. However, section 16(b) provides for recovery of the "profits realized" by the defendant. Damages that a defendant must pay because of a rule 10b-5 claim arising out of a transaction that also generates a short-swing profit would probably offset the "profits realized" within the meaning of section 16(b).

E. Common Law Liability for Insider Trading

1. Introduction [§522]

As discussed at the very beginning of this chapter, the majority rule at common law was that a director or officer who bought or sold stock without disclosing inside information normally was not liable to the purchaser or seller, partly on the theory that directors and officers owed a fiduciary duty only to the corporation, not to shareholders (*see supra*, §361). In contrast, several modern cases have held that as a matter of common law, insider trading *does* constitute a breach of fiduciary duties owed by the insider to the *corporation*—specifically, a breach of the duty not to use corporate assets (the inside information) for other than corporate purposes. Under this approach, the *corporation* can recover profits made by insider trading. [**Diamond v. Oreamuno,** 24 N.Y.2d 494 (1969); **Brophy v. Cities Service Co.,** 70 A.2d 5 (Del. 1949); *but see* **Schein v. Chasen,** 313 So. 2d 73 (Fla. 1975); **Freeman v. Decio,** 584 F.2d 186 (7th Cir. 1978)—contra]

2. Common Law Liability Compared to Liability Under Section 16(b) [§523]

Like liability under section 16(b), common law liability runs against insiders and in favor of the corporation. In other respects, however, common law liability differs from liability under section 16(b):

a. Scope [§524]

The common law theory applies to all corporations. In contrast, section 16(b) applies only to corporations with a class of equity securities required to be registered under section 12 of the 1934 Act.

b. Defendants [§525]

Under the common law theory, recovery can be had against any corporate insider who trades on inside information. In contrast, recovery under section

16(b) is allowed only against officers, directors, or more-than-10% beneficial owners.

c. **Short-swing requirement [§526]**

The common law theory is available even though the purchase and sale did not occur within a six-month period. In contrast, section 16(b) is applicable only to a purchase and sale that occurs within a six-month period.

d. **Informational requirement [§527]**

The common law theory applies only if an insider uses inside information. In contrast, section 16(b) applies whether or not inside information is used.

3. **Common Law Liability Compared to Liability Under Rule 10b-5 [§528]**

Liability under the common law also differs from rule 10b-5 liability, in that it runs to the corporation rather than to the injured purchaser or seller. In other respects, the two kinds of liability are highly comparable. However, they do differ in some ways.

a. **No purchaser or seller requirement [§529]**

Under rule 10b-5, the plaintiff must be either a purchaser or a seller. In contrast, the common law theory permits recovery by the corporation even when the corporation was neither a purchaser nor a seller.

b. **Tippees, etc. [§530]**

Common law liability has so far been imposed only against corporate insiders. It is still unclear whether courts would allow recovery under the common law theory against noninsiders (such as tippees), which may be allowed under rule 10b-5 under certain conditions (*see supra*, §§419-426, 428).

Chapter Seven:
Rights of Shareholders

CONTENTS

Chapter Approach

This chapter details shareholders' rights with respect to voting, transferring shares, inspecting corporate records, and bringing direct and derivative actions. It also considers the fiduciary obligations of controlling shareholders. A great deal of important information is covered in this chapter. Some key things to remember for exam purposes are discussed below.

1. Voting Rights

Generally shareholders may vote (i) for the *election and removal of directors*, (ii) to *amend the articles or bylaws*, and (iii) on *"fundamental" corporate changes*. Besides that rule, the things you should know about voting rights are:

a. Straight voting

Remember that except for the election of directors, or if the articles otherwise provide, shareholders are generally entitled to *one vote per share*.

b. Cumulative voting

Most states permit cumulative voting for directors, which means that each shareholder is given *one vote per share for each director to be elected* and may cast all of the votes for one person or divide them up as he sees fit. The purpose is to give minority shareholders a voice on the board. You may have to memorize the formula for electing directors by cumulative voting so that you can calculate the ability of particular shareholders to elect directors. Keep in mind that the majority shareholders may wish to employ devices such as staggering directors' terms, removing directors elected by the minority, and reducing the size of the board, to avoid the effects of cumulative voting.

c. Voting by proxy

A proxy is a power granted by a shareholder to exercise his voting rights. If you see a proxy question on your exam, make sure that the proxy is in writing and is being exercised during its statutory effective period. Remember too that, unless coupled with an interest, a proxy is *revocable* at any time.

(1) Proxy solicitation

This is a likely source of exam questions. In publicly held corporations, nearly all shareholders vote by proxy. Management solicits proxies for reelection of directors and approval of corporate actions. Occasionally, insurgent groups try to take control of the corporation through a proxy solicitation. Most exam questions will want you to apply the *federal proxy rules* to these situations. These rules forbid misstatements or omissions of *material* facts in proxy materials. In addition, the rules contain detailed *disclosure requirements*, particularly with respect to director-nominees and committees. Generally, shareholder proposals must be included in corporate proxy materials. If this issue comes up on your exam, however, be aware of the lengthy list of exceptions.

(a) Remedies

The SEC may institute a suit for a violation of section 14(a) or the proxy rules. The proxy rules also provide for a *private cause of action* for material misstatements or omissions with respect to proxy solicitations. For these private actions, the crucial elements are: materiality, causation (although this is satisfied by a showing of materiality), standing, and fault. Remember that fairness is no defense. Rescission and damages are the remedies available under this private action.

(b) Expenses

An important possible exam issue is whether corporate funds may be used to reimburse the expenses of a proxy fight. Remember that *management's expenses* may be reimbursed for (i) soliciting proxies to obtain a quorum, and (ii) a proxy fight involving corporate policy, not personnel. *Insurgents* never have a *right* to reimbursement of their proxy expenses, but the corporation may voluntarily reimburse the expenses of insurgents who win a contest involving policy.

d. Combining votes for control—close corporations

If your exam question involves a *close corporation*, the shareholders may be able to control corporate policy through the following voting devices: shareholder voting agreements, agreements requiring greater-than-majority approval, shareholder agreements binding votes as directors, and voting trusts.

2. Restrictions on Transfer of Shares

Transfer restrictions are often used by close corporations to limit the number of shareholders, prevent entry of unwanted shareholders, or avoid a shift of control. (These restrictions are also used on certain classes of shares by large corporations.) If this comes up in an exam question, remember that, to be valid, the restriction must be *reasonable* and *noted conspicuously* on the certificate. Also, recall that restrictions are not favored and will be strictly construed.

3. Shareholders' Right to Inspect Corporate Records

Generally, a shareholder acting for a *proper purpose* has a right to inspect corporate books and records at reasonable times. At common law, the shareholder has the burden of proving a proper purpose. Most statutes, however, shift the burden to the corporation to prove improper purpose. To determine whether a purpose is proper, ask yourself whether the shareholder is seeking inspection *primarily to protect his interest as a shareholder*, rather than as a potential business rival or litigant.

4. Fiduciary Obligations of Controlling Shareholders

A controlling shareholder owes a fiduciary duty to minority shareholders to act *with good faith and inherent fairness* toward them. The obligation is even greater in close corporations. Thus, when a question arises concerning a controlling shareholder's business dealings with the corporation, ask whether the transactions are fair. The burden of proof is on the controlling shareholder. Likewise, if a controlling shareholder causes a fundamental corporate change, ask whether it promotes his own self-interest at the expense of the minority. Be sure that when the controlling shareholder deals with the minority, he makes a *full disclosure*.

Although a controlling shareholder may sell his control stock at a *premium*, the following transactions are forbidden: A bare sale of directorships or corporate offices is invalid. Similarly, under the theory of corporate action, transactions where controlling shareholders are considered to have usurped a corporate opportunity are breaches of the fiduciary duty, as are sales where the controlling shareholder persuades the minority to sell on less favorable terms than he receives. It is also a breach for a controlling shareholder to sell control to a transferee whom he knows will deal unfairly with the corporation.

5. Shareholder Suits

Direct suits by shareholders, which concern the breach of duties *owed to shareholders as individuals*, are rare exam topics. In contrast, derivative suits, which concern the breach of duties *owed to corporations*, are exam favorites. Whenever a breach of a duty owed to the corporation arises, consider whether a shareholder derivative suit is appropriate. Ask yourself: Have the *corporate remedies* been exhausted (*e.g.*, has a demand for suit been made on directors and, if required, on shareholders)? Is the plaintiff now *a shareholder*, and was he a shareholder at the time of the wrong? Does the plaintiff *fairly and adequately represent* the interests of the other shareholders? Note that any defense that would have been available if the corporation had brought the suit is available in a derivative suit.

Since the cause of action belongs to the corporation, so does any *recovery or settlement*. At this point, you will want to consider whether the plaintiff-shareholder is entitled to *reimbursement* for expenses and whether officers and directors are entitled to *indemnification*. Many courts order reimbursement of a victorious plaintiff's expenses if the suit has resulted in a substantial benefit to the corporation. Every state permits the corporation to reimburse the expenses of officers or directors who win on the merits. However, where a director or officer settles or loses a suit, he may be reimbursed for litigation expenses only, indemnified for the settlement, or denied protection altogether depending upon (i) the state statute and (ii) whether he acted in good faith, with reasonable care, and believed he was acting in the best interests of the corporation.

A. Voting Rights

1. Right to Vote—In General [§531]

Subject to certain exceptions for close corporations (*supra*, §§191-206), shareholders generally have no right to exercise direct management or control over ordinary corporate affairs. However, they may control the corporation *indirectly* to some extent through their voting rights. Shareholders generally have the right to vote (i) for the *election and removal of directors;* (ii) to *amend the articles or bylaws*; and (iii) on *"major corporate action"* or *"fundamental changes"* (*e.g.*, sale of all the assets, merger, consolidation, and dissolution).

a. Who may vote [§532]

The right to vote at a meeting of the shareholders belongs to persons who are shareholders on a certain date—called the *record date*—according to the corporation's records. Statutes in many states provide that the record date is the date the notice of the meeting is sent or the day before notice is sent. Many statutes also allow the articles or bylaws to designate some other record date. [*See, e.g.*, Del. Gen. Corp. Law §213(a)—"record date" cannot be more than 60 days, nor less than 10 days, prior to shareholders' meeting]

(1) Sale of shares after record date [§533]

The corporation must permit the owner of the shares as of the record date to vote, even if he no longer owns the shares at the time of the shareholders' meeting. But the new owner can protect himself by requiring the record owner to give him a *proxy* (*see infra*, §558). In any event, a record owner who votes in a way that injures the new owner may be liable to the new owner for damages. [*In re* **Giant Portland Cement Co.**, 21 A.2d 697 (Del. 1941)]

> **EXAM TIP**   **gilbert**
>
> Be sure to remember that because the record date is set in advance of a shareholders' meeting, there can be persons who own shares on the meeting date who **do not have the right to vote** (because they purchased their shares after the record date), and persons who do not own shares on the meeting date who **do have the right to vote** (because they sold their shares after the record date). As will be discussed *infra*, voting rights can be aligned with meeting day ownership if the post-record-date seller gives his buyer a **proxy** to vote the shares.

b. Restrictions on right [§534]

Voting rights are not "inherent" in any class of stock. Generally, shares may be either voting or nonvoting, or may have multiple votes per share. [Del. Gen. Corp. Law §151(a)] A few statutes have been interpreted to preclude nonvoting stock. [**C.A. Cavendes Sociedad Financiera v. Florida National Banks**, 565 F. Supp. 254 (M.D. Fla. 1982)]

(1) **Maximum votes per shareholder [§535]**

A limit on the number of votes that any shareholder may have, regardless of the number of shares he owns, has been upheld. [**Providence & Worcester Co. v. Baker,** 378 A.2d 121 (Del. 1977)]

(2) **Publicly issued common stock [§536]**

A number of state regulatory agencies prohibit the issuance of common stock without voting rights or with unequal voting rights. In addition, the major national stock exchanges, prodded by the SEC, forbid listed companies from reducing the voting rights of existing common stock (but do permit issuance of *new* common stock with restricted voting rights).

2. Shareholders' Meetings [§537]

Whereas some informality is accepted as to actions by directors (*see supra*, §225), this is not generally true as to actions by the shareholders. In most states, shareholders can act only at meetings duly called and noticed, at which a quorum (usually a majority of the shares entitled to be voted, unless otherwise provided in the articles) is present, by resolution passed by a specified percentage of the shares present (usually a majority, but a greater percentage may be required for certain shareholder resolutions).

a. Timing of meeting [§538]

Statutes usually require an *annual meeting* of the shareholders for the election of directors. In addition, *special meetings* are authorized whenever called by a designated corporate officer, by the holders of some designated percentage of the voting shares (*e.g.*, 10%), or by "such other persons as may be provided in the articles or bylaws." [Del. Gen. Corp. Law §211(d)]

b. Notice [§539]

Written notice must generally be given some period in advance of the shareholders' meeting—*e.g.*, not less than 10 nor more than 60 days before the meeting. The notice must specify the place, date, and hour of the meeting, and the general nature of the business to be transacted. [Del. Gen. Corp. Law §222]

EXAM TIP   **gilbert**

It is not uncommon for an exam to test the *notice requirements* for shareholders' meetings. All shareholders entitled to vote must be given notice, typically between 10 and 60 days before the meeting. Typically, the notice must include the place, date, and hour of the meeting and, if the meeting is a special meeting, the purpose of the meeting. If proper notice is not given, action taken at the meeting can be *voided*.

---

c. Withdrawal of quorum [§540]

Courts are divided on the question of whether a shareholder meeting that begins with a quorum present may validly continue to transact business after shareholders withdraw, leaving less than a quorum remaining. [*Compare* **Levisa**

Oil Corp. v. Quigley, 234 S.E.2d 257 (Va. 1977)—meeting may not continue when majority shareholders withdraw to protect their interests; *with* **Duffy v. Loft, Inc.,** 151 A. 223 (Del. 1930)—meeting may continue despite withdrawal of person holding proxies for shares necessary for a quorum]

(1) Statutory view [§541]

Some statutes provide that the meeting may continue notwithstanding the withdrawal of shareholders necessary for a quorum. [Cal. Corp. Code §602(b)]

d. Informal action [§542]

Statutes permit shareholder action to be taken without a meeting, upon the unanimous *written consent* of all shareholders entitled to vote or simply upon the written consent of the number of shareholders (*e.g.,* majority) required to take the action. But in the case of nonunanimous consents, prompt notice must be given to *all* shareholders of whatever action was approved. [*See* Del. Gen. Corp. Law §228]

3. Shareholder Voting

a. Straight voting [§543]

Unless the articles otherwise provide, in all matters other than the election of directors, a shareholder who is entitled to vote has *one vote* for each share held. The shareholder vote is determined by counting the number of votes for or against each proposition. Anything over 50% of the votes cast thus controls in the absence of some greater requirement in the articles. (*See infra,* §634.)

(1) Distinguish—statutory provisions [§544]

However, to effect certain fundamental changes in the corporate structure (*e.g.,* dissolution, merger, certain amendments of articles), statutes frequently require a higher percentage of shareholder approval. (*See infra,* §§1103, 1137, 1146, 1163.)

b. Cumulative voting for directors [§545]

Straight voting allows the holders of a bare majority of the shares complete control over the minority (except where statutes require a higher percentage of shareholder approval). To assure some representation on the board for a minority holding some significant percentage of the shares, shareholders may be granted the right to vote *cumulatively* for directors. [Cal. Corp. Code §708]

(1) Mechanics [§546]

Each share is given one vote for each director to be elected. Thus, if a shareholder owns 10 voting shares, and there are five directors to be elected, the shareholder has 10 votes for each director, or a total of 50 votes. She may then "cumulate" her votes—meaning that she can cast them all for one director, some for one and some for another, or any other way she chooses.

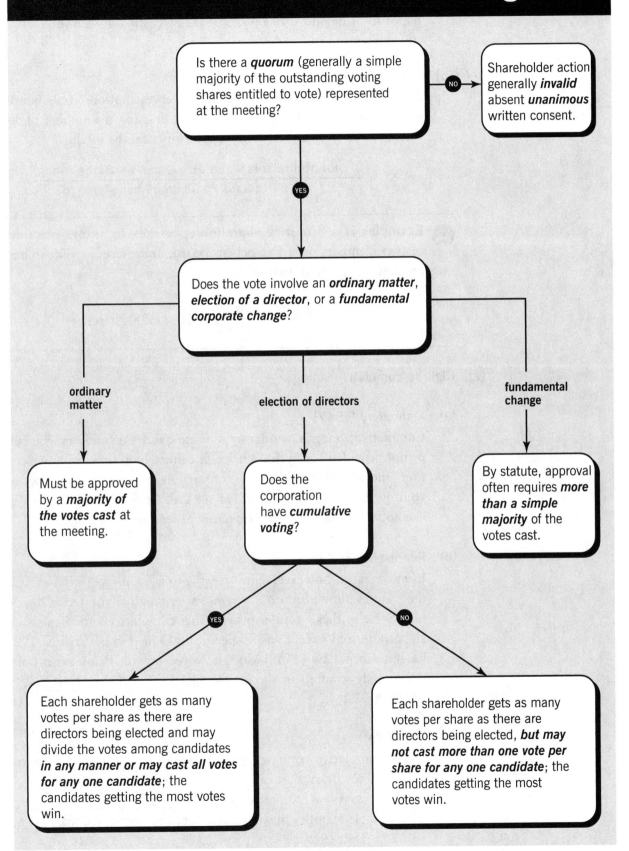

Is there a **quorum** (generally a simple majority of the outstanding voting shares entitled to vote) represented at the meeting?

NO → Shareholder action generally **invalid** absent **unanimous** written consent.

YES ↓

Does the vote involve an **ordinary matter**, **election of a director**, or a **fundamental corporate change**?

ordinary matter

Must be approved by a **majority of the votes cast** at the meeting.

election of directors

Does the corporation have **cumulative voting**?

fundamental change

By statute, approval often requires **more than a simple majority** of the votes cast.

YES → Each shareholder gets as many votes per share as there are directors being elected and may divide the votes among candidates **in any manner or may cast all votes for any one candidate**; the candidates getting the most votes win.

NO → Each shareholder gets as many votes per share as there are directors being elected, **but may not cast more than one vote per share for any one candidate**; the candidates getting the most votes win.

(a) Effect

Where five directors are to be elected, a shareholder holding approximately 17% of the shares can insure the election (and prevent the removal) of one director on the board by casting all her votes for a single director.

(b) Formula

The number of shares needed to assure representation on the board varies with the number of shares outstanding and the number of directors to be elected. The following formula can be used:

$$X > \frac{Y \text{ (no. of directors wanted)} \times Z \text{ (no. of shares voting)}}{1 + T \text{ (total no. of directors being elected)}}$$

Example: If a minority shareholder wishes to assure election of two members on a five-person board, and there are 600 shares outstanding, she needs at least—

$$X > \frac{2 \times 600}{1 + 5} \quad X > 200 \text{ shares}$$

(2) Right to cumulative voting

(a) Mandatory [§547]

Cumulative voting is mandatory in some states; *i.e.*, it exists whether or not provided for in the articles, it cannot be refused in any election, and any provision to the contrary in the articles or bylaws is void. [Cal. Corp. Code §708; *but see* Cal. Corp. Code §301.5(a)—exempts corporations listed on national securities exchanges]

(b) Permissive [§548]

In most states, however, cumulative voting is only permissive; *i.e.*, the statutes allow, *but do not require*, cumulative voting for directors. Some of these statutes provide that cumulative voting exists in all corporations except where specifically denied in the articles. [*See* Pa. Bus. Corp. Law §1758] Most, however, provide that it exists only if expressly granted in the articles. [Del. Gen. Corp. Law §214; RMBCA §7.28]

1) Note

If cumulative voting exists only where provided for in the articles (or bylaws), it can always be eliminated by whatever percentage vote is required to amend the articles (or bylaws)—often a simple majority of shares. [**Maddock v. Vorclone Corp.**, 147A. 255 (Del. 1929)]

(3) Devices to avoid cumulative voting [§549]

In corporations that have cumulative voting, the majority may attempt to curtail the minority's right to representation on the board in a number of ways, only some of which are valid.

(a) Staggering terms of directors [§550]

The fewer directors being elected at any one time, the greater the number of shares needed to assure representation (*see* formula above). Consequently, the majority may seek to amend the articles or bylaws to stagger the terms of directors (*e.g.*, only three members of nine-person board elected each year for a three-year term), in order to cut down the impact of the minority's cumulative voting rights.

1) Statutory prohibition [§551]

To prevent this, staggering of elections is prohibited by statute in some states where cumulative voting is mandatory. All directors must be elected each year. [Cal. Corp. Code §301(a)]

2) Distinguish—case law [§552]

Absent such statutes, the cases are split. [**Bohannan v. Corporation Commission**, 313 P.2d 379 (Ariz. 1957); **Humphrey v. Winous Co.**, 133 N.E.2d 780 (Ohio 1956)—permitting staggered terms; **Wolfson v. Avery**, 126 N.E.2d 701 (Ill. 1955)—statute authorizing staggered terms violated state constitutional requirement of cumulative voting]

3) Minimum directors in each class [§553]

The cumulative voting statute may require a minimum number of directors in each class, because a three-class board with one director in each would effectively negate cumulative voting. Most statutes permit no more than three classes, thus requiring that at least one-third be elected each year. A few permit four classes. [*See, e.g.*, N.Y. Bus. Corp. Law §704]

(b) Removal of directors elected by minority [§554]

If the majority shareholders could remove the directors elected by the minority, the benefits of cumulative voting would be eliminated.

1) Statutory limitation [§555]

To prevent this, many statutes provide that the majority shareholders may remove the entire board, but that no individual director can be removed during his term if the votes against his removal would be sufficient to elect him through cumulative voting. [N.Y. Bus. Corp. Law §706(c)]

a) Distinguish

Some such statutes provide that this limitation on the shareholders' power to remove a director applies only to removing an individual director *without cause*. [Del. Gen. Corp. Law §141(k)]

2) Removal for cause [§556]

In any event, some states provide that individual directors can be *removed by court action for cause* (*e.g.*, breach of fiduciary duty to the corporation), regardless of shareholder votes for retention. Some statutes authorize such action on motion of a state official or a designated percentage of the shareholders. [N.Y. Bus. Corp. Law §706(d)]

(c) Reducing size of the board [§557]

Reducing the number of board members may decrease minority representation. As the above formula indicates, the fewer directors being elected, the more shares will be needed by the minority to assure a seat on the board. For example, if there are five directors, a shareholder holding 17% of the outstanding shares may obtain representation. However, if the number of directors is reduced to three, that shareholder has no assurance of representation (because this would take more than 25%).

4. Voting by Proxy

a. Definition [§558]

A "proxy" is a power granted by a shareholder to another person to exercise the shareholder's voting rights. The term "proxy" is also sometimes applied to the person to whom the power is given, but here such a person will be referred to as a "proxy holder." A proxy holder is normally an agent of the shareholder, although in some cases the proxy holder has an independent interest in the subject matter of the proxy. (*See infra*, §562.)

b. Formalities [§559]

A proxy normally must be in writing.

c. Revocability [§560]

Like most other agency powers, a proxy is normally revocable at any time. A shareholder may revoke the proxy by notifying the proxy holder, by giving a new proxy to someone else, or by personally attending the meeting and voting the shares.

(1) Shareholder's death or incapacity [§561]

The death or incapacity of a shareholder ordinarily does not revoke a proxy, unless written notice is given to the corporation before the vote is counted. [RMBCA §7.22; Cal. Corp. Code §705(c)]

(2) Irrevocable proxies [§562]

A proxy may be made irrevocable if, but only if, it *expressly* so states and it is *"coupled with an interest"*—i.e., the proxy holder has an independent interest in the subject matter of the proxy.

(a) Interest in shares themselves [§563]

The general common law rule is that the interest required to make a proxy irrevocable must be an interest in the *shares* themselves, not in the corporation. [*In re* Chilson, 168 A. 82 (Del. 1933); *but see* Deibler v. Chas. H. Elliott Co., 81 A.2d 557 (Pa. 1951)]

e.g. **Example:** Shareholder borrows money from Creditor. Shareholder pledges her shares to Creditor as security for repayment, and gives him an irrevocable proxy to vote her shares until the loan is repaid. [150 A.L.R. 308] The interest of Creditor in the shares qualifies to make the proxy irrevocable.

e.g. **Example:** Shareholder agrees to sell her shares to P. She gives P an irrevocable proxy to vote her shares, pending a transfer of the shares on the corporation's books. The interest of P in the shares qualifies to make the proxy irrevocable.

(b) Interest in corporation [§564]

Statutes in many states now provide that certain types of interest in the *corporation*, rather than in the shares that are the subject of the proxy, can support an irrevocable proxy. These include the interests of persons who have extended credit to the corporation partly in consideration of the proxy, persons who have agreed to serve as corporate employees on condition that they receive a proxy, and parties to shareholder voting agreements. [RMBCA §7.23]

(c) Termination of interest [§565]

Even when a proxy is irrevocable because coupled with an interest, it becomes revocable when the interest that supports the proxy terminates (*e.g.*, when a loan that supports the proxy is repaid). [RMBCA §7.23]

EXAM TIP

It is important to note that a proxy will not be irrevocable just because it says that it is. If an exam question tells you that a shareholder of record gave a proxy to someone and then either tried to vote the shares personally at the meeting or gave a proxy to yet another person, you should generally find that the *shareholder* (or second proxy holder) *has the right to vote the shares*. The shareholder's showing up to vote the shares or giving a subsequent proxy *revokes* the first proxy. And this is true even if the first proxy says that it is irrevocable *unless* the first proxy was coupled with an interest (*e.g.*, the first proxy holder purchased the shares from the shareholder of record after the record date).

d. Proxy solicitation [§566]

In publicly held corporations, almost all shareholders vote by proxy. Typically, the management of a publicly held corporation solicits proxies from the shareholders, both for reelection of directors and to approve various types of actions that require shareholder approval. Occasionally, insurgent groups attempt to obtain control of the corporation through a proxy solicitation.

(1) State regulation [§567]

Prior to the 1930s, state courts sometimes invalidated a proxy solicitation, and set aside corporate elections pursuant to the solicitation, if the solicitation misrepresented material facts or was grossly deficient in disclosing relevant information. Generally, however, state regulation of proxy solicitation was inadequate. This led to federal regulation, in the form of section 14(a) of the Securities Exchange Act of 1934 and the federal proxy rules (*see* below). State law has also improved in this area. The Delaware courts, for example, now hold that in self-interested transactions involving a controlling shareholder, if the controlling shareholder seeks approval of the transaction by a vote of the minority shareholders, it has a duty to disclose all material facts. [**Lynch v. Vickers Energy Corp.,** 383 A.2d 278 (Del. 1977); **Weinberger v. UOP, Inc.,** 457 A.2d 701 (Del. 1983)]

(2) Federal proxy rules [§568]

Section 14(a) of the 1934 Act provides that it is unlawful for any person, in contravention of SEC rules and regulations, to solicit any proxy with respect to any security registered under section 12 of the 1934 Act. Acting under section 14(a), the SEC has adopted the proxy rules, which regulate the solicitation of proxies. [Exchange Act Rules 14a-1 *et seq.*]

(a) Securities covered [§569]

The federal proxy rules apply to any solicitation of proxies, oral or written, in connection with any security registered under section 12 of the 1934 Act. Section 12 requires registration of securities traded on national securities exchanges or equity securities that are held by at least 500 persons and issued by a corporation having total assets exceeding $10 million (*see supra*, §364).

1) Nonmanagement solicitation of ten or fewer shareholders [§570]

The proxy rules do not apply to a solicitation of 10 or fewer shareholders made on behalf of persons other than management. [Exchange Act Rule 14a-2]

(b) "Proxy" and "solicitation" defined [§571]

The definitions of "proxy" and "solicitation" are extremely broad. "Proxy" means "every proxy, consent, or authorization within the meaning of section 14a of the Act. The consent or authorization may take the form of failure to object or to dissent." [Exchange Act Rule 14a-1(f)] "Solicitation" includes: (i) a request for a proxy; (ii) a request to execute, not to execute, or to revoke a proxy; or (iii) furnishing a form of proxy or other communication to shareholders under circumstances reasonably calculated to result in procuring, withholding, or revoking a proxy. [Exchange Act Rule 14a-1(l)]

1) Continuous plan [§572]

These definitions have been given a very expansive interpretation that goes well beyond a formal request for a proxy. For example, a letter sent to shareholders seeking authorization to inspect the corporation's shareholder list constituted a solicitation of proxies under the proxy rules, because it was part of "a continuous plan" intended to end in a solicitation of proxies and to prepare the way for success in that solicitation. [**Studebaker Corp. v. Gittlin**, 360 F.2d 692 (2d Cir. 1966)]

2) Safe harbor for certain communications between shareholders [§573]

A safe harbor provision under the proxy rules excludes communications between shareholders from the definition of "solicitation" if the communications (i) do not solicit proxy voting authority and (ii) are sent by persons who have no material interest in the solicitation other than their interest as shareholders. [Exchange Act Rule 14a-2(b)(1)]

a) Communications about proxy voting [§574]

Under this provision, shareholders—particularly institutional investors—may communicate with each other about proxy voting without the risk that those communications would be deemed a solicitation under the sweeping definition of that term in the proxy rules. [*See* Securities Exchange Act Release No. 34-31326 (1992)]

3) Broadcast or published communications [§575]

A person who has filed a definitive proxy statement (*i.e.,* an informational statement that must be distributed to the shareholders under the proxy rules) with the SEC can broadcast or publish communications in advertisements, speeches, or columns without having first sent copies of the definitive proxy statement to those to whom the communications are distributed. [Exchange Act Rule 14a-3(f)]

4) Relaxed preliminary filing requirements [§576]

A preliminary filing of soliciting materials is not required except for the proxy and the proxy statement. This allows newspaper ads and similar materials to be published without prior review by the SEC. [Exchange Act Rule 14a-6]

(c) Scope of proxy rules [§577]

The proxy rules serve five different purposes:

1) Transactional disclosure [§578]

One purpose of the proxy rules is to require full disclosure in connection with transactions that shareholders are being asked to approve, such as mergers, certificate amendments, or election of directors. This purpose is accomplished in the first instance by rule 14a-3 and schedule 14A. Rule 14a-3 provides that no solicitation of proxies that is subject to the proxy rules may be made unless the person being solicited "is concurrently furnished or has previously been furnished with a written proxy statement containing the information specified in schedule 14A." Schedule 14A, in turn, lists in detail the information that must be furnished when specified types of transactions are to be acted upon by the shareholders. Rule 14a-3 and schedule 14A are backed up by rule 14a-9, which provides that no solicitation subject to the proxy rules may contain any statement that is false or misleading with respect to any material fact or omit a material fact.

2) Periodic disclosure [§579]

The proxy rules also require certain forms of annual disclosure. Much of this disclosure is only very loosely related to any specific action that the shareholders are asked to vote upon.

a) Annual report [§580]

For example, rule 14a-3 provides that when proxies for the election of directors are solicited on behalf of a corporation that is subject to the proxy rules, the corporation must send an annual report to its shareholders, either in advance of or concurrently with the proxy statement. This annual report to shareholders must be distinguished from the annual report on form 10-K that the corporation must file with the SEC. The contents of the annual report to shareholders are governed by rule 14a-3. The report must include, among other things, the corporation's financial statements; selected financial data; and management's discussion and analysis of the corporation's financial condition and results of operations ("MD & A"). Either the annual report or the proxy statement must prominently feature an undertaking to furnish a copy of the form 10-K to any shareholder, without charge, upon written request.

b) Proxy statement [§581]

In addition to transactional disclosure and the information that must be provided in the annual report, the proxy rules require a great deal of nontransactional information in the proxy statement.

1/ Compensation and conflicts of interest [§582]

Under schedule 14A, items 7 and 8, the proxy statement for an annual meeting at which directors are being elected must disclose the compensation of the CEO and the four most highly paid executives and the executive officers as a group (including not only salary, but also bonuses, deferred compensation, stock options, and the like), and significant conflict-of-interest transactions during the corporation's last fiscal year involving, among others, directors, executive officers, and 5% beneficial owners.

2/ Committees [§583]

The proxy statement also must disclose a variety of information concerning the corporation's audit, compensation, and nominating committees.

a/ In general [§584]

The proxy statement must state whether or not the corporation has standing audit, compensation, and nominating committees, or committees performing similar functions. If the corporation has such committees, the proxy statement must identify each committee member, state the number of committee meetings held by each committee during the last fiscal year, and describe briefly the functions performed by the committees.

b/ Audit committee [§585]

In connection with the audit committee, the proxy statement must discuss the independence of the members of the committee and must report, among other things, whether the committee has reviewed and discussed the audited financial statements with management and whether the audit committee has a written charter. (If it does, the charter must be included in the proxy statement at least once every three years.) The proxy statement must also disclose that the board of directors has determined that the committee either has or does not have a member who is a financial expert.

c/ Compensation committee [§586]

In connection with the compensation committee, the proxy statement must report, among other things, the committee's compensation policies applicable to the corporation's executive officers, including the specific relationship of corporate performance to executive compensation and the bases for the CEO's compensation, including the factors and criteria upon which the CEO's compensation was based.

d/ Nominating committee [§587]

If the corporation does not have a nominating committee, or a committee performing similar functions, the proxy statement must state the basis for the board's view that it is appropriate for the corporation not to have such a committee. If the corporation does have a nominating committee, the proxy statement must report, among other things, whether the nominating committee has a charter (and if so must either make a copy of the charter on its website or include a copy of the charter in the proxy statement at least once every three years). The proxy statement must also discuss the independence of the members of the nominating committee.

3/ Information required when corporation not soliciting proxies [§588]

In the case of an annual meeting at which directors are to be elected, a corporation with securities registered under section 12 must distribute an annual report and certain other information (such as information relating to conflict-of-interest transactions and compensation), even if the corporation is not soliciting proxies. [Securities Exchange Act §14(c), Regulation 14C, and Schedule 14C]

3) Proxy contests [§589]

Proxy rule 14a-11 regulates proxy contests, in which insurgents try to oust incumbent directors. Basically, rule 14a-11 is an adaptation of the salient concepts of other proxy rules to the special circumstances of a proxy fight. Its main bite is to require the filing of certain information by insurgents.

4) Communications with other shareholders [§590]

Proxy rules 14a-7 and 14a-8 provide mechanisms through which shareholders can communicate with each other.

5) Mechanics of proxy voting [§591]

Still another purpose of the proxy rules is to regulate the mechanics of proxy voting itself. This is done, somewhat indirectly, through rule 14a-4, which governs the form of proxy (*see infra*).

EXAM TIP   **gilbert**

Proxy issues come up from time to time in essay questions. Be sure to remember the basics. If a corporation calls for a shareholder vote on a matter, proxies will be solicited, and if the corporation's shares are registered under section12, ***all material facts concerning the matter must be disclosed***. The corporation's annual report must also be delivered to shareholders if directors are to be elected.

(d) Form of proxy [§592]

Under the proxy rules, a form of proxy providing for the election of directors must set forth the names of persons nominated for directors. The form of proxy must also clearly provide the means for a shareholder to withhold authority to vote for each nominee. A proxy executed by the shareholder in such a way as not to withhold authority to vote for the election of any nominee will be deemed to grant such authority, provided that the proxy so states in boldface type. [Exchange Act Rule 14a-4]

(e) Shareholder proposals [§593]

Under the proxy rules, the corporation must include shareholder proposals in the corporate proxy materials, provided certain conditions are met. [Exchange Act Rule 14a-8] To be eligible under rule 14a-8, the proponent must have held continuously for at least one year at least 1% or $2,000 in market value of securities entitled to be voted on the proposal. The proposal and its supporting statement may not exceed 500 words.

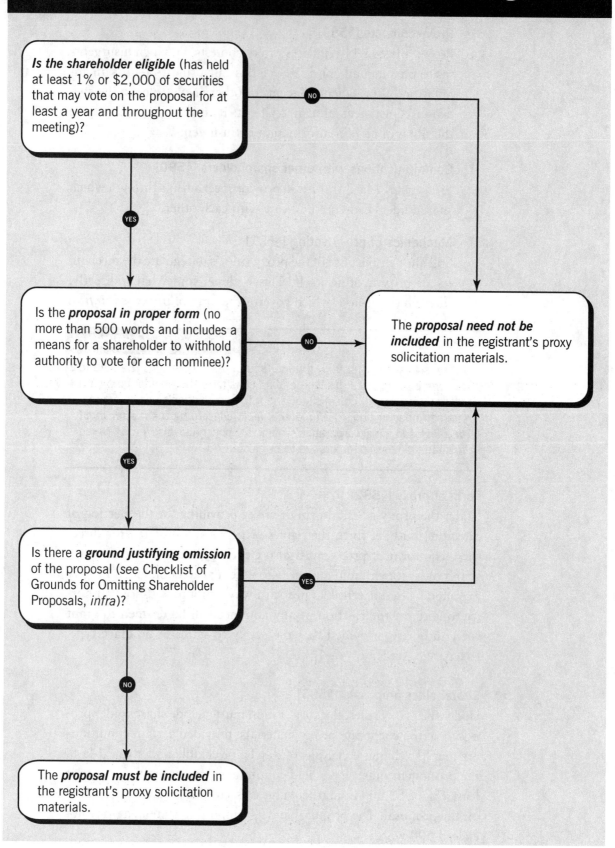

Is the shareholder eligible (has held at least 1% or $2,000 of securities that may vote on the proposal for at least a year and throughout the meeting)?

NO →

YES ↓

Is the **proposal in proper form** (no more than 500 words and includes a means for a shareholder to withhold authority to vote for each nominee)?

NO →

YES ↓

Is there a **ground justifying omission** of the proposal (*see* Checklist of Grounds for Omitting Shareholder Proposals, *infra*)?

YES →

NO ↓

The **proposal must be included** in the registrant's proxy solicitation materials.

The **proposal need not be included** in the registrant's proxy solicitation materials.

1) **Exceptions [§594]**

The corporation is not required to include a shareholder proposal under the following circumstances:

a) **Not proper subject of shareholder action under state law [§595]**

If, under the laws of the state in which the corporation is incorporated, the proposal is not a proper subject for action by shareholders, the corporation is not required to include the shareholder proposal. Whether a proposal is a proper subject for action by shareholders will depend on the applicable state law. A proposal that mandates certain action by the board of directors may not be a proper subject matter for shareholder action, while a proposal recommending or requesting such action may be a proper subject. [Exchange Act Rule 14a-8(i)(1)]

b) **Violation of law [§596]**

If the shareholder proposal would require the corporation to violate state or federal law or the law of a foreign jurisdiction to which the corporation is subject, the corporation need not include it. [Exchange Act Rule 14a-8(i)(2)]

c) **False or misleading statement [§597]**

If the shareholder proposal or supporting statement is false or misleading, the corporation does not have to include it. [Exchange Act Rule 14a-8(i)(3)]

d) **Redress of personal claim or grievance [§598]**

If the shareholder proposal concerns the redress of a personal claim or grievance against the corporation or any other person, or is designed to result in a benefit to the shareholder or to further a personal interest that is not shared with the other shareholders at large, the corporation need not include it. [Exchange Act Rule 14a-8(i)(4)]

e) **Relates to operations accounting for less than five percent of assets or business [§599]**

If the shareholder proposal relates to operations that account for less than 5% of the corporation's total assets and less than 5% of its net earnings and gross sales, and is not otherwise significantly related to the registrant's business, the corporation does not have to include it. [Exchange Act Rule 14a-8(i)(5)] *Note:* In adopting the 5% standard, the SEC stated that shareholder proposals must be included in the proxy statement, notwithstanding their failure to reach the 5% threshold, "if a significant relationship to the issuer's business is demonstrated on the face of the resolution or supporting statement." [Exchange Act Release No. 19,135 (1982)] The meaning of "significantly related" is not limited to economic significance.

Example: A shareholder submitted a proposal calling on the board to appoint a committee to report to the shareholders on whether the production methods of a supplier of pate de foie gras caused undue distress, pain, or suffering to the animals involved and, if so, whether further distribution of the product should be discontinued until a more humane production method was developed. The corporation had annual revenues of $141 million, annual profits of $6 million, and assets of $78 million. Its sales of pate de foie gras were $79,000, gave rise to a net loss of $3,121, and the corporation had only $34,000 in assets related to pate. Thus, none of the company's net earnings, and less than .05% of its assets, were implicated by the shareholder proposal. The court held, however, that in light of the ethical and social significance of the shareholder proposal, the shareholder had shown a likelihood of prevailing on the merits with regard to the issue of whether the proposal was "otherwise significantly related" to the corporation's business. [**Lovenheim v. Iroquois Brands, Inc.,** 618 F. Supp. 554 (D.D.C. 1985)]

Example: A shareholder proposal requested that a corporation's board initiate a policy mandating no further purchases of tobacco stock, and that the corporation divest itself of all tobacco stocks. The SEC staff concluded that the proposal was "otherwise significantly related" to the corporation's business, and was not a matter relating to ordinary business operations.

f) Other exceptions [§600]

The corporation need not include a shareholder proposal in its proxy statement if:

(i) The proposal deals with a *matter beyond the registrant's power* to effectuate;

(ii) The proposal deals with a matter relating to the *conduct of ordinary business operations*;

(iii) The proposal relates to an *election to office*;

CHECKLIST OF GROUNDS FOR OMITTING SHAREHOLDER PROPOSALS

gilbert

MANAGEMENT MAY EXCLUDE A SHAREHOLDER'S PROXY SOLICITATION PROPOSAL IF THE PROPOSAL IS:

- ☑ *Not a proper subject* for shareholder action

- ☑ One that would require the registrant to *violate any law*

- ☑ *False or misleading*

- ☑ Related to *redress of a personal claim* not shared with other shareholders in general

- ☑ Related to *operations that involve less than 5%* of assets, earnings, and sales and is otherwise not significantly related to the corporation's business

- ☑ Related to *issues over which the registrant has no power to control*

- ☑ Related to conduct of the registrant's *ordinary business operations* not involving important political or social issues

- ☑ Related to *election to the registrant's board*

- ☑ *Counter to a proposal to be submitted by the registrant*

- ☑ Moot because the corporation has *already substantially implemented the proposal*

- ☑ *Substantially duplicative of an earlier proposal*

- ☑ Related to the *amount of a dividend*

- ☑ *Substantially the same as a proposal previously rejected* by shareholders at a previous meeting (but the rules vary according to the vote received at those previous meetings)

       (iv) The proposal conflicts with *a proposal to be submitted by the corporation* at the same meeting;

       (v) The corporation has already *substantially implemented* the proposal;

       (vi) The proposal is substantially *duplicative* of a proposal submitted to the corporation by another shareholder that will be included in the corporation's proxy material for the meeting;

       (vii) The proposal relates to *specific amounts of cash or stock dividends*; or

       (viii) The proposal deals with substantially the *same subject matter as a prior proposal* that was submitted *within the previous five years*, is submitted for a meeting to be held within three years of its last submission, and either: (i) the proposal was submitted at only one meeting during the previous five years and received less than 3% of the votes, or (ii) the proposal was submitted at two meetings during the previous five years and received less than 6% of votes at the time of its second submission, or (iii) the proposal was submitted at three or more meetings during the previous five years and received less than 10% of votes at the time of its last submission.

       [Exchange Act Rule 14a-8(i)(6) - (13)]

2) Private right of action [§601]

A shareholder whose proposal is rejected by a corporation on the ground that the proposal can be excluded under one of the exceptions to rule 14a-8 can bring a private right of action against the corporation to contest the corporation's rejection.

(f) Providing shareholder lists or mailing communications [§602]

A shareholder who wishes to communicate with the other shareholders is entitled either (i) to be supplied with a list of shareholders, or (ii) to have his communication included with the corporate proxy materials if the shareholder pays the cost. (With very limited exceptions, the choice between (i) and (ii) is the corporation's, not the shareholder's.) [Exchange Act Rule 14a-7]

(g) Remedies for violation of proxy rules

1) Administrative remedies [§603]

The SEC may institute suit for violation of section 14(a) of the proxy rules (*e.g.*, to enjoin the solicitation, to bar a party from voting improperly obtained proxies, or to order a new election).

2) Private suits [§604]

The proxy rules also create an implied private right of action in the individual investor. [**J.I. Case Co. v. Borak,** 377 U.S. 426 (1964)] Typically, such actions are brought under rule 14a-9, which prohibits solicitation by means of any proxy statement, form of proxy, notice of meeting, or other communication, written or oral, containing any statement that is false or misleading with respect to any material fact, or that omits to state any material fact necessary to make the statements therein not false or misleading.

a) Materiality [§605]

To establish materiality for purposes of a rule 14a-9 action, there must be "a showing of a substantial likelihood that, under all the circumstances, the omitted fact would have assumed actual significance in the deliberations of the reasonable shareholder"—or, to put it differently, a showing of "a substantial likelihood that the disclosure of the omitted fact would have been viewed by the reasonable investor as having significantly altered the 'total mix' of information made available." [**TSC Industries, Inc. v. Northway, Inc.,** 426 U.S. 438 (1976)] It is not enough simply to show that the information "might" have been considered important by a reasonable shareholder, because such a standard could force management to disclose so much trivial data that the real issues in the proxy solicitation could be obscured. [**TSC Industries, Inc. v. Northway, Inc.,** *supra*]

Example: The board of C Corp. solicits proxies from C's shareholders for approval of a proposed merger with D Corp. The fact that C's directors, who were recommending approval of the merger, were nominees of D, would be material, because reasonable shareholders would likely take such fact into consideration in deciding whether to follow the directors' recommendation. [**Mills v. Electric Auto-Lite Co.,** 396 U.S. 375 (1970)]

Compare: Where full disclosure has been made concerning the extent of a parent corporation's voting control over a subsidiary, mere failure to disclose that officers of the parent are also serving as officers of the subsidiary is not necessarily material, because in light of the disclosures made as to the parent's voting control, the officers' status is not necessarily a matter that a reasonable shareholder would have considered important in voting on the proposed merger. [**TSC Industries, Inc. v. Northway, Inc.**, *supra*]

b) Neutralization of misleading statements [§606]

A materially misleading statement concerning an issue may be neutralized, for liability purposes, by correct statements about the issue elsewhere in the proxy statement. However, this will not invariably be the case. "[N]ot every mixture with the true will neutralize the deceptive. If it would take a financial analyst to spot the tension between the one and the other, whatever is misleading will remain materially so, and liability should follow." [**Virginia Bankshares, Inc. v. Sandberg**, 501 U.S. 1083 (1991)]

c) Statements of reasons and beliefs [§607]

A knowingly false statement of reasons, opinions, or beliefs in a proxy statement—such as a knowingly false statement that the board believes a proposed transaction is fair—can be made the basis of liability under the proxy rules (including private actions), even though the statement is made in conclusory terms. [**Virginia Bankshares, Inc. v. Sandberg**, *supra*] Of course, the statements must be material, but statements concerning the views of the board on a proposed transaction will normally be material.

1/ Qualification [§608]

A knowingly false statement of reasons, opinions, or beliefs is actionable only when, in addition to being a false or misleading description of the true views of the person who makes it, the statement is *objectively false* or misleading. For example, if a proxy statement says that the board believes a proposed transaction to be fair, and the board does not have that subjective belief, but the transaction is objectively fair, the statement, although false, would not be actionable. The reason for this qualification is a concern that "to recognize liability on mere disbelief or undisclosed motive without any demonstration that the proxy statement was false or misleading about its subject could lead to strike suits and frivolous litigation." [*Id.*]

a/ Note

This qualification on the basic holding of *Virginia Bankshares* is unlikely to have much practical significance, because it would be rare to find a case with evidence of disbelief or undisclosed motivation but no proof that the statement is objectively defective.

d) Causation [§609]

A false or misleading statement in a proxy statement will not give rise to a private action unless it is the cause of a shareholder vote that the proxy statement solicits. However, a showing of materiality normally satisfies the causation requirement. Accordingly, where a shareholder seeks to set aside or enjoin a transaction on the ground that shareholder approval was solicited by a proxy statement that involved misstatements or omissions, she need do nothing more to prove causation than to prove materiality. [**Mills v. Electric Auto-Lite Co.**, *supra*; **Gaines v. Haughton**, 645 F.2d 761 (9th Cir. 1981), *cert. denied*, 454 U.S. 1145 (1982)]

1/ Where management or parent controls majority of stock [§610]

If the management or a parent owns or controls a majority of the stock, so that it can cause shareholder approval of the relevant transaction without any votes from the minority, false or misleading statements in a proxy statement will not normally give rise to liability in a private action by the minority shareholders. The theory is that the false statements could not have caused a loss to the minority, because the transaction would have been approved even without their votes. [**Virginia Bankshares, Inc. v. Sandberg**, *supra*, §607]

a/ Exception [§611]

In *Virginia Bankshares,* the Supreme Court left open whether minority shareholders would have a cause of action, when their votes were not necessary for a transaction, if the false or misleading statements in the proxy statement led the minority shareholders to lose a state remedy (*e.g.*, led them to forgo the exercise of appraisal rights). In **Wilson v. Great American Industries, Inc.**, 979 F.2d 924 (2d Cir. 1992), the court held that minority shareholders did have a right of action in such cases. [*See also* **Howing Co. v. Nationwide Corp.**, 972 F.2d 700 (6th Cir. 1992), *cert. denied*, 507 U.S. 1004 (1993)]

e) Standing [§612]

Even a shareholder who did not grant a proxy on the basis of a misleading solicitation has standing to challenge the solicitation. The injury that a shareholder suffers from corporate action pursuant to a deceptive proxy solicitation flows from the damage done to the corporation, rather than from the damage inflicted directly upon the shareholder. The damage suffered results not from the deceit practiced on the shareholder alone, but rather from the deceit practiced on the shareholders as a group. [**Cowin v. Bresler**, 741 F.2d 410 (D.C. Cir. 1984); **Stahl v. Gibralter Financial Corp.**, 967 F.2d 335 (9th Cir. 1992)]

f) **Fault required [§613]**

Under rule 10b-5 scienter is required, so that mere negligence will not suffice as the basis of a private action to impose liability. [**Ernst & Ernst v. Hochfelder**, *supra*, §373] It is unclear whether mere negligence is sufficient to impose liability in an action for violation of rule 14a-9 of the proxy rules. In **Shidler v. All American Life & Financial Corp.**, 775 F.2d 917 (8th Cir. 1985), the Eighth Circuit held that the plaintiff in a private action under section 14(a) had to establish *some fault*—i.e., section 14(a) does not create strict liability for misrepresentations or misleading statements. In **Gould v. American-Hawaiian Steamship Co.**, 535 F.2d 761 (3d Cir. 1976), the Third Circuit held that negligence is sufficient, on the ground that the language of section 14(a) of the 1934 Act does not suggest a scienter requirement. [*See also* **Gerstle v. Gamble-Skogmo, Inc.**, 478 F.2d 1281 (2d Cir. 1973)] However, in **Adams v. Standard Knitting Mills, Inc.**, 623 F.2d 422 (6th Cir. 1980), the Sixth Circuit held that scienter must be established in a suit against accountants under rule 14a-9, and strongly intimated that it would apply a scienter requirement in all rule 14a-9 suits.

PROXY RULE VIOLATIONS—SUMMARY OF CRUCIAL ELEMENTS IN A PRIVATE CASE **gilbert**

A PRIVATE PLAINTIFF MUST SHOW THE FOLLOWING IN ORDER TO BRING A PRIVATE CAUSE OF ACTION FOR VIOLATION OF THE PROXY RULES:

☑ *Materiality*—A substantial likelihood that disclosure of the truth or an omitted fact would have been viewed by the reasonable investor as having significantly altered the "total mix" of information available.

☑ *Causation*—The false or misleading statement caused the shareholder vote that the proxy solicited; usually satisfied merely by showing materiality.

☑ *Standing*—Must have been a shareholder when the vote was taken, but need not have granted a proxy on the basis of the misleading solicitation.

☑ *Fault*—At least negligence is required; some courts require scienter.

g) Fairness no defense [§614]

A materially misleading solicitation entitles the complainant to relief regardless of whether the matter acted upon was fair to the corporation and its shareholders. Otherwise, a judicial finding of fairness could be used to bypass the shareholders' right to make an informed choice after full disclosure. [**Mills v. Electric Auto-Lite Co.**, *supra*]

h) Nature of relief available [§615]

The federal courts are empowered to award whatever relief will effectuate the purposes of the statute, which may include both prospective and retroactive remedies. [**J.I. Case Co. v. Borak**, *supra*, §604]

1/ Rescission [§616]

If necessary and otherwise equitable, a court may rescind an action that was approved by the shareholders as a result of a misleading proxy solicitation (*e.g.*, by setting aside a corporate merger). [**J.I. Case Co. v. Borak**, *supra*]

2/ Monetary damages [§617]

Monetary damages are also recoverable if they can be shown. [**Mills v. Electric Auto-Lite Co.**, *supra*]

(h) Jurisdiction [§618]

Federal courts have exclusive jurisdiction in any suit for violation of the proxy rules. Any related claim for violation of state law may be joined with the federal claim under the doctrine of pendent jurisdiction.

e. Expenses incurred in proxy contest [§619]

Because the expenses involved in a large-scale proxy fight may be extremely large, the question whether corporate funds may be used to reimburse those expenses is extremely important.

(1) Reimbursement of management's expenses [§620]

The corporation may properly pay the normal expense of preparing and soliciting proxies to obtain a quorum for the annual meeting. In the event of a proxy contest, the corporation may also properly reimburse reasonable amounts expended by management, as long as the matter in controversy is one of corporate policy, rather than one of personnel (*i.e.*, one in which management seeks simply to retain its office). [**Steinberg v. Adams,** 90 F. Supp. 604 (S.D.N.Y. 1950)] Management may use corporate funds to fully inform the shareholders concerning the relevant issues and to protect the corporation against a "raid" by wealthy insurgents. [**Rosenfeld v. Fairchild Engine & Airplane Corp.**, 309 N.Y. 168 (1955); 51 A.L.R.2d 860]

(2) Insurgents' expenses [§621]

Unlike management, insurgents do not have a right to reimbursement of their proxy expenses, even if they win. However, the corporation can voluntarily reimburse the reasonable expenses of insurgents who win a proxy contest involving policy (rather than personnel), on the ground that they have conferred a benefit on the corporation, at least if the shareholders ratify the reimbursement. [**Rosenfeld v. Fairchild Engine & Airplane Corp.**, *supra*]

5. Other Methods to Combine Votes for Control—Close Corporations [§622]

Various voting devices may be used by shareholders (particularly in close corporations) to assure control of corporate policies.

a. Shareholder voting agreements [§623]

Shareholders (often those owning a majority of the stock) may agree with other shareholders to vote in a specified way for a specified period of time. They may agree for a variety of reasons—*e.g.*, as a condition of the other shareholders investing in the corporation. Such agreements usually concern voting for the election of certain directors, but may also cover other matters subject to shareholder vote (amendment of the articles, dissolution, etc.).

(1) Pooling agreements [§624]

A "pooling agreement" is a particular kind of voting agreement whereby shareholders (none of whom usually owns a majority of the stock) agree to vote their shares together in a specified way (or as the majority of them decides) for a specified period.

(2) Validity of shareholder voting agreements [§625]

Early cases often refused to enforce shareholder voting agreements (particularly if all shareholders were not parties to the agreement), on the ground that shareholders could not irrevocably separate their voting rights from their ownership rights. However, shareholder voting agreements are generally upheld today, as long as they are made for a proper purpose and work no fraud on creditors or other stockholders. [**E.K. Buck Retail Stores v. Harkert**, 62 N.W.2d 288 (Neb. 1954)]

(a) Purpose of agreement [§626]

Shareholders generally may vote their shares as they please and are permitted to combine their votes to serve certain of their own purposes, *e.g.*, to elect themselves as directors.

(b) Consideration [§627]

Pooling agreements have sometimes been challenged for lack of consideration. [**Roberts v. Whitson**, 188 S.W.2d 875 (Tex. 1945)] Most courts, however, find sufficient consideration in the shareholders' exchange of mutual promises to vote their shares in a specified way. Alternatively, pooling agreements have been upheld on the theory that the combining of votes for control gives each shareholder a sufficient "interest" in the shares of the other that their agreement is enforceable as a grant of an *irrevocable proxy* (*supra*, §§562-565). [**Abercrombie v. Davies,** 130 A.2d 338 (Del. 1957)]

(c) Statutory authority [§628]

Statutes today frequently authorize shareholders to enter into agreements respecting the voting of their shares. [Cal. Corp. Code §706(a)—applicable to close corporations only; N.Y. Bus. Corp. Law §620(a)] Some statutes limit the duration of such agreements.

(d) Agreements limited to shareholder action [§629]

The agreements under discussion concern only shareholder action (*e.g.*, voting for directors, amendment of articles, etc.). The validity of shareholder agreements insofar as they seek to bind the parties in voting as directors is considered below (*see infra*, §§636-641).

(3) Self-executing agreements [§630]

Sometimes, the parties to a pooling agreement may attempt to make it "self-executing" by requiring each shareholder to execute and deposit a *proxy* with an agent to vote the shares.

(a) But note

This self-executing plan may not work if any of the shareholders decides to revoke her proxy. Even though she may have expressly agreed not to revoke, her proxy may be held revocable because it is not coupled with "an interest." (Some courts have not regarded a pooling agreement as creating a sufficient "interest" in each other's shares to render the proxy irrevocable [*In re* **Chilson,** *supra,* §563], but this approach has been modified by statute in a number of states (*see supra*, §564).) Consequently, the other shareholders will have to sue for enforcement of the pooling agreement; they cannot rely on the proxy.

(b) And note

Even where the proxies are held irrevocable, the self-executing arrangement may be viewed as a *voting trust*, in which event it must comply with special requirements (below). [**Abercrombie v. Davies,** *supra*] Statutes in some states will prevent this result. [*See, e.g.*, Cal. Corp. Code §706(c)—shareholders' voting agreements shall not constitute voting trusts]

(4) Remedy for breach [§631]

If the voting agreement is enforceable, the remedy usually sought in the event of breach is *specific performance*, *i.e.*, a court order compelling the shareholder to vote her shares as agreed. Equitable relief would appear to be justified on the ground that the legal remedy (damages) is usually inadequate.

(a) Statutes [§632]

Statutes in many states expressly authorize specific performance of shareholder voting agreements [*See, e.g.,* Cal. Corp. Code §706(a); RMBCA §7.31(b)]

(b) When fewer than all shareholders participate [§633]

Absent statutory authorization, however, some courts have refrained from granting specific performance of pooling agreements to which *fewer than all* of the shareholders were parties. [**Ringling Bros.-Barnum & Bailey Combined Shows, Inc. v. Ringling,** 53 A.2d 441 (Del. 1947); *but see* **Weil v. Berseth,** 220 A.2d 456 (Conn. 1966)—contra]

b. Agreements requiring greater-than-majority approval [§634]

Minority shareholders in a close corporation may seek to achieve a certain degree of control (or, more precisely, a veto power) by obtaining the agreement of the other shareholders (in a contract, or through a charter or bylaw provision) that no shareholder action may be taken without a unanimous (or some percentage greater than majority) vote.

(1) Modern trend [§635]

The modern trend of judicial decisions permits such devices. [*See, e.g.,* **Katcher v. Ohsman,** 97 A.2d 180 (N.J. 1953)] Many statutes now expressly authorize greater-than-majority voting requirements if provided for in the articles of incorporation. [N.Y. Bus. Corp. Law §616—*reversing* **Benintendi v. Kenton Hotel, Inc.,** 294 N.Y. 112 (1945); RMBCA §7.27]

c. Shareholder agreements binding votes as directors [§636]

In addition to agreeing how they will vote as shareholders, the shareholders of a close corporation may seek to control more detailed matters of corporate policy, *e.g.,* who will be the corporate officers, what will be the salaries, how much will be paid in dividends. These are "management" questions, traditionally committed to the board of directors (*supra,* §183).

(1) Less-than-unanimous agreements [§637]

When fewer than all the shareholders are parties to agreements seeking to bind the directors, most courts have held them *unenforceable*, reasoning that corporate directors are charged with fiduciary duties to the corporation and any agreement that seeks to restrict or limit their actions as directors is therefore void. It is contrary to public policy to have a "passive board." [**McQuade v. Stoneham & McGraw,** *supra,* §193]

(a) But note

Some more recent decisions, recognizing the special nature and needs of close corporations, have upheld such nonunanimous agreements—at least where no nonparty shareholder claimed prejudice to herself as a result. [**Galler v. Galler,** *supra,* §194; **Glazer v. Glazer,** 374 F.2d 390 (5th Cir. 1967)]

(2) Unanimous agreements [§638]

When all the shareholders are parties to such agreements, courts have been quicker to uphold them—at least when no damage to creditors or the public has been shown. [**Clark v. Dodge,** *supra,* §193] But even unanimous agreements have been held unenforceable if they involve "substantial impingements" on the discretion of the board. [**Long Park, Inc. v. Trenton-New Brunswick Theatres Co.,** *supra,* §193]

(3) Statutes [§639]

In more recent decades, a number of special statutes applicable to close corporations have validated shareholder agreements that bind the discretion of directors. Some require that such agreements be unanimous [N.Y. Bus. Corp. Law §620(b)], while others do not [Del. Gen. Corp. Law §§350, 354].

(a) Notice [§640]

A number of these statutes require that these agreements be included in a provision of the articles of incorporation. [*See, e.g.,* N.Y. Bus. Corp. Law §620(a)] Some go further and require that the provision be noted conspicuously on all share certificates. [N.Y. Bus. Corp. Law §620(g)]

1) Estoppel [§641]

It has been held that a shareholder who promised, but failed, to fulfill these statutory requirements is estopped from denying the validity of a shareholder agreement to which he was a party. [**Zion v. Kurtz,** 50 N.Y.2d 92 (1980)]

d. Voting trusts [§642]

A voting trust is another device employed by shareholders to assure control. Each shareholder transfers *legal title* of her shares to a trustee, in return for a transferable "voting trust certificate" that evidences her equitable ownership of the shares involved and carries the right to dividends and other distributions of assets. Because the right to vote follows legal title, the trustee has the voting right for the shares involved for the life of the trust.

(1) Formalities [§643]

Statutes in most states require such trust agreements to be in writing, filed with the corporation, and open to inspection by all shareholders and owners of voting trust certificates. [Del. Gen. Corp. Law §218(a)]

(a) Failure to comply with statutory requirements [§644]

Although some courts have invalidated voting trusts that do not comply with the statute, others have nonetheless enforced voting trust agreements when the policy of the voting trust statute has been fulfilled.

[**Oceanic Exploration Co. v. Grynberg,** 428 A.2d 1 (Del. 1980)—all shareholders had notice of the voting trust agreement even though it was not filed with corporation]

(2) Duration [§645]

Most statutes limit the period for which such trusts may be created (the usual term being 10 years). [RMBCA §7.30(b)] Others have no time limits. [Del. Gen. Corp. Law §218]

(a) Extensions [§646]

Most statutes permit a voting trust to be extended for additional terms—usually on condition that only the assenting shareholders shall be so bound. [RMBCA §7.30(c)]

(3) Authority of voting trustees [§647]

The scope of the trustees' authority to vote depends on the terms of the voting trust agreement. This almost always extends to voting for the election of directors. But absent explicit authority in the voting trust agreement, most courts hesitate to allow the trustees to vote on such extraordinary matters as sale of all of the corporation's assets, dissolution of the corporation, or termination or extension of the voting trust. [**Brown v. McLanahan,** 148 F.2d 703 (4th Cir. 1945); *compare* **Clarke Memorial College v. Monaghan Land Co.,** 257 A.2d 234 (Del. 1969)]

(a) Fiduciary duty [§648]

In any event, voting trustees are held to a fiduciary duty to the beneficiaries of the trust in exercising their authority. [**Brown v. McLanahan,** *supra*]

(4) Rights of holder of voting trust certificate [§649]

Other than voting, the shareholder's rights generally remain intact. The shareholder is still entitled to receive dividends, inspect corporate records, etc., and even bring a representative suit (*infra*).

POOLING AGREEMENT VS. VOTING TRUST— A COMPARISON		gilbert
	POOLING AGREEMENT	**VOTING TRUST**
PURPOSE	Any proper purpose	Any proper purpose
DURATION	Ordinarily can be perpetual	10-year maximum in most states, but renewable
SHARE OWNERSHIP	Shareholders retain both legal and beneficial ownership	Legal ownership transferred to trustee; shareholders retain beneficial ownership

B. Restrictions on Transfer of Shares

1. **Restrictions Imposed by Articles, Bylaws, or Shareholder Agreement [§650]**

   Stock transfer restrictions are frequently used in close corporations to limit the total number of shareholders (often to enable the corporation to retain statutory benefits as a "close corporation"; *see supra*, §§175-195), to prevent the entry of unwanted shareholders, or to avoid a major shift in control. Larger corporations on occasion may also limit the transferability of a certain class of shares—*e.g.*, to restrict ownership to a certain group, such as employees. Usually, stock transfer restrictions will be in the corporation's articles or bylaws. Sometimes, however, they are contained in a separate agreement among the shareholders.

   a. **Types of restrictions [§651]**

   The two most common types of restrictions on transferability of shares are the right of first refusal and the mandatory buy-sell provision.

   (1) **Right of first refusal [§652]**

   A right of first refusal is a provision giving the corporation or the other shareholders (or both) a first option to buy the stock before any shareholder may sell or otherwise transfer shares to a third party.

   (2) **Mandatory buy-sell [§653]**

   A mandatory buy-sell provision stipulates that on the occurrence of a designated event (*e.g.*, death of a shareholder, termination of employment), the corporation or other shareholders *must* buy the stock, and the shareholder (or the shareholder's estate) *must* sell to the corporation or other shareholders.

   b. **Validity of restrictions**

   (1) **Common law—reasonableness requirement [§654]**

   The right to transfer is deemed an inherent right of property ownership, and at common law total restraints or effective prohibitions on the transferability of shares were usually held invalid. To be valid at common law, a restriction on transfer must be "reasonable" in view of the needs of the particular corporation and shareholders involved. [**Allen v. Biltmore Tissue Corp.**, 2 N.Y.2d 534 (1957)]

   (a) **"Consent" restrictions [§655]**

   Thus, at common law, a provision that "these shares are nontransferable," or "nontransferable without the consent of each other shareholder," was usually held invalid as an unreasonable restraint on alienation. [**Rafe v. Hindin**, 29 A.D.2d 481 (1968)]

   1) **Special circumstances [§656]**

   Provisions requiring the consent of other shareholders or directors may be upheld under special circumstances. [**Penthouse Properties, Inc. v. 1158 Fifth Ave., Inc.,** 256 A.D. 685 (1939)—corporation owned cooperative apartment house in which shareholders were tenants; restriction requiring shareholders' consent to stock transfer upheld because right of occupancy went with it]

2) Modern decisions [§657]

Some more recent decisions have shown a greater tolerance for consent restrictions and upheld them when not an unreasonable method of limiting corporate control to particular individuals. [**Gray v. Harris Land & Cattle Co.,** 737 P.2d 475 (Mont. 1987)]

(b) Restrictions as to whom shares may be transferred [§658]

Restrictions limiting the type of persons to whom the shares may be transferred will be upheld if the restriction is reasonable under the circumstances (*e.g.*, provisions against selling shares to persons engaged in businesses that compete with the corporation).

(c) Right of first refusal [§659]

A right of first refusal (option) for a limited period of time in favor of the corporation or other shareholders (or both) will almost always be upheld as a reasonable restraint.

---

e.g. **Example:** "No sale of these shares to a nonshareholder shall be made until the holder first offers them to the corporation on the same terms and conditions as offered to the nonshareholder; and the corporation shall have 30 days thereafter within which to purchase same on such terms."

(d) Options to purchase [§660]

Similarly, provisions giving the corporation an option to purchase the shares in question at a fixed price or book value are usually upheld—even where the shares are now worth much more than the price. More than a large disparity between the option price and current market value must be shown to render an option agreement unreasonable. [**Evangelista v. Holland,** 537 N.E.2d 589 (Mass. 1989); **Concord Auto Auction, Inc. v. Rustin,** 627 F. Supp. 1526 (D. Mass. 1986)]

1) Termination of employment [§661]

Contractual provisions giving the corporation the right to repurchase the shares of an employee at a designated price upon termination of employment "at-will" have been enforced—even when the purpose for the firing was to acquire the stock at a low price. *Rationale:* Employees who agree both (i) to their being fired at will and (ii) to a particular buy-back formula are held to their bargain. [**Ingle v. Glamore Motor Sales,** 73 N.Y.2d 183 (1989)]

a) But note

Other courts have reasoned that employment at will may *not* be terminated for "any reason at all." The contractual relation implies that the employee will not be fired for *opportunistic* reasons rather than for reasons related to job performance. [**Jordan v. Duff & Phelps, Inc.,** 815 F.2d 429 (7th Cir. 1987)]

(2) Statutes [§662]

Today, a large number of states have statutes dealing with the validity of stock transfer restrictions.

(a) "Reasonable" restrictions [§663]

Some statutes simply codify the common law, authorizing "reasonable" restrictions on the transfer of shares. [Cal. Corp. Code §204(b)]

(b) Detailed restrictions [§664]

Others deal with such restrictions in more detail. For example, the Delaware statute authorizes the following types of stock transfer restrictions, which may appear in the articles, bylaws, or separate shareholder agreements: (i) provisions giving the corporation or other shareholders a right of first refusal for a reasonable time; (ii) provisions giving the corporation or other shareholders the right to consent to a proposed transfer; (iii) mandatory buy-sell provisions; (iv) restrictions on transfer to designated classes of persons "unless manifestly unreasonable"; and (v) "any other lawful restriction on transfer." [Del. Gen. Corp. Law §202]

1) And note

Even if the stock transfer restriction is held not to be authorized by statute, the corporation nevertheless is given the *option* to acquire whenever shares are sought to be transferred at a "fair price" to be determined by agreement of the parties or by the court. [Del. Gen. Corp. Law §349]

(3) Limitation—proper fund available for repurchase [§665]

Even if the stock transfer restriction is otherwise valid, where the corporation seeks to repurchase its own shares pursuant to the transfer restriction, a number of states require that the corporation have available funds from a proper source (*e.g.*, surplus) with which to make the repurchase (*see infra*, §§1057-1059). [**Van Kampen v. Detroit Bank & Trust Co.,** 199 N.W.2d 470 (Mich. 1972); *but see* **Lewis v. Powell,** 203 So. 2d 504 (Fla. 1967)—contra]

c. Shares subject to restriction

(1) Common law [§666]

Courts at common law split on whether stock transfer restrictions can be enforced with respect to shares *already issued* at the time the restrictions were adopted. Some hold that the corporation has the power, through amendment of its articles or bylaws (*see infra*, §§1145 *et seq.*), to alter existing shareholder rights—even where the shareholder neither knew nor consented to the restriction. [**Tu-Vu Drive-In Corp. v. Ashkins**, 61 Cal. 2d 283 (1964); *but see* **B&H Warehouse, Inc. v. Atlas Van Lines, Inc.**, 490 F.2d 818 (5th Cir. 1974)—contra]

(a) Removal of restriction [§667]

There is a similar split on whether stock transfer restrictions can be removed over the objection of dissenting stockholders. [**Silva v. Coastal Plywood & Timber Co.**, 124 Cal. App. 2d 276 (1954)—upholding bylaw retroactively removing stock transfer restrictions; *but see* **Bechtold v. Coleman Realty Co.**, 79 A.2d 661 (Pa. 1951)—contra]

(2) Statutes [§668]

Some modern statutes provide that stock transfer restrictions can be enforced only against shares issued *subsequent* to adoption of the restriction. Such restrictions cannot be enforced against the transfer of shares already issued, unless the owner consents. [Cal. Corp. Code §204(b); Del. Gen. Corp. Law §202(b)]

d. Transactions subject to restriction [§669]

Because restrictions on alienation of property are disfavored as a matter of public policy, stock transfer restrictions may be *strictly construed*. Provisions that contain only general restraints (*e.g.*, covering "all sales or transfers") are often interpreted as applying only to *voluntary* sales. Therefore, in the absence of specific language, the restriction may be held inapplicable to transfers on death [**Vogel v. Melish**, 196 N.E.2d 402 (Ill. 1964)], to a sale of shares in bankruptcy, or to pledges of shares as security for a loan (no transfer of title).

e. Notice requirement [§670]

Unless "noted conspicuously" on the *certificate itself*, a lawful stock transfer restriction is of no effect against a person who otherwise had no knowledge of the restriction at the time of transfer. [RMBCA §6.27(b); U.C.C. §8-204]

(1) Actual knowledge [§671]

This applies, of course, only to "innocent" persons. One who has *actual* knowledge of a stock transfer restriction is bound by it, even if it is not "conspicuously noted" on the face of the certificate. [RMBCA §6.27(b); U.C.C. §8-204]

(2) "Noted conspicuously" [§672]

The requirement that the restriction be "noted conspicuously" on the certificate means only that it reasonably appear from the face of the certificate that the shares are subject to some sort of transfer restriction. The restriction itself need not be set forth in full text. [**Ling & Co. v. Trinity Savings & Loan Association**, 482 S.W.2d 841 (Tex. 1972)]

(3) "Innocent" transferee [§673]

Without such notice, an innocent transferee of the certificate (whether a donee or purchaser) is entitled to have the shares transferred into his name on the books of the corporation and thereafter to receive dividends, vote the shares, etc. Moreover, he takes free and clear of the stock transfer restriction—so he can thereafter resell his shares to another without regard to the restriction.

EXAM TIP   **gilbert**

Share transfer restrictions are common in close corporations, so it would not be surprising for a share transfer restriction issue to arise on your exam. Remember, to be valid, a restriction must be *reasonable*, and to be upheld against a third-party purchaser, the existence of the restriction must be *noted conspicuously* on the share certificate.

C. Shareholders' Informational Rights

1. Types of Books and Records [§674]

The books and records of a corporation fall into several basic categories—shareholder lists; minutes of board meetings, shareholders' meetings, board committees, and officer committees; financial records, such as books of account and monthly, quarterly, and annual period summaries; and business documents, such as contracts, correspondence, and office memoranda.

2. Common Law [§675]

At common law, a shareholder acting for a proper purpose has a right to "inspect" (examine) the corporate books and records at reasonable times. The shareholder has the burden of alleging and proving a proper purpose for inspection. [**Albee v. Lamson & Hubbard Corp.**, 69 N.E.2d 811 (Mass. 1946)]

3. Statutes [§676]

In most states today, shareholder inspection rights are granted by statutes. Many of these statutes apply only to certain kinds of shareholders, such as those who are record holders of at least 5% of the corporation's stock, or who have been record holders for at least six months. [N.Y. Bus. Corp. Law §624] The statutes are normally interpreted to preserve the proper-purpose test, but to place on the corporation the burden of proving that the shareholder's purpose is improper. [**Crane Co. v. Anaconda Co.**, 39 N.Y.2d 14 (1976)] Moreover, those statutes that are limited to only certain kinds of shareholders, or only certain books and records, are usually interpreted to *supplement* the common law, so that a suit for inspection that does not fall within the statute can still be brought under the common law. [**Tucson Gas & Electric Co. v. Schantz**, 428 P.2d 686 (Ariz. 1967); *but see* **Caspary v. Louisiana Land & Exploration Co.**, 707 F.2d 785 (4th Cir. 1983)]

a. Kind of books and records sought [§677]

The burden of proof under a statute may be affected by the kind of books and records that are sought. For example, the Delaware statute provides that if inspection is sought of shareholder lists, the burden is on the corporation to prove that the information is being sought for an improper purpose. For other corporate records, the burden is on the shareholder to prove proper purpose. [Del. Gen. Corp. Law §220(c)]

4. Proper vs. Improper Purposes [§678]

In determining what constitutes a proper or improper purpose, the basic test is whether the shareholder is seeking inspection to protect her interest as a shareholder, or instead is acting for a nonshareholder purpose, such as furthering her interest as a potential business rival or as a litigant on a personal, nonshareholder claim. [**Rosentool v. Bonanza Oil & Mine Corp.**, 352 P.2d 138 (Or. 1960)]

a. Recognized purposes [§679]

Among the purposes the courts have recognized as *proper* for exercising the inspection right are the following: (i) to determine whether the corporation is being properly managed or whether there has been managerial misconduct, at least if the shareholder alleges some specific concerns [**Skouras v. Admiralty Enterprises, Inc.**, 386 A.2d 674 (Del. 1978)]; (ii) to determine the corporation's financial condition [**Riser v. Genuine Parts Co.**, 258 S.E.2d 184 (Ga. 1979)]; and (iii) to determine the value of the shareholder's stock [**Friedman v. Altoona Pipe & Steel Supply Co.**, 460 F.2d 1212 (3d Cir. 1972)].

b. Multiple purposes [§680]

As long as the primary purpose is a proper one, the fact that the shareholder has an improper secondary purpose usually will not defeat the claim. [**General Time Corp. v. Talley Industries**, 240 A.2d 755 (Del. 1968)]

c. Inspection of shareholders list [§681]

Most courts are reluctant to deny a shareholder access to the shareholders list, because such access is often vital to the exercise of other shareholder rights and will seldom if ever harm the corporation through disclosure of business secrets.

(1) Proxy fights [§682]

Inspection of a shareholders list to enable a shareholder to make a take-over bid or engage in a proxy contest with management is normally considered a proper purpose, because it is reasonably related to the interest of the shareholder.

(2) Shareholder litigation [§683]

Similarly, it is a proper purpose to inspect the shareholders list as a means to seek the solicitation of other shareholders to participate in shareholder litigation against management or even the corporation. [**Compaq Computer Corp. v. Horton**, 631 A.2d 1 (Del. 1993)]

CHECKLIST OF PROPER PURPOSES FOR INSPECTION **gilbert**

THE FOLLOWING ARE PURPOSES THAT COURTS HAVE FOUND SUFFICIENT TO ALLOW INSPECTION OF PERTINENT RECORDS:

☑ To *determine* whether the corporation is being *properly managed*

☑ To *investigate managerial misconduct*

☑ To *determine* the *value* of the shareholder's stock

☑ To *enable* the shareholder to make a *takeover bid* or engage in a *proxy fight*

☑ To *seek shareholders to participate in litigation* against management or the corporation

(3) Social or political interests [§684]

In **State ex rel. Pillsbury v. Honeywell, Inc.**, 191 N.W.2d 406 (Minn. 1971), Pillsbury was a shareholder of Honeywell, Inc. Pillsbury opposed the Vietnam war, and asked Honeywell to produce its shareholder ledger and all corporate records dealing with weapons and munitions manufacture. Pillsbury admitted that his sole motive in purchasing Honeywell stock was to persuade Honeywell to cease producing munitions, but argued that the desire to communicate with fellow shareholders was per se a proper purpose. Honeywell argued that a proper purpose contemplates a concern with investment return. The court held for Honeywell, finding that Pillsbury's motivation (to force Honeywell to cease production of bombs) was not a proper purpose germane to his economic interest as a shareholder.

(a) Note

The authority of *Honeywell* is questionable. *Honeywell* purported to apply Delaware law. However, in **Credit Bureau Reports, Inc. v. Credit Bureau of St. Paul, Inc.**, 290 A.2d 691 (Del. 1972), the Delaware Supreme Court reiterated its prior holdings that, under the Delaware statute, the desire to solicit proxies for a slate of directors is reasonably related to the shareholder's interest as a shareholder and that any secondary purpose is irrelevant. The court went on to repudiate *Pillsbury* to the extent that it is inconsistent with these holdings. [*See* **General Time Corp. v. Talley Industries, Inc.**, 240 A.2d 755 (Del. 1968); *and see* **The Conservative Caucus Research, Analysis & Education Foundation, Inc. v. Chevron Corp.**, 525 A.2d 569 (Del. 1987)]

5. Mandatory Disclosure of Information [§685]

In contrast to the law governing the shareholder's inspection right, which puts the initiative on the individual shareholder, various federal and state statutes require corporations to make affirmative disclosure of certain information.

a. Securities Exchange Act of 1934 [§686]

Extensive disclosure requirements are imposed on corporations whose stock is registered under section 12 of the Securities Exchange Act of 1934.

(1) Reports [§687]

Such corporations must file with the SEC, and any securities exchange on which the stock is listed, reports disclosing their financial condition and certain types of material events. These reports are open to inspection by the public. Under section 13 of the Act, and the rules promulgated under the Act, such corporations must file a form 10-K annually, a form 10-Q quarterly, and a form 8-K within four business days after the occurrence of certain specified events.

(a) Information included [§688]

The form 10-K must include audited financial statements; management's discussion of the corporation's financial condition and results of operations; and disclosure concerning legal proceedings, developments in the corporation's business, executive compensation, conflict-of-interest transactions, and other specified issues. The form 10-Q must include quarterly financial data prepared in accordance with generally accepted accounting principles; a management report; and disclosure concerning legal proceedings, defaults on senior securities, and other specified issues. Among the matters that trigger an 8-K report are a change in control of the corporation, the acquisition or disposition of a significant amount of assets, a change of accountants, a change in control, and the resignation of a director or top executive.

(2) Proxy rules [§689]

Under the proxy rules (*supra*, §§568-618), corporations whose stock is registered under section 12 must annually disclose certain information to shareholders, such as the compensation of the chief executive officer and the four most highly compensated officers other than the CEO, unless the compensation of such an officer is less than $100,000; details on the operation of stock option and pension plans; and transactions with insiders during the previous year involving amounts in excess of $60,000.

b. State statutes [§690]

State laws vary greatly as to the amount of information that must be provided by corporations incorporated in the jurisdiction.

(1) Report to state [§691]

Most states require corporations incorporated in the jurisdiction to file an annual report with an appropriate state officer, such as the secretary of state, providing at least certain minimal information, *e.g.*, the names and addresses of its directors and officers, the address of its principal business office, its principal business activity, and the name and address of its agent for the service of process upon the corporation. [RMBCA §16.22]

(2) Report to shareholders [§692]

In addition, some states require corporations to send an annual report to shareholders containing financial statements. For example, under the Model Act, a corporation must furnish its shareholders with annual financial statements that include a balance sheet, an income statement, and a statement of changes in shareholders' equity. If financial statements are prepared for the corporation on the basis of generally accepted accounting principles, the annual financial statements furnished to the shareholders must also be prepared on that basis. If the annual financial statements are reported upon by a public accountant, the accountant's report must accompany them. If not, the statements must be accompanied by a statement of the president or the person responsible for the corporation's accounting records: (i) stating his reasonable belief whether the statements were prepared on the basis of generally accepted accounting principles and, if not, describing the basis of preparation; and (ii) describing any respects in which the statements were not prepared on the basis of accounting consistent with the statements prepared for the preceding year.

D. Fiduciary Obligations of Controlling Shareholders

1. Introduction [§693]

Where a controlling shareholder serves as a director or officer, he owes fiduciary obligations to the corporation in those capacities. Even where a controlling shareholder does not serve as a director or officer, he may owe fiduciary obligations to the minority shareholders in exercising his control.

a. Business dealings with corporation [§694]

Although a controlling majority shareholder may validly contract with the corporation, he cannot exploit the corporation at the expense of the minority. Thus, if the contract is unfair—as where the price terms are not those that would be set in an arm's-length bargain—the controlling shareholder has breached his fiduciary obligation to the minority. [**Sinclair Oil Corp. v. Levien,** *supra*, §320]

(1) Parent-subsidiary dealings [§695]

The most common cases in which there are dealings between a controlling shareholder and a corporation are those in which the controlling shareholder is a parent and the corporation is a subsidiary with minority ownership. [**Sinclair Oil Corp. v. Levien,** *supra*]

(2) Burden of proof [§696]

When a transaction between a corporation and its controlling shareholder is challenged, as in a derivative suit by minority shareholders, the burden is on the controlling shareholder to prove the transaction's fairness. [**Sinclair Oil Corp. v. Levien,** *supra*]

(3) A.L.I. test [§697]

The A.L.I.'s Principles of Corporate Governance provide that a controlling shareholder who enters into a transaction with the corporation fulfills the duty of fair dealing to the corporation with respect to the transaction if:

(i) The transaction is *fair* to the corporation when entered into; or

(ii) The transaction is ***authorized in advance or ratified*** by disinterested shareholders, following disclosure concerning the conflict of interest and the transaction, and does not constitute a waste of corporate assets at the time of the shareholder action.

[A.L.I. Prin. Corp. Gov. §5.10]

(a) Burden of proof—general rule [§698]

If the transaction was authorized in advance by disinterested directors, or authorized in advance or ratified by disinterested shareholders following disclosure, the party challenging the transaction has the burden of proof. The party challenging the transaction normally also has the burden of proof if the transaction was ratified by disinterested directors. If the transaction was not so authorized or ratified, the controlling shareholder has the burden of proof, except as provided below. [A.L.I. Prin. Corp. Gov. §5.10]

(b) Transactions in the ordinary course of business [§699]

If a transaction between a controlling shareholder and the corporation was in the ordinary course of the corporation's business, a party who challenges the transaction has the burden of coming forward with evidence that the transaction was unfair, whether or not the transaction was authorized in advance or ratified by disinterested directors or disinterested shareholders. [A.L.I. Prin. Corp. Gov. §5.10]

b. Corporate opportunities [§700]

A controlling shareholder is subject to the corporate opportunity doctrine. (*See supra,* §§321-335.) However, the rules that apply to a controlling shareholder in this respect are not as strict as the rules that apply to directors and officers, because controlling shareholders are typically themselves corporations engaged in business and seeking new opportunities.

(1) A.L.I. approach [§701]

The A.L.I.'s Principles of Corporate Governance provide that a controlling shareholder may not take advantage of a corporate opportunity unless:

(i) The taking of the opportunity is *fair* to the corporation; or

(ii) The taking of the opportunity is *authorized in advance or ratified by disinterested shareholders*, following disclosure of the conflict of interest and the corporate opportunity, provided the taking of the opportunity is not equivalent to a waste of corporate assets.

[A.L.I. Prin. Corp. Gov. §5.12]

(a) A.L.I. definition of a corporate opportunity [§702]

The A.L.I. defines "corporate opportunity" in the *controlling shareholder context* as any opportunity to engage in a business activity that:

(i) Is developed or received by the controlled corporation, or comes to the controlling shareholder primarily by virtue of its relationship to the controlled corporation; or

(ii) Is held out to shareholders of the controlled corporation as being a type of business activity that will be within the scope of the corporation's business and will not be within the scope of the controlling shareholder's business.

[A.L.I. Prin. Corp. Gov. §5.12]

c. Fundamental changes [§703]

A controlling shareholder also owes a duty of fairness in causing fundamental changes, such as mergers or amendments of the articles of incorporation, that may promote its own self-interest at the expense of the minority. (*See infra*, §§1184-1206.)

EXAM TIP   **gilbert**

A controlling shareholder owes a fiduciary duty to minority shareholders to *act with good faith and inherent fairness* toward them. The obligation is even greater in close corporations. Thus, when a question arises concerning a controlling shareholder's business dealings with the corporation, ask whether the transactions are fair. The *burden* of proof is on the *controlling shareholder*. Likewise, if a controlling shareholder causes a fundamental corporate change, ask whether it promotes his own self-interest at the expense of the minority. Be sure that when the controlling shareholder deals with the minority, he makes a *full disclosure*.

---

2. Transactions in Corporate Control [§704]

In any transaction in which control of the corporation is material, the controlling shareholders must act with "good faith and inherent fairness" toward the minority. [**Jones v. H.F. Ahmanson & Co.**, 1 Cal. 3d 93 (1969)]

Example: There were relatively few shares of X Corp. outstanding, and they sold at a very high price. Accordingly, the marketability of the shares was highly impaired. The controlling shareholders transferred their shares to Holding

Co., which they had formed. Holding Co. then "went public," which allowed the controlling shareholders to cash out part of their investment, and greatly increased the value and marketability of the remainder. In contrast, the minority shareholders in X were stuck with shares that were even less marketable than before. The controlling shareholders of X Corp. violated their fiduciary duties by engaging in a transaction that, with no business justification, increased the marketability of their own shares and decreased the marketability of the minority's shares, without affording the minority an opportunity to participate. [**Jones v. H.F. Ahmanson & Co.,** *supra*]

---

3. Obligations of Shareholders in Close Corporations [§705]

Shareholders in a close corporation owe each other an even stricter duty than controlling shareholders in publicly held corporations. It has been said that such shareholders owe each other the same duty of utmost good faith and loyalty that is owed by partners to each other. This duty is owed by all shareholders in a close corporation, majority and minority. [**Donahue v. Rodd Electrotype Co.,** 328 N.E.2d 505 (Mass. 1975); **Helms v. Duckworth,** 249 F.2d 482 (D.C. Cir. 1957)]

a. Equal treatment doctrine [§706]

Several important cases have suggested that in a close corporation there must be equal treatment of all shareholders, or, at least, all shareholders must be afforded equal opportunities. Thus, in the *Donahue* case, *supra*, the court held that controlling shareholders of a close corporation who cause the corporation to acquire some of their shares must see that minority stockholders have an equal opportunity to sell a proportionate number of shares to the corporation at an identical price.

(1) "Equality" [§707]

What constitutes "equality" for these purposes may not always be clear. In general, it is not unequal to treat actors differently if there is a legitimate difference between the actors upon which the different treatment is based. For example, shareholder-employees do not have to be offered the same salaries if one shareholder is a highly skilled executive and the other has no training in business.

(2) Minority view [§708]

In **Nixon v. Blackwell,** 626 A.2d 1366 (Del. 1993), the Delaware Supreme Court took a contrary view, holding that shareholders did not have to be treated equally for all purposes, and in particular that different categories of shareholders in a close corporation did not have the right to be treated equally in terms of corporate arrangements affecting the liquidity of their stock.

b. Legitimate business purpose [§709]

The majority shareholders of a close corporation cannot sever a minority shareholder from the corporate payroll, or refuse to reelect him as a salaried officer and director, without a legitimate business purpose. [**Wilkes v. Springside Nursing Home, Inc.,** 353 N.E.2d 657 (Mass. 1976)]

c. **Obligation of minority shareholders [§710]**

A minority shareholder in a close corporation cannot use a veto power unreasonably, as by refusing to vote for dividends when the accumulation of undistributed earnings will lead to a foreseeable tax penalty to the corporation. [**Smith v. Atlantic Properties, Inc.,** 422 N.E.2d 798 (Mass. 1981)]

4. **Disclosure [§711]**

A controlling shareholder must make full disclosure when dealing with the minority shareholders, as when making a tender offer for their shares [**Lynch v. Vickers Energy Corp.,** *supra*, §567], or when causing the corporation to deal with minority shareholders, as when calling redeemable stock that the minority shareholders could convert to another class of shares [**Zahn v. Transamerica Corp.,** 162 F.2d 36 (3d Cir. 1947)].

5. **Sale of Control [§712]**

Controlling shareholders may also owe fiduciary duties to other shareholders in transactions involving sale of controlling stock at a premium or the transfer of control in connection with a sale of their stock.

a. **General rule [§713]**

The general rule is that a controlling shareholder has the right to sell his controlling stock at a premium; *i.e.*, for an above-market price that is not available to other shareholders. [**Zetlin v. Hanson Holdings, Inc.,** 48 N.Y.2d 684 (1979); **Clagett v. Hutchison,** 583 F.2d 1259 (4th Cir. 1978)]

(1) **Rationale**

This rule reflects the fact that controlling stock normally sells at a higher price than noncontrolling stock. The rule also serves a policy purpose by facilitating the transfer of control from less efficient to more efficient hands.

(2) **Equal opportunity doctrine [§714]**

Some commentators have urged that where a purchaser offers to purchase control of a corporation at a premium, the controlling shareholders owe a fiduciary duty to provide all shareholders with an equal opportunity to participate; *i.e.*, the controlling shareholder must arrange that the offer be made to all shareholders on a pro rata basis. [78 Harv. L. Rev. 505]

---

e.g. **Example:** Suppose S owns 51% of C Corp.'s stock. Under the equal opportunity doctrine, if a purchaser offers to buy S's 51% of C Corp.'s stock at a premium above-market price, S could not sell his shares alone, but instead would be required to ask the minority shareholders if they wanted to participate in the 51% offer on a pro rata basis.

(a) Comment [§715]

There is little case support for this doctrine, and it has been specifically rejected in various cases.

(b) A.L.I. rule [§716]

Under the A.L.I. Principles of Corporate Governance, a controlling shareholder has the same right to dispose of voting shares as any other shareholder, including the right to sell those shares for a price that is not made proportionally available to other shareholders. However, the controlling shareholder does not satisfy the duty of fair dealing to the other shareholders if:

(i) The controlling shareholder *does not make disclosure* concerning the transaction to other shareholders with whom the controlling shareholder deals in connection with the transaction; or

(ii) It is apparent from the circumstances that the *purchaser is likely to violate the duty of fair dealing* and obtain a significant financial benefit for the purchaser or an associate.

[A.L.I. Prin. Corp. Gov. §5.16]

(c) Impact of Jones v. H.F. Ahmanson & Co. [§717]

In **Jones v. H.F. Ahmanson & Co.**, *supra*, §704, the California Supreme Court held that controlling shareholders were under a duty to act toward minority shareholders with "good faith and inherent fairness . . . in any transaction in which control of the corporation is material." Although that case did not involve a sale of control, the theory on which it was decided could be extended to sale-of-control cases. As of now, however, the doctrine has found little judicial acceptance in straight sale-of-controlling-stock cases.

b. Exceptions [§718]

The general rule, that control can be sold at a premium, is subject to a number of exceptions in cases where there is something more than a straight sale of controlling stock at a premium.

(1) Bare sale of office [§719]

While a sale of control stock at a premium is permissible, a bare sale of directorships or other corporate offices is invalid. Thus, a controlling shareholder cannot transfer control of the board for consideration if the transfer of control of the board is not simply incidental to a transfer of an amount of stock that is sufficient in itself to carry control. Accordingly, if a person (i) controls the board although he owns only a small amount of stock, and (ii) transfers control of the board in connection with a sale of his stock at a premium (by a series of resignations and simultaneous appointment of the purchaser's nominees), the appointment of the purchaser's nominees is voidable at the suit of a shareholder, and the seller must account for the premium. [**Caplan v. Lionel Corp.,** 20 A.D.2d 301, *aff'd*, 14 N.Y.2d 679 (1964)—transfer of control of board in connection with sale of only 3% of outstanding shares held a wrongful "sale of office"]

(a) Damages [§720]

In case of a bare sale of office, the amount that the controlling shareholder receives for transferring control belongs to the corporation.

(b) Exception [§721]

It is not improper for a selling shareholder to arrange for the resignations of existing officers and directors and the appointment of a new board chosen by the purchaser, as part of a sale of controlling stock, if the block of shares sold constitutes either a majority of the outstanding stock or an amount sufficiently large to carry control "as a practical certainty," so that the purchaser could have forced the changes of office herself, even if the seller had not facilitated the change of office. [**Essex Universal Corp. v. Yates,** 305 F.2d 572 (2d Cir. 1969); 13 A.L.R.3d 361]

1) Test [§722]

What constitutes control "as a practical certainty" is a question of fact. In a publicly held corporation, something less than 51% will usually suffice; *i.e.*, large blocks of shares may carry voting control even though short of a majority. [*See* **Essex Universal Corp. v. Yates,** *supra*—indicating that 28% of outstanding shares of publicly held corporation may satisfy the test]

(2) Theory of corporate action [§723]

Suppose a prospective purchaser, P, wants to acquire complete control of the assets and business of corporation C, and proposes to make an offer to C *to buy C's assets*, or have C *merge* with a corporation that P controls. If C's controlling shareholders instead convince P to purchase just their stock, at a premium, the minority shareholders may assert that the controlling shareholders have diverted a corporate opportunity from C to themselves. This is the theory of "corporate action." It has been successfully employed by minority shareholders in several cases. [**Commonwealth Title Insurance & Trust Co. v. Seltzer,** 76 A. 77 (Pa. 1910); **Dunnett v. Arn,** 71 F.2d 912 (10th Cir. 1934); **Roby v. Dunnett,** 88 F.2d 68 (10th Cir.), *cert. denied*, 301 U.S. 706 (1937)]

(a) Comment

The problem with this theory is that a controlling shareholder cannot be compelled to sell his shares at a price he does not accept. A knowledgeable controlling shareholder therefore might be able to avoid the application of this theory by (i) allowing P to make an offer to C, (ii) voting to reject the offer to C, and (iii) then waiting for an offer from P to purchase his controlling shares.

(3) Sales involving fraud or nondisclosure [§724]

A controlling shareholder violates his fiduciary duty to the remaining shareholders if, as part of the sale of stock at a premium, he deals with minority shareholders without disclosing the terms of his sale.

Example: In some cases, especially where the buyer wants more stock than the controlling shareholder owns, the premium paid to the controlling shareholder may depend on the controlling shareholder convincing minority shareholders to sell their stock to the buyer. In such cases, the controlling shareholder must disclose to the minority shareholders the premium that he is to receive.

---

(4) Sale of control to transferee who plans to deal unfairly with corporation [§725]

Controlling shareholders breach their fiduciary duties to the minority shareholders if they transfer their controlling shares to a person or group whom they know or have reason to know will deal unfairly with the corporation.

(a) Looting [§726]

The principal type of case in this category is a sale of controlling shares to a purchaser whom the controlling shareholder *knows or has reason to know* intends to loot the corporation. [**Gerdes v. Reynolds**, 28 N.Y.S.2d 622 (1941); **Insuranshares Corp. v. Northern Fiscal Corp.**, 35 F. Supp. 22 (E.D. Pa. 1940)]

1) Knowledge of purchaser's intent [§727]

Usually in such cases there is no question, by the time of the trial, that the purchaser did loot. The main problem is whether the controlling shareholder knew or had reason to know of the purchaser's intent at the time of the sale.

a) Terms of sale may put controlling shareholder on inquiry [§728]

Typically, these cases concern a corporation whose assets are highly liquid (*e.g.*, investment companies whose assets consist of readily marketable securities). Because the value of the stock in such a corporation can be determined with a high degree of precision (because liquid assets are easy to value, and there is normally no goodwill attached to the business), payment of a premium significantly above the fair value of the shares may be enough to put the controlling shareholder on notice that the purchaser intends to recover the premium by looting the corporation's assets. [**Gerdes v. Reynolds,** *supra*]

e.g. **Example:** Bank held controlling shares in C Corp. Bank sold its shares to a purchaser, whom Bank knew had a long history of business failures, outstanding fraud judgments, and no apparent assets with which to pay for the shares. Under such circumstances, it was reasonably foreseeable that the purchaser would be likely to loot C Corp., which he did. Bank's sale to such a purchaser was a breach of duty to C and C's minority shareholders. [**De Baun v. First Western Bank & Trust Co.,** 46 Cal. App. 3d 686 (1975)]

2) No duty to investigate [§729]

In the absence of some ground for suspicion, however, a seller of control stock generally does not have an affirmative obligation to investigate the purchaser's plans to determine whether looting or fraud is intended or likely. [**Swinney v. Keebler Co.,** 480 F.2d 573 (4th Cir. 1973); **Levy v. American Beverage Corp.,** 265 A.D. 208 (1942)]

3) Damages [§730]

Where the controlling shareholder knows or has reason to know that the purchaser plans to deal unfairly with the corporation, he is accountable to the minority shareholders for the premium that he received (*i.e.,* the amount by which the purchase price exceeded the fair value of his stock) and for any damage caused to the corporation by the purchasers. [**Gerdes v. Reynolds,** *supra*]

4) Plans to deprive corporation of profits [§731]

Even if the controlling shareholder has no reason to expect looting, he is accountable where he knows or has reason to know that the purchaser intends to use control to prevent the corporation from realizing profits it otherwise would have obtained.

e.g. **Example:** In **Perlman v. Feldmann,** 219 F.2d 173 (2d Cir. 1955), the controlling shareholder of a steel company sold his controlling shares to a group of steel consumers. Steel was in short supply, and the purchasers paid a premium for the control of stock in order to obtain the steel company's output at artificially low prices. The court held that the controlling shareholder had breached his fiduciary duties to the minority shareholders, and ordered him to account for that portion of the price that exceeded the fair value of his stock.

SALE OF CONTROL—A SUMMARY   **gilbert**

ALTHOUGH THE GENERAL RULE IS THAT A MAJORITY OR CONTROLLING SHAREHOLDER MAY SELL HER CONTROLLING INTEREST AT A PREMIUM, THERE ARE EXCEPTIONS WHERE:

☑ The controlling shareholder is in reality *selling directorships or other corporate offices* (*e.g.*, where a nonmajority shareholder sells her stock at a premium and causes the controlling directors to resign)

☑ An outside party seeking control of the corporation proposes to purchase the corporation's assets or to merge with the corporation and the controlling shareholder *convinces the outsider to purchase only his shares*

☑ The controlling shareholder *deals with the minority shareholders without making full disclosure* of the terms of his sale (*e.g.*, where the controlling shareholder must first purchase shares from the minority shareholders in order to sell sufficient control to a third party at a premium)

☑ The controlling shareholder *knows that the transferee will loot the corporation*

E. Shareholder Suits

1. Introduction [§732]

Court actions brought by shareholders fall into two categories: (i) a *direct action* on the shareholder's own behalf (or on behalf of a class of shareholders to which he belongs) for injury to his interest *as a shareholder*; or (ii) a *derivative suit* filed on *behalf of the corporation* for injury done to the corporation for which it has failed to sue.

2. Direct (Individual) Suits [§733]

Where management has abridged a contractual or statutory duty owed directly *to the shareholder* as an individual (*e.g.*, refusing to permit shareholder inspection of corporate records), the shareholder may bring a suit on *his own behalf*—*i.e.*, a direct (or individual) suit.

a. Class action [§734]

If the alleged misconduct affects the rights of a number of shareholders, the suit may be maintained as a class action, in which case the individual shareholder sues as the *representative* of the class of shares that has been damaged. *Examples:* Management denies all shareholders preemptive rights in new stock issuance; or corporate insider fails to disclose material information when purchasing shares from a number of existing shareholders.

3. Derivative Suits [§735]

If management (or a third party) has abridged a duty *owed to the corporation* (*e.g.*, officers loot the corporate treasury, or customer fails to pay for goods purchased from corporation), and the corporation fails to enforce its cause of action, a shareholder may bring a suit on behalf of the corporation—*i.e.*, a derivative suit.

a. Nature of action [§736]

The derivative suit is a creature of equity. It was conceived to permit a shareholder to redress injuries done directly to the corporation (injuring the shareholder only indirectly or derivatively), where management has refused to enforce the corporate cause of action, usually because recovery is sought against management for breach of fiduciary duty. [**Sax v. World Wide Press, Inc.**, 809 F.2d 610 (9th Cir. 1989)]

(1) Who benefits [§737]

A derivative suit enforces the corporation's cause of action, and any recovery usually belongs to *the corporation* rather than the plaintiff-shareholder. (But the plaintiff-shareholder may be entitled to reimbursement for expenses in obtaining such recovery; *see infra*, §823.)

(2) Distinguishing direct suits from derivative suits [§738]

It must be determined initially whether the shareholder's action is properly direct or derivative in nature. (This is significant because derivative suits are subject to a series of prerequisites—including security-for-expenses statutes, *infra*, §798—that do not apply to direct suits.) While borderline cases may be difficult to classify, the basic test is which party has the cause of action—*i.e.*, whether the injury was suffered by the corporation or directly by the shareholder—and to whom the defendant's *duty* ran.

(a) Direct actions

1) Illustrations [§739]

The following kinds of shareholder actions have been held *direct* (individual) rather than derivative in nature, because the immediate injury is to the shareholder rather than the corporation.

####### a) Action to compel dividend [§740]

Directors of XYZ Corp. refuse to declare a dividend, in order to depress the value of the shares. Shareholder action to compel payment of dividend is a direct action (injury to the shareholder), and a class action in such a case would be proper. [**Knapp v. Bankers Securities Corp.**, 230 F.2d 717 (3d Cir. 1956)]

####### b) Action to challenge reorganization reducing shareholder's influence [§741]

Shareholder complains of reorganization allegedly diluting

his voting influence in the corporation. This is a direct suit (again a class action may be proper). [**Eisenberg v. Flying Tiger Line, Inc.,** 451 F.2d 267 (2d Cir. 1971)]

2) Significance of relief sought [§742]

In cases that are difficult to classify, courts may characterize the action as direct when the plaintiff-shareholder seeks only injunctive or prospective relief. [**Grimes v. Donald**, 673 A.2d 1207 (Del. 1996)—suit sought a declaration that the board of directors abdicated its responsibility to the company by too broadly delegating its authority to the CEO]

(b) "Special duty" cases—still direct actions [§743]

Cases occasionally arise in which the corporation has sustained immediate injury, but the action is nevertheless deemed direct because of some "special duty" owed to the plaintiff-shareholder.

Example: A suit by a shareholder/pledgor against a director/pledgee for dissipating the corporation's assets has been held to be a direct action. Even though the injury was to the corporation, thus giving rise to a derivative action as well, there was a "special duty" owed arising out of the pledge arrangement. [**Citibank, N.A. v. Data Lease Financial Corp.,** 828 F.2d 686 (11th Cir. 1987)]

Example: A suit by a corporation against one of its directors for looting the assets of the corporation's subsidiary has been held to be a direct action. Even though the injury was to the subsidiary corporation, on whose behalf the parent corporation could have brought a derivative suit, there was a special fiduciary duty owed by the director to the parent corporation-shareholder. [**General Rubber Co. v. Benedict,** 215 N.Y. 18 (1915)]

(c) Close corporation exception [§744]

Some courts have held that minority shareholders of a close corporation may bring a direct action against controlling shareholders for breach of fiduciary duty, thus enabling the plaintiffs to avoid the special restrictions and defenses of a derivative suit. [**Barth v. Barth**, 659 N.E.2d 559 (Ind. 1995)] The Principles of Corporate Governance approve this exception if it does not (i) unfairly expose the corporation or the defendants to a multiplicity of actions, (ii) materially prejudice the interests of creditors in the corporation, or (iii) interfere with a fair distribution of the recovery among all interested persons. [A.L.I. Prin. Corp. Gov. §7.01(d)] Other courts have adhered to the traditional rule that a shareholder must redress an injury to the corporation through a derivative suit. [**Bagdon v. Bridgestone, Firestone, Inc.,** 916 F.2d 379 (7th Cir. 1990)]

(d) Securities acts violations—derivative action [§745]

A derivative action will lie for violations of the federal securities acts where the violation constitutes a breach of management's duties to the corporation.

---

e.g. Example: Where a violation of rule 10b-5 results in injury to the corporation (as distinct from its shareholders), a derivative action will lie if the corporation fails to sue. (*See supra*, §735.)

---

e.g. Example: Under section 16(b), recovery of "short swing profits" by insiders belongs to the corporation. If it fails to sue, the statute authorizes a minority shareholder to sue on its behalf (*supra*, §493). (*Note*: This is a statutory action, rather than a true derivative suit, and as a consequence, it is not subject to the same procedural limitations, *see infra*, §§783, 808.)

---

b. Prerequisite to suit—exhaustion of corporate remedies [§746]

Because a derivative suit seeks to enforce a corporate cause of action, the plaintiff must first show that he has exhausted his remedies within the corporate structure. This is an essential element of the plaintiff's cause of action, and thus it must be specifically *pleaded and proven*. [Fed. R. Civ. P. 23.1; Cal. Corp. Code §800(b)(2)]

(1) Demand on directors [§747]

Because only the board of directors is authorized to bring suit on behalf of the corporation, a shareholder, before proceeding with a derivative suit, must make a sincere effort to induce the directors to remedy the wrong complained of. His complaint must "allege with particularity the efforts, if any, made by the plaintiff to obtain the action he desires from the directors or comparable authority . . . and the reasons for his failure to obtain the action or for not making the effort." [Fed. R. Civ. P. 23.1]

(a) When excused [§748]

Demand on the directors may be excused if the shareholder demonstrates that it would be "futile," *i.e.*, when all or a majority of the directors (i) are "interested" in that they themselves are the alleged wrongdoers or are "controlled" by them, (ii) have failed to exercise reasonable care to prevent the wrong by fully informing themselves about the challenged transaction to the extent reasonably appropriate under the circumstances, *or* (iii) could not have used sound business judgment because the challenged transaction was so egregious on its face. [**Marx v. Akers**, 88 N.Y.2d 189 (1996)]

1) Note—majority approval does not excuse demand [§749]

Most courts hold that in the absence of negligence, self-interest, or other indication of bias, the fact that a majority of the directors merely *approved* the transaction under attack does not itself excuse the demand; *i.e.*, it does *not* follow that these directors will refuse to remedy the error of their business judgment when it is brought to their attention. [**Kamen v. Kemper Financial Services, Inc.,** 939 F.2d 458 (7th Cir. 1991); **Aronson v. Lewis,** 473 A.2d 805 (Del. 1984); **Lewis v. Graves,** 701 F.2d 245 (2d Cir. 1983)]

2) Model statutes—"universal demand" [§750]

Both model statutes provide that demand should be excused only on a showing that "irreparable injury" to the corporation would result. [A.L.I. Prin. Corp. Gov. §7.03(b); RMBCA §7.42] This view has now been adopted by nearly half the states.

3) Violations of federal law [§751]

If the derivative suit charges a violation of federal law, the scope of the demand requirement is determined by state rule unless this would be inconsistent with the policies underlying the federal law. [**Kamen v. Kemper Financial Services, Inc.,** 500 U.S. 90 (1991)]

(b) Effect of directors' rejection of demand [§752]

If a derivative suit alleges wrongdoing by a majority of the directors (or by persons who control them), the board's decision not to sue will not prevent the derivative suit. [**Lewis v. Curtis,** 671 F.2d 779 (3d Cir. 1982)]

1) Note

Even if a demand is required because a majority of the directors "merely approved" the challenged transaction (*see supra*), some courts have held that it does not necessarily follow that their decision not to sue will end the matter. [**Galef v. Alexander,** 615 F.2d 51 (2d Cir. 1980)—participation by directors insufficient to excuse a demand may nonetheless disqualify directors from barring derivative suit]

(c) "Business judgment, honestly exercised" [§753]

Where the matter complained of does not involve wrongdoing by the directors or by persons who control them (*e.g.*, where plaintiff-shareholder complains that a third party has breached a contract with the corporation and wants the corporation to bring suit for damages), the board's good faith refusal to sue bars the action. If the directors reasonably conclude that there is no likelihood of recovery, or that the costs of suit would outweigh any recovery, courts may refuse to allow a derivative suit. *Rationale:* A court will not interfere with a good faith exercise of discretion by the board elected to make business judgments for the corporation. [**United Copper Securities Co. v. Amalgamated Copper Co.**, 244 U.S. 261 (1917)]

1) Reasonable diligence [§754]

The derivative suit will not be barred, however, if plaintiff-shareholder's well-pleaded allegations of fact create a reasonable doubt that the board exercised reasonable business judgment in declining to pursue the cause of action. [**Levine v. Smith**, 591 A.2d 194 (Del. 1991)]

a) Discovery not permitted [§755]

The Delaware Supreme Court, however, has held that a plaintiff-shareholder is not entitled to discovery in connection with showing that demand was wrongfully refused. Rather, the plaintiff must rely on public sources of information or on his right to inspect corporate records (*see supra*, §§674-692). [**Rales v. Blasband**, 634 A.2d 927 (Del. 1993)]

(d) Derivative suit against less than a majority of the directors [§756]

If a derivative suit alleges wrongdoing by a minority of the directors, courts have held that the suit may be barred if the disinterested director majority makes a good faith business judgment that the suit is not in the corporation's best interests. [**Untermeyer v. Fidelity Daily Income Trust**, 580 F.2d 22 (1st Cir. 1978)] In contrast, the New Jersey Supreme Court has recently applied a "modified business judgment rule" in a shareholder suit against a company's officers for mismanagement, barring the action if: (i) the members of the board were independent and disinterested, (ii) the board acted in good faith and with due care in their investigation of the shareholder's allegations, *and* (iii) the board's decision was reasonable. [*In re* **PSE & G Shareholder Litigation**, 801 A.2d 295 (N.J. 2002)]

1) Discovery permitted [§757]

The *PSE & G* case also held that the plaintiff-shareholder was entitled to discovery of the steps the board took to inform itself about its decision.

(e) Special litigation committee in derivative suit alleging wrongdoing by a majority of directors [§758]

A board of directors (a majority of which may be interested) may appoint a special committee of disinterested directors, which may be advised by special counsel, to determine whether the suit would be in the corporation's best interest. Most courts have held that the good faith decision of such a committee to terminate the suit is governed by the business judgment rule. [**Auerbach v. Bennett**, 47 N.Y.2d 619 (1979)]

1) **Limited judicial review [§759]**

The court will determine whether the special committee was truly disinterested and whether its procedures and methodology of investigation were sufficient. [**Auerbach v. Bennett,** *supra*]

a) **Note on burden [§760]**

Some courts have explicitly placed the burden of proving independence, good faith, reasonableness of investigation, and reasonable bases for the special committee's conclusions on the corporation seeking to dismiss the derivative suit. [**Zapata Corp. v. Maldonado,** 430 A.2d 779 (Del. 1981); *and see* RMBCA §7.44(e)—adopts this position]

b) **"Independence" [§761]**

Several recent decisions note that "independence" focuses on *impartiality* and *objectivity*, but mere acquaintanceship and social interaction are not per se bars. Rather the question turns on whether there is any *substantial reason* that the director cannot base a decision only on the *merits*, *i.e.,* what is in the corporation's best interests. [**Einhorn v. Culea,** 612 N.W.2d 78 (Wis. 2000); *In re* **Oracle Corp. Derivative Litigation,** 824 A.2d 917 (Del. 2003)]

2) **Distinguish—court's independent judgment [§762]**

Some decisions further provide that the court *may* also apply its *own* independent business judgment (as well as consider matters of public policy) as to whether termination of the derivative suit is in the corporation's best interest. [**Zapata Corp. v. Maldonado,** *supra*; **Kaplan v. Wyatt,** 499 A.2d 1184 (Del. 1985)—emphasizing that this step is within court's discretion]

a) **Burden of proof [§763]**

It has been held in cases where a majority of the directors are charged with self-dealing that the court must determine whether the defendant-directors will be able to show that the transaction complained of was fair and reasonable to the corporation (*see supra,* §291). [**Alford v. Shaw,** 358 S.E.2d 323 (N.C. 1987)]

3) **Distinguish—general review only [§764]**

Other decisions hold that courts should abstain from imposing their own business judgments. Rather, the court should consider a variety of factors—the likelihood of a judgment in the plaintiff's favor, the expected recovery as compared to out-of-pocket costs, whether the corporation took corrective action, and whether dismissal would allow any defendant with control to retain a significant improper benefit—and determine whether the special committee's decision is reasonable and principled. [**Houle v. Low,** 556 N.E.2d 51 (Mass. 1990)]

4) Minority view [§765]

It has been held that directors charged with misconduct have no power to select a special litigation committee. Rather, if the derivative suit alleges wrongdoing by a majority of the board, the corporation may request the court to appoint a "special panel" to act in place of the board of directors. [**Miller v. Register & Tribune Syndicate, Inc.,** 336 N.W.2d 709 (Iowa 1983)] This procedure is also *authorized* by the Model Act. [RMBCA §7.44(f)]

5) Violations of federal law [§766]

If the derivative suit charges a violation of federal law, the question of whether a special litigation committee may terminate the suit by deciding that it is not in the corporation's best interest depends on (i) whether the relevant state law allows the board to delegate such decisions to a committee of disinterested directors, and (ii) whether it would be consistent with the federal law allegedly violated. [**Burks v. Lasker,** 441 U.S. 471 (1979)]

a) Section 10(b) [§767]

Neither the policies underlying rule 10b-5 nor the disclosure requirements of the federal proxy rules are offended by permitting a special litigation committee to terminate a derivative suit alleging a violation of section 10(b) or of section 14(a) of the Securities Exchange Act of 1934. [**Lewis v. Anderson,** 615 F.2d 778 (9th Cir. 1979)]

(2) Demand on shareholders [§768]

In a number of states, the plaintiff in a derivative suit must also make a demand on the shareholders—although this is often qualified by some phrase such as "if necessary." [Fed. R. Civ. P. 23.1] (California and New York require only that demand be made on the directors. [Cal. Corp. Code §800(b)(2); N.Y. Bus. Corp. Law §626(c); *and see* RMBCA §7.42])

(a) When excused [§769]

Demand on the shareholders is usually excused if the alleged wrongdoing is beyond the power of the shareholders to "ratify." [**Continental Securities Co. v. Belmont,** 206 N.Y. 7 (1912)]

Derivative suit questions are common on law school exams. If someone (*e.g.*, an officer, a director, a third-party contractor—often one related to an officer, director, or majority shareholder) has breached a duty owed to the corporation and the corporation has not sought a remedy for the breach, a shareholder derivative suit may be appropriate. However, be sure to note that the shareholder has some hurdles to jump before bringing suit, the first being that *corporate remedies must have been exhausted*. Most notably, the shareholder usually must have *made a demand* on the board and/or shareholders that the corporation bring suit. However, a few jurisdictions will excuse such a demand if it would be futile or the shareholders have ratified the wrong.

1) **Fraud [§770]**

Courts are split on whether a majority of the disinterested shareholders may "ratify" an alleged fraud on the corporation by its directors. [**Claman v. Robertson,** 128 N.E.2d 429 (Ohio 1955)—fraud ratifiable; **Mayer v. Adams,** 141 A.2d 458 (Del. 1958)—contra]

2) **Illegal acts [§771]**

It has been held that shareholders have no power to ratify illegal acts by the directors that cause injury to the corporation (*e.g.*, antitrust violations), and hence no demand need be made prior to a derivative suit. [**Rogers v. American Can Co.,** 305 F.2d 297 (3d Cir. 1962)]

3) **Negligence, unreasonable business judgment [§772]**

Shareholders do have power to ratify alleged negligence or unreasonable business judgment by the directors. Hence, the demand is not excused under those circumstances. [**Smith v. Brown-Borhek Co.,** 200 A.2d 398 (Pa. 1964)]

4) **Lack of prior authorization [§773]**

Similarly, shareholders may ratify actions by the board that are voidable due to lack of prior authorization (*e.g.*, no shareholder approval). [**Continental Securities Co. v. Belmont,** *supra*]

5) **Nonratifiable wrongs [§774]**

Even if the wrongdoing is not ratifiable, some courts still require a demand on shareholders so as to inform them and give them an opportunity to take appropriate action—such as removing the directors, electing new ones who will cause the corporation to sue, or determining that the suit is not in the corporation's best interest. [**Bell v. Arnold,** 487 P.2d 545 (Colo. 1971)]

6) Cost of demand as excuse [§775]

Courts are split on the question of whether a shareholder demand should be excused when the shareholders are so numerous and widespread as to make the cost of such demand extremely expensive. [**Levitt v. Johnson,** 334 F.2d 815 (1st Cir. 1964)—demand excused; **Saigh v. Busch,** 403 S.W.2d 559 (Mo. 1966)—contra]

(b) Effect of shareholders' refusal to sue [§776]

If a demand on the shareholders is required (*i.e.,* if the alleged wrongdoing is subject to ratification by the shareholders, or if the jurisdiction requires that the shareholders be informed of the suit) and the majority of disinterested shareholders make a good faith decision not to sue, the derivative suit ordinarily may not be maintained. [**S. Solomont & Sons Trust, Inc. v. New England Theatres Operating Corp.,** 93 N.E.2d 241 (Mass. 1950)] *Rationale:* The shareholder body has power to determine what is in the best interests of the corporation.

1) Limitation [§777]

Of course, the ratification or refusal to sue must be by a *disinterested* majority—not by shareholders who were the direct or indirect wrongdoers or beneficiaries of the allegedly wrongful transaction.

c. Qualifications of plaintiff

(1) Shareholder status [§778]

A few states require that the plaintiff be a "registered" shareholder or shareholder "of record" in order to bring a derivative suit. However, most also permit suit to be initiated by a "beneficial" or "equitable" owner of shares—*e.g.,* the holder of a voting trust certificate, or the purchaser of shares who has not yet been recorded on the corporation's books. [**Theodora Holding Corp. v. Henderson,** 257 A.2d 398 (Del. 1969); Cal. Corp. Code §800(b)(1)]

(a) Convertible bondholders [§779]

Some classes of creditors have the right to exchange their debt for shares (*e.g.,* owners of bonds that are convertible into stock). Courts are split on whether such creditors are "equitable" owners of shares. [*Compare* **Harff v. Kerkorian,** 324 A.2d 215 (Del. 1974)—debtholder until conversion takes place; *with* **Hoff v. Sprayregan,** 52 F.R.D. 243 (S.D.N.Y. 1971)—Securities Exchange Act includes convertible bonds within definition of "equity security"]

(b) Multiple derivative suits [§780]

The shareholder of a parent corporation has a sufficient economic interest in a subsidiary of the parent to bring a derivative suit on the subsidiary's cause of action. [**Blasband v. Rales,** 971 F.2d 1034 (3d Cir. 1992)]

(c) Action after merger or dissolution [§781]

The Principles of Corporate Governance permit a person who has ceased to be a shareholder because of a merger or dissolution in which he did not acquiesce to bring a derivative suit on behalf of the terminated corporation if no others are eligible to assert the claim. [A.L.I. Prin. Corp. Gov. §7.02(a)(2); *compare* **Pessin v. Chris-Craft Industries, Inc.,** 181 A.D.2d 66 (1992)—when plaintiff's corporation (ABC) has been merged into XYZ and plaintiff has received XYZ stock in exchange for ABC stock, plaintiff cannot bring a derivative suit asserting a claim on behalf of ABC that arose before the merger; plaintiff was not an XYZ shareholder at the time of the alleged wrongdoing and his XYZ stock was not acquired by "operation of law" (*see infra,* §785)]

(d) Direct action possible by former shareholders [§782]

One who is no longer a shareholder normally cannot maintain a derivative suit. However, where he sold his shares *without knowledge* of management's wrongdoing, and the wrong would otherwise go *unremedied,* a former shareholder may be allowed a *direct* action against the wrongdoers to compensate for the loss in value of the shares sold. [**Watson v. Button,** 235 F.2d 235 (9th Cir. 1956)]

1) Illustration

A and B were the sole shareholders of XYZ Corp. A looted the corporate treasury, unbeknownst to B. Then, A and B sold their shares to C. Later, B discovered A's wrongdoing and realized that she received less for her shares because of it.

a) No derivative action possible

B cannot maintain a derivative suit on behalf of XYZ because she is no longer a shareholder of record. Nor can C maintain such an action, because of the contemporaneous ownership requirement. Furthermore, because the sole shareholder, C, is barred from suing on behalf of the corporation, the corporation itself is barred. [**Kirk v. First National Bank,** 439 F. Supp. 1141 (M.D. Ga. 1977)]

b) Direct action permitted

Under these circumstances, courts permit the innocent former shareholder (B) to bring a direct action against the wrongdoer (A) for the amount by which the fraud or mismanagement reduced the value of the shares sold because the wrong would otherwise go unremedied. [**Watson v. Button,** *supra*]

(2) Contemporaneous ownership [§783]

Most states require the plaintiff to have been a shareholder at the time of the alleged wrongdoing. Shareholders cannot complain of wrongs that occurred *before* they purchased their shares. [Fed. R. Civ. P. 23.1; RMBCA §7.41(i); Cal. Corp. Code §800(b)(1)]

(a) Underlying rationale [§784]

One historic purpose is to prevent so-called "strike suits"—actions stirred up by persons who search out corporate irregularities, buy a few shares, and file suit to secure a private settlement, rather than to obtain recovery for the corporation. (The current rule, however, requires that any amount received in settlement be paid over to the corporation; *see infra*, §815.) Another reason for the rule is that one not a shareholder at the time of the alleged wrongdoing suffers no injury and thus should not be permitted to sue. [**Home Fire Insurance Co. v. Barber,** 93 N.W. 1024 (Neb. 1903)]

(b) Exceptions

1) "Operation of law" [§785]

The contemporaneous ownership requirement generally does not apply if the plaintiff acquires her shares "by operation of law from a holder who was a holder at the time of the transaction" complained of (*e.g.*, by inheritance). [Cal. Corp. Code §800(b)(1)]

2) Securities Exchange Act section 16(b) [§786]

The contemporaneous ownership requirement is expressly inapplicable to shareholder suits for short-swing profits under section 16(b), which really are not true derivative suits. [**Dottenheim v. Murchison,** *supra*, §493]

3) Injustice [§787]

A few state statutes also waive the rule of contemporaneous ownership if it is shown "that there is a strong prima facie case in favor of the claim asserted on behalf of the corporation" and that without such suit serious injustice will result. [Pa. Bus. Corp. Law §1782(b); Cal. Corp. Code §800(b)(1)]

4) Continuing wrongs [§788]

Where the wrong is continuing in nature, the plaintiff need not have owned the shares at the inception of the wrong. [**Palmer v. Morris,** 316 F.2d 649 (5th Cir. 1963)—corporation sold assets to defendant at unduly low price before plaintiff became shareholder but received payments for shares after plaintiff was shareholder]

(c) **Corporation may be barred where controlling shareholder disqualified—"piercing corporate veil" [§789]**

Where the controlling shareholder of a corporation acquires the shares *after* the alleged wrongdoing, the shareholder is clearly barred by the contemporaneous shareholder requirement from maintaining a derivative suit against the former management. And in such cases, equitable considerations may require that the *corporation itself* also be barred. [**Bangor Punta Operations, Inc. v. Bangor & Aristook Railroad,** 417 U.S. 703 (1974)]

Example: A purchases all of the stock of XYZ Corp. from B for a fair price. A cannot maintain a derivative suit charging B with mismanagement during the time B owned the controlling shares. Nor will A be permitted to cause XYZ Corp. to file a suit against B under these circumstances. *Rationale*: Equity will not permit a controlling shareholder to use the corporate veil to obtain indirectly that which he could not recover directly. Because he bargained for and received the controlling shares for a fair price, the seller's prior acts of corporate mismanagement caused the purchaser no injury. To allow the corporation to recover would in effect allow the purchaser to recoup what he voluntarily paid for the shares. [**Bangor Punta Operations, Inc. v. Bangor & Aristook Railroad,** *supra*]

---

1) **"Unfair" price [§790]**

This rationale does not apply, however, if the price paid did not reflect the earlier wrongdoing by the seller. [**Rifkin v. Steele Platt,** 824 P.2d 32 (Colo. 1991)—corporation may recover for seller's breach of fiduciary duty prior to sale]

(3) **Fair and adequate representative [§791]**

At least under the Federal Rules [Fed. R. Civ. P.23.1; *and see* RMBCA §7.41(2)], it must appear that the plaintiff-shareholder "fairly and adequately" represents the interests of the shareholders generally in enforcing the rights of the corporation. [**Hornreich v. Plant Industries, Inc.,** 535 F.2d 550 (9th Cir. 1976)—action dismissed where it appeared motive of plaintiff-shareholder was to force corporation to settle direct suit by plaintiff against it]

CHECKLIST OF PREREQUISITES TO BRINGING A SHAREHOLDER DERIVATIVE SUIT **gilbert**

TO BRING A SHAREHOLDER DERIVATIVE SUIT, THE PLAINTIFF MUST:

☑ Have *made a demand* on the directors and/or (in a number of states) the shareholders

☑ Be a *shareholder of record* or a *beneficial or equitable owner* of stock

☑ Have *owned stock at the time of the alleged wrong* or have had it devolve upon her by operation of law from one who was a shareholder at the time of the alleged wrong*

☑ *Fairly and adequately represent* the interests of the corporation and other shareholders

*There are exceptions under Securities Exchange Act section 16(b), where the wrong is continuing, and, in a few states, where injustice would otherwise result.

d. Procedural issues in derivative suits

(1) Pleadings [§792]

Under most statutes, the plaintiff-shareholder's complaint must allege a qualification to sue (contemporaneous share ownership), exhaustion of corporate remedies (demand on directors and shareholders, if necessary), and the wrong or injury to the corporation. [Fed. R. Civ. P. 23.1]

(a) Verify pleadings [§793]

Although the plaintiff is required, under the Federal Rules, to verify the pleadings, he need not personally understand the allegations. He may properly rely on the judgment of another person (*i.e.*, his attorney). [**Surowitz v. Hilton Hotels Corp.**, 383 U.S. 363 (1966)]

(2) Legal representation—conflict of interest problem [§794]

Although the corporation is joined as a defendant as an indispensable party, the action is still brought on its behalf; its interests are ordinarily adverse to the other defendants (especially where its officers and directors are charged with wrongdoing). Thus, most courts hold that it is improper for the corporation attorney, or any other lawyer, to represent *both* the corporation and the real defendants. They must retain separate counsel. [**Cannon v. U.S. Acoustics Corp.**, 398 F. Supp. 209 (N.D. Ill. 1975); *and see* Legal Ethics Summary]

(a) Attorney-client privilege [§795]

The corporation is a "client" of its attorney; thus, communications between the corporation's lawyer and either the corporation's control group of managers or its lower level executives are privileged. [**Upjohn Co. v. United States**, 449 U.S. 383 (1981)]

(3) Right to jury trial

(a) General rule [§796]

Because a derivative suit is an equitable action, a jury trial often is *not* available in state courts. [**Rankin v. Frebank Co.,** 47 Cal. App. 3d 75 (1975)] But some states do provide a right to a jury trial. [**Finance, Investment & Rediscount Co. v. Wells,** 409 So. 2d 1341 (Ala. 1981)]

(b) Federal actions [§797]

In federal actions, the Seventh Amendment right to a jury trial has been held to apply to those issues upon which the *corporation* would have had a right to a jury trial had it brought the action. Thus, for example, where the issue is the corporation's right to recover damages for fraud, the plaintiff is entitled to a jury trial. [**Ross v. Bernhard,** 396 U.S. 531 (1970)—decision applicable to federal litigation only, as Seventh Amendment is not binding on states]

e. Security for expenses [§798]

To discourage "strike suits" (*supra*, §784), a few states (now less than a dozen) have statutes that require the plaintiff-shareholder in a derivative suit, under certain circumstances, to *post a bond* or other security to indemnify the corporation against certain of its litigation expenses in the event the plaintiff loses the suit.

(1) When plaintiff must post security [§799]

Statutes vary considerably as to when security is required.

(a) Mandatory posting of security [§800]

Under some statutes, the plaintiff is required to post security if he owns less than a specified percentage of outstanding shares (*e.g.*, 5%); or less than a specified dollar amount of the corporation's stock (*e.g.*, $25,000 or $50,000). [N.Y. Bus. Corp. Law §627]

1) May aggregate holdings [§801]

In these states, if several shareholders join in bringing the action (or join after the action is filed), their holdings may be aggregated to avoid the security requirement. [**Baker v. MacFadden Publications, Inc.,** 300 N.Y. 325 (1950)]

2) Acquiring shares after action is filed [§802]

It is unclear whether a plaintiff may avoid the security requirement by acquiring the specified percentage or dollar amount after suit is filed. [**Haberman v. Tobin,** 626 F.2d 1101 (2d Cir. 1980)—suit dismissed, but plaintiff repeatedly disregarded judge's orders]

(b) Discretionary posting of security [§803]

Other statutes make the posting of security discretionary with the court. For example, they may provide that the trial judge is authorized to order the plaintiff to deposit security if it appears "that there is no reasonable possibility that the action will benefit the corporation or its shareholders." [Cal. Corp. Code §800(c)] One statute authorizes the court to deny a request for security if the plaintiff can show that it would "impose undue hardship . . . and serious injustice would result." [Pa. Bus. Corp. Law §1782(c)]

(2) Who is entitled to security [§804]

Under most statutes, only the *corporation* is entitled to move for the posting of security; and the bond or other security posted runs only in its favor. [N.Y. Bus. Corp. Law §627]

(a) But note

A few statutes also permit officers or directors who are defendants in the action to demand security. [Cal. Corp. Code §800(c)]

(3) Expenses to be covered [§805]

Most statutes require the security to cover all expenses reasonably incurred by the corporation as the result of the derivative suit, including *attorneys' fees*—plus whatever litigation expenses the corporation may legally or contractually be required to pay by way of *indemnification* to its officers or directors as defendants in the action (*infra*, §§829-845). [Cal. Corp. Code §800(d)]

(a) Limitation

Some states limit the total amount of security that may be required. [*See, e.g.,* Cal. Corp. Code §800(d)—$50,000]

(4) When liability or security matures [§806]

Under a few statutes, it is enough that the plaintiff-shareholder loses the derivative suit, *i.e.*, the defendant corporation is *automatically* entitled to recourse against the bond or other security, although the amounts are to be determined by the court. [N.D. Bus. Corp. Act §86] Other statutes are more restrictive, allowing recourse against the plaintiff only if the court finds that the derivative suit was brought "without reasonable cause." [N.J. Bus. Corp. Act §3-6(2)]

(5) Applicability of state statutes to derivative suits in federal court

(a) In diversity cases [§807]

State security-for-expenses statutes are deemed "substantive" for purposes of the *Erie* doctrine. Thus, in federal derivative suits based on diversity of citizenship jurisdiction, the federal court must apply whatever security statute is applied in the local state courts. [**Cohen v. Beneficial Industrial Loan Corp.,** 337 U.S. 541 (1949)]

(b) In cases under federal securities act [§808]

State security-for-expenses statutes do not apply where the derivative suit is based on violation of the Securities Act of 1934. Here, the federal court is exercising federal question jurisdiction, and the Act has been held to reflect a congressional intent that shareholders be afforded access to federal tribunals without the constraint of such state statutes. [**McClure v. Borne Chemical Co.,** 292 F.2d 824 (3d Cir. 1961)]

(6) Distinguish—liability for court costs [§809]

Quite apart from security-for-expenses statutes, a plaintiff-shareholder who loses is liable for the court costs incurred by the prevailing parties—the same as any other litigant. (*See* Civil Procedure Summary.)

(a) No attorneys' fees [§810]

In most states, recoverable court costs do not include attorneys' fees. (Some states are contra.) Under the Model Act and the Principles of Corporate Governance, the court may order payment of reasonable attorneys' fees incurred by defendants if it finds that a derivative action was brought "without reasonable cause." [RMBCA §7.46(2); A.L.I. Prin. Corp. Gov. §7.04(d); *and see* Fed. R. Civ. Proc. 11, discussed in Civil Procedure Summary]

f. Defenses [§811]

In general, any defense that could have been asserted had the corporation brought the action (*e.g.,* statute of limitations) can also be asserted in the plaintiff-shareholder's derivative suit—plus certain equitable defenses assertable only against the plaintiff personally.

(1) Personal defenses [§812]

A derivative suit is a proceeding in equity, and laches, unclean hands, pari delicto, and other so-called equitable defenses may therefore be asserted to bar the plaintiff's action.

Example: A shareholder who *participated* or *acquiesced* in the wrong complained of cannot maintain a derivative suit on behalf of the corporation. Her conduct would be viewed as "unclean hands," precluding equitable relief. [*But see* **Kullgren v. Navy Gas & Supply Co.,** 149 P.2d 653 (Colo. 1934)—contra]

g. Res judicata [§813]

Judgment on the merits or a court-approved settlement in a derivative suit is res judicata to the claims asserted in the suit. Because the suit was maintained on behalf of the corporation, judgment on the merits *for or against* the defendants bars any further suits for the same wrong—either by the corporation itself, or by any other shareholders in derivative suits.

h. Settlement and recovery [§814]

Because the cause of action belongs to the corporation, so does any settlement or judgment (except in the "unusual circumstances" noted below). The plaintiff-shareholder benefits only indirectly, through any increase in the value of stock.

(1) Private settlements barred [§815]

If a plaintiff-shareholder personally receives any consideration to discontinue the action, it is held in trust for the corporation and must be paid over. [**Clarke v. Greenberg**, 296 N.Y. 146 (1947)]

(2) Procedural requirements [§816]

Most states require that settlement or dismissal of derivative suits be subject to *court approval* after some form of notice to all shareholders. [Fed. R. Civ. P. 23.1; RMBCA §7.45]

(a) Without notice and court approval [§817]

Absent such notice and approval, the settlement or dismissal will not be given res judicata effect; *i.e.*, other shareholders or the corporation may be permitted to sue again. [**Papilsky v. Berndt**, 466 F.2d 251 (2d Cir. 1972)]

(b) Judicial approach to approval [§818]

A proposed settlement must be fair and reasonable to the corporation. Among the circumstances that courts consider are: (i) the validity of the claims, (ii) the difficulties in enforcing the claims, (iii) the amount of proposed settlement, (iv) the collectibility of any judgment, (v) the expense of litigation, and (vi) the views of all parties involved. [**Polk v. Good**, 507 A.2d 531 (Del. 1986)]

1) Burden of proof [§819]

Proponents of the settlement bear the burden of proof that the settlement is in the best interests of the corporation. [***In re* General Tire & Rubber Co. Securities Litigation**, 726 F.2d 1074 (6th Cir. 1984)]

(3) Shareholders may recover under "unusual circumstances" [§820]

Under special circumstances, recovery in a derivative suit may be ordered paid directly to certain shareholders rather than to the corporate treasury.

(a) Corporation dissolved [§821]

If the corporation has been dissolved and *all creditors paid*, no purpose would be served by ordering it paid to the corporation, and therefore the court may properly order any recovery paid to the shareholders.

(b) Corporate recovery would benefit those not entitled [§822]

Where a corporate recovery would benefit certain shareholders not entitled to it, the court may order the money paid to other shareholders. For example, in **Perlman v. Feldmann** (*supra*, §731), a shareholder sold "control" of the corporation to a buyer who made it a captive supplier and thereby deprived the corporation of profits it otherwise would have made. The former controlling shareholder was ordered to account for the improper profits that he made on the sale. However, these profits were ordered paid to the remaining shareholders rather than to the corporation to prevent the buyer (new controlling shareholder) from participating in the recovery.

(c) Comment

This kind of "bypass" of the corporate treasury is tantamount to the court's declaring a dividend from the corporation to the innocent shareholders. It will ordinarily be done only when the rights of creditors are not prejudiced.

i. Reimbursement to plaintiff for litigation expenses [§823]

If victorious, the plaintiff-shareholder may be entitled to reimbursement from the corporation for litigation expenses, including reasonable attorneys' fees.

(1) Common fund doctrine [§824]

At least where the derivative suit results in a monetary recovery to the corporation, such reimbursement is based on the equitable doctrine that one who has obtained a "common fund" for the benefit of others (here, the other shareholders) is entitled to reimbursement. [**Fletcher v. A.J. Industries Inc.**, 266 Cal. App. 2d 313 (1968)]

(2) "Substantial benefit" to corporation [§825]

Even in the absence of a monetary recovery, many courts order reimbursement to a successful plaintiff if the derivative suit has resulted in a *substantial benefit* to the corporation. [**Bosch v. Meeker Cooperative Light & Power Association**, 101 N.W.2d 423 (Minn. 1960)—election of directors held illegal; **Mills v. Electric Auto-Lite Co.**, *supra*, §605—management's proxy statement held violative of proxy rules]

(a) Derivative suit not required [§826]

It has been held that a plaintiff may obtain reimbursement for litigation expenses in any suit (including an individual action) that results in a substantial benefit to the corporation. A derivative suit (or a class action) is not required. [**Tandycrafts, Inc. v. Initio Partners**, 562 A.2d 1162 (Del. 1989)]

(3) Amount of fee [§827]

Courts have used two basic approaches in determining the amount of the fee to be awarded. Some courts award a percentage of the amount recovered for the corporation ("salvage value" approach). [*In re* **Oracle Securities Litigation,** 131 F.R.D. 688 (N.D. Cal. 1990)] However, the majority approach today focuses on the time counsel spent on the case, adjusted to reflect the quality of the work done and the risk assumed by the lawyer ("lodestar" approach). [**Lindy Bros. Builders v. American Radiator & Standard Sanitary Corp.,** 487 F.2d 161 (3d Cir. 1973)]

(a) Middle position [§828]

The Principles of Corporate Governance *permit* either the salvage value or lodestar approaches, but sets a percentage of recovery as a ceiling on the maximum fee allowable. [A.L.I. Prin. Corp. Gov. §7.17]

EXAM TIP   **gilbert**

If an exam question involves a settlement or recovery in a shareholder derivative suit, there are three key points to remember:

(i) The *plaintiff cannot privately settle* the case.

(ii) Settlements generally *must be approved* by the court.

(iii) Any recovery usually *goes to the corporation* and not to the shareholder who brought the suit (although a victorious shareholder usually is entitled to reimbursement for litigation expenses, including reasonable attorneys' fees).

---

j. Indemnification of officers and directors [§829]

Statutes in all states govern the extent to which the corporation may properly indemnify its directors or officers (or other employees or agents) for expenses incurred in defending suits against them for conduct undertaken in their official capacity. These statutes apply not only to derivative suits, but also to direct actions by the corporation, its shareholders, or third parties (*e.g.,* the state for a criminal violation; or an injured party for a tort).

(1) Scope of statutes [§830]

In some states, such statutes constitute the exclusive basis upon which indemnification is permitted. Any broader provision in the corporation's articles or bylaws is void as contrary to public policy. [RMBCA §8.58] Other states permit the subject to be governed by the articles or bylaws, shareholder agreements, or votes of the shareholders or directors. [Cal. Corp. Code §317(g); Del. Gen. Corp. Law §145(f); N.Y. Bus. Corp. Law §721]

(2) "Official capacity" [§831]

Courts have been generous in construing the scope of coverage afforded by indemnification statutes. Not only are directors and officers entitled to indemnification when sued for breach of duty to the corporation or for a

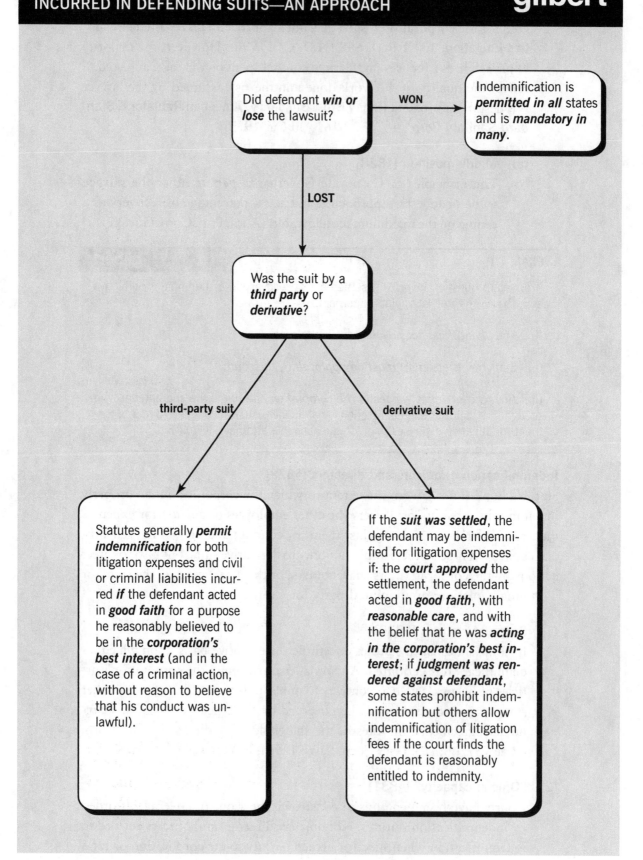

Did defendant win or lose the lawsuit?

WON → Indemnification is **permitted in all** states and is **mandatory in many**.

LOST

Was the suit by a third party or derivative?

third-party suit

Statutes generally **permit indemnification** for both litigation expenses and civil or criminal liabilities incurred **if** the defendant acted in **good faith** for a purpose he reasonably believed to be in the **corporation's best interest** (and in the case of a criminal action, without reason to believe that his conduct was unlawful).

derivative suit

If the **suit was settled**, the defendant may be indemnified for litigation expenses if: the **court approved** the settlement, the defendant acted in **good faith**, with **reasonable care**, and with the belief that he was **acting in the corporation's best interest**; if **judgment was rendered against defendant**, some states prohibit indemnification but others allow indemnification of litigation fees if the court finds the defendant is reasonably entitled to indemnity.

wrong committed on behalf of the corporation, but also for actions that are more tangential to their official roles. [**Heffernan v. Pacific Dunlop GNB Corp.,** 965 F.2d 369 (7th Cir. 1992)—director failed to disclose information to buyer when selling his shares in corporation]

(3) Where defendant wins [§832]

As long as the director or officer accused of wrongdoing *wins on the merits*, there is generally no problem. Every state permits the corporation to reimburse him for his litigation expenses, including attorneys' fees, in defending the action.

(a) Rationale [§833]

Public policy favors indemnification where the director or officer is vindicated. Indemnification encourages capable directors and officers to seek and retain corporate office and to resist unfounded charges against them. Moreover, it discourages minority shareholders from filing frivolous derivative suits, knowing that the defendants will contest such suits vigorously because their expenses will be paid by the corporation if they win. [**Solimine v. Hollander,** 19 A.2d 344 (N.J. 1941)]

(b) Indemnification as discretionary or mandatory [§834]

In some states, reimbursement is discretionary with the board. But under many statutes, the corporation is required to indemnify a director or officer where successful on the merits (some add "or otherwise") in defense of a derivative suit or direct action against her in her capacity as director or officer. [Cal. Corp. Code §317(d); N.Y. Bus. Corp. Law §724; Del. Gen. Corp. Law §145]

1) "Or otherwise" [§835]

A director or officer is considered to have successfully defended, and thus is entitled to indemnification, even if the suit is dismissed because of a "technical" defense—*e.g.,* statute of limitations, improper service of process—and the dismissal does not mean "moral exoneration." [**Waltuch v. ContiCommodity Services, Inc.,** 88 F.3d 87 (2d Cir. 1996)]

2) "Fees on fees" [§836]

Courts have split on whether the statutory provision—that the corporation's indemnification must include "attorneys' fees actually and necessarily incurred as a result" of defending the suit—covers legal fees incurred by the director or officer in *suing the corporation* to secure the required indemnification. [**Baker v. Health Management Systems, Inc.,** 98 N.Y. 2d 80 (2002)—no; **Stifel Financial Corp. v. Cochran,** 809 A.2d 555 (Del. 2002)—yes]

(4) Where defendant settles or loses [§837]

The statutes vary significantly on the extent to which the indemnification is permissible when the officer or director loses the lawsuit or the suit is settled. Many statutes distinguish between third-party suits and derivative suits:

(a) Third-party suits [§838]

If the suit against the director or officer is by an outsider (*e.g.*, the state, in criminal action; an injured party, in tort action), statutes generally permit indemnification for both litigation expenses and whatever civil or criminal liabilities are incurred (money paid out in settlement, judgment, or fines) provided that the disinterested directors or shareholders (or independent legal counsel) determine that the defendant director or officer acted in *good faith* for a purpose reasonably believed to be in the best interests of the corporation and (where a criminal action was involved) there was no reason to believe that the action involved was unlawful. [N.Y. Bus. Corp. Law §722(b); Del. Gen. Corp. Law §145(a); *and see* Cal. Corp. Code §317(b)]

(b) Derivative suits [§839]

However, where the suit against the director or officer is a derivative action charging him with wrongdoing toward the corporation, the statutes in most states are much stricter.

1) Suit settled [§840]

If the derivative suit is settled prior to judgment, most statutes permit indemnification of the officer or director for his *litigation expenses*, including attorneys' fees, provided (i) the settlement was made with court approval, and (ii) the defendant is determined to have acted in good faith, with reasonable care, and with the belief that he was acting in the best interest of the corporation, such determination being made by a majority of the disinterested directors or shareholders, or by the court. [Cal. Corp. Code §317(c), (e)]

a) Amount paid in settlement [§841]

If the above (or similar) conditions are met, some states also permit the corporation to indemnify the director or officer for amounts paid in settlement. [N.Y. Bus. Corp. Law §722(c)]

b) Public policy [§842]

Even if the statute is not the exclusive basis for indemnification, and even if a bylaw requires the corporation to reimburse all litigation expenses regardless of the good faith of the director or officer, it has been held that public policy places limits on the corporation's ability to pay. [**Waltuch v. ContiCommodity Services, Inc.,** *supra*—denying reimbursement under these circumstances]

2) Judgment against defendant [§843]

When a director or officer in a derivative suit is adjudged to have acted dishonestly, or in bad faith, or to have obtained an improper personal gain, some statutes *prohibit* indemnification by the corporation, and this applies to both his litigation expenses and any liability imposed upon the director or officer. [N.Y. Bus. Corp. Law §721; *and see* Cal. Corp. Code §317(g)—prohibiting indemnification if director acts in "reckless disregard" of duty]

a) Rationale

It would destroy the purpose of the derivative suit if the corporation could make the errant director or officer "whole" for the consequences of this breach of duty to the corporation.

b) Distinguish

But statutes allow the corporation to indemnify the errant director or officer for his litigation expenses including attorneys' fees (but not the damages assessed against him) in the derivative suit—if the court finds "such person is fairly and reasonably entitled to such indemnity." [Del Gen. Corp. Law §145; Cal. Corp. Code §317(c)(1); N.Y. Bus. Corp. Law §722]

(5) Advancing expenses [§844]

Most statutes also authorize the corporation to advance expenses in defending these suits prior to final disposition of the matter, as long as the directors and officers agree to repay the advance if it is ultimately determined that they are not entitled to it under the indemnification statute or properly authorized bylaws. [RMBCA §8.53; Cal. Corp. Code §317(b); Del. Gen. Corp. Law §145(e); N.Y. Bus. Corp. Law §723(c)] Thus, the corporation may agree to *advance* expenses even though the eventual result in the suit (*e.g.*, director found guilty of wrongdoing) would bar the corporation from *paying* the expenses. [**Citadel Holding Corp. v. Roven**, 603 A.2d 818 (Del. 1992)]

(a) Security not required [§845]

Most statutes provide that the director's undertaking to repay need not be secured and may be accepted without reference to financial ability to repay. [RMBCA §8.53(b)]

k. Insurance against derivative suit liability [§846]

Most states have statutes that authorize a corporation to purchase and maintain insurance to protect the corporation against liability to its directors and officers for indemnification as authorized by law, and to protect the directors and officers against *any liability* arising out of their service to the corporation and against the expense of defending suits asserting such liability. (Sometimes, but not always, the directors and officers pay a portion of the insurance premium to reflect the cost of their coverage.)

(1) Statutes [§847]

Some statutes are quite permissive and authorize the corporation to maintain such insurance against any liability or expense incurred by a director or officer acting in an official capacity whether or not the corporation has power to indemnify the director or officer for the alleged misconduct. [Del. Gen. Corp. Law §145(g); Cal. Corp. Code §317(i); RMBCA §8.57]

(a) Distinguish

Other statutes prohibit a corporation's insuring its officers or directors against liability for acts involving deliberate dishonesty or where the wrongdoer "personally gained a financial profit or other advantage to which he was not legally entitled." [N.Y. Bus. Corp. Law §726(b); *and see* A.L.I. Prin. Corp. Gov. §7.20(a)(2)]

(a) Comment

To the extent that such insurance is permitted, it may enable a corporation to do indirectly (by paying insurance premiums) that which it could not do directly (indemnifying officers and directors against liability for breach of duty to corporation).

(b) Public policy

Merely insuring against liability for acts of negligence is no doubt permissible. But if the insurance purports to insure against liability for intentional dishonesty or self-dealing by directors, it may be unenforceable as contrary to public policy.

4. Distinguish—Suits by Directors or Officers [§848]

Some state statutes permit directors or officers to bring suits on behalf of the corporation. These are generally subject to fewer restrictions than shareholders' derivative suits (*e.g.*, no prior demand on the board of directors or shareholders is required). [N.Y. Bus. Corp. Law §720(b)]

Chapter Eight:
Capitalization of the Corporation

CONTENTS

Chapter Approach

This chapter concerns the capitalization of the corporation through the issuance of shares, and the regulations incident thereto. Some important areas for exam purposes are as follows:

1. **Stock Subscriptions**

   Subscriptions are agreements to purchase shares from the corporation. If such an agreement appears on your exam, first determine whether the agreement was entered into before or after formation of the corporation. *Post-incorporation* agreements are binding contracts; *pre-incorporation* agreements, however, vary in enforceability. A pre-incorporation agreement may be found to be merely a continuing offer and, thus, unenforceable. Most statutes eliminate the problem by making pre-incorporation subscriptions irrevocable for a designated period (*e.g.*, six months) in the absence of a contrary agreement.

2. **Consideration Required to Be Paid for Shares**

   Statutes generally regulate the form and the amount of consideration the corporation must receive for its shares.

   a. **Form**

      Remember that under traditional statutes "money paid, labor done, or property actually acquired" is valid consideration, while an executory promise generally is not. However, modern statutes permit shares to be issued for a promise of future payment or services.

   b. **Amount**

      A corporation must receive full payment for its shares. To determine whether shares have been paid for in full, start by checking to see whether the shares are par or no-par value shares. Remember that, ordinarily, par value shares must be sold for at least par value, or they are considered "watered." Watch out for stock that has either been sold for *less than par value* (discount shares) or issued in exchange for *overvalued property or services*. *No-par* value stock eliminates the watered stock problem because it may be sold at whatever price is deemed *reasonable* by the board.

3. **Fiduciary Duties of Promoters**

   If an exam question concerns a promoter selling property to the corporation, note that the promoter has a fiduciary duty of *full disclosure*. If the promoter fails to make a full disclosure with respect to his dealings with the corporation, the corporation may sue for either rescission or damages.

4. **Preemptive Rights**

   At common law, a shareholder has a right to subscribe to the number of shares in a *new* issuance that will preserve his proportionate interest in the corporation. Remember that, when recognized, preemptive rights can be enforced by specific performance to compel issuance to the plaintiff, damages, or an injunction against the issuance of shares in violation of preemptive rights.

5. Statutes Regulating Issuance of Shares

State statutes regulating the issuance of shares are known as "blue sky" laws. Some impose civil or criminal penalties for fraud in connection with the issuance of shares. All require that persons who sell securities be licensed. The most comprehensive blue sky laws require that the stock be registered with the appropriate state official.

Probably more important for exam purposes are the *federal securities laws*. The Securities Act of 1933 establishes the framework for federal regulation. The most important thing to remember is that no interstate facilities or mails may be used to offer to sell a security unless a *registration statement* has been filed with the SEC. You should also know that *written* offers to sell must always satisfy the requirements for a statutory prospectus (*i.e.*, set forth the key information from the registration statement), and actual sales or deliveries of securities may be made only after the effective date of the registration statement and a prospectus must accompany or precede the delivery of any security.

Be aware, however, that certain securities and transactions are *exempt from the registration requirements*. In particular, watch for the following *exempt transactions*: (i) ordinary trading transactions between individual investors in securities that have already been issued, (ii) transactions by a securities broker, provided she is not acting as an underwriter and the time for initial distribution of the securities has passed, (iii) transactions by an issuer not involving a public offering (*i.e.*, private placements), and (iv) offerings made entirely to residents of the issuer's state.

Finally, note that a question may ask you to consider the *remedies* for a violation of the securities laws. If so, first ask yourself whether the securities are required to be registered. If so, and if the registration statement contains a misstatement or omits a material fact, recall that *any person* acquiring the securities without knowledge thereof has an action for damages against those connected with the issuance of shares or the registration statement (*e.g.*, the corporation, directors, underwriters, experts, etc.). Note that the corporation is absolutely liable, but the others may defend on the ground that they exercised due diligence. If the securities are exempt, only the original purchaser is entitled to recover and only the issuer or other sellers may be held liable. Also, the purchaser has a cause of action against a seller for failure to comply with the federal requirements (*e.g.*, registration, delivery of prospectus, etc.).

A. Shares—In General

1. **What a Share Represents [§849]**

    A "share" represents the stockholder's proprietary interest in the corporation. Specifically (unless provided otherwise), a share represents the right to receive dividends as declared by the board, the right to receive a portion of the corporate assets on liquidation and, if voting shares are involved, the right to vote.

2. **What a Share Does Not Represent [§850]**

    Ownership of a share does *not* entitle the holder to any specific asset of the corporation or any interest in its assets as a whole. Title to corporate assets is in the corporation and cannot be conveyed by the shareholders.

B. Classes of Shares—Preferences

1. **Introduction [§851]**

    Shares of one or more classes may be authorized in the articles. All shares have equal rights except as otherwise provided in the articles.

2. **Common [§852]**

    Common stock represents the residual ownership of the corporation. The common stockholders are entitled to pro rata dividends, without priority or preference over any other stock. Normally, the common stockholders have voting rights and are entitled to the final share in the distribution of assets on liquidation.

    a. **Classes [§853]**

        A corporation may have more than one class of common stock (*e.g.*, "Common A" and "Common B"), with one class having certain rights that the other does not, or with one class entitled to certain priorities over the other. In such cases, the stock with the rights or priorities is, in effect, "preferred stock" (below).

3. **Preferred [§854]**

    Preferred stock is a class of stock having some sort of preference over other classes of stock—generally as to dividends or liquidation rights.

    a. **Classes or series [§855]**

        There may be several classes or series of preferred (*e.g.*, "Preferred A" and "Preferred B")—one with distinct priorities over the other, and both with priority over the common stock.

    b. **Redemption rights [§856]**

        Preferred stockholders may be given the right to compel the corporation to repurchase the shares if it has legally available funds to do so. (*See infra*, §§1052-1053.) This is known as a right of redemption. Frequently, the articles will require the corporation to maintain a *sinking fund* for this purpose (*i.e.*, accumulations of earnings not available for dividend distribution).

c. Particular preferences [§857]

The following are the special rights or priorities (preferences) most often given to preferred stock. As indicated above, these rights exist only if expressly conferred by the articles.

(1) Preference in receipt of dividends [§858]

The most frequent preference (and the most important) is to give preferred stock the right to receipt of dividends—*i.e.*, dividends must be paid to it at a specified rate (*e.g.*, 5% of par value or $5 per share) before dividends are paid to the holders of common stock. Whether the right to dividends is cumulative or noncumulative depends on what is provided in the articles.

(a) Cumulative [§859]

Holders of cumulative preferred shares have the right to receive payment of the designated dividend each year, whether or not there are sufficient earnings to pay it. Nonpayment in a given year does not destroy the right; the dividends "cumulate" until paid. In the absence of a specific provision, there is ordinarily no method of forcing the corporation to pay (absent abuse of discretion by the directors, below). But no amounts may be paid as dividends on inferior classes of stock until the current dividend and all arrears are paid on the cumulative preferred shares.

(b) Noncumulative [§860]

The general view is that where dividends are determined to be "noncumulative," the shareholder is entitled to dividends only if and when declared by the board. The right does not accumulate and is completely lost as to any year in which a dividend is not declared. This is true even if there are earnings available from which to pay the dividends. Absent an abuse of discretion, the shareholder cannot force the directors to declare dividends. [**Guttman v. Illinois Central Railroad**, 189 F.2d 927 (2d Cir. 1951)]

(2) Participation rights [§861]

In addition to preference in receipt of dividends, holders of preferred shares are sometimes given the right to participate with the common shares in any remaining funds available for distribution after the preferred dividend has been paid. Again, the terms and extent of such participation (whether pro rata, or different amounts for each class) are as fixed in the articles.

d. Convertibles [§862]

Preferred stockholders may be given the right to convert their shares into common stock under specified circumstances.

4. Derivatives [§863]

Newer types of securities may be "derived" from stock because their value largely depends on the value of the corporation's stock. A frequently used example is a *warrant*, which is issued by the corporation and gives the owner the option to buy the stock on designated terms.

C. Authorization and Issuance of Shares

1. Introduction [§864]

This portion of the summary deals primarily with so-called "primary" stock sales; *i.e.*, the *original issuance* of shares by a corporation, as distinguished from later resale of the shares by the issuee.

2. Authorization [§865]

Whatever shares are issued must be *authorized* by the articles or charter of the corporation (*e.g.*, "This corporation shall be authorized to issue 1,000 shares of capital stock, each share shall have a par value of $100, and the par value of all shares authorized shall be $100,000"). [RMBCA §2.02]

a. When all authorized shares issued [§866]

If all of the shares authorized under the articles have already been issued, no further shares can be issued until there is an *amendment* to the articles (*infra*, §§1145 *et seq.*) authorizing a larger number of shares.

> **EXAM TIP** **gilbert**
>
> Be sure to remember that a corporation cannot issue more shares than are authorized. Issuance beyond the number of shares authorized requires *amendment of the articles of incorporation*.

3. Issuance [§867]

Issuance is the process by which all or part of the corporation's authorized shares are sold. Issuance requires action by the board of directors accepting an offer to subscribe for shares of the corporation, and directing the secretary to issue appropriate share certificates upon receipt of the specified consideration.

a. Legislative control [§868]

The sale and issuance of shares by a corporation is subject to detailed regulation under federal and state statutes. (*See* discussion below.)

b. Shares outstanding [§869]

Once shares have been issued, they are referred to as "outstanding."

c. Repurchase of shares outstanding [§870]

Under certain circumstances, the corporation may be authorized to repurchase its shares. (*See infra*, §§1054-1071.) If it does so, it may either:

(1) *Cancel the shares* (in which case the shares would no longer be issued, thereby increasing the number of shares that the corporation could thereafter issue within its authorized capital); or

(2) *Hold repurchased shares as treasury stock.* Such stock is no longer outstanding, but the shares are still considered to be issued. Treasury stock may, however, be resold by the corporation subject to rules different from those for the sale of unissued shares. The Model Act eliminates treasury stock and provides that reacquired stock is automatically canceled. [RMBCA §6.31]

D. Stock Subscriptions

1. Definition [§871]

Stock subscriptions are agreements by subscribers to purchase stock or other securities to be issued by the corporation. Such agreements may be made prior to incorporation (it is often one of the functions of a promoter to obtain such subscriptions); or they may be made after formation as the corporation seeks to obtain or increase its capital.

2. Offer and Acceptance Problems

a. Post-incorporation subscriptions [§872]

If a subscription agreement is made between a subscriber and a corporation already in existence, it plainly constitutes a binding contract, obligating the subscriber to purchase (and the corporation to issue and sell) the securities in question. Ordinary contract principles of offer and acceptance apply.

b. Pre-incorporation subscriptions [§873]

It was less clear at common law whether a subscription for shares in a corporation yet to be formed constitutes an enforceable contract.

(1) Majority view—subscription as "continuing offer" [§874]

Most courts at common law held that a pre-incorporation subscription is *not* an enforceable agreement on the theory that because the corporation is not yet in existence (and the promoters have no power to bind the corporation, *see supra*, §§130-137), there is no contract. Thus, a pre-incorporation subscription is considered a mere "continuing offer" by the subscriber to purchase shares of the corporation—when, as, and if it comes into existence—which may be revoked by the subscriber before acceptance by the corporation.

(2) Minority view—subscription irrevocable as contract among subscribers [§875]

To avoid that result, some courts held that a pre-incorporation subscription has a dual character. In addition to being an offer to the corporation (above), it is deemed to be a *contract among the subscribers* based on their mutual promises to become shareholders upon formation of the corporation and acceptance of their offers. As such, it is binding and irrevocable at the outset.

(3) Statutes [§876]

Statutes in most states today eliminate the problem by making pre-incorporation subscriptions irrevocable for a designated period of time in the absence of contrary agreement. [*See, e.g.,* Del. Gen. Corp. Law §165—six months; RMBCA §6.20(a)—same]

EXAM TIP   **gilbert**

Subscription questions appear from time to time in exam questions. Statutes in most states have simplified the issue. Generally, a **pre-incorporation** subscription is **irrevocable** by the subscriber for a statutory period (*e.g.,* six months), while a subscription with an **existing corporation** is governed by ordinary contract law (which generally means that it is a **revocable offer until accepted** by the corporation and an **enforceable contract** once the corporation accepts).

E. Consideration Required to Be Paid for Shares

1. Introduction [§877]

Statutes in most states regulate both the *form* and *amount* of consideration that the corporation must receive on issuance of its shares.

2. Form of Consideration [§878]

Many states have statutory restrictions on the kinds of consideration for which shares may be issued. In such states, typically, shares may be issued only for "*money paid, labor done, or property actually acquired.*"

a. Executory consideration [§879]

Under restrictive statutes, executory promises generally are *not* legal consideration for the issuance of shares. Thus, *unsecured promissory notes* (executory promises to pay in the future) and executory promises to transfer assets or render services in the future are not lawful consideration. *Rationale:* This prohibition assures that a corporation's capital consists of substantial assets and prevents the issuance of stock as "fully paid" when the corporation has not actually acquired that which was promised. [**Sohland v. Baker,** 141 A. 277 (Del. 1927)]

(1) Distinguish—secured obligations [§880]

An adequately secured promissory note is generally regarded as legal consideration for share issuance, the *collateral* being regarded as "property actually acquired." [**General Bonding & Casualty Insurance Co. v. Moseley,** 222 S.W. 961 (Tex. 1920)]

(2) Exceptions [§881]

More modern statutes permit issuing shares in exchange for a promise of future payment or services. [RMBCA §6.21(b)] Indeed, the Model Act permits issuing shares in exchange for any tangible or intangible property or benefit to the corporation.

EXAM TIP   **gilbert**

Exam questions sometimes test on the type of consideration that the corporation may accept for stock. Many states follow the *traditional rule* that stock may be sold *only for money paid, labor done, or property actually acquired*. Thus, for example, if a question tells you that a corporation issues shares in exchange for a shareholder's promise to act as the corporation's manager for the next two years, or in exchange for a promissory note, you should recognize that the consideration is improper and, consequently, the shares have not been properly issued—unless the facts tell you that the corporation is in a jurisdiction following the *modern* approach.

---

3. Amount of Consideration [§882]

The price that the corporation must receive for shares issued as "fully paid" depends on whether the shares have a par value.

a. Par value shares [§883]

Generally, shares with a par value must be sold for consideration worth *at least par value*. [Del. Gen. Corp. Law §153(a)]

(1) Exception—to remedy impairment of capital [§884]

Some courts hold that a going concern (as distinguished from one just beginning business) whose *capital is impaired* may sell its shares at "the best price obtainable"—even for less than par—for the purpose of recuperating itself. [**Handley v. Stutz**, 139 U.S. 417 (1891)]

(2) "Watered stock" liability [§885]

Except in the circumstance just noted, par value shares sold for less than par are *not* "fully paid" (regardless of what the share certificate itself may state). Such stock is said to be "watered."

(a) Remedies for creditors [§886]

If the corporation becomes insolvent, its creditors may be able to recover from the shareholders the amount by which their shares were "watered."

1) Which creditors may sue [§887]

Courts are split on whether all corporate creditors may impose such liability, or only those who extended credit *after* the shares were issued; *i.e.*, the issue is whether prior creditors can be said to have been prejudiced by the issuance of watered stock. The answer depends on which theory of liability the court adopts:

####### a) Misrepresentation theory—subsequent creditors [§888]

Most courts regard the issuance of par value stock as an implied representation to its creditors that the corporation has received assets equivalent in value to the par value of the shares issued. Under this approach, only those creditors who extended credit after the shares were issued are entitled to complain of watered stock. These subsequent creditors are presumed to have extended credit *in reliance* on the corporation having received par value for its shares. However, the defendant-shareholder may prove that the subsequent creditor did not rely. [**Hospes v. Northwestern Manufacturing & Car Co.**, 50 N.W. 1117 (Minn. 1892)]

b) Trust fund theory—all creditors [§889]

A minority view imposes liability for stock watering on the theory that the capital stock of the corporation constitutes a trust fund for all of its creditors. Under this theory, a shareholder who has received shares having a par value in excess of the assets transferred to the corporation is liable to *any creditor*—prior or subsequent—with or without notice, and irrespective of reliance. [**Wood v. Dummer**, 30 F. Cas. 435 (C.C.D. Me. 1824)]

c) Statutory obligation [§890]

Some statutes codify, or have been interpreted as codifying, the trust fund theory. [Del. Gen. Corp. Law §162; **Hanewald v. Bryan's Inc.**, 429 N.W.2d 414 (N.D. 1988)]

2) Extent of liability—determining value of consideration [§891]

Most courts held that if the parties in good faith believed that the value of the property or services given to the corporation was equal to the par value of the shares issued, the stock was not watered. The effect is that watered stock liability exists only where there is *intentional overvaluation* of the assets being received by the corporation.

a) Note

Most states today have statutes embodying this rule. For example, the Delaware statute provides, "In the absence of actual fraud in the transaction, the judgment of the directors as to the value of such consideration shall be *conclusive*." [Del. Gen. Corp. Law §152]

b. No-par value shares [§892]

All states today authorize the issuance of no-par value stock. One purpose of no-par stock is to permit a corporation to issue stock in return for present market value. No-par was developed to *eliminate* the problem of watered stock liability. No-par shares may be sold at *whatever price* is determined to be *reasonable* by the board of directors.

(1) Effect of statutes requiring stated value [§893]

Most statutes require that the directors (or shareholders) determine (or state) the value of the consideration to be received by the corporation for no-par shares. [Del. Gen. Corp. Law §153(b)] In such event, no-par shares cannot be issued unless the assets are in fact worth their stated value; otherwise, the shares are "watered" and all the rules and consequences discussed above apply. [**G. Loewus & Co. v. Highland Queen Packing Co.,** 6 A.2d 545 (N.J. 1939)]

c. Actual situation today [§894]

Watered stock liability suits are much less frequent today than in the past. One reason is that many states have some sort of regulatory statute ("blue sky" laws, *infra*, §§926-933) controlling the form and amount of consideration for which shares may be issued. The result is that shares are rarely issued for less than a fair and adequate consideration to the corporation.

d. Model Act and California rule [§895]

The Model Act (which has been adopted by a number of states) and California have *eliminated* the designations of par and no-par. Shares may be sold at *whatever price* the board of directors determines in good faith to be their value. [RMBCA §6.21; Cal. Corp. Code §409(a)]

EXAM TIP   **gilbert**

The rules that govern the price at which a corporation may issue stock differ depending on whether the corporation is governed by the law of a state following the traditional par value approach or a more modern approach, such as that of the Model Act. In states following the *traditional par value approach*, you must determine whether or not the stock has a par value. If the stock has a par value, it *cannot be sold for less than par* (and, as will be discussed later, at least the aggregate par value for all such shares issued must be placed in a "stated capital" account). *No par stock* may be sold for *any amount* that the directors deem adequate, which is basically true of all stock sold in states following the more modern Model Act-type approach.

F. Fiduciary Duties of Promoters

1. Duty to Corporation [§896]

Promoters are the persons who procure commitments for capital and other instrumentalities that will be used by the corporation after it is formed. They owe a fiduciary duty to the corporation that is formed. [**Post v. United States,** 407 F.2d 319 (D.C. Cir. 1968)] Problems typically arise when, after formation, a promoter sells property that he owns to the corporation (for cash or for shares).

a. Duty of disclosure [§897]

A promoter owes the corporation a fiduciary duty of *full disclosure* as to any dealings with it in which he has a personal interest. This requires a full revelation of the promoter's interest in the property being sold to the corporation, and *all material facts* that might affect the corporation's decision to purchase—perhaps including the extent of the promoter's profit on the transaction.

b. **Effect of promoters taking all the stock with no plan to issue additional shares [§898]**

Where the promoters become the *sole* shareholders of the corporation, and there is no plan to issue shares to others as part of the original capitalization, a failure to disclose their adverse financial interest is not deemed a violation of their fiduciary duty to the corporation at common law—on the theory that they cannot conceal something from themselves.

c. **Effect of plan to issue additional shares [§899]**

The result may be different where, although the promoters were the only stockholders at the outset, a *further issue* to innocent subscribers was contemplated as *part of the original capitalization*. Initially, there was a split of authority on whether the *corporation* (under a new board of directors or through a derivative suit) could maintain an action against the original shareholders (promoters) for nondisclosure.

(1) Massachusetts rule [§900]

Most courts follow the "Massachusetts rule," which permits the corporation to maintain such an action. [**Old Dominion Copper Mining & Smelting Co. v. Bigelow**, 89 N.E. 193 (Mass. 1909)] *Rationale:* The original capitalization of the corporation is viewed as a single transaction even though the shares are issued in stages, and sale to innocent subscribers is viewed to have been intended as part of the original capitalization, so that the promoters' sale of their assets will not be deemed to have been approved by *all* the shareholders absent full disclosure to them. [**Northridge Cooperative Section No. 1, Inc. v. 32nd Avenue Construction Corp.**, 2 N.Y.2d 514 (1957)]

(2) Federal rule [§901]

The federal courts formerly held that no action could be maintained by the corporation. [**Old Dominion Copper Mining & Smelting Co. v. Lewisohn**, 210 U.S. 206 (1908)] *Rationale:* The corporation was considered a legal entity whose status could not be affected by a subsequent enlargement of its membership. Because the corporation could not sue before the innocent shareholders came in, it could not sue afterwards.

2. Effect of Securities Laws [§902]

The whole problem of promoters' fiduciary duties to a corporation organized by them is now also governed by state and federal laws regulating the issuance of corporate securities. (*See* full discussion *infra*, §§925 *et seq*.) In general, these laws make *mandatory* full disclosure of all material facts affecting the value of property received by the corporation in consideration for issuance of its shares. In particular, the Securities Act of 1933 requires disclosure of any shares issued or amounts paid to promoters within the previous two years and the consideration given by the promoter for the shares. Furthermore, some state laws stipulate that the corporation *must* receive a *fair and adequate consideration* for each issuance.

a. Result of violation [§903]

Violation of such laws may result in penal sanctions against the promoters. Civil remedies are also available to the corporation and/or the innocent shareholders allowing them to recover the amount by which they have been damaged.

G. Preemptive Rights

1. Definition [§904]

A shareholder's preemptive right is the right to subscribe to that amount of shares in a new issuance that will preserve his existing proportionate interest in the corporation. In this way, preemptive rights protect the shareholder's voting percentage and proportionate interest in the net worth of the corporation.

a. Common law [§905]

At common law, preemptive rights were *inherent*—they existed even if not provided for in the articles or bylaws. [**Stokes v. Continental Trust Co.,** 78 N.E. 1090 (N.Y. 1906)]

b. Statutes [§906]

Today, statutes in practically every state regulate preemptive rights.

(1) Implied [§907]

A minority of statutes reflect policies favoring preemptive rights, and thus provide that such rights exist unless expressly denied in the articles. [Tex. Bus. Corp. Act §2.22-1]

(2) Expressly granted [§908]

Other statutes are aimed at restricting preemptive rights because they hinder financing, and accordingly these statutes provide that no shares shall have preemptive rights unless expressly granted in the articles. [Del. Gen. Corp. Law §102(b); RMBCA §6.30(a)]

(3) Close corporations [§909]

Preemptive rights are more important in the case of small, closely held corporations. Where close corporations are treated separately by statute, preemptive rights are almost always provided.

2. When More Than One Class of Shares Exists [§910]

If a corporation has more than one class of shares (*e.g.,* common and preferred) and each class has different rights as to voting, dividends, and liquidation, it may be impossible to preserve the proportionate interest of each class exactly when a new class of shares possessing such rights is issued.

a. Statutes [§911]

Some statutes simply allow this problem to be resolved in the articles. [Del. Gen. Corp. Law §102(b)] Others authorize the board to apportion the new issues so as to "preserve as nearly as practicable" the relative rights of the different classes—and make the board's apportionment final absent fraud or bad faith. [N.Y. Bus. Corp. Law §622(d)]

3. **Authorized But Unissued Shares [§912]**

The general rule at common law was that preemptive rights applied only to new issues resulting from an *increase in the authorized capital* of the corporation. Thus, where the shares involved had been previously authorized but were not issued at the time of the original stock issuance, preemptive rights were denied—on the theory that the proportionate interest of each shareholder should be calculated in terms of the number of shares originally authorized.

a. **Statutes [§913]**

Some statutes resolve the problem by providing that, unless otherwise stated in the articles, there are no preemptive rights in shares sold within six months of their original authorization. Thereafter, preemptive rights apply. [RMBCA §6.30(b)(iii)]

4. **Shares Sold for Consideration Other Than Cash [§914]**

Most courts hold that preemptive rights apply only to shares issued for cash, and not to shares issued in exchange for property or personal services rendered to the corporation or shares issued to accomplish a merger. *Rationale:* It is more important to allow the corporation to obtain unique property or services by issuing its shares than to protect minority shareholders against dilution.

a. **Statutes [§915]**

Of those statutes that deal with the problem, most deny preemptive rights in shares issued for noncash consideration unless otherwise provided in the articles. [RMBCA §6.30(b)(3)(iv)]

CHECKLIST OF SITUATIONS WHERE PREEMPTIVE RIGHTS DO NOT APPLY — gilbert

PREEMPTIVE RIGHTS DO NOT APPLY WHEN:

- ☑ The *articles deny* preemptive rights (in some states) or *fail to grant them* (in a majority of states)
- ☑ The shares issued are of a *different class* than the shares of the person seeking to assert preemptive rights
- ☑ The shares issued are part of the *originally authorized stock* (although some states limit this to shares sold within six months of their original authorization)
- ☑ The shares issued are sold for *noncash consideration*

---

5. **Remedies [§916]**

When recognized, preemptive rights can be enforced either by: (i) suit for *specific performance* to compel issuance to the plaintiff of authorized shares in an amount necessary to retain his proportionate interest; (ii) *damages* computed on the basis of the difference between the subscription price of that amount of newly issued shares and their market value (on the theory that plaintiff can then acquire the shares on the market); or (iii) a court of equity *enjoining* the corporation from issuing shares in violation of the preemptive rights. [**Stokes v. Continental Trust Co.**, *supra*, §905]

6. Equitable Limitations on Issuance of New Shares [§917]

Regardless of whether preemptive rights are recognized, courts have recognized "quasi-preemptive rights," thereby forbidding majority shareholders or directors from causing an *unfair dilution* of the minority's interest by issuing shares to themselves at less than fair value. [**Bennett v. Breuil Petroleum Corp.**, 99 A.2d 236 (Del. 1953)]

Example: X Corp. has 600 shares outstanding, owned equally by A, B, and C. The value of the shares is $10 each. A and B (also directors) cause X Corp. to issue to them 600 new shares for $5 each. C's interest is diminished in value from $2,000 to approximately $1,500.

a. Fiduciary obligation [§918]

Other courts have simply held that the majority (as directors and as shareholders) owe a fiduciary duty to the minority, and that their issuing shares to themselves for less than fair value, or to obtain or perpetuate control, is a "fraud" upon the minority shareholder. Under this approach, a court of equity may *set aside the unfair issuance* even if there were preemptive rights that the minority failed to exercise. [**Katzowitz v. Sidler**, 24 N.Y.2d 512 (1969)—new shares issued at $100 per share, when book value was $1,800; but minority shareholder lacked funds to exercise his preemptive rights]

(1) Breach of duty [§919]

Thus, it is a breach of fiduciary duty, irrespective of the existence of preemptive rights, for directors to obtain control by issuing shares to themselves or their associates, even at a fair price, unless the directors can show a bona fide corporate purpose for the issuance, which purpose could not have been accomplished substantially as effectively by alternative means. [**Schwartz v. Marien**, 34 N.Y.2d 487 (1975)] (For further discussion of fiduciary duties owed by majority shareholders to minority, *see supra*, §§693 *et seq.*)

b. Significance of rule 10b-5 [§920]

Apart from common law "equitable limitations," it is a violation of rule 10b-5 for directors to cause the corporation to issue stock to themselves or their associates at an unfairly low price or for the purpose of obtaining or perpetuating control. Such an issuance is a "fraud" on the corporation within the meaning of rule 10b-5, and if the corporation fails to sue, a derivative action may be filed by a minority shareholder against the directors involved. (*See supra*, §745.)

H. Underwriting

1. **Defined [§921]**

   Underwriting is the process whereby a securities dealer takes stock from a corporate issuer and arranges for its sale to the public.

2. **"Firm Commitment" Underwriting [§922]**

   In a "firm commitment" underwriting, the underwriters insure the sale of the entire issue by purchasing it outright from the corporation. The underwriters then seek to market the stock to the public.

3. **"Best Efforts" Underwriting [§923]**

   In a "best efforts" underwriting, the underwriters sell the issuer's securities on a commission basis and are bound only to use their special skills and efforts to attempt sale of the issue. They are not responsible for any unsold stock.

FIRM COMMITMENT VS. BEST EFFORTS UNDERWRITING	**gilbert**
FIRM COMMITMENT	**BEST EFFORTS**
The underwriter **buys the securities from the issuer** and then resells them to a dealer or the public.	The underwriter sells the issuer's securities **on a commission basis**, agreeing to use its best efforts but **not guaranteeing** that it will sell all of the securities.

4. **Statutory Regulation [§924]**

   Underwriters are subject to strict regulation under both federal and state laws, which (among other things) generally require full disclosure of the compensation arrangements with the issuer and subject the underwriter to the same anti-fraud prohibitions applicable to the issuer (below).

I. Statutes Regulating Issuance of Shares

1. **In General [§925]**

   Both state and federal laws have been enacted regulating the issuance of securities. Because federal laws expressly do **not** completely preempt the field [Securities Act of 1933 §18], a corporate issuer must often comply with **both** state and federal regulations.

2. State Regulation—"Blue Sky" Laws [§926]

State statutes regulating the issuance of securities are known as "blue sky" laws (their constitutionality resting on the legitimate state interest in preventing "schemes which have no more basis than so many feet of blue sky"). [**Hall v. Geiger-Jones Co.,** 242 U.S. 539 (1917)] Every state has some type of blue sky law; many have special regulatory bodies charged with administration and enforcement of these laws. There are three basic types of blue sky laws (states combining the features of more than one type):

a. Fraud type [§927]

Some laws simply impose civil or criminal sanctions for fraud in connection with the issuance of securities. No permit or registration is required to issue securities, and there is generally no special administrative agency charged with enforcement of the statute. No state uses this method alone.

b. License type [§928]

All states have laws requiring that various persons who sell securities—brokers, dealers and agents of corporate issuers—register with the state and submit certain information.

c. Securities registration type [§929]

The most comprehensive type of blue sky law requires that stock be registered (or "qualified") with an appropriate state officer or agent prior to issuance. The Uniform Securities Act, adopted by a majority of the states, provides three methods of registration:

(1) Registration by notification [§930]

Some laws require a description of the issuer and shares to be issued, and the shares must be sold as described. The purpose of such laws is simply disclosure; unless the state regulator objects, filing automatically qualifies the shares.

(2) Registration by qualification [§931]

However, other laws provide for *substantive review* of the proposed issuance by a state official who can prevent issuance if it fails to meet statutory requirements, *e.g.*, that it is "fair, just, and equitable."

(3) Registration by coordination [§932]

Some states provide that securities registered under the federal scheme may be issued by submitting essentially the same information as is required under the Securities Act of 1933 to the state official who then declares the registration to be effective.

d. Federal restriction of "merits" review [§933]

In 1996, section 18 of the Securities Act of 1933 was amended to exempt "covered securities" from Blue Sky *substantive* regulation. "Covered securities" are those traded on all stock exchanges approved by the Securities and Exchange Commission. States still may, however, continue to bring fraud proceedings, and to require filing, even in respect to "covered securities," solely for purposes of notice, coordination, and filing-fee charges.

3. Federal Regulation [§934]

The *Securities Act of 1933* [15 U.S.C. §77] establishes the basic framework for federal regulation of the public distribution of securities through use of interstate commerce or the mails. It provides for a *registration-type* system of regulation, the purpose of which is to assure *full disclosure* of all pertinent facts to any prospective investor. The agency charged with enforcement is the Securities and Exchange Commission ("SEC"). Note that the SEC has no power to disapprove a proposed issuance; its only power is to compel *disclosure* of all pertinent details.

a. Registration statement [§935]

Basically, the 1933 Act forbids the use of interstate facilities or the mails to offer to sell a security, unless a registration statement has been filed with the SEC. [Securities Act §5(c)]

(1) Waiting period [§936]

During the time between filing the registration statement and the date that it becomes "effective" (a time known as the "waiting period"), no *written* offer to sell a security may be made through interstate facilities or the mails unless it satisfies the requirements for a "statutory prospectus," essentially, a document disclosing key information from the registration materials (*see infra,* §947). (This rule on written offers also applies after the effective date.) [Securities Act §5(b)(1)]

(2) After effective date [§937]

Actual sales of securities, or deliveries after sale, through interstate facilities or the mails may be made only after the "effective date" [Securities Act §5(a)]—and a prospectus must either accompany or precede the delivery of any security [Securities Act §5(b)(2)].

b. Integrated disclosure [§938]

Corporations subject to the reporting requirements of the Securities Exchange Act of 1934 whose shares are actively traded (as defined) may incorporate by reference their 1934 Act filings in their 1933 Act registration statements. [Securities Act Release No. 6331 (1981)]

(1) "Shelf" registration [§939]

Corporations may also offer securities over a two-year period after the effective date of a registration statement that automatically incorporates by reference subsequently filed 1934 Act reports. [Securities Act Rule 415] This permits these corporations to sell securities "off the shelf" when they feel market conditions are favorable.

c. Relevant terms

(1) "Offer to sell" [§940]

This term includes "every attempt or offer to dispose of, or solicitation of an offer to buy, a security or interest in a security, for value." [Securities Act §2(3)] It has been broadly interpreted to include all activities that, under the circumstances, are designed to stir public interest in a security. [*In re* **Carl M. Loeb, Rhoades & Co.,** 38 S.E.C. 843 (1959)—publicity in advance of a proposed issuance]

EXAM TIP   gilbert

Keep in mind that the term *"offer to sell"* under section 5 is *broader than it is under state contract law*. Information may not be released if it would have the effect of *whetting the public's appetite* for the securities. Thus, before filing, issuers may not publicly disclose who will be underwriting the securities or any other information designed to procure or solicit advance interest in the securities.

---

(2) "Security" [§941]

This includes not only stock, bonds, and most promissory notes, but also any offering that constitutes an investment contract or certificate of interest or participation in any profit-sharing agreement, regardless of form. [Securities Act §2(1)]

(a) Test [§942]

The test is "whether the scheme involves an investment of money in a common enterprise with profits to come *solely* from the efforts of others." [**SEC v. W.J. Howey Co.,** 328 U.S. 29 (1946)] Some courts have expanded this to include profit schemes wherein "the efforts made by those other than the investor are the undeniably significant ones." [**SEC v. Glenn W. Turner Enterprises, Inc.,** 474 F.2d 476 (9th Cir. 1973)]

EXAM TIP   gilbert

If your exam includes a question in which you must determine whether something is a security under the 1933 Act (and many exams do include such a question), you should *state the traditional Howey test* (an investment contract is any profit-making scheme whereby a person invests his money in a common enterprise and expects to make a profit solely from the efforts of others, who are responsible for management). But you should *then note the more expansive test* discussed above.

(b) Application [§943]

The term "security" has thus been applied to a wide variety of interests—*e.g.,* fractional interests in oil royalties or mineral leases, percentages of patent rights or fruit orchards, and interests in limited partnerships, mortgages, or deeds of trust. But it has been held not to apply to an employer-financed pension plan because the employee made no monetary investment and the fund's income came mainly from employer contributions rather than the efforts of the fund's managers. [**International Brotherhood of Teamsters v. Daniel,** 439 U.S. 551 (1979)]

1) Sale of business [§944]
Sale of all of the stock of a company *is* the sale of "securities." Even though the sale is simply a method to transfer ownership of a business, the stock has all of the traditional characteristics of a security. [**Landreth Timber Co. v. Landreth,** 471 U.S. 681 (1985)]

2) Promissory notes [§945]
Some promissory notes are not subject to the federal securities acts. A four-factor test is used to determine whether the note bears a "strong family resemblance" to a "noninvestment" type of financial instrument. The note *is* a "security" if: (i) the *purchasers*, or (ii) other *reasonable persons* conceive of it as an investment, (iii) the notes are *commonly traded* as investments, and (iv) the note is *not subject to some other federal regulation*. [**Reves v. Ernst & Young,** 494 U.S. 56 (1990)]

(3) "Registration statement" [§946]
A registration statement is a detailed statement of all matters pertaining to the proposed issuance. The form is designed to force *disclosure* of all factors that may affect the fairness of the issue and the financial status of the corporation. Full details must be provided as to the issuer's property and business; the identity and background of all corporate officers and directors; the compensation they receive; the nature of the security being offered; sales costs, underwriting commission and discounts; and the like. [Securities Act §7]

(4) "Statutory prospectus" [§947]
A statutory prospectus is a document, filed with the registration statement, that sets forth the key information contained in the statement. [Securities Act §10] As noted above, a copy of the prospectus (but not the registration statement) must be given to every buyer of securities covered by the registration statement.

(5) "Effective date" [§948]
The registration statement becomes effective 20 days after filing unless the SEC agrees to an earlier date. If the SEC requires further information, it notifies the corporation that amendments to the registration statement are necessary. Such amendments start the 20-day period again, unless the SEC consents to an acceleration of the effective date. [Securities Act §8]

d. Exempt securities [§949]

The Act lists a number of types of securities that are exempt from the Act's registration requirements, *e.g.*, certain short-term commercial paper, securities issued by governmental bodies or charitable institutions, and securities subject to other government regulation (such as bank securities or insurance policies). [Securities Act §3(a)]

(1) But note

Even exempt securities are subject to the Act's *anti-fraud* rules. (*See infra*, §1004.)

e. Exempt transactions [§950]

In addition to securities that are exempted from registration, certain transactions also are exempted. It is important to distinguish exempted *securities* from exempted *transactions*. If the security *itself* is exempted, as above, it can be sold and resold without ever being subject to the registration requirements of section 5. On the other hand, if only the *transaction* is exempt, that transaction is not subject to section 5, but a later transaction in the same securities might be. For example, if XYZ Corp. issues stock to A under a *transaction* exemption, and A later transfers the stock to B, the transfer to B may not be exempt. However, if the *security* issued by XYZ to A is exempt, the transfer from A to B would be exempt. The following types of transactions are exempted from the registration requirements of the 1933 Act. (*Note*: The *anti-fraud rules* of the Act may still apply; *see infra*, §1004.)

(1) Ordinary trading transactions ("casual sales" exemption) [§951]

The Act exempts "*transactions* by any person *other than* an issuer, underwriter, or dealer." [Securities Act §4(1)] This covers ordinary trading transactions between individual investors in securities that have already been issued—in contrast to sales by issuers and others participating in transactions connected with the initial distribution of securities. [**SEC v. Chinese Consolidated Benevolent Association**, 120 F.2d 738 (2d Cir. 1941)]

EXAM TIP | **gilbert**

Remember that the registration requirements of the 1933 Act apply *only to issuers, underwriters, and dealers*. The majority of everyday securities transactions, therefore, are exempt from registration.

(a) Not applicable to secondary distributions [§952]

The exemption does *not* cover public offerings by a person who acquired the shares from an issuer in a "private placement" (below) if that person took the shares with a *view to public distribution*. Such persons are considered underwriters regardless of whether they are otherwise engaged in the securities business. [Securities Act §2(11); **Gilligan, Will & Co. v. SEC**, 267 F.2d 461 (2d Cir. 1959)]

(b) Not applicable to sales by control persons [§953]

The exemption also does not cover public offerings by persons who have a *control relationship* with the issuer. As to such offerings, the control persons are themselves considered issuers under the Act; and those who distribute the securities for them are underwriters. [*In re* **Ira Haupt & Co.,** 23 S.E.C. 589 (1946)]

1) "Casual sales" by control persons [§954]

However, *rule 144* under the Securities Act exempts sales to the public by control persons of small amounts of securities within designated time periods. (For details on rule 144, *see infra*, §§963-968.)

(2) Dealer sales [§955]

Transactions by a dealer (securities broker) are exempt, except where (i) she is acting as an underwriter of the securities, or (ii) during the initial distribution of the securities (first 40 days following registration). [Securities Act §4(3)]

(3) Private placements [§956]

Transactions by an issuer "not involving any public offering" are exempt. [Securities Act §4(2)] This applies to an offering to a relatively small number of private subscribers who are *sufficiently experienced or informed* that the disclosure requirements are not necessary for their protection (*i.e.*, they are "able to fend for themselves") and who are acquiring the shares *as an investment* rather than for resale to the public. [**SEC v. Ralston-Purina Co.,** 346 U.S. 119 (1953)]

(a) Requirement of available information [§957]

A high degree of business or legal sophistication by the offerees is not enough to gain the private placement exemption. The offerees *must* have either (i) *full disclosure* of the information that a registration statement would have provided, or (ii) *access* to such information (through an employment or family relationship or by economic bargaining power). [**Doran v. Petroleum Management Corp.,** 545 F.2d 893 (5th Cir. 1977)]

1) Note—number of offerees not decisive [§958]

The number of offerees is *not* decisive. Depending on the availability of information, an offering to a few persons may be public and an offering to many persons may be private. (But the *size of the offering is* a significant factor.) [**Doran v. Petroleum Management Corp.,** *supra*]

2) Rule 506 offerings [§959]

Under rule 506 (which is within regulation D, *infra,* but based on section 4(2)), an issuer may sell an *unlimited* amount of securities to "accredited investors" (defined *infra*, §960) and up to 35 other purchasers, but the issuer must reasonably believe that these other purchasers (or their purchaser representatives) have such knowledge and experience that they are capable of evaluating the offering *and* they must be furnished detailed information (as defined).

(b) Small offerings under regulation D [§960]

During any 12-month period, an issuer may, without providing *any* information, sell securities:

1) Up to $1 million to *any number* of purchasers—if the issuer is not an investment company or registered under the Securities and Exchange Act of 1934 (*supra*, §364) [Securities Act Rule 504]; or

2) Up to $5 million to *accredited investors*. [Securities Act §4(6)] "Accredited investors" include financial institutions, business development companies, large charitable or educational institutions, the issuer's directors and executive officers, and wealthy individuals (as defined). [Securities Act Rules 501, 505] In addition to accredited investors, the issuer may add up to *35 ordinary purchasers* if it provides detailed information (as defined) to all purchasers. [Securities Act Rule 505]

(c) Investment intent [§961]

Each purchaser in a private offering or one under regulation D must acquire the securities as an investment, and not for resale or distribution to the public. Ordinarily, each purchaser is required to sign a letter of intent to this effect so that shares issued pursuant to this exemption are commonly known as "letter stock" or "restricted securities."

1) Legal imprint [§962]

To assure that the purchasers take the shares for investment, many corporations print a notice on the face of the share certificates to the effect that "these shares have been issued pursuant to an exemption from registration, and may not be freely traded until registered, or further exemption established," and instruct their transfer agents not to transfer shares bearing such imprint.

2) Resale of restricted securities—rule 144 [§963]

Such legend imprint renders shares issued under a private offering exemption nonmarketable until registered, or until some further exemption from registration is established. Rule 144 creates an exemption for resale of such shares (and shares owned by control persons; *supra*, §954).

a) **Sales by noncontrol persons [§964]**
Purchasers who are not control persons may sell *any* amount if: (i) they have owned the securities for three years and the shares are listed on a national exchange or quoted through an approved automated system, or (ii) they have owned the securities for four years and the issuer has provided specified current public information.

b) **Sales by control persons [§965]**
The following requirements must be met for sales by control persons:

1/ **Public information [§966]**
There must be specified current public information concerning the issuer.

2/ **Holding period [§967]**
No resales at all of restricted securities are generally permitted within the first two years following issuance of the shares.

3/ **Limitation on amount sold [§968]**
After two years, purchasers who are control persons can sell during each *three-month* period shares equal to as much as 1% of the total shares outstanding in the same class (or 1% of the average weekly volume of shares traded on national securities exchanges or automated quotation systems during the preceding four weeks, whichever is greater).

4/ **Notice requirement [§969]**
If more than 500 shares are to be sold, or if the sales price exceeds $10,000, the shareholder must file with the SEC a signed notice of intent to sell the securities concurrently with placing the sale order with the broker. The purpose is to allow the SEC to monitor the marketing of such securities.

3) **Resale of restricted securities in another private placement [§970]**
If shares issued under a private offering exemption are resold in a transaction that would have initially qualified as a private offering (*e.g.*, sale to an accredited investor, *supra*, §959), there has been no public distribution. Thus, the person who resold the shares is not an underwriter (*but see supra*, §952). [**Ackerberg v. Johnson,** 892 F.2d 1328 (8th Cir. 1989)]

a) Resale to institutional buyers

Under rule 144A, unregistered shares of a class not publicly traded may be sold at any time to an institution that has investments of over $100 million.

(4) Intrastate offerings [§971]

Where the offering and sale is made *entirely* to residents of the same state in which the issuer resides and is doing business, the issue is exempt from registration. (A corporation is said to "reside" in the state of incorporation.) [Securities Act §3(a)(11)]

(a) Note

The exemption is strictly construed. Thus, it is lost where securities are *inadvertently offered* to an out-of-state resident, even if no sale is ever made to that person. Good faith reliance on the offeree's representation of residence is apparently no defense if it proves to be false. [Securities Act Rule 147]

EXAM TIP — **gilbert**

This point is worth repeating. On an exam, be sure that the offering is *truly intrastate*. A single offer to a nonresident can destroy the section 3(a)(11) exemption regardless of how compelling the facts are.

---

(5) Other exemptions [§972]

The 1933 Act also authorizes the SEC to exempt other issuances where the SEC finds that registration is not necessary by reason of the small amount involved or the *limited character of the offering*. [Securities Act §3(b)]

(a) Regulation A [§973]

For a public offering not exceeding *$5 million* in any 12-month period, the SEC permits an *abbreviated offering circular* containing basic information about the stock and its issuer, in lieu of the more detailed registration statement otherwise required. After review by the SEC, the offering circular must be distributed to prospective purchasers of the stock.

(b) Rule 145 [§974]

Another provision provides *limited registration* requirements for securities issued pursuant to certain transactions *formally approved by the shareholders* of the issuer, pursuant to statute or the articles— *e.g.*, certain mergers, acquisitions, transfers of assets and reclassification of shares (*see infra*, §§1102, 1137, 1147).

(c) Small business issues [§975]

Another regulation permits the offering through a simplified system of an unlimited dollar amount of securities by a "small business issuer"—defined as one with: (i) under $25 million in revenue in the last fiscal year and (ii) no more than $25 million in outstanding securities with the public. [Securities Act Regulation S-B]

f. Remedies—anti-fraud provisions [§976]

The 1933 Act provides both civil and criminal sanctions for violation of its registration requirements or any fraud in connection with the issuance of the securities or the filing of the registration statement.

(1) False registration statement—section 11 [§977]

If the registration statement, when it becomes effective, contains a *misstatement or omission of material fact*, any person acquiring the securities without knowledge of the misstatement or omission has an action for damages (the amount she lost on the investment) against various persons connected with the issuance.

(a) Who may sue [§978]

This remedy is granted to *any person who has acquired* the securities—not just the original issuee. But a person cannot sue if she *knew* of the misstatement or omission when she acquired the securities. [Securities Act §11(a)]

1) Privity not required [§979]

No privity is required between the plaintiff and the parties sought to be held liable.

2) Must prove shares were part of that offering [§980]

If plaintiff acquired her shares in the market *subsequent to distribution* of the registered offering, she must prove that the shares she acquired were *part of that offering*, rather than shares issued at some other time.

(b) Elements of plaintiff's action [§981]

The plaintiff need not prove fraud in the tort sense, or even any intentional wrongdoing. Subject to certain defenses (*see* below), the plaintiff need only show that *some material fact was omitted or misrepresented* in the registration statement.

1) Materiality [§982]

"Material" covers all matters that an average, prudent investor needs to know before being able to make an intelligent, informed decision on whether to buy the security.

2) Damages [§983]

The plaintiff must also prove damages.

3) Reliance and causation need not be shown [§984]

It is *not* necessary for the plaintiff to prove that she *relied* on the misrepresentation or omission, or that it *caused* the loss in value of the security. The fact that it was "material" (above) is enough for liability.

a) Exception [§985]

If the plaintiff acquires her shares *after* the corporation publishes an earnings statement for the 12-month period following the effective date of registration, the plaintiff must prove reliance, *i.e.*, that the falsity in the registration statement *caused* her to purchase. [Securities Act §11(a)] (Even here, however, the plaintiff need not prove that she personally *read* the statement—she could have been relying on investment advice given her by others who had.)

EXAM TIP gilbert

The prima facie case for a violation of section 11 is very simple. The plaintiff generally need show only two things—*a material misstatement and damages*. The plaintiff need *not* show that the misstatement caused his loss. Nor need the plaintiff show any kind of intent.

(c) Who may be held liable [§986]

Liability may extend to the *corporation*, its *directors* and persons who are named as being or about to become its directors, all persons who *sign* the registration statement, the *underwriter*, and *experts*—such as accountants, engineers, and other professionals (including *lawyers*)—who are identified as having prepared or certified the registration statement or any report or valuation in connection therewith. [Securities Act §11(a)]

1) Liability of experts [§987]

The responsibility of lawyers, accountants, and other experts is normally limited to those parts of the registration statements *made on their authority*. [Securities Act §11(a)]

(d) Defenses

1) Corporation [§988]

The issuer is *absolutely liable* for any material misstatement or omission in the registration statement. [Securities Act §11(b)] The only possible issuer defense is that plaintiff *knew* of the untruth or omission at the time she acquired the shares (*see* above).

2) Others—"due diligence" defense [§989]

All other persons to whom liability extends under section 11 (above) may avoid liability by *proving* that they exercised *due diligence* with respect to the information in that part of the registration statement for which they are sought to be held liable.

a) Signers, directors, underwriters, etc. [§990]

Generally, these persons must prove that, after reasonable investigation, they had reasonable ground to believe that the statements were true and complete as required. [Securities Act §11(b)(3)(A)] The standard of "reasonableness" is that required of a prudent person in the management of her own property. [Securities Act §11(c)]

STANDARDS OF DUE DILIGENCE UNDER SECTION 11—A SUMMARY		gilbert
PARTY	**STANDARD**	**HOW MET**
CORPORATION	*Absolutely liable*	Not applicable
SIGNERS REVIEWING STATEMENTS OF NONEXPERTS	*Reasonable belief* that the statement was true	Act as a *prudent person* would in the management of his own property
SIGNERS REVIEWING STATEMENTS OF EXPERTS	*No reason to believe* that the statement was false	*Generally met automatically* unless facts show a potential for problems
EXPERTS	*Reasonable belief* that statement was true	Must make *reasonable investigation* into the facts

1/ Personal investigation required [§991]

It is *no defense* that these persons had no knowledge of the misstatements or omissions or that they had been associated with the issuer for only a limited time. They must show not merely that they made inquiry of responsible corporate officers or employees, but also that they *reasonably investigated* the corporation's affairs *personally*. The defendant cannot escape liability by taking management's representations at face value. [**Escott v. Barchris Construction Corp.**, 283 F. Supp. 643 (S.D.N.Y. 1968)]

2/ Distinguish—portions made on authority of expert [§992]

However, as to those portions of a registration statement made on the authority of an *expert* (*e.g.*, financial statements certified by accountant or valuations certified by appraiser), "due diligence" is established as long as the party-defendant had no reasonable ground to disbelieve the expert's statement. [Securities Act §11(b)(3)(C)]

b) Experts [§993]

As to those parts of the registration statement made on their authority, experts must prove that, after reasonable investigation, they had reasonable ground to believe such parts were true and complete. [Securities Act §11(b)(3)(B)]

(e) Measure of recovery [§994]

The plaintiff is entitled to *actual damages*. This is considered to be the purchase price minus the resale price, but if she has not sold by the time she sues, damages may not exceed the difference between the purchase price and the market value of the security at the time suit is brought. [Securities Act §11(e)]

1) Reduction of damages [§995]

A defendant may reduce liability by proving that the plaintiff's damages were not attributable to the part of the registration statement as to which the liability is asserted. [Securities Act §11(e)]

(2) General civil liability—section 12 [§996]

The 1933 Act expressly imposes civil liability on any person who *offers or sells* a security: (i) in violation of section 5 (requiring registration, delivery of a prospectus, etc.) [Securities Act §12(a)(1)], or (ii) through means of interstate commerce or the mails by use of material misstatements or omissions (*i.e.*, not limited to the registration statement) [Securities Act §12(a)(2)].

(a) Scope [§997]

Liability for misstatements or omissions under section 12 arises only in connection with a public offering. It does not extend to statements in a private sales contract. [**Gustafson v. Alloyd Co.**, 513 U.S. 561 (1995)]

(b) Who may sue [§998]

This right of action is afforded only to the original purchaser. There must be a showing of *privity* with the seller.

1) Distinguish

Under section 11, above (misrepresentation or omissions in the registration statement), *any* holder is entitled to sue; no privity is required.

(c) Who may be held liable [§999]

By its terms, section 12 applies only to "persons who offer or sell" a security, so that, apparently, only the *issuer and other sellers* can be held liable under section 12.

1) Distinguish

Under section 11, liability can be imposed on *any person* connected with the registration statement; thus, liability extends to officers, directors, lawyers, accountants, etc.

(d) Defenses [§1000]

Liability under section 12(a)(2) for misstatements or omissions is conditioned on the plaintiff's proving that she did not know of them. Also there is no liability if the defendant proves that he did not and, in the exercise of reasonable care, could not know of them.

(e) Measure of recovery [§1001]

The plaintiff may sue to rescind or, if she no longer owns the security, to recover damages (the amount she lost on the investment).

(3) Criminal liability—section 17 [§1002]

The 1933 Act also makes it unlawful for *any* person to offer or sell securities through the mails or in interstate commerce by means of "any device or scheme to defraud" or "by means of any misstatement or omission" of material fact. [Securities Act §17]

LIABILITY UNDER THE 1933 ACT—A SUMMARY **gilbert**

LIABILITY CAN BE IMPOSED FOR VIOLATIONS OF THE 1933 ACT UNDER:

SECTION 11	Imposes *civil liability for misstatements* in a registration statement, whether or not intentional
SECTION 12(a)(1)	Imposes *civil liability* on persons who *issue an unregistered security* that was required to be registered under the Act
SECTION 12(a)(2)	Imposes *civil liability* on persons who issue a security by means of a *false statement* in an oral or written offer
SECTION 17	Imposes *criminal penalties* on persons who offer to sell a security by means of any *fraudulent misstatement or omission*

(a) Implied right of action [§1003]

Unlike sections 11 and 12, which expressly create a civil cause of action for violation, section 17 simply provides that the acts are "unlawful" (*i.e.*, criminal liability). However, some courts have *implied* a civil remedy against persons who violate section 17, but most recent authority has refused to do so. [**Finkel v. Stratton Corp.**, 962 F.2d 169 (2d Cir. 1992)]

(4) Remedies applicable to exempt securities [§1004]

Note that the anti-fraud provisions of sections 12 and 17 apply to the "offer or sale" of securities *whether or not* the securities are required to be registered. Thus, they cover transactions and securities that are *exempt from the registration* requirements of the 1933 Act (*supra*, §§950-975) and therefore beyond the reach of section 11 (which applies only to omission and falsity in the registration statement; *see* above).

(5) Indemnification agreements—enforceability [§1005]

Frequently, persons outside the issuing company who play some role in connection with a stock issuance (particularly underwriters) may bargain for an indemnification agreement—whereby the company and/or its controlling shareholders agree to hold the underwriters harmless from any liability they incur for Securities Act violations.

(a) Willful violations [§1006]

If the underwriter (or other indemnified party) has *knowledge* of the violations, the indemnification agreement is *unenforceable* as a matter of law. *Rationale:* One cannot insure himself against his own willful wrongdoing, and to allow indemnity in such cases would encourage flaunting of the Act. [**Globus v. Law Research Service, Inc.**, 418 F.2d 1276 (2d Cir. 1969)]

(6) Distinguish from rule 10b-5 [§1007]

As discussed *supra* (§§365 *et seq.*), none of the anti-fraud provisions of the 1933 Act are as broad as section 10(b) of the 1934 Act and rule 10b-5.

(a) Scope [§1008]

Rule 10b-5 protects *sellers* as well as buyers.

(b) Procedure [§1009]

Even as to buyers, an action under rule 10b-5 has certain *procedural advantages* over sections 11 and 12; *e.g.*, it *may* avoid the strictures on damages under the latter (*supra*, §§994, 1001).

(c) Costs [§1010]

Moreover, under sections 11 and 12, a court may assess *unsuccessful* plaintiffs with the *costs of suit* (including attorneys' fees) and may require plaintiffs to post advance *security* for such costs.

(d) Scienter [§1011]

Thus, despite the fact that sections 11 and 12 eliminate the plaintiffs' need to prove scienter, most purchaser-plaintiffs prefer to maintain a civil action under rule 10b-5, rather than under the anti-fraud provisions of the 1933 Act.

Chapter Nine: Distributions to Shareholders

CONTENTS

Chapter Approach

Chapter Approach

The subjects of this chapter, dividends and the redemption or repurchase of shares, are more likely to arise as subissues rather than as major exam topics. Nevertheless, it is important for you to know at least the following rules:

1. **Dividends**

   In discussing issues concerning dividends, keep in mind that shareholders do not have a right to dividends; payment of dividends is ordinarily within the business judgment of the directors. When a cash or property dividend has been declared, investigate the *source* of the dividend. In a number of states, these dividends may be paid only out of a surplus of net assets over stated capital. Check the surplus account from which the dividend is to be paid. Some states restrict the use of certain accounts and prohibit the use of reappraisal surplus for dividends. Be aware that *all* states prohibit dividends when the corporation is insolvent or the payment of the dividend would render it insolvent.

   If the directors have declared an illegal dividend, recall that they are personally liable to the corporation to the extent of the injury to creditors and preferred shareholders. As for shareholder liability, if the corporation is *solvent*, shareholders who receive an illegal dividend without knowledge of its illegality are entitled to keep it, but if the corporation is *insolvent*, the shareholders who receive an illegal dividend are *absolutely* liable to return it.

2. **Redemption and Repurchase of Shares**

   a. **Redemption**

      If a corporation wishes to retire certain shares (usually a preferred class) for the benefit of the common shares, consider redemption, by which the corporation pays the stipulated redemption price and the shareholders must relinquish their shares. Redeemed shares are canceled (and in states following the traditional par value approach, stated capital is reduced accordingly). Note that even in states limiting payment of dividends to certain funds, a corporation can redeem out of *any available funds* (surplus or stated capital). Most importantly, check to see that the corporation has the power to redeem—*i.e.*, is that power *expressly provided in the articles or bylaws*?

   b. **Repurchase**

      All states have statutes authorizing corporations to *repurchase* their own shares. A provision in the articles or bylaws is *not* required. In states following the traditional par value approach, repurchased shares are not automatically canceled; they remain issued as "treasury stock." In other states, repurchased shares revert to being "authorized, but unissued." Unlike redemption, a repurchase may be made only under the same conditions that a cash or property dividend may be paid; *i.e.*, only when there is a surplus and only out of certain surplus accounts in states following the traditional approach.

c. Limitations

When faced with a redemption or repurchase problem, ask whether the corporation is *insolvent* or whether the redemption or repurchase will render it insolvent. If so, redemption and repurchase are not permitted. Then ask whether the redemption or repurchase will leave the corporation with *sufficient assets to cover liquidation preferences* of outstanding shares. If not, the redemption or repurchase generally will not be permitted. Finally, ask whether a discretionary redemption or repurchase serves a *bona fide corporate purpose*, rather than the personal interests of directors or insiders. Note that the remedies for unlawful redemption or repurchase are generally the same as those available for illegal dividends.

A. Dividends

1. Definition [§1012]

A "dividend" is any distribution of *cash* or *property* paid to shareholders on account of their share ownership.

2. Right to Dividends [§1013]

The general rule is that payment of dividends is a matter within the business judgment of the board of directors. The shareholders ordinarily have no right to dividends, even if funds are available. The directors alone determine if and when dividends are to be declared, and the amounts of the dividends. [**Gottfried v. Gottfried,** 73 N.Y.S.2d 692 (1947)]

a. Equitable limitation [§1014]

If a complaining shareholder can show that the board's refusal to declare dividends is in *bad faith* or so unreasonable as to amount to an *abuse of discretion*, a court of equity may intervene. Thus, if the directors (on behalf of the majority shareholders) are attempting to abuse the minority by refusing to declare dividends notwithstanding huge earned surpluses (and/or generous salaries to the majority), equity may intervene to protect the minority by compelling distribution of some reasonable portion of the available surplus. [**Dodge v. Ford Motor Co.,** *supra*, §158]

(1) Caution [§1015]

It should be emphasized that equity will not intervene unless there is palpable abuse or bad faith by the directors. The *Dodge* case is one of the few reported decisions where this has been found. [*See also* **Miller v. Magline, Inc.,** 256 N.W.2d 761 (Mich. 1977)]

(2) Fiduciary duty in close corporations [§1016]

The duty that shareholders of a close corporation owe each other (*supra*, §705) may affect the power to declare dividends held by the majority shareholders (or a minority that has a veto power). [**Smith v. Atlantic Properties, Inc.**, 422 N.E.2d 798 (Mass. 1981)—court may order declaration of dividends to avoid federal tax penalty for undue accumulation of earnings]

3. Source of Lawful Dividends [§1017]

There are two main approaches concerning payment of dividends—the traditional approach and the modern approach. The traditional approach is tied to the concept of par value, and dividends can be paid only from certain accounts. States following the modern approach have done away with the accounting classifications based on par value and allow dividends to be paid from any source.

a. Traditional par value approach [§1018]

Under the traditional approach, money received by the corporation when it issues par value stock generally must be placed into an account, usually called the "stated capital" account. This account must always contain at least an amount equal to the aggregate par value of all outstanding par value shares.

---

e.g. Example: Bigco's articles of incorporation authorize the issuance of 1,000 shares having a par value of $50 each. Bigco sells 500 of the shares for $75 each. Because Bigco has 500, $50 par value shares outstanding, it must have at least $25,000 (500 × $50) in its stated capital account. It *may* place the extra $12,500 that it received from the sales into the stated capital account or into a surplus account (often called "paid-in" surplus; *see infra*, §1028).

---

(1) Dividends payable only from surplus [§1019]

In states following the traditional par value approach, cash or property dividends are payable only when the corporation has a surplus—an excess of net assets (total assets minus total liabilities) over stated capital. In these states, dividends cannot be paid out of the corporation's stated capital. [*See, e.g.*, N.Y. Bus. Corp. Law §510(b)]

> **EXAM TIP**   **gilbert**
>
> It is important to remember the source of funds limitation on dividends in states following the traditional par value approach. In such states, dividends generally cannot be paid unless the corporation has *assets in excess of its stated capital* (*i.e.*, a surplus).

(a) Underlying rationale [§1020]

Traditionally, a corporation's stated capital represented amounts contributed by the shareholders to allow the corporation to operate. Creditors were entitled to rely on such amounts for payment of debts incurred by the corporation (*supra*, §§882-891). Therefore, except under designated special circumstances (*infra*, §§1028-1032), stated capital could not be returned to the shareholders as dividends—at least while creditors of the corporation remained unpaid.

(b) Exception—"wasting asset" corporations [§1021]

The restriction prohibiting payment of dividends out of stated capital generally prohibits a corporation from paying dividends when the corporation's stated capital has become impaired (*e.g.*, by virtue of operating losses or depreciation write offs). Any profits on earnings must be used to repair the deficit in stated capital. However, most states following the traditional par value approach recognize an exception to this rule for corporations engaged in the exploitation of a "wasting asset," *i.e.*, an asset such as an oil well or patent that is to be consumed over a period of time and not replaced. [Del. Gen. Corp. Law §170(b); N.Y. Bus. Corp. Law §510(b)] Subject to some limitations, these statutes permit corporations to pay dividends out of net profits computed without a deduction for the depletion (*i.e.*, depreciation) of the value of the wasting asset. In effect, they permit a return of capital to the shareholders in the form of dividends.

(c) "Nimble dividends" permitted in some states [§1022]

Some states permit payment of dividends out of *current net profits* regardless of impairment of the capital account. A corporation's net profits generally are its earnings during a specific accounting period, with adjustments as required by good accounting practices (*e.g.*, appropriate reserves for depreciation, bad debts, etc.). Typically, these states broaden the accounting period over which the corporation's net profits are computed for dividend purposes. For example, Delaware permits dividends out of earnings during the current and preceding years (rather than during just the current accounting period). [Del. Gen. Corp. Law §170]

(d) California rule [§1023]

California has an even more liberal dividend policy. Broadly, a corporation is permitted to pay cash or property dividends as long as its total assets after such payment are at least equal to 1¼ times its liabilities *and* its current assets are at least equal to its current liabilities. [Cal. Corp. Code §500(b)] Under this rule, as long as the asset value requirements are met, dividends may be paid even though the corporation has no current profits, and even though the amount contributed as its capital is impaired.

1) Valuation of assets [§1024]

The value of corporate assets must be determined in conformity with generally accepted accounting principles. Specifically, the value may include goodwill or capitalized research and development expenses. [Cal. Corp. Code §500(b)]

(2) Restrictions as to type of surplus account from which dividends may be paid [§1025]

Besides the prohibition on any dividend payment while capital is impaired, states following the traditional par value approach also have statutory restrictions on payment of cash or property dividends from certain kinds of surplus accounts.

(a) Earned surplus [§1026]

"Earned surplus" is the total net profits retained by the corporation during all of its previous years of operation, *i.e.*, its profits offset by its losses, and further reduced by dividends paid out in previous years.

> **Example:** XYZ Corp. has been in business three years. During the first year, it had an operating loss of $5,000. During the second year it had profits of $20,000. In the third year it broke even and, for the first time, paid a dividend of $10,000. XYZ now has an earned surplus of $5,000 (-$5,000 + $20,000 - $10,000).

1) As source of dividends [§1027]

Earned surplus is a proper source of cash and property dividends in all states. Indeed, earned surplus may ordinarily be the only proper source of such dividends in a few states.

(b) Paid-in surplus [§1028]

"Paid-in surplus" occurs where par value shares are sold for more than par; where no-par value shares are sold for more than their stated value (so that not all of the consideration received for no-par shares is allocated to stated capital); or from gifts to the corporation.

> **Example:** XYZ Corp. sells 1,000 shares of its $10 par value shares for $12,500. The $2,500 excess over par value is paid-in surplus. Similarly, if XYZ Corp. sells 1,000 shares of its no-par shares for $5,000, the directors designating $1,000 as the stated value of such shares, the $4,000 excess over stated value is paid-in surplus.

1) As source of dividends [§1029]

Most states following the traditional approach *permit a distribution of dividends out of paid-in surplus*. [N.Y. Bus. Corp. Law §510(b)] Other states are more restrictive. In some, dividends may not be paid out of paid-in surplus unless the fair value of the remaining assets is at least 25% of the total liabilities. [R.I. Bus. Corp. Act §7-1.1-41]

(c) Capital reduction surplus [§1030]

Capital reduction surplus arises when the par value or stated value of no-par shares has been reduced by the corporation. There are a variety of methods for reducing capital. In many states, capital may be reduced by amending the articles of incorporation. (*See infra*, §§1145-1161.) In some states, capital reduction can be accomplished only pursuant to special statutory procedures. [Del. Gen. Corp. Law §§242, 244]

1) Purpose [§1031]

A frequent reason for reducing stated capital is to remedy a capital impairment (*e.g.*, deficits incurred by operating losses in past years). When capital is reduced, the surplus created by the reduction is "capital reduction surplus." Such surplus can be used to offset the prior deficit so that future earnings can be available for dividends, instead of having to be used to "repair" the deficit in the capital account.

2) As source of dividend [§1032]

In most states following the traditional approach, any capital reduction surplus in excess of that needed to "repair" the capital account may properly be used as a source of cash and property dividends to the shareholders—subject, however, to restrictions similar to those for dividends from paid-in surplus (*supra*, §1028).

3) Shareholder approval [§1033]

If the capital reduction is accomplished by amending the articles of incorporation, shareholder approval is required. Some states require such approval for *all* methods of capital reduction. Other states allow the board of directors to reduce capital without shareholder approval, *e.g.*, by canceling stock that has been reacquired. [N.Y. Bus. Corp. Law §515]

4) Appraisal rights [§1034]

Some statutes give preferred shareholders appraisal rights (*i.e.*, the right to demand the corporation to repurchase their shares for a fair price) if a capital reduction adversely affects their interests (*e.g.*, preference on liquidation). [N.Y. Bus. Corp. Law §806(b)(6)]

(d) Reappraisal (revaluation) surplus [§1035]

Surplus may also be created by a corporation revaluing assets that have appreciated in value over acquisition cost.

---

e.g. **Example:** XYZ Corp.'s home office is located on land that cost the corporation $100,000 but now has a fair market value of $500,000. By changing the balance sheet value of the land, a "revaluation" surplus of $400,000 is created.

---

1) As source of dividend [§1036]

Surplus created by unrealized appreciation in asset value is not a proper source of dividends in some states. Other states allow surplus from reappraisal of assets to be used like paid-in surplus or capital reduction surplus. [**Randall v. Bailey,** 23 N.Y.S.2d 173 (1940); **Klang v. Smith's Food & Drug Centers, Inc.,** 702 A.2d 150 (Del. 1997)—although case involved *repurchase* of shares, test is same for legality of *dividend*]

2) Scope of duty in revaluation [§1037]

Directors have reasonable latitude in reappraising assets and liabilities. They need only act "in good faith, on the basis of acceptable data, by methods that they reasonably believe reflect present values, and arrive at a determination of the surplus that is not so far off the mark as to constitute actual or constructive fraud." [**Klang v. Smith's Food & Drug Centers, Inc.,** *supra*]

(3) Notice to recipient shareholder [§1038]

Where dividends are paid out of any source other than earned surplus, many states also provide that the corporation must notify the receiving shareholders as to the source of the funds distributed. [Cal. Corp. Code §507; N.Y. Bus. Corp. Law §510(c)]

b. Modern Model Act approach [§1039]

The Model Act has generally done away with par value and the accounting classifications based on par value. It authorizes cash or property dividends as long as the corporation's total assets are at least equal to its total liabilities. [RMBCA §6.40(c)] The value of the corporation's assets may be based upon any "fair method that is reasonable under the circumstances." [RMBCA §6.40(d)]

4. Other Restrictions

a. Insolvency as restriction on dividends [§1040]

Virtually all states forbid dividends of any type if the corporation is in fact insolvent, or if payment of the dividend would render the corporation insolvent. [N.Y. Bus. Corp. Law §510(a)]

(1) "Insolvency" defined [§1041]

"Insolvency" is defined in two ways. In the bankruptcy sense, a corporation is insolvent if its *liabilities exceed its assets*. In the equity sense, a corporation is insolvent if it is unable to meet its debts as they mature, *i.e., insufficient cash* to pay its bills, regardless of the value of its assets. [N.Y. Bus. Corp. Law §102(a)(8)] If a corporation is insolvent—or a dividend payment would render it insolvent—in either sense, it may not legally pay a dividend.

b.   **Protection of preferred stock as restriction on dividends [§1042]**

Holders of preferred shares are generally entitled to payment upon liquidation before any distribution to holders of common stock (*see infra*, §1179). In some states, a corporation cannot pay a cash or property dividend from any source if the payment would endanger the liquidation preference of shares having such a preference (*i.e.*, if net assets after the payment would be less than the liquidation preference) unless the dividend is paid to that class of shares alone. [Cal. Corp. Code §502]

c.   **Contractual restrictions on dividends [§1043]**

Especially because of the ease in creating capital reduction surplus to "repair" deficits from previous operating losses (*see supra*, §§1030-1032), dividend statutes provide relatively little protection to creditors as long as the corporation is not insolvent (*see supra*, §§1040-1041). As a consequence, institutions that make large, long-term loans may place protective covenants in the loan agreement limiting dividends that might jeopardize repayment of the loan. Similar provisions may be required by underwriters in connection with the public issuance of bonds or preferred stock.

5.   **Remedies for Illegal Dividends**

a.   **Personal liability of directors [§1044]**

Directors who declare a dividend from an unlawful source, or under conditions that render payment illegal, are jointly and severally liable to the corporation for the benefit of creditors or preferred shareholders affected by the illegal dividend.

(1)   **Defenses [§1045]**

Early cases held that the directors' liability was absolute, but modern statutes and cases recognize a number of defenses. Usually directors are not liable if they voted against the distribution, were absent from the meeting, or relied in good faith (*i.e.*, after making inquiries reasonable under the circumstances) on financial statements showing that the funds were properly available for the payment. [Del. Gen. Corp. Law §§172, 174; N.Y. Bus. Corp. Law §§717, 719]

PAYMENT OF DIVIDENDS—A SUMMARY

gilbert

TRADITIONAL PAR VALUE APPROACH	Dividends may be paid from *surplus* only; a few states allow payment from current profits, even if stated capital is impaired. If dividends are paid from any source other than earned surplus, shareholders must be given notice of the source.
MODERN MODEL ACT APPROACH	Dividends may be paid from *any source*.
LIMITATIONS	Under either approach, dividends *cannot be paid if* the corporation is *insolvent* or would be *rendered insolvent* by the payment, payment would *jeopardize preferential rights*, or payment would *breach a contractual restriction*.
LIABILITY FOR IMPROPER DIVIDENDS	Directors who *voted for* the dividend *are personally liable*.* They may seek contribution from other directors who voted for the dividend and from shareholders who took the dividend knowing that it was improper. If the corporation is insolvent, corporate creditors can seek to recover from shareholders directly, but cannot do so if the corporation is solvent. *Directors have a defense if they relied in good faith on financial statements showing that funds were properly available.

(2) Amount of liability [§1046]

Some statutes allow the corporation to recover the full amount of the unlawful dividend. [RMBCA §8.33] Most, however, limit the recovery to the amount of injury suffered by the creditors and preferred shareholders, *e.g.*, the amount of liabilities owed to the creditors and the amount by which the dividend impaired liquidation preferences of the preferred shares. [N.Y. Bus. Corp. Law §719]

(3) Contribution among directors [§1047]

Any director held liable for unlawful dividends is normally entitled to compel contribution from other directors who could also be held liable (*i.e.*, those with no defense). [RMBCA §8.33; Del. Gen. Corp. Law §174(b)]

(a) Contribution from shareholders [§1048]

Most statutes also permit directors held liable to compel contribution from shareholders who received the unlawful dividend *with knowledge* of the illegality. [RMBCA §8.33(b); N.Y. Bus. Corp. Law §719(d)]

b. Personal liability of shareholders

(1) Where corporation insolvent [§1049]

If the corporation is insolvent (or is rendered insolvent by the dividend distribution), the shareholders who receive the illegal dividend are often held *absolutely* liable to return it to the corporation for the benefit of the creditors or preferred shareholders affected by the dividend. *Rationale:* The distribution by an insolvent corporation constitutes a *fraudulent conveyance* (no consideration given by the shareholder), and such a conveyance is void against creditors or those entitled to priority. [**Wood v. National City Bank,** 24 F.2d 661 (2d Cir. 1928)]

(a) Direct action possible [§1050]

Creditors (or preferred shareholders) affected by the dividend can bring a direct action against the shareholders receiving the illegal dividend. [Unif. Fraud. Transfer Act §7]

(2) Where corporation solvent [§1051]

Where the corporation's solvency is not affected by the distribution, shareholders who receive the payments *innocently*—not knowing that the dividend is from an improper source or under illegal conditions—are generally held entitled to retain them. [**McDonald v. Williams,** 174 U.S. 397 (1899)]

B. Redemption and Repurchase of Shares

1. Redemption [§1052]

A "redemption" involves the corporation's acquisition of some or all of a class of its outstanding shares by paying a stipulated redemption price (usually something in excess of par or stated value in states following the traditional par value approach) to the shareholders, who must then surrender their certificates. Redeemed shares are usually canceled and stated capital (shares outstanding) reduced accordingly. The chief purpose of redemption is usually to retire shares with dividend preferences, for the benefit of the common shares.

a. Source of funds to redeem [§1053]

In most states, a corporation is permitted to redeem out of *any available funds*, *i.e.*, any kind of surplus or even stated capital—even in most states following the traditional par value approach. [N.Y. Bus. Corp. Law §513(c)] *Rationale:* Having conferred upon the corporation the power to redeem, the shareholders are deemed to consent even to the impairment of capital if required for this purpose. Similarly, because redemption must be expressly authorized in the articles or bylaws, creditors are deemed to have notice of the possibility that capital will be reduced by a redemption.

2. Repurchase of Shares [§1054]

A "repurchase" of shares by the corporation is distinguished from a "redemption" in that a repurchase is not effected pursuant to a provision in the articles.

a. Effect of repurchase [§1055]

In most states following the traditional par value approach, repurchased shares generally are not automatically canceled. The shares remain issued. Hence, a repurchase in such states has no effect on stated capital. Instead the shares become *treasury shares* (*supra*, §870), which can be resold by the corporation at any price—even for less than their par value. In states following the modern approach, repurchased shares simply revert to being authorized, but unissued, shares unless the articles of incorporation provide otherwise. [RMBCA §6.31(a)]

b. Power to repurchase [§1056]

Whereas the power to redeem shares must be expressly reserved in the articles, at common law, a corporation generally was deemed to have the inherent right to repurchase its own shares, providing it acted in good faith. (*See infra*, §1067.) All states now have statutes authorizing the corporation to repurchase its own shares.

c. Source of funds for repurchase [§1057]

Most statutes permit a corporation to repurchase its shares under the same conditions that they permit payment of a cash or property dividend, *i.e.*, only if the corporation has a surplus. [N.Y. Bus. Corp. Law §513(a)]

(1) States following traditional approach [§1058]

In most states following the traditional par value approach, shares may be repurchased with funds from earned, paid-in, or capital reduction surplus accounts (*supra,* §§1027, 1029, 1032).

EXAM TIP   gilbert

Although a repurchase and a redemption each involve the corporation buying out-standing shares, they are treated quite differently in states following the ***traditional*** par value approach. In such states, a redemption is ***not*** subject to the limitation that generally restricts the source of funds for a ***repurchase to surplus***. A ***redemption*** may be made from ***any available funds***, because shareholders and creditors are deemed to have notice of this possibility since the option to redeem must be included in the corporation's articles of incorporation.

(a) Exceptions—repurchases out of stated capital [§1059]

In states following the traditional approach, generally, repurchases cannot be made if there is no surplus. However, many statutes authorize a corporation to repurchase its own shares out of *stated capital* for the following limited purposes:

(i) To collect or compromise a *debt, claim, or controversy with a shareholder*;

(ii) To pay dissenting shareholders for *appraisal rights* in merger proceedings (*infra,* §§1073-1094); or

(iii) To *eliminate fractional shares*.

[N.Y. Bus. Corp. Law §513(b)]

(2) Modern approach [§1060]

Under the modern approach, shares may be repurchased with funds from any source, so long as the corporation is not insolvent and will not be rendered insolvent by the repurchase (*see infra*). [*See* RMBCA §6.31]

3. Further Limitations on Repurchase and Redemption [§1061]

A repurchase or redemption of shares has the same effect as a dividend—*i.e.*, distributing assets of the corporation to shareholders, thereby putting them beyond the reach of creditors and, often, of senior shareholders. Thus, limitations similar to those imposed on dividend distributions (*supra,* §§1017-1043) are imposed on redemptions and repurchases of shares.

a. Insolvency limitation [§1062]

No redemption or repurchase is permitted if the corporation is insolvent, or if the effect of the redemption or repurchase would be to render the corporation insolvent in either the bankruptcy or equity sense. [N.Y. Bus. Corp. Law §513(a)]

(1) Time of valuation [§1063]

The corporation's solvency has usually been determined at the time that payment on the redemption or repurchase is made, rather than at the time the corporation bound itself to redeem or repurchase. Thus, even if the corporation was solvent when it entered into an agreement to repurchase certain shares in the future, the agreement is unenforceable if at the time payment is due, the corporation has become insolvent. [**Neimark v. Mel Kramer Sales, Inc.,** 306 N.W.2d 278 (Wis. 1981)]

(a) **Promissory note**

1) **Common law [§1064]**

Pursuant to this rule, at common law most courts have held that if a solvent corporation gives a promissory note in repurchasing its shares, the note can be enforced only as long as the corporation remains solvent. If the corporation becomes insolvent, further payments are unenforceable. [**McConnell v. Estate of Butler,** 402 F.2d 362 (9th Cir. 1968)—on bankruptcy of corporation, holder of note issued to repurchase shares was subordinated to claims of other corporate creditors; *but see* **Williams v. Nevelow,** 513 S.W.2d 535 (Tex. 1974)—contra]

2) **Statutes [§1065]**

Statutes in a number of states have adopted the contrary view. If the promissory note was given when the corporation could properly repurchase its shares, the note may subsequently be enforced as an ordinary debt of the corporation. [Del. Gen. Corp. Law §160; RMBCA §6.40(e)]

(b) **Surplus requirement [§1066]**

In addition to the rule that a repurchase agreement cannot be enforced at a time when the corporation is insolvent, some courts have also held that the corporation must meet the *surplus test* when each payment is made. [**Mountain State Steel Foundries, Inc. v. Commissioner,** 284 F.2d 737 (4th Cir. 1960); *but see* **Neimark v. Mel Kramer Sales, Inc.,** *supra*—contra]

b. **Bona fide corporate purposes—equitable limitations [§1067]**

In addition to the foregoing restrictions, courts have held that any discretionary redemption or repurchase must serve some bona fide *corporate purpose* (such as to eliminate dissident shareholders)—rather than merely to serve the *personal interests* of the directors or "insiders."

(1) **Repurchase or redemption favoring "inside" shareholders prohibited [§1068]**

A repurchase or redemption cannot be used to favor "inside" shareholders at the expense of others (*e.g.,* buying out the shares of "insiders" when the outlook for the corporation is bleak, or conversely, buying out "outsiders" when prospects for the corporation are bright). [**Zahn v. Transamerica Corp.,** *supra*, §711]

(2) Protection from corporate "raider" [§1069]

A corporate purpose must be shown when a corporation purchases the shares of a "corporate raider" to prevent his obtaining control, *e.g.*, when directors cause the corporation to purchase shares from a shareholder who otherwise threatens to seize control; or the directors cause the corporation to purchase shares of other shareholders to prevent the "raider" from obtaining them. If the purchases are made solely for the purpose of perpetuating the officers and directors in their jobs, this is not a bona fide corporate purpose. But if there is reason to believe that the corporate takeover by the "raider" would jeopardize the interests of the corporation generally, the repurchase may be justified. [**Cheff v. Mathes,** 199 A.2d 548 (Del. 1964)]

(a) Distinguish—rule 10b-5 [§1070]

Where directors cause the corporation to repurchase or redeem shares for the personal benefit of the directors rather than for bona fide corporate purpose, the corporation, as purchaser of the shares, is deemed "defrauded," and is entitled to maintain an action against the directors under rule 10b-5. (*See* detailed discussion *supra*, §§365-481.)

4. Remedies for Unlawful Redemption or Repurchase [§1071]

Generally, the same remedies available for illegal dividends are available against directors and shareholders for unlawful redemptions or repurchases of shares. (*See* detailed discussion *supra*, §§1044-1051.)

Chapter Ten:
Fundamental Changes
in Corporate Structure

CONTENTS

Chapter Approach

This chapter concerns fundamental corporate changes (principally, mergers, sales of substantially all assets, amendments of the articles (certificate) of incorporation, and dissolution), and the shareholder rights they trigger. The most important areas for exam purposes are as follows:

1. **Appraisal Rights of Shareholders**

    Whenever you encounter a fundamental corporate change on an exam, consider whether the dissenting shareholders have appraisal rights *requiring the corporation to buy their shares* at "fair value" (or sometimes "fair market value"). Keep in mind that the exercise of appraisal rights often involves an elaborate procedure, such as notice by the shareholder of intent to demand payment, notice by the corporation that the proposed action was authorized, demand for payment by the dissenters, and payment by the corporation of the amount it determines to be the fair value of the shares. If the dissenting shareholders reject the corporation's estimate of fair value, the court determines fair value. Also, appraisal rights are often exclusive—*i.e.*, a shareholder who is entitled to appraisal may not be able to seek other forms of relief.

2. **Statutory Merger**

    A statutory merger occurs when one corporation is *absorbed into another* pursuant to statutory provisions. This is normally accomplished by the "surviving" corporation issuing its shares to the shareholders of the "disappearing" corporation. In a statutory merger case, consider whether the merger requires approval by the shareholders of each corporation and whether dissenting shareholders have appraisal rights. Generally, a merger must first be approved by the board. Thereafter, it must be approved by the shareholders of each corporation. Dissenters are usually entitled to appraisal rights. However, in *"short-form" mergers*, neither corporation's shareholders are entitled to vote on the plan, and only the subsidiary's shareholders have appraisal rights. Furthermore, under many statutes, only the shareholders of the disappearing corporation in a "small-scale" merger have approval and appraisal rights. Also, some statutes deny appraisal rights if the corporation's stock is listed on a national securities exchange or is held by over 2,000 shareholders.

3. **De Facto Mergers**

    Watch for a question where a corporation attempts to circumvent the approval and appraisal rights of shareholders by (i) acquiring substantially all of a corporation's assets in exchange for stock or (ii) acquiring a majority of a corporation's stock in exchange for stock. Remember that some courts have held that a transaction that has the *effect* of a statutory merger is *deemed to be a merger* for purposes of voting and appraisal rights.

4. **Sale of Substantially All Assets**

    A sale, not in the ordinary course of business, of substantially all of a corporation's assets requires the approval of both the board and the shareholders. Most statutes also grant appraisal rights for shareholders dissenting from a sale of substantially all of the corporate assets.

5. Amendment of Articles

Generally, amendments to the articles (or certificate) of incorporation must be approved by the board and the shareholders. If the amendment will particularly affect a certain class, the approval of that class may also be required. Some states give appraisal rights to dissenters where, for example, the amendment adversely alters or abolishes a preferential right; excludes or limits a right to vote; alters or abolishes a preemptive right; or creates, alters, or abolishes a redemption right. Remember, however, that some states do not provide appraisal rights for any article amendments.

6. Dissolution and Liquidation

Dissolution terminates the corporation's status as a legal entity; *liquidation* terminates the corporation's business. For voluntary dissolution, approval by the board and a majority of the outstanding shares is normally required. Shareholders usually may bring an action for involuntary dissolution when, for example, the directors are deadlocked and irreparable injury is threatened; the directors are acting in an illegal, oppressive, or fraudulent manner; the shareholders are deadlocked; or the corporate assets are being misapplied or wasted. Most statutes also allow the state to institute dissolution proceedings on specified grounds (*e.g.*, fraud in obtaining the certificate of incorporation).

After dissolution, the corporation must "liquidate" or "wind up" its affairs by paying its debts and distributing the remaining assets. On liquidation, creditors are paid first. Known creditors must be given notice of dissolution. A creditor must present its claim within a given time period, or the claim will be barred. After the creditors are paid, every shareholder is generally entitled to a pro rata portion of the net assets remaining. However, preferred shares usually have a liquidation preference, which entitles their holders to payment before any distribution to holders of common stock.

7. Limitations on Power of Controlling Shareholders

Fundamental changes that increase the ownership or change the rights of controlling shareholders are subject to judicial review for fairness. Such changes may, for example, provide a way for controlling shareholders to "freeze out" minority shareholders through a sale of substantially all assets to a corporation owned by the controlling shareholder, a cash-out merger, or a reverse stock split. Many courts require that a freeze-out serve a legitimate business purpose; other courts do not require a business purpose, but do require that the transaction meet the standard of entire fairness. "Going private" transactions, either through freeze-outs or self-tenders (tender offers by a corporation for its minority shares), are subject to extensive federal regulation, which includes disclosure provisions and an anti-fraud provision similar to rule 10b-5.

8. Tender Offers

In a tender offer, a bidder makes an offer to the shareholders of a target corporation to tender their shares for cash or securities. Because a tender offer addresses the shareholders in their individual capacities, it is not a corporate transaction from the target's perspective, and gives rise to neither shareholder voting nor appraisal rights in the target's shareholders, in the absence of special statutory provisions. Similarly, a tender offer generally does not require approval by the bidder's shareholders or give rise to appraisal rights in those shareholders, unless consummation of the tender offer would amount to a de facto merger under the law of the bidder's state of incorporation.

Tender offers are regulated in many ways by federal securities laws. For example, a person (or group) who acquires more than 5% of a corporation's securities that are registered under the Securities Exchange Act must file a schedule 13D disclosure form. Similarly, anyone making a tender offer for registered securities must file a schedule 14D disclosure form. Furthermore, the Exchange Act regulates certain terms of tender offers—e.g., the period during which they must remain open—and requires the target corporation's management to either (i) recommend acceptance or rejection of the offer to the shareholders, (ii) remain neutral, or (iii) state that it is unable to take a position.

Section 14(e) of the Exchange Act prohibits material misstatements or omissions and fraudulent or manipulative acts in connection with a tender offer or a solicitation favoring or opposing a tender offer. Because this section was designed to protect the shareholders of the target, neither the bidder nor the target corporations may sue for damages under section 14(e), although they may seek injunctive relief. Target shareholders who tender their shares based on misleading information may sue for both damages and injunctive relief; even nontendering shareholders may be able to sue, provided they can show damages.

Because state statutes also regulate tender offers, an exam question may also require you to discuss the effect of such a statute. If a state statute is applicable, you should discuss whether the statute violates either the U.S. Constitution's Supremacy Clause (by conflicting with the federal regulation of tender offers) or the Commerce Clause (by regulating interstate commerce or imposing an excessive burden on interstate commerce).

A. Introduction

1. Major Fundamental Changes [§1072]

Fundamental changes in a corporation's structure are subject to special statutory requirements. The major fundamental changes are statutory mergers, sales of substantially all assets, amendment of the articles (certificate) of incorporation, and dissolution. Tender offers are also subject to special rules.

B. Appraisal Rights

1. In General [§1073]

Statutes in most states provide that shareholders who "dissent" from statutory mergers or certain other kinds of fundamental corporate changes may require the corporation to purchase their shares at the "fair value" or "fair market value" of the shares—usually excluding any element of appreciation or depreciation resulting from anticipation or execution of the merger or other change. [Del. Gen. Corp. Law §262; RMBCA §§13.01-13.03, 13.20-13.28, 13.30-13.31; Cal. Corp. Code §§1300 *et seq.*]

2. Valuation [§1074]

Most statutes provide that a dissenting shareholder has the right to be paid the "fair value" of his stock. Some statutes provide that a shareholder has the right to be paid the "fair market value" of his stock.

a. "Fair value" statutes [§1075]

Under statutes that provide that a dissenter must be paid the fair value of his shares, the two leading methods of valuation are the "Delaware block method" and the methods of modern finance.

(1) Delaware block method [§1076]

Traditionally, fair value was determined by applying the so-called "Delaware block method" of valuation. Under this method, the court separately determines the value of a corporation's stock by assigning a value to several elements of valuation (usually market value, earnings value, and asset value, and sometimes dividend value) and then assigning a weight to each element. The value of the stock is then calculated as the weighted average of the applicable valuations. For example, in **Piemonte v. New Boston Garden Corp.**, 387 N.E.2d 1145 (Mass. 1987), the Massachusetts Supreme Court approved the following weighting by the lower court:

Market Value	-	10%
Earnings Value	-	40%
Asset Value	-	50%

(a) Market value [§1077]

The market value is the price at which the corporation's shares were being traded on the market just prior to announcement of the transaction. The weight given to market value will depend in part on how deep the market was, *i.e.*, whether there was extensive or only limited trading in the corporation's stock.

(b) "Investment" or "earnings" value [§1078]

"Investment" or "earnings" value is usually measured by determining the corporation's average annual earnings during some number of years (usually five) before the event that triggers appraisal rights, and then capitalizing (*i.e.*, multiplying) that average by a selected multiplier. [**Tri-Continental Corp. v. Battye,** 74 A.2d 71 (Del. 1950); **Francis I. duPont & Co. v. Universal City Studios, Inc.,** 312 A.2d 344 (Del. 1973), *aff'd*, 334 A.2d 216 (Del. 1975)]

(c) Asset value [§1079]

Asset value is normally based on the liquidation value of the corporation's assets. [**Poole v. N.V. Deli Maatschappij,** 243 A.2d 67 (Del. 1968)]

(d) Dividend value [§1080]

Dividend value, based on the stream of dividends that the corporation has traditionally paid, is sometimes taken into account, but often no separate weight is given to this element, on the ground that it largely reflects the same value as earnings. [**Francis I. duPont & Co. v. Universal City Studios, Inc.,** *supra*]

(2) Modern financial methods [§1081]

A more modern approach to the valuation of stock for appraisal purposes is to allow proof of value to be made by any technique or method that is generally considered acceptable in the financial community. This approach was adopted by Delaware in **Weinberger v. UOP, Inc.,** *supra*, §567, and is also adopted in New York by statute [N.Y. Bus. Corp. Law §623(h)(4)]. However, non-Delaware courts that have used the Delaware block method in the past may continue to do so. [*See* **Leader v. Hycor, Inc.,** 479 N.E.2d 173 (Mass. 1985)]

b. "Fair market value" statutes [§1082]

Some statutes provide that a dissenter should be paid "fair market value" (rather than "fair value"). Under such statutes, market price may be determinative unless the market is very thin or reflects aberrational factors.

c. Minority and marketability discounts [§1083]

After the value of the corporation has been determined for appraisal purposes, some courts reduce the value of dissenting shares by applying minority discounts, marketability discounts, or both. In effect, minority and marketability discounts are second-step adjustments. In the first step, the court values the entire corporation, and then assigns a pro rata share of that value to each share of stock. In the second step (if there is one), the court discounts (reduces) the pro rata value of each dissenting share by a certain percentage.

(1) Minority discounts [§1084]

The theory of a minority discount is that because a minority shareholder lacks corporate decisionmaking power, the value of a minority share is less than its pro rata share of corporate value.

(2) Marketability discounts [§1085]

Some courts apply a marketability discount to minority shares in close corporations, on the ground that because shares in such corporations are not easily marketable, the fair value of such a share is less than the pro rata share of the corporation's value than the share represents.

(3) Acceptance [§1086]

Some courts apply minority discounts, marketability discounts, or both, to determine the value of shares that are owned by shareholders who have dissented from a fundamental change, such as a merger. Generally speaking, the courts seem more ready to accept marketability discounts than minority discounts. A few courts accept both. Two leading cases, **Cavalier Oil Corp. v. Harnett,** 564 A.2d 1137 (Del. 1989) and *In re* **Valuation of Common Stock of Mcloon Oil Co.,** 565 A.2d 997 (Me. 1989), reject both. That is the general modern trend, although the trend is far from uniform.

(4) Mandatory buyouts [§1087]

Most courts have held that a minority discount should not be applied when a corporation elects to buy out a shareholder who petitions for dissolution under a statutory mandatory buyout provision. (*See infra,* §1170.) In part, this position rests on the theory that if the minority shareholder had proved her case in the dissolution proceeding, and the corporation had been dissolved, each shareholder would have been entitled to the same amount per share. No consideration would be given, in dissolution, to whether the shares were controlling or noncontrolling. A mandatory buyout pursuant to a dissolution proceeding should be treated the same way. Furthermore, if a minority discount were applied in such cases, an unscrupulous controlling shareholder could engage in misconduct and unfairness to pressure minority shareholders to seek dissolution, and then buy the minority out at a discounted price.

3. Procedure [§1088]

To qualify as a "shareholder" for purposes of the appraisal statutes, a shareholder must often follow an elaborate statutory procedure. The corporation must also follow an elaborate procedure in response. Details vary from state to state, but the procedure stated in the Model Act is typical:

a. Notice to the corporation [§1089]

First, the shareholder must deliver to the corporation, before the vote is taken, written notice of her intent to demand payment for her shares if the proposed action is effectuated, and must not vote her shares in favor of the proposed action. [RMBCA §13.21(a)]

b. Notice by the corporation [§1090]

If the proposed corporate action is authorized at a shareholders' meeting, the corporation must deliver a written notice to all shareholders who gave the notice of intent to demand payment and did not vote in favor of the transaction. The notice to dissenters must be sent no later than 10 days after the corporate action was taken, and must:

(i) Supply a *form* for demanding payment;

(ii) State the *address* to which a demand for payment must be sent, and where and when stock certificates must be deposited;

(iii) Inform shareholders *to what extent transfer of their shares will be restricted* after their demand for payment is received;

(iv) *Set a date* by which the demand for payment must be made, which may not be less than 40 nor more than 60 days after the date the notice to the shareholder is delivered;

(v) *State the corporation's estimate* of the fair value of the shares; and

(vi) Be accompanied by a copy of the *relevant statutory provisions*.

[RMBCA §13.22]

c. Demand for payment [§1091]

After receiving this notice, the shareholder must then demand payment from the corporation and deposit her stock certificates with the corporation. [RMBCA §13.23]

d. Corporate response [§1092]

As soon as the proposed corporate action is taken, or upon receipt of a demand for payment, the corporation must pay each dissenter who has complied with the procedural requirements the amount the corporation estimates to be the fair value of the shares, plus accrued interest. The payment must be accompanied by:

(i) *Financial statements*;

(ii)   A statement of the corporation's estimate of the *fair value* of the shares;

(iii)   A statement of the *dissenter's rights* if the shareholder is dissatisfied with the payment; and

(iv)   A copy of the *relevant statutory provisions*.

[RMBCA §13.25]

e.   Appraisal proceedings [§1093]

A shareholder who is dissatisfied with the amount of the payment that the corporation makes must notify the corporation in writing of her estimate of the fair value of the shares and demand payment of that estimate (minus the amount that the corporation has paid). If the corporation is unwilling to pay the amount demanded, it must petition the court within 60 days of receiving the demand to determine fair value. (If it does not petition the court within 60 days, it must pay the amount demanded.) All dissenters whose demands remain unsettled must be made parties to the proceeding. The court may appoint one or more appraisers to receive evidence and recommend a decision on the question of fair value. The dissenters are entitled to the same discovery rights as parties in other civil proceedings. [RMBCA §13.30] A shareholder who fails to notify the corporation in writing, within 30 days after receiving payment, of her demand to be paid her fair estimate of the value of her shares, waives the right to demand payment as a dissenting shareholder.

f.   Costs [§1094]

The costs of an appraisal proceeding, other than counsel and expert fees, are assessed against the corporation, except that the court may assess these costs against all or some of the dissenters, in amounts that the court finds equitable, to the extent the court finds the dissenters acted arbitrarily, vexatiously, or not in good faith. The court may also assess counsel and expert fees, in amounts the court finds equitable, against the corporation if the court finds the corporation did not substantially comply with the statutory requirements, or acted arbitrarily, vexatiously, or not in good faith. [RMBCA §13.31]

C.   Statutory Mergers

1.   In General [§1095]

A statutory merger is a corporate combination in which one corporation is legally absorbed into another. To accomplish a statutory merger, shares of the corporation that will not survive the merger (the "disappearing corporation") are converted into shares or other securities of the corporation that will survive the merger (the "survivor"), other stock or securities, property, cash, or other interests, as the case may be, pursuant to the terms of the plan of merger. Under the statute, the disappearing corporation is thereby absorbed into the survivor, and the disappearing corporation's shareholders become shareholders in the survivor. [Del. Gen. Corp. Law §251(a)(e); RMBCA §§11.01, 11.03, 11.05, 11.06]

a. Consolidation [§1096]

A consolidation is similar to a merger, except that in a consolidation two or more existing corporations combine to form a wholly new corporation. Because the requirements for merger and consolidation are virtually identical, and the consolidation technique is rarely employed, the balance of this section will focus on mergers.

2. Effect of Merger [§1097]

When a merger becomes effective, the disappearing corporation ceases to exist. The survivor succeeds, by operation of law, to all of the disappearing corporation's rights, assets, and liabilities. [Del. Gen. Corp. Law §259; RMBCA §11.06; Cal. Corp. Code §1107(a)]

a. Effect on corporate contracts [§1098]

Because the survivor succeeds to the disappearing corporation's rights, assets, and liabilities by operation of law, the disappearing corporation's contracts— even contracts that are not ordinarily assignable and, indeed, even contracts that are not assignable by their terms—are generally taken over by the survivor by operation of law.

EXAM TIP   **gilbert**

It is important to remember that in a merger the disappearing corporation's **assets and obligations do not disappear**—they continue with the corporation that survives. The same generally is **not true** when one corporation buys substantially all of another corporation's assets. (*See infra*, §§1137-1143.) Generally, in a sale of assets the buyer does not become liable on the seller's obligations. This distinction could be important when deciding how to structure a takeover.

---

(1) Exception

A contract may specifically provide that it is not assignable in a merger. Furthermore, a court may imply such a term in an appropriate case.

3. Board Approval [§1099]

A merger is begun when the board of directors of each constituent corporation adopts a plan or agreement of merger. Normally, this plan or agreement must set forth:

(i) The *terms and conditions* of the merger, including the manner of converting shares of the constituents into shares of the survivor;

(ii) The *mode* of putting these terms into effect;

(iii) A statement of *any amendments to the survivor's articles* (certificate) of incorporation to be effected by the merger; and

(iv) Any *other terms* agreed upon.

[Del. Gen. Corp. Law §251(b); RMBCA §11.01; Cal. Corp. Code §1101]

4. Notice [§1100]

If the plan of merger must be approved by the shareholders, the corporation must notify each shareholder, whether or not entitled to vote, of the shareholders' meeting at which the plan is to be submitted for approval. The notice must indicate that a purpose of the meeting is to vote on the plan, and the plan or a summary of the plan must be included. If a shareholder intends to seek appraisal rights, he generally must give the corporation notice of his intent to do so (*see supra*, §1089) after receiving this notice.

5. Shareholder Approval [§1101]

After the merger plan or agreement is adopted by the board, it normally must be submitted to the shareholders of each constituent corporation for their approval.

a. Percentage of approval required [§1102]

Because of the importance of mergers, most statutes require approval by a stated percentage of the outstanding shares, rather than approval by a majority of those shares that are present at the meeting at which the merger is considered. Traditionally, the statutes required two-thirds of the outstanding shares, but most statutes now require a *majority of the outstanding shares*. Some statutes require only a simple majority vote, not a majority of outstanding shares. The Model Act requires that more shares vote in favor of the merger than vote against it, at a meeting at which at least a majority of the votes entitled to be cast on the merger are present.

b. Class voting [§1103]

A number of statutes provide that under certain conditions a merger must also be approved by a designated percentage of each class of shareholders, whether or not otherwise entitled to vote. [Cal. Corp. Code §1201—approval of each class required, except that no approval by nonvoting preferred shareholders is necessary if no change in the rights, privileges, or preferences of the class]

6. Appraisal rights [§1104]

Shareholders who dissent from a merger, and follow certain procedures, normally have a right to be paid the fair value of their shares. (*See supra*, §§1073-1094.)

a. Exclusivity of appraisal rights [§1105]

Under some statutes, dissenting shareholders who have an appraisal right may not be permitted to invoke another remedy to challenge or upset the merger. (*See infra*, §1202.)

7. Mergers that Do Not Require Shareholder Approval [§1106]

There are two kinds of cases in which approval of one or both corporations' shareholders may not be required for a merger—"short-form" mergers and "small-scale" mergers.

a. Short-form mergers [§1107]

Many statutes provide special rules for the approval of a merger between a parent and a subsidiary in which the parent owns a designated percentage of the stock—normally 90%. [Del. Gen. Corp. Law §253; RMBCA §11.04; Cal. Corp. Code §1110(b)] Such mergers are known as "short-form" mergers.

(1) Merger effected by boards of directors [§1108]

Typically, under these statutes, a short-form merger does not require the approval of either the parent's or the subsidiary's shareholders. Instead, the merger can be effected simply by the boards of the parent and the subsidiary, or, under some statutes, by the board of the parent alone.

(a) Rationale

Because the parent owns almost all the subsidiary's stock, approval of the subsidiary's shareholders would be a foregone conclusion.

(2) Appraisal rights [§1109]

Although the subsidiary's shareholders do not have the right to vote on a short-form merger, they do have appraisal rights. However, the parent's shareholders have neither voting nor appraisal rights.

b. Small-scale mergers [§1110]

Some statutes provide that approval by the shareholders of the *survivor* corporation is not required if:

(i) The voting stock of the survivor issued to effect the merger does not constitute more than a certain percentage—usually one-sixth—of the outstanding shares of voting stock immediately after the merger, and

(ii) The merger does not make any change in the survivor's articles (certificate) of incorporation.

[Del. Gen. Corp. Law §251(f); RMBCA §11.03(g); Cal. Corp. Code §1201(b)] *Rationale:* Such mergers are not economically or legally significant to the survivor and its shareholders.

(1) Appraisal rights [§1111]

Following this same rationale, in such cases the survivor's shareholders have no appraisal rights.

(2) Shareholders of disappearing corporation [§1112]

The small-scale merger statutes affect only the survivor corporation. Approval by the shareholders of the disappearing corporation is still required, because the merger is economically significant to that corporation. These shareholders also have appraisal rights.

8. Mergers that Do Not Trigger Appraisal Rights [§1113]

Some statutes deny appraisal rights for certain mergers even though the merger requires shareholder approval.

a. Exceptions based on nature of merger [§1114]

As noted above, in a short-form merger, the minority shareholders of the subsidiary have appraisal rights, but the parent's shareholders do not. (*See supra*, §1109.) Likewise, in a small-scale merger, the shareholders of the disappearing corporation have appraisal rights, but the shareholders of the survivor do not. (*See supra*, §1111.)

b. Exceptions based on nature of stock

(1) Stock listed on national exchange or by a large number of shareholders [§1115]

Some statutes provide that a merger does not give rise to appraisal rights in the case of a corporation whose stock is listed on a national securities exchange. Some statutes also eliminate appraisal rights in the case of any corporation with 2,000 or more shareholders, whether or not the stock is listed on a securities exchange [Del. Gen. Corp. Law §262(k)], or a very large number of shareholders. Such a provision is sometimes referred to as a "market out."

(a) Rationale

The theory of the market-out exception is that in such cases the shareholder has an assured market for the stock, and therefore does not need an appraisal right to be able to get out of the corporation when it undergoes a fundamental change. Moreover, it is thought that where stock is traded on an organized market, it is unlikely that the appraisal valuation would differ significantly from the market price of the stock. Similarly, if a corporation has a large number of shareholders, the market is likely to be about as deep as it is on some stock exchanges.

CHECKLIST OF MERGERS THAT MIGHT NOT TRIGGER APPRAISAL RIGHTS **gilbert**

BE ON THE LOOKOUT FOR QUESTIONS INVOLVING THE FOLLOWING MERGERS THAT MIGHT NOT TRIGGER APPRAISAL RIGHTS UNDER STATE LAW:

☑ Stocks listed on a *national securities* exchange or of corporations that have *many* (e.g., > 2,000) *shareholders*

☑ *Short-form mergers*—shareholders of the surviving (parent) corporation generally do not have appraisal rights

☑ *Small-scale mergers*—shareholders of the surviving corporation do not have appraisal rights in some states

---

(2) Carve-outs from market-out exception

(a) California [§1116]

The California statute eliminates appraisal rights as to shares traded on the New York or American Stock Exchange, and as to certain over-the-counter stocks, *except* where the appraisal is demanded by shareholders holding 5% or more of the outstanding shares. [Cal. Corp. Code §1300(b)]

1) Rationale

If a block of shares that large entered the market, it would sell at a distress price, even in a well-organized market. Furthermore, the fact that so many shareholders prefer appraisal rights to selling their stock on the market provides a good indication that appraisal is not being sought merely as a nuisance tactic.

(b) Model Act [§1117]

The market-out provision of the Model Act does not apply to certain conflict-of-interest transactions. In such cases, if appraisal is otherwise available, it is not made unavailable because the corporation's stock is listed on a major exchange, or has 2,000 shareholders and more than $20 million in assets. The statute is complex, but generally speaking the exception to the market-out provision applies when any of the corporation's shares or assets are being acquired, pursuant to a corporate action that triggers appraisal rights, by a person who either:

1) Was, during the year preceding the corporate action, the *owner of 20% or more of the corporation's voting power;*

2) Directly or indirectly had, during that one-year period, the *power to cause the appointment or election of 25% or more of the directors*; or

3) Was, during that one-year period, a *senior executive or director* of the corporation who will receive, as a result of the corporate action, a financial benefit not generally available to other shareholders.

9. Articles of Merger Must Be Filed with State [§1118]

After a plan of merger is approved by the directors and shareholders, articles of merger are executed by each party to the merger. The articles generally must indicate the parties' names, set forth any changes that were made to the survivor's articles of incorporation as part of the merger, and be filed with the state.

REQUIREMENTS TO UNDERTAKE A STATUTORY MERGER—A SUMMARY

gilbert

THE STEPS REQUIRED TO UNDERTAKE A STATUTORY MERGER ARE AS FOLLOWS:

First, the *board of directors* (generally of both corporations*) must adopt a resolution to undertake a merger, setting forth the terms and conditions of the merger, the mode of putting the terms into effect, any amendments that will be made to the articles, etc.

Second, if the merger must be approved by the shareholders (and most must be**), all *shareholders*—whether or not entitled to vote—must be given *notice* of the meeting at which the vote will be taken. The notice must set forth at least a summary of the merger plan. This enables the shareholders to decide whether they plan to exercise their appraisal rights and give the required notice before a vote is taken (see *supra,* §1089).

Third, the *shareholders generally must approve* the merger at the shareholders' meeting by a specific statutory percentage (traditionally two-thirds of all outstanding shares, now usually a majority of outstanding shares, in some states a majority of the votes cast at the meeting).

Finally, articles of merger, setting forth the details of the merger, must be filed with the state.

---

*Short-form mergers may not require approval by the directors of the subsidiary, depending on the statute.

**Short-form mergers may not require approval by the shareholders of either the surviving or the disappearing corporations, and small-scale mergers may not require approval by the shareholders of the surviving corporation.

D. De Facto Mergers

1. Introduction [§1119]

The explicit statutory rules that govern voting and appraisal rights in mergers often differ considerably from the explicit statutory rules that govern voting and appraisal rights for other kinds of corporate combinations, such as acquisitions by one corporation of the stock or assets of another. For example, a merger normally requires shareholder approval. In contrast, under the literal terms of most statutes, an acquisition of assets or stock normally does not. A merger normally triggers appraisal rights. In contrast, under the literal terms of most statutes, an acquisition of stock or assets normally does not. Under a few statutes, including Delaware, even a sale of substantially all assets does not trigger appraisal rights. Accordingly, there are certain anomalies in the statutes, in that if only the explicit rules are considered, corporate combinations that are virtually identical in substance give rise to radically different shareholder rights, depending solely on the form in which management chooses to cast the combination. To address these anomalies, some courts have created the de facto merger doctrine and some states have legislatively codified the doctrine.

2. Acquisition of Substantially All Assets in Exchange for Stock (Stock-for-Assets Combinations) [§1120]

Suppose one corporation acquires substantially all of the assets of another (the "transferor") in exchange, not for cash, but for its own stock. As part of the agreement the acquiring corporation assumes the transferor's liabilities, and the transferor agrees to dissolve and liquidate. In that case, the two corporations are combined, as in a merger: the liabilities and the assets of the two corporations are combined; the transferor corporation disappears; and the shareholder groups of the two corporations are combined. [**Farris v. Glen Alden Corp.**, 143 A.2d 25 (Pa. 1958); **Rath v. Rath Packing Co.**, 136 N.W.2d 410 (Iowa 1965)]

a. Comment

It is true that in an acquisition of assets, stock in the acquiring corporation is issued to the transferor corporation, while in a merger, stock in the survivor corporation is issued directly to the disappearing corporation's shareholders. However, if the agreement requires the transferor corporation to immediately liquidate and distribute the stock to its shareholders, this difference is only one of form.

3. Acquisition of Majority Stock in Exchange for Stock (Stock-for-Stock Combinations) [§1121]

Alternatively, suppose an acquiring corporation acquires a majority of the stock of another corporation in exchange for its own stock. From the perspective of the acquiring corporation's shareholders, the transaction is functionally equivalent to a merger, at least where the acquired corporation is then dissolved. The assets and liabilities of the two corporations are combined, as in a merger; one corporation disappears, as in a merger; and the two shareholder groups are combined, as in a merger. [**Applestein v. United Board & Carton Corp.**, 159 A.2d 146, *aff'd*, 161 A.2d 474 (N.J. 1960)]

4. De Facto Merger Doctrine [§1122]

To protect the rights of shareholders in such stock-for-assets and stock-for-stock combinations, some courts hold that a transaction that has the effect of a merger is deemed to be a merger for purposes of voting and appraisal rights. Under this *de facto merger doctrine*, if one corporation acquires substantially all of another corporation's assets and assumes its liabilities in exchange for stock of the acquiror that is distributed to the transferor corporation's shareholders, the transaction will require the approval of the acquiring corporation's shareholders and will trigger appraisal rights for those shareholders. The same rule would apply to the shareholders of a corporation that acquired a majority of another corporation's stock in exchange for the acquiring corporation's stock. The test is whether the transaction has "all the characteristics and consequences," or the "indicia," of a merger. [**Farris v. Glen Alden Corp.**, *supra*; **Applestein v. United Board & Carton Corp.**, *supra*; **Rath v. Rath Packing Co.**, *supra*]

5. "Equal Dignity" Rule [§1123]

Some courts have rejected the de facto merger doctrine. In particular, the Delaware courts say that the various forms of combination all have "equal dignity," and the requirements of one form are irrelevant to others. Under this view, the form and label that management attaches to a corporate combination determines whether the transaction requires shareholder approval and triggers appraisal rights. [**Hariton v. Arco Electronics, Inc.,** 188 A.2d 123 (Del. 1963); **Heilbrunn v. Sun Chemical Corp.,** 150 A.2d 755 (Del. 1959)]

6. **Statutes [§1124]**
   Several states have statutes that effectively eliminate the de facto merger problem by codifying the doctrine and treating corporate combinations on the basis of substance rather than form.

   a. **California [§1125]**
      The California statute illustrates this approach.

      (1) **Reorganizations [§1126]**
          The statute creates a new category of corporate combinations, called "reorganizations." [Cal. Corp. Code §§181, 1200] The following are all considered "reorganizations" under the California statute:

          (a) *Merger reorganization*—A merger other than a short-form merger.

          (b) *Exchange reorganization*—An acquisition by one corporation of more than 50% of the stock in another, wholly or partly in exchange for shares of the acquiring corporation.

          (c) *Sale-of-assets reorganization*—An acquisition by one corporation of substantially all of the assets of another, wholly or partly in exchange either for the acquiring corporation's shares or for debt securities that are not adequately secured and have a maturity greater than five years.

      (2) **Shareholder rights [§1127]**
          If a combination is a reorganization, as defined above, shareholders have the following voting and appraisal rights under the California statute:

          (a) **Shareholder approval required [§1128]**
              A merger or sale-of-assets reorganization must be approved by a majority of the shareholders of both constituent corporations. [Cal. Corp. Code §§15, 117] An exchange reorganization must be approved by shareholders of the acquiring corporation. [Cal. Corp. Code §§1200, 1201(a)]

              1) **Exception—small-scale acquisitions [§1129]**
                 Approval by the shareholders of the acquiring or surviving corporation is not required if the persons who were shareholders immediately before the reorganization (or the corporation itself)

end up owning at least five-sixths of the stock of the acquiring or surviving corporation, provided that the reorganization does not require amendment of the corporation's articles.

(b) Appraisal rights [§1130]

If a reorganization requires approval by a corporation's shareholders under the California statute, the shareholders of that corporation are also given appraisal rights if they dissent from the proposed reorganization (subject to the California market-out exception for securities traded on national exchanges (*supra*, §1116)). [Cal. Corp. Code §1300(a), (b)]

7. New York Stock Exchange Rules [§1131]

Like the California statute, a rule of the New York Stock Exchange requires shareholder approval of certain corporate combinations regardless of form. Under that rule, with certain limited exceptions, shareholder approval is required for the issuance of common stock, or securities convertible into or exercisable for common stock, if (i) the common stock to be issued or issuable will have voting power equal to 20% or more of the voting power outstanding before the issuance; or (ii) the number of shares of common stock to be issued or issuable is equal to 20% or more of the number of shares of common stock outstanding before the issuance. Among the exceptions to the rule are sales of stock for cash in a public offering. Certain other major exchanges have equivalent rules. Note that the New York Stock Exchange rule only requires shareholder approval; it does not provide appraisal rights. (Of course, appraisal rights might be triggered under state law if the issuance of shares occurs in connection with a transaction that gives rise to appraisal rights under state law, such as a statutory merger or a de facto merger in those states that adopt the de facto doctrine.)

8. Model Act [§1132]

The Model Act includes a provision that is similar to the New York Stock Exchange rule. Under section 6.21(f) of the Model Act, an issuance of shares, or other securities or rights excercisable for shares, requires shareholder approval if: (i) the shares, or other securities or rights, are issued for consideration other than cash or cash equivalents, and (ii) the voting power of the shares that are issued and issuable as a result of the transaction comprise more than 20% of the voting power of the shares of the corporation that were outstanding before the transaction. Like the New York Stock Exchange rule, section 6.21(f) only requires shareholder approval; it does not confer appraisal rights. As in the case of the New York Stock Exchange rule, however, appraisal rights may be available if the issuance falls under some other provisions of the Model Act that provides for appraisal rights, such as the merger provisions.

a. Distinguish

One major difference between the Model Act rule and the New York Stock Exchange rule is that the Model Act rule applies not just to listed corporations, but rather to all corporations that are incorporated in a state that has adopted the rule. Another difference is that the only sanction for violating the New York Stock Exchange rule is that shares that are issued without the shareholder approval required under the rule cannot be listed on the Exchange. In contrast, if a corporation that is incorporated in a state that has adopted the Model Act rule issues or attempts to issue shares without the approval required by that rule, the issuance can be enjoined or rescinded.

E. Triangular Mergers

1. Introduction [§1133]

Triangular mergers are a special form of merger. There are two types of triangular mergers—conventional and reverse.

2. Conventional Triangular Merger [§1134]

A conventional (or "forward") triangular merger works like this: Assume that ParentCo and X Corp. want to engage in a merger in which ParentCo will be the survivor and X Corp.'s shareholders will end up with 100,000 shares of ParentCo. In a traditional merger, this would be accomplished by having ParentCo issue 100,000 shares to X Corp.'s shareholders. In a conventional triangular merger, ParentCo instead begins by creating a new subsidiary, SubCo. ParentCo then transfers 100,000 shares of its own stock to SubCo, in exchange for all of SubCo's stock. X Corp. is then merged into SubCo. However, instead of issuing its own stock to X Corp.'s shareholders, SubCo issues the 100,000 shares of ParentCo stock that it owns. The net result is that X Corp.'s shareholders end up with 100,000 shares of ParentCo stock, just as they would in a traditional merger with ParentCo itself. However, X Corp.'s business is owned by ParentCo only indirectly—through SubCo, its wholly owned subsidiary—rather than directly by ParentCo itself, as in a traditional merger.

a. Purpose

A major purpose for using this technique is that ParentCo may want to avoid assuming X Corp.'s liabilities. In a traditional merger between ParentCo and X Corp., ParentCo would succeed to X Corp.'s liabilities by operation of law. By using a triangular merger, ParentCo may be able to insulate itself from direct responsibility for X Corp.'s liabilities, because X Corp. is merged into SubCo, not into ParentCo.

3. Reverse Triangular Merger [§1135]

A reverse triangular merger begins like a conventional triangular merger: ParentCo creates a subsidiary, SubCo, and transfers 100,000 shares of ParentCo stock to SubCo in exchange for all of SubCo's stock. In a conventional triangular merger, X Corp. would then be merged into SubCo. In a reverse triangular merger, however, SubCo is merged into X Corp. The merger agreement provides that all previously outstanding X Corp. shares are automatically converted into the 100,000 shares of ParentCo owned by SubCo, and all SubCo shares are automatically converted into X Corp. shares. As a result, SubCo disappears, because it is merged into X Corp. X Corp. becomes a wholly owned subsidiary of ParentCo, because ParentCo owned all the

SubCo shares, and all the SubCo shares are converted into X Corp. shares, so that ParentCo now owns all of the shares of X Corp. The shareholders of X Corp., in turn, now own 100,000 ParentCo shares, because all X Corp. shares are converted into ParentCo shares.

a. Purpose

Like a conventional triangular merger, a reverse triangular merger may insulate ParentCo from X Corp.'s liabilities, because X Corp. ends up as a subsidiary of ParentCo, rather than merging into ParentCo. In addition, however, X Corp.'s legal status as a corporation is preserved. This could be important where X Corp. has valuable rights under contracts, leases, licenses, or franchises that might be lost in a merger in which it is not the survivor.

METHODS OF MERGING CORPORATIONS— A COMPARISON	**gilbert**
TYPE OF MERGER	**METHODOLOGY**
REGULAR STATUTORY MERGER	X Corp shares are converted into A Corp shares or other securities or interests pursuant to the plan of merger. X Corp disappears, and A Corp is liable on X Corp's obligations.
SHORT-FORM MERGER	Same as above, but A Corp already owns most of X Corp's shares (e.g., 90%) and approval of X Corp's shareholders and directors generally is not required.
DE FACTO MERGER	A Corp purchases substantially all of the assets of X Corp in exchange for A Corp stock, or acquires most of X Corp's stock in exchange for A Corp stock, and assumes X Corp's liabilities; this is treated as a merger in some states.
CONVENTIONAL (FORWARD) TRIANGULAR MERGER	A Corp creates a subsidiary, SubCo, and transfers A Corp stock to SubCo in exchange for SubCo stock. SubCo then exchanges its A Corp stock for all of the stock of X Corp, X Corp disappears into SubCo, and SubCo becomes liable on X Corp's obligations; A Corp is not directly liable on X Corp's obligations.
REVERSE TRIANGULAR MERGER	A Corp creates a subsidiary, SubCo, and transfers A Corp stock into SubCo in exchange for SubCo's stock. SubCo then merges into X Corp under an agreement that provides that all previously outstanding X Corp stock will be converted into shares of SubCo, and all SubCo shares will be converted into X Corp stock. As a result, SubCo disappears and X Corp becomes a subsidiary of A Corp. A Corp is not directly liable for X Corp's obligations and X Corp's corporate identity is preserved.

4. Voting and Appraisal Rights in Triangular Mergers [§1136]

Triangular mergers may also be used to erode voting and appraisal rights. For example, in a merger of SubCo into X Corp., the subsidiary (SubCo) rather than the parent (ParentCo) is a party to the merger. Literally, therefore, only SubCo's shareholders have voting and appraisal rights. Because SubCo's only shareholder is ParentCo, and because ParentCo obviously will vote its stock in SubCo in favor of the merger, ParentCo's shareholders would not have voting and appraisal rights. In **Terry v. Penn Central Corp.**, 668 F.2d 188 (3d Cir. 1981), it was argued that such a merger is a de facto merger as to ParentCo. However, the court rejected this argument, partly because the Pennsylvania statute, which governed the transaction, had earlier been amended with the purpose of rejecting the de facto merger theory.

F. Sale of Substantially All Assets

1. Shareholder Approval

a. Approval normally required [§1137]

At common law, a sale of substantially all assets normally required unanimous shareholder approval, on the theory that it violated an implied contract among the shareholders to maintain the corporation in business. Today, virtually every state has a statute authorizing such a sale upon approval by the board and a requisite percentage of the shareholders. Because of the importance of a sale of substantially all assets, most statutes require approval by a stated percentage of the outstanding shares, rather than approval by a majority of those shares that are present at the meeting at which the merger is considered. Traditionally, the statutes required two-thirds of the outstanding shares, but most statutes now require a majority of the outstanding shares. Some statutes require only a simple majority vote, not a majority of outstanding shares. The Model Act requires that more shares vote in favor of the sale of assets than vote against it, at a meeting at which at least a majority of the votes entitled to be cast on the sale are present.

EXAM TIP   **gilbert**

The *basic procedure* for approving a *sale of substantially all assets*, and indeed, for approving any fundamental corporate change that will be discussed *infra*, is similar to the procedure for adopting a merger:

* First, the *directors must adopt a resolution* to undertake the fundamental change;

* Second, the *directors must notify the shareholders* of the meeting at which shareholder approval will be sought to undertake the fundamental change (*see supra*, §§538-539); and

* Third, the *shareholders must* approve the change by a statutorily provided vote (often more than a simple majority of the shares at the meeting).

Note: Most fundamental corporate changes—other than a sale of substantially all assets—also require a fourth step: *filing a document with the state* describing the fundamental change (*e.g.,* articles of merger, articles of amendment).

---

b. Exception for sales made in ordinary course of business [§1138]

Some statutes explicitly exclude sales in the ordinary course of business from the requirement of shareholder approval. [RMBCA §12.01; Cal. Corp. Code §1001(a)(2)] Under such a statute, if, for example, a corporation was organized to build and sell a single office building, the sale of the building would not require shareholder approval. Even where the statute does not explicitly so provide, courts have treated sales in the ordinary course of business as outside the statutory requirement of shareholder approval, on the theory that even at common law, where unanimous shareholder approval was required, sales made in the ordinary course of business were excepted, because they were deemed to be in furtherance (rather than in breach) of the implied contract among the shareholders. [**Jeppi v. Brockman Holding Co.,** 34 Cal. 2d 11 (1949)]

c. Exception for corporations in failing circumstances [§1139]

There is a split of authority on whether the requirement of shareholder approval applies when a corporation is insolvent or in failing circumstances or financial distress. [*See* **Teller v. W.A. Griswold Co.,** 87 F.2d 603 (6th Cir. 1937)—statute inapplicable; **Michigan Wolverine Student Cooperative v. William Goodyear & Co.,** 22 N.W.2d 884 (Mich. 1946)—contra]

d. Exception for mortgages, pledges, etc. [§1140]

Most statutes do not require shareholder approval for the corporation's execution of a mortgage or other lien on corporate assets for the purpose of securing a corporate obligation. [RMBCA §12.01; Cal. Corp. Code §1000]

e. Other exceptions [§1141]

The Model Act also excludes transfers of a corporation's assets to a wholly owned subsidiary of the corporation and pro rata distributions of the corporation's assets to its shareholders.

EXAM TIP   **gilbert**

A good way to test on the sale of substantially all assets is by asking about a transaction that does *not require shareholder approval*:

* *Sales in the ordinary course of business*, even of substantially all assets;

* *Mortgages and pledges*, even if they encumber substantially all of a corporation's assets;

* Sales by corporations in *failing circumstances* (in some states), even if they are of substantially all of a corporation's assets;

* Sales by a *corporation to a subsidiary* (in some states), even if they are of substantially all of a corporation's assets; and

* *Pro rata distributions of assets to shareholders* (in some states), even if the assets constitute substantially all of the corporation's assets.

---

2. **Appraisal Rights [§1142]**

Where a sale of substantially all assets requires shareholder approval, most statutes also provide dissenting shareholders with appraisal rights.

a. **Exceptions**

A few statutes do not confer appraisal rights in connection with the sale of assets. [*See* Del. Gen. Corp. Law §262] California provides appraisal rights for a sale of substantially all assets only if the consideration for the sale consists of either stock or long-term unsecured securities of the acquiring corporation. [Cal. Corp. Code §§181, 1300]

3. **What Constitutes "Substantially All Assets" [§1143]**

In determining whether a sale of assets includes "substantially all assets" for purposes of the statute, the question is not simply the percentage of assets sold, but rather whether the assets sold constitute substantially all of the corporation's operating assets, account for most of the corporation's revenues, or are vital to the operation of the corporation's business. [**Katz v. Bregman**, 431 A.2d 1274, *appeal denied sub nom.* **Plant Industries Inc. v. Katz**, 435 A.2d 1044 (Del. 1981)]

a. **Model Act [§1144]**

Under Model Act section 12.01, no approval of the shareholders of a corporation is required to: (i) sell the corporation's assets in the *usual and regular course of business*; (ii) *encumber* the corporation's assets, whether or not in the usual and regular course of business; (iii) *transfer the corporation's assets to a wholly owned subsidiary*; or (iv) *distribute assets pro rata to the shareholders*. A sale of assets that is not described in section 12.01 requires approval of the corporation's shareholders if the sale would leave the corporation without a significant continuing business activity. If a corporation retains a business activity that represented at least 25% of the corporation's total assets at the end of its most recently completed fiscal year, and 25% of either income from continuing operations before taxes or revenues from continuing operations for that fiscal year, the corporation will conclusively be deemed to have retained a significant continuing business activity.

G. Amendment of Articles

1. **In General [§1145]**

Fundamental changes in the corporation may be effected through amendment of the corporate articles. Some amendments may be pure formalities (*e.g.*, changing the name of the corporation). Others may substantially change or impair the rights of the shareholders (*e.g.*, making cumulative preferred shares noncumulative). Still others may substantially affect the corporation itself (*e.g.*, changing the corporation's business purpose).

2. **Vote Required [§1146]**

An amendment of the corporation's articles normally must be approved by the board and the shareholders. Because of the importance of an amendment of the certificate, most statutes require approval by a stated percentage of the outstanding shares, rather than approval by a majority of those shares that are present at the meeting at which the merger is considered. Traditionally, the statutes required two-thirds of the outstanding shares, but most statutes now require a majority of the outstanding shares. Moreover, some statutes require only a simple majority vote, not a majority of outstanding shares. The Model Act requires that more shares vote in favor of the amendment than vote against it, at a meeting at which at least a majority of the votes entitled to be cast on the amendment are present.

a. Class voting [§1147]

Under many statutes, amendments that would have certain designated effects on the shares of a given class must be approved not only by the shareholders as a whole, but also by the class voting separately—whether or not stock of the class is otherwise entitled to vote. For example, under the Model Act an amendment to the articles of incorporation requires the approval of each class of shareholders—even those classes not entitled to vote under the articles of incorporation—if it would effect an exchange or reclassification of all or part of the shares of the class into shares of another class; increase or decrease the authorized shares of the class; limit or deny a preemptive right; change shares of the class into a different number of shares of the same class; change the rights, preferences, or limitations of the class; create a new class of shares having superior financial rights or preferences; increase the rights, preferences, or number of shares of any class that have superior financial rights or preferences; or have certain other effects. [RMBCA §10.04]

b. Special provisions [§1148]

Statutes may also contain special provisions placing limitations on certain kinds of amendments. For example, under the Delaware statute, an amendment restricting transferability of shares is not binding on shares already issued, unless approved by the holders of the shares in question. [Del. Gen. Corp. Law §202(b)] Under the California statute, an amendment reducing the number of directors to less than five cannot be adopted over the opposition of more than 16-2/3% of the outstanding shares. [Cal. Corp. Code §212(a)]

c. Effect of provision in articles requiring higher percentage [§1149]

Under most statutes, the articles may validly require a higher (but not a lower) percentage of shareholder approval for any proposed amendment than would otherwise be required by the statute. [Del. Gen. Corp. Law §§216, 242(b)(1); RMBCA §7.27; Cal. Corp. Code §904(a)(5)] Similarly, most courts will enforce shareholder agreements requiring a higher percentage of shareholder approval than would otherwise be required by statute. (*See supra*, §634.)

3. Appraisal Rights [§1150]

Many states give appraisal rights in connection with certain kinds of article amendments. For example, under the Model Act, shareholders have a right to be paid the fair value of their shares if they dissent from an amendment with respect to a class or series of shares that reduces the number of shares of the class or series owned by the shareholder to a fraction of a share and the corporation has the obligation or right to repurchase the fractional share so created. [RMBCA §13.02(a)(4)] However, many statutes do not provide appraisal rights in connection with article amendments.

4. **Constitutional Issues**

   a. **Contract between state and corporation [§1151]**

      The Supreme Court early held that, for purposes of constitutional law, a certificate of incorporation is a contract between the incorporating state and the corporation, and therefore is within the Contract Clause of the Constitution, which prohibits states from impairing the obligation of contracts. [**Trustees of Dartmouth College v. Woodward**, 17 U.S. 518 (1819); U.S. Const. art. I, §10]

   b. **Contract among shareholders [§1152]**

      Subsequently, the Supreme Court held that the certificate of incorporation was also a contract among the shareholders, and therefore, it could not be changed without their unanimous consent. [**Geddes v. Anaconda Copper Mining Co.,** 254 U.S. 590 (1921)]

   c. **Result—limited state power [§1153]**

      The result was to set limits on the power of a state to regulate corporations organized under its laws and also on the power of the shareholders—absent unanimity—to amend the articles of incorporation or make any fundamental change in the corporation that could be regarded as a change in their "contract."

   d. **Reserved power clauses [§1154]**

      In response, the states amended their general corporation laws to include "reserved power clauses," *i.e.*, provisions reserving to the state the power to alter, amend, or repeal its corporation laws as regards corporations incorporated after the adoption of the provisions. These reserved power clauses are deemed to be part of the "contract" between the state and the corporation and are therefore given effect by the courts.

   e. **Shareholder amendment [§1155]**

      State corporations laws were also amended to permit the shareholders of corporations to amend the articles of incorporation or adopt other fundamental changes with less-than-unanimous consent. These provisions were also given effect.

   f. **Today [§1156]**

      Most existing corporations have been either organized or reorganized under statutes that contain reserved-power and shareholder-amendment provisions. Because the granting of any corporate charter is subject to these provisions, the incorporators are deemed to have consented to them. Therefore, the problem whether an amendment to the articles of incorporation constitutes an impairment of contract is relatively minor today.

   g. **Remaining problems [§1157]**

      The remaining problems are (i) whether there are any constitutional or implied contractual limitations on the power of the state to amend its laws in a way that affects corporations incorporated *prior to* the adoption of a reserved power clause, and (ii) whether there are any limits on the power of a state to regulate, or on the power of shareholders to amend the articles of, corporations incorporated after adoption of a reserved power clause.

(1) Limitations on powers of state

(a) Changes affecting corporation's business [§1158]

In the case of general laws that apply only to the corporation's business activities, as opposed to the rights and duties of shareholders, it is clear today that the state's power to change the law is not limited by *Dartmouth College, supra.* For example, the state may enact general laws restricting or prohibiting certain businesses even though such businesses were proper at the time the corporation was originally organized, and even though the law affects a corporation incorporated prior to the adoption of a reserved power clause.

(b) Changes affecting persons [§1159]

On the other hand, there may still be some limitations on the state power to regulate the rights of shareholders, directors, officers, or corporate creditors, as such, even where reserved power clauses are in effect. Specifically, a state cannot eliminate "vested property rights" or "impair the obligations of contract of third persons." [**Coombes v. Getz,** 285 U.S. 434 (1932)] In *Coombes,* creditors of a corporation filed an action against its directors under a provision of state law that made directors liable for corporate funds embezzled or misappropriated by officers. While the action was pending, the relevant state law provision was repealed. The Supreme Court held that the repeal was ineffective as to the plaintiff-creditors because it would not be permitted to affect their "vested" rights against the directors.

1) Rationale

The rationale of **Coombes v. Getz** was that the exercise of a state's reserved powers is still subject to the limitations of the United States Constitution. Such state action may constitute a taking without compensation in violation of the Due Process Clause.

(2) Limitations on shareholders' power

(a) "Vested-property-rights" theory [§1160]

In the past, the vested-property-rights theory also constituted a significant limitation on shareholder power to amend the certificate. Many cases struck down certain kinds of amendments that seriously altered shareholder rights—particularly the rights of preferred shareholders to receive accrued but unpaid dividends—where the type of amendment in question was not explicitly authorized by the statute in force at the time the corporation was organized. [**Keller v. Wilson & Co.,** 190 A. 115 (Del. 1936)] However, other courts rejected this approach [**McNulty v. W. & J. Sloane,** 34 A.D.2d 284 (1945)], and even those courts that accepted this approach allowed equivalent results to be reached through other techniques, such as mergers. [**Federal United Corp. v. Havender,** 11 A.2d 331 (Del. 1940)] This problem is largely historical, because most existing corporations have been organized or reorganized under statutes that explicitly authorize almost every conceivable type of shareholder amendment, and because modern courts are generally unsympathetic to the vested-rights theory.

(b) Fairness [§1161]

A much more significant limitation is that of fairness. Recall that controlling shareholders owe a broad fiduciary duty to minority shareholders with respect to the exercise of corporate control (*supra,* §693). Accordingly, when a controlling shareholder causes a corporation to amend its articles in a manner that arguably benefits that shareholder, a minority shareholder can complain that the amendment is fraudulent or unfair. [**Bove v. The Community Hotel Corp.,** 249 A.2d 89 (R.I. 1969)] The fairness issue frequently arises in attempts to recapitalize a corporation in a manner that adversely affects the rights, preferences, or privileges of a certain class of shareholders—*e.g.*, reducing the dividend rate on preferred shares, making the dividends noncumulative instead of cumulative, or issuing a new class of preferred with priorities senior to the class already outstanding.

EXAM TIP   gilbert

Today, as a general rule, states may amend corporate law and corporations may amend their articles of incorporation in almost any manner. There are only a few restrictions: The states may not be able to amend corporate law in such a way as to eliminate *vested property rights* or impair obligations of contracts with third parties. And majority shareholders may not cause an amendment to be adopted that is unfair to minority shareholders.

H. Dissolution and Liquidation

1. Introduction [§1162]

Dissolution involves the termination of a corporation's status as a *legal entity*. Dissolution falls into two basic categories, voluntary and involuntary. Voluntary dissolution occurs as a result of a decision of the corporation, acting through appropriate corporate organs. Involuntary dissolution is forced upon the corporation by the courts. To be distinguished from dissolution is the related process of liquidation, which involves termination of the corporation's business.

2. Voluntary Dissolution [§1163]

For voluntary dissolution, the statutes typically require a vote of the board recommending a plan of dissolution to the shareholders, and approval of the plan by the shareholders. Because of the importance of dissolution, most statutes require approval by a stated percentage of the outstanding shares, rather than approval by a majority of those shares that are present at the meeting at which the merger is considered. However, some statutes require only a simple majority vote, not a majority of outstanding shares. The Model Act requires that more shares vote in favor of the dissolution than vote against it, at a meeting at which at least a majority of the votes entitled to be cast on the dissolution are present. [RMBCA §14.02] Some statutes have much different requirements. For example, in California board approval is not required, and 50% shareholder approval is sufficient. [Cal. Corp. Code §1900]

EXAM TIP   **gilbert**

Note that there are *two types of dissolution*: voluntary and involuntary. In many states *voluntary* dissolution can be undertaken through a process similar to that used to undertake other fundamental corporate changes (board resolution, notice, shareholder vote, and filing with the state). *Involuntary* dissolution follows a different path—requiring judicial action (*see infra*).

---

3. Involuntary Dissolution [§1164]

Involuntary dissolution may be precipitated by shareholders, the state, or, under some statutes, the directors.

a. Action by shareholders or directors

(1) Nonstatutory involuntary dissolution [§1165]

The original rule at common law was that, absent statutory authority, courts had no jurisdiction to grant dissolution at the request of a minority shareholder. [**Leventhal v. Atlantic Finance Corp.,** 55 N.E.2d 20 (Mass. 1944)] Eventually, however, some (although not all) courts took the position that they could grant dissolution for fraud, dissension, deadlock, abuse to minority shareholders, or gross mismanagement, even in the absence of a statute providing for dissolution on those grounds. [**Miner v. Belle Isle Ice Co.,** 53 N.W. 218 (Mich. 1892); **Lichens Co. v. Standard Commercial Tobacco Co.,** 40 A.2d 447 (Del. 1944)] However, nonstatutory dissolution is rarely granted.

(2) Involuntary dissolution under statute [§1166]

Today, statutes in most states set forth grounds under which shareholders can bring judicial proceedings to force dissolution.

(a) Grounds [§1167]

These statutes vary widely as to the grounds for involuntary dissolution. However, the Model Act includes many of the typical grounds. It provides that a court can dissolve a corporation in a proceeding by a shareholder if any of the following grounds are established:

(i) The *directors are deadlocked* in the management of the corporate affairs, the shareholders are unable to break the deadlock, and because of the deadlock irreparable injury to the corporation is threatened or being suffered, or the business and affairs of the corporation can no longer be conducted to the advantage of the shareholders generally;

(ii) The directors or those in control of the corporation have acted, are acting, or will act in a manner that is *illegal, oppressive, or fraudulent*;

(iii) The *shareholders are deadlocked* in voting power and have failed, for a period that includes at least two consecutive annual meeting dates, to elect successors to directors whose terms have expired; or

(iv) The corporate *assets* are being *misapplied or wasted*.

[RMBCA §14.30(2)]

(b) Application to close corporations [§1168]

As a practical matter, involuntary dissolution is highly unlikely to be ordered except in closely held corporations. In such corporations, however, dissolution is a very important remedy, especially for oppression by those in control. The statutes are gradually increasing the grounds for involuntary dissolution to include oppression and like grounds, and the courts are increasingly giving the statutes an expansive reading and are readier than in the past to order dissolution. Although some cases focus on the wrongfulness of the conduct of those who are in control [**Baker v. Commercial Body Builders, Inc.,** 507 P.2d 387 (Or. 1973)], the trend is to focus on whether the conduct of those in control frustrates the reasonable expectations of those not in control [*In re* **Kemp & Beatley, Inc.,** 64 N.Y.2d 63 (1984); **Meiselman v. Meiselman,** 307 S.E.2d 551 (N.C. 1983)].

(c) Who can bring action [§1169]

Under some statutes, there is a limitation on shareholder standing to sue for involuntary dissolution. Under the California statute, for example, a shareholder petition for dissolution can be filed only by one of the following:

(i) *One-third of the shareholders* (other than those alleged to have participated personally in management wrongdoing, where that is the ground on which dissolution is sought);

(ii) *Any shareholder of a statutory close corporation*;

(iii) *Any shareholder* of any corporation, where the ground for dissolution is *expiration of the period* for which the corporation was formed; or

(iv) *Any other person authorized in the articles* to bring such an action.

[Cal. Corp. Code §1800(a)]

(d) Mandatory buyout [§1170]

Under some statutes, noncomplaining shareholders may avoid involuntary dissolution by purchasing (or causing the corporation to purchase) the shares of the complaining shareholders at their fair cash value as determined by the court. [Cal. Corp. Code §2000] Normally, under these statutes, if the other shareholders or the corporation make an election to buy out the complaining shareholder, the latter must sell her shares.

1) Distinguish—voluntary dissolution [§1171]

A similar mandatory buyout right exists under the California statute where *voluntary dissolution* is initiated by 50% of the shareholders. The other 50% of the shareholders have the option to prevent dissolution by purchasing the shares of those who want to dissolve. [Cal. Corp. Code §2000]

4. Dissolution Under Shareholder Agreement [§1172]

Courts may also order dissolution to give effect to a preexisting agreement among the shareholders. For example, close-corporation agreements sometimes provide that upon the happening of certain defined events (*e.g.*, completion of a certain project), each shareholder (or certain designated shareholders) will have the option to require dissolution of the corporation. Such agreements are valid and will be given effect, even if not specifically authorized by statute. [**Leventhal v. Atlantic Finance Corp.**, *supra*, §1165]

5. Action by Directors [§1173]

Some statutes permit directors to petition for involuntary dissolution on specified grounds. [Cal. Corp. Code §1800(a)—one-half of the directors can petition for dissolution on the same grounds as shareholders]

6. Action by State [§1174]

Most statutes also allow designated state officials to institute dissolution proceedings on specified grounds. For example, the Model Act authorizes the secretary of state to begin proceedings for administrative dissolution if a corporation does not pay any franchise tax within 60 days after it is due, or does not deliver its annual report to the secretary of state within 60 days after it is due. [RMBCA §§14.20-14.21]

7. Liquidation

a. Nature of liquidation [§1175]

Dissolution does not in itself terminate the corporate business. After dissolution, the corporation must still "liquidate" or "wind up" its affairs, pay or make provision for payment of its debts, and distribute its remaining assets or sell the remaining assets and distribute the proceeds. Under the Model Act, for example, a dissolved corporation continues its corporate existence, and may carry on any business that is appropriate to wind up and liquidate its business affairs, including: (i) collecting its assets; (ii) disposing of properties that will not be distributed in kind to its shareholders; (iii) discharging or making provision for discharging its liabilities; (iv) distributing its remaining property among its shareholders according to their interests; and (v) doing every other act necessary to wind up and liquidate its business and affairs. However, the corporation may not carry on any business that is not necessary to wind up and liquidate its business affairs. [RMBCA §14.05]

b. Management [§1176]

During the liquidation or winding-up process, the corporation continues under the management of the board. However, if the directors continue to operate the business of the corporation after dissolution beyond the period reasonably required for the winding-up process, they may be held personally liable for the corporation's debts. [**Borbein, Young & Co. v. Cirese**, 401 S.W.2d 940 (Mo. 1966)]

EXAM TIP **gilbert**

Note that dissolution does not mean that the corporation is instantly terminated—it *continues on* so that the directors may *wind up its affairs*. They are not personally liable for carrying on any business, or entering into any contracts appropriate for winding up the corporation's affairs.

---

c. Rights of shareholders on dissolution

(1) Where corporation has only common stock [§1177]

Where a corporation has only common stock, the general rule is that on liquidation every shareholder is entitled to a pro rata portion of the net assets remaining after the claims of creditors have been paid or provided for.

(a) Form of distribution [§1178]

Under most statutes, liquidating distributions to the holders of common stock normally can be made either in cash or (if practicable) in property. [Cal. Corp. Code §2006] In the absence of unanimous consent, the corporation ordinarily cannot discriminate among shareholders by adopting a plan of distribution under which unique property is distributed to certain designated shareholders, while cash is distributed to others (*e.g.*, giving cash to minority shareholders, while giving irreplaceable corporate assets (patents, etc.) to majority shareholders). [*In re* **San Joaquin Light & Power Co.**, 52 Cal. App. 2d 814 (1942)]

(2) Where corporation has preferred stock [§1179]

If there is a class of preferred stock outstanding, the certificate of incorporation will usually provide that shares of that class are entitled to a liquidation preference. This means that the net assets remaining after creditors have been paid must be applied to payment of the preferred stock's liquidation preference before any distribution is made to holders of common stock.

d. Rights of creditors

(1) Notice [§1180]

A corporation remains liable on its debts after dissolution. In winding up, the first priority is to pay these debts. To expedite liquidation, however, some statutes create a time limit within which a creditor must file a claim in the dissolution proceedings. Creditors who do not file a claim within this period are thereafter barred from bringing suit on their claims.

(a) Disposition by written notice [§1181]

The Model Act provides that a dissolved corporation may give known claimants written notice of dissolution. The notice must state a deadline, at least 120 days after the date of the notice, by which the dissolved corporation must receive a claim. The notice must state that the claim will be barred if not received by the deadline. If a claimant who was given such notice does not present the claim to the dissolved corporation by the deadline, the claim is barred. The claim is also barred if a claimant whose claim was presented and rejected does not begin a proceeding to enforce the claim within 90 days from the effective date of the rejection notice. [RMBCA §14.06]

(b) Disposition by publication [§1182]

The Model Act also provides that a dissolved corporation may publish notice of its dissolution in a newspaper of general circulation in the county where the dissolved corporation's principal office (or, if the corporation had no principal office in the state, its registered office) is or was last located. The notice must request that persons with claims against the corporation present them in accordance with the notice.

The notice must describe the information that has to be included in a claim, provide a mailing address where the claim may be sent, and state that a claim will be barred unless a proceeding to enforce it is begun within three years after the publication of the notice. All claims against the dissolved corporation, including unknown claims, contingent claims, and known claims that were not the subject of individual written notice, are then barred unless a proceeding to enforce the claim is brought within three years after the newspaper notice. [RMBCA §14.07]

(2) Right to trace corporate assets [§1183]

If the corporation's assets are distributed prior to satisfaction of creditors' claims, an unpaid creditor who is not barred by the failure to present a timely claim may recover from the transferee shareholders, to the extent of the shareholder's pro rata share of the claim or the corporate assets distributed to the shareholder in liquidation, whichever is less. A shareholder's total liability for all claims may not exceed the total amount of assets distributed to the shareholder.

I. Limitations on Power of Controlling Shareholders to Effect Fundamental Changes in Corporate Structure

1. Fiduciary Duties Owed by Controlling Shareholders to Minority—Fairness [§1184]

Recall that controlling shareholders owe a broad fiduciary duty to minority shareholders with respect to the exercise of corporate control (*supra*, §693). This duty is particularly relevant to fundamental changes in which the controlling shareholders are self-interested (*e.g.*, a merger between Corporation C, in which S owns a majority of stock, and Corporation D, which is wholly owned by S). Such transactions are subject to a requirement of fairness and can be set aside if unfair. [**Sterling v. Mayflower Hotel Corp.**, 93 A.2d 107 (Del. 1952)]

2. Freeze-Outs [§1185]

Often a controlling shareholder wishes to eliminate ("freeze out") minority shareholders from any further participation in the corporate enterprise. Among the techniques sometimes used to effect a freeze-out of minority shareholders are the following:

a. Sale of substantially all assets [§1186]

A sale of substantially all assets may be used to freeze out minority shareholders by causing the corporation, C, to sell its assets to a controlling shareholder, S, or to a corporation that S controls, for cash. The minority shareholders in C end up with stock in a corporation that holds only cash (and which is normally dissolved), while S ends up with 100% ownership of the corporate business. [**Theis v. Spokane Falls Gaslight Co.,** 74 P. 1004 (Wash. 1904); **Matteson v. Ziebarth,** 242 P.2d 1025 (Wash. 1952)]

b. Mergers [§1187]

Most merger statutes now permit the surviving corporation in a merger to issue cash, rather than stock, in exchange for stock of the disappearing corporation. This creates another freeze-out technique: Assume that S is the majority shareholder of Corporation C and owns all of the stock of Corporation D. S then arranges a "cash-out merger" of C into D, in which D issues cash rather than stock to C's minority shareholders. Here again, the minority shareholders in C end up with stock in a corporation that holds only cash, and S ends up with all of the corporate business. [**Weinberger v. UOP, Inc.,** *supra,* §1081] (Much the same result can be achieved if D issues debentures or redeemable preferred instead of cash.)

c. Reverse stock splits [§1188]

Most statutes empower a corporation to involuntarily eliminate fractional shares (*i.e.,* shareholdings representing less than one full share) by paying any holder of fractional shares the value of the fractional shares in cash. This gives rise to another freeze-out technique. Under this technique, the corporation effects a reverse stock split by amending its certificate to drastically reduce the number of outstanding shares, and then pays off (and thereby ousts) shareholders who own fractional shares as a result of the reverse split.

---

e.g. **Example:** Corporation C amends its certificate to cause every 1,000 existing shares to become one share. Each person holding less than 1,000 shares thus ends up owning a fractional share, and then is frozen out when C exercises its right to eliminate fractional shares.

---

d. Two kinds of freeze-out [§1189]

Freeze-outs can be placed into two categories. In some cases, a freeze-out is effected by a combination of two preexisting business *enterprises* (not simply two preexisting corporate *entities*). In other cases (*e.g.,* a reverse stock split or a cash-out merger into a shell corporation), there is no change in the business enterprise, but only a change in the corporate entity, its ownership, or both.

e. Permissibility of freeze-outs [§1190]

The courts have taken two different lines on whether freeze-outs are permissible.

(1) Business purpose required [§1191]

Many courts hold that a freeze-out is permissible if, but only if, it is effected for a business purpose. [**Coggins v. New England Patriots Football**

Club, Inc., 492 N.E.2d 1112 (Mass. 1986)] Normally, the business-purpose test requires a showing that eliminating the minority shareholders will increase corporate income or assets, *i.e.*, will make the pie bigger, rather than simply redistributing the value of the enterprise from the minority shareholders to the controlling shareholders.

(a) Operating efficiency [§1192]

The clearest business purpose for a freeze-out is a combination between two preexisting business enterprises (most typically, a controlling parent and a partially owned subsidiary) that will result in operating efficiencies.

(b) Increase corporate income or assets [§1193]

Some cases accept a business purpose even in the absence of a combination of two different business enterprises, where it can be shown that elimination of the noncontrolling shareholders will increase corporate income or assets. [**Alpert v. 28 Williams St. Corp.,** 63 N.Y.2d 557 (1984)] At least one case permitted a reverse stock split technique to be used for elimination of a very small minority interest (0.01%) by analogizing the transaction to a short-form merger. [**Teschner v. Chicago Title & Trust Co.,** 322 N.E.2d 54 (Ill. 1974)] In another case, however, it was held that such a transaction was subject to attack if no compelling business purpose was shown. [**Clark v. Pattern Analysis & Recognition Corp.,** 87 Misc. 2d 385 (1976)]

(2) Entire fairness suffices [§1194]

Delaware does not require a business purpose for a freeze-out. However, any self-interested combinations, including freeze-outs, must meet the standard of entire fairness under Delaware law. [**Weinberger v. UOP, Inc.,** *supra*, §1187; **Rabkin v. Philip A. Hunt Chemical Corp.,** 498 A.2d 1099 (Del. 1985)] Under Delaware law, a controlling or dominating shareholder who stands on both sides of a transaction bears the burden of proving the transaction's entire fairness (except in the case of a short-form merger, *see infra*). [**Weinberger v. UOP, Inc.,** *supra*] Normally, the burden of establishing entire fairness rests upon controlling or dominating shareholders. However, an informed approval of the transaction by an independent committee of disinterested directors, or by the minority shareholders, shifts the burden of proof on the issue of fairness to the shareholder-plaintiff. Nevertheless, even if such informed approval is given, an entire-fairness analysis remains the standard of judicial review. [*Id.*]

3. Effect of Securities Acts [§1195]

In addition to having rights under state law, a shareholder objecting to a merger (or other fundamental change) may be able to bring an action for violation of rule 10b-5 or the federal proxy rules if the transaction required shareholder approval and the controlling shareholder did not make full disclosure of all material facts surrounding the transaction or has not complied with SEC rule 13e-3 (*see infra*, §§1197 *et seq.*) (*See supra*, §§365-475, 568-618.) However, where there has been full disclosure, and compliance with SEC rule 13e-3, if applicable, a complaining shareholder's remedies, if any, must be found under state law.

4. Self-Tender [§1196]

Another technique for effectively eliminating most or all minority shareholders is to cause the corporation to make a tender offer for the minority shares (a "self-tender"). This is technically not a freeze-out, because it is not involuntary: A shareholder is not legally required to tender her shares in a self-tender. As a practical matter, however, she may have little economic alternative, because the self-tender may have an adverse effect on nontendering shareholders by drying up the market for their stock, causing delisting of the corporation's stock, etc.

5. Going-Private Transactions—Rule 13e-3

a. In General [§1197]

Transactions that eliminate public ownership, whether through a freeze-out or a self-tender, are sometimes known as "going-private" transactions. Rule 13e-3 of the Securities Exchange Act governs going-private transactions that involve corporations with equity securities registered under that Act.

b. Definition [§1198]

A "rule 13e-3 transaction" includes:

(1) A *purchase* of any equity security by the corporation;

(2) A *tender offer* for any equity security made by the corporation; and

(3) A *solicitation of proxies* in connection with a merger or similar corporate transaction, a sale of substantially all assets, or a reverse stock split, if the effect of the transaction is (i) to cause any class of the corporation's equity securities registered under the 1934 Act to be held of record by *fewer than 300 persons*, or (ii) to cause any class of the corporation's equity securities that is listed on a national securities exchange to be *delisted*.

c. Requirement of filing and disseminating information [§1199]

An issuer that proposes to engage in a rule 13e-3 transaction must file and disseminate a schedule 13e-3. The schedule 13e-3 must include information on alternative means to accomplish the relevant purpose, the reasons for the structure and timing of the transaction, and the benefits and detriments of the transaction to the corporation and minority shareholders (including the federal tax consequences). The schedule 13e-3 must also state whether the corporation "reasonably believes that the rule 13e-3 transaction is fair or unfair to unaffiliated security holders" and must discuss "in reasonable detail the material factors upon which the belief . . . is based." According to an instruction to the schedule, such factors will normally include:

(1) Whether the consideration offered to minority shareholders constitutes *fair value* in relation to current market prices, historical market prices, net book value, going concern value, and liquidation value;

(2) The *purchase price* paid by the issuer for the securities during the preceding two fiscal years;

(3) *Any report, opinion, or appraisal* obtained from outside parties; and

(4) *Firm offers* made by an outsider during the preceding 18 months in connection with a proposed combination.

d. Anti-fraud rule [§1200]

If a going-private transaction falls under rule 13e-3, the transaction is subject to an anti-fraud rule that is comparable to rule 10b-5, but does not contain the "in connection with the purchase and sale of securities" limitation of rule 10b-5.

6. Effect of Appraisal Rights [§1201]

If a transaction triggers appraisal rights, those rights are sometimes deemed exclusive of other remedies. Just when, and to what extent, appraisal rights will be exclusive is a complex question that depends on the terms of the relevant statute, the ground on which the transaction is attacked, and the precise remedy sought.

a. Statutes that explicitly make appraisal exclusive remedy [§1202]

Some statutes explicitly make appraisal rights an exclusive remedy. For example, the Pennsylvania statute provides that if a shareholder dissents from a transaction, he is limited to his appraisal rights, and if he does not dissent, he is conclusively presumed to have consented. [Pa. Bus. Corp. Act §1515(B)]

(1) But note

Even under this kind of statute, the availability of appraisal rights normally does not preclude an attack based on the grounds that:

(a) The transaction is *not authorized* under the statute;

(b) The *procedural steps* required to effectuate the transaction (*e.g.*, a shareholder vote) were not properly taken; or

(c) Shareholder approval of the transaction was obtained through *misrepresentation* or without disclosure of material facts.

b. Statutes that make appraisal rights exclusive with certain exceptions [§1203]

A number of statutes provide that appraisal rights are exclusive with certain exceptions. For example, the statute may provide that the appraisal right is exclusive in the absence of fraud. In this context, "fraud" may be deemed to include not only misrepresentation, but also gross unfairness. The Model Act includes an exclusivity rule, but provides that appraisal is not exclusive if the transaction in question was not properly authorized (or "effectuated"), was procured as a result of fraud or material misrepresentation, involved certain kinds of conflicts of interest, or involved noncash payments to shareholders. [RMBCA §13.02(d)]

c. Statutes that do not explicitly make appraisal exclusive remedy

(1) Injunctive relief or rescission [§1204]
The general rule is that in the absence of explicit statutory language, the mere availability of appraisal rights does not preclude shareholders from seeking injunctive relief or rescission for fraud (using that term in the broad sense to include unfair self-dealing by fiduciaries). However, some cases suggest that the availability of appraisal rights precludes a suit for injunctive relief or rescission even in the absence of explicit statutory language. [**Pupecki v. James Madison & Co.**, 382 N.E.2d 1030 (Mass. 1978); **Blumenthal v. Roosevelt Hotel, Inc.**, 202 Misc. 988 (1952)]

(2) Monetary damages [§1205]
Even statutes that do not explicitly make the appraisal remedy exclusive are often interpreted to preclude a shareholder from bringing a suit based on the transaction in which he asks only for monetary damages measured by the value of his stock. [**Adams v. United States Distributing Corp.**, 34 S.E.2d 244 (Va. 1945)]

(3) Delaware view [§1206]
The Delaware statute grants appraisal rights only in connection with mergers. However, the Delaware courts recognize that the appraisal remedy may not be adequate in certain cases, particularly where fraud, misrepresentation, self-dealing, deliberate waste of corporate assets, or gross and palpable overreaching are involved. [**Weinberger v. UOP, Inc.**, *supra*, §1194; **Rabkin v. Philip A. Hunt Chemical Corp.**, *supra*, §1194] Under Delaware law, whether the appraisal remedy is exclusive depends on the ground of the shareholders' complaint and the kind of merger involved.

(a) Ground of complaint
Under Delaware law, if a merger involves a cash-out of minority shareholders, the basic test is one of entire fairness. The concept of entire fairness includes fair dealing (how the transaction was timed, initiated, structured, negotiated, disclosed, and approved) and fair price. The test for fairness is not bifurcated; the two elements are considered together. [**Weinberger v. UOP, Inc.**, *supra*] Appraisal is the exclusive remedy only if the shareholders' complaint is limited to "judgmental factors of valuation." [**Rabkin v. Philip A. Hunt Chemical Corp.**, *supra*]

(b) Short-form merger

Delaware has a different rule in the case of a short-form merger, (*i.e.*, a merger between a parent corporation and a subsidiary corporation in which the parent owns 90% or more of the stock). Such a merger does not require the consent of either the subsidiary's board or its shareholders. In **Glassman v. Unocal Exploration Corp.,** 777 A.2d 242 (Del. 2001), the Delaware Supreme Court held that the concept of fair dealing has no place in the case of such a merger, because there is no "dealing" between the parent and the subsidiary. Accordingly, assuming that full disclosure has been made, the only issue that can arise in such a merger is adequacy of price. Because that issue can be fully dealt with in an appraisal proceeding, under Delaware law if full disclosure has been made, absent fraud or illegality *appraisal is the exclusive remedy* in the case of a short-term merger. Most or all other courts would probably take the same position. However, the court in *Glassman* went on to say that the determination of fair value in such cases must be based on all relevant factors, including elements of future value where appropriate. So, for example, if a merger was timed to take advantage of a depressed market, or a low point in the company's cyclical earnings, or to precede an anticipated positive development, the appraised value must be adjusted to account for those factors. That is true even though these are exactly the types of issues that are frequently raised in entire-fairness claims.

J. Tender Offers

1. Terminology

a. Raider [§1207]

The term "raider" refers to a person (normally, although not necessarily, a corporation) that makes a tender offer. The term is somewhat invidious; a more accurate term is *bidder*.

b. Target [§1208]

The corporation whose shares the bidder seeks to acquire is referred to as the target.

c. White knight [§1209]

Often the management of a target of a tender offer realizes that it will be taken over, but prefers a takeover by someone other than the original bidder. The management therefore solicits competing tender offers from other corporations. These more friendly corporations are known as "white knights."

d. Lock-up [§1210]

A "lock-up" is a device that is designed to protect one bidder (normally, a friendly bidder) against competition by other bidders (deemed less friendly). The favored bidder is given an option to acquire selected assets or shares in the target at a favorable price under designated conditions. These conditions usually involve either defeat of the favored bidder's attempt to acquire the corporation, or the occurrence of events that would make that defeat likely.

e. Crown jewels [§1211]

To defeat or discourage a takeover bid by a disfavored bidder, the target's management may sell or (more usually) give to a white knight a lock-up option that covers the target's most desirable business or, at least, the business most coveted by the disfavored bidder—its "crown jewels."

f. Standstill [§1212]

A target may seek an accommodation with a shareholder who has acquired a significant amount of stock, under which the shareholder agrees to limit his future stock purchases—hence, *standstill*. In the typical standstill agreement, the shareholder makes one or more of the following commitments: (i) it will not increase its shares above designated limits for a specified period of time; (ii) it will not sell its shares without giving the corporation a right of first refusal; (iii) it will not engage in a proxy contest; and (iv) it will vote its stock in a designated manner in the election of directors, and perhaps on other issues. In return, the corporation typically agrees to give the shareholder board representation, to register the shareholder's stock under the Securities Act on demand, and not to oppose the shareholder's acquisition of stock up to the specified limit.

g. Junk bonds [§1213]

A "junk bond" is a bond that has an usually high risk of default (and is therefore below investment grade), but correspondingly, carries an unusually high yield.

h. No-shop clauses [§1214]

A board of a corporation that enters into an agreement for a merger or other corporate combination (whether with a white knight or otherwise) may enter into a "no-shop agreement" that it will not shop around for a more attractive deal.

i. Greenmail [§1215]

"Greenmail" is a payment by a potential target to a potential bidder to buy back the shares in the corporation that the bidder already holds, normally at a premium. In exchange, the potential bidder agrees not to pursue a takeover bid. Some persons are suspected of purchasing shares with the object of collecting greenmail from frightened boards.

j. Fair-price provision [§1216]

A "fair-price provision" requires that a supermajority (usually 80%) of the voting power of a corporation must approve any merger or similar combination with an acquiror who already owns a specified interest in the corporation (usually 20% of the voting power). The supermajority vote is not required under certain conditions—most notably, if the transaction is approved by a majority of those directors who are not affiliated with the acquiror and were directors at the time the acquiror reached the specified level of ownership of the company, or if certain minimum-price criteria and procedural requirements are satisfied. A fair-price provision discourages purchasers whose objective is to seek control of a corporation at a relatively cheap price, and discourages accumulations of large blocks, because it reduces the options an acquiror has once it reaches the specified level of shares.

k. Poison pill [§1217]

A "poison pill" is a device adopted by a potential or actual takeover target to make its stock less attractive to a bidder. Under one kind of pill, the corporation issues a new series of preferred stock, or other rights, that gives existing shareholders the right to redeem the stock at a premium price after certain events, like a takeover. A *"flip-in poison pill"* allows all existing holders of target company shares, except the acquiror, to buy additional shares at a bargain price. A *"flip-over poison pill"* allows existing holders to convert into the acquiror's shares at a bargain price in the event of an unwelcome merger. The pill is intended to deter a takeover bid by making a bid very costly.

l. Leveraged buyout [§1218]

A "leveraged buyout" is a combination of a management buyout and a high degree of leverage. A *management buyout* ("MBO") is the acquisition for cash or nonconvertible senior securities of the business of a public corporation, by a newly organized corporation in which members of the former management of the public corporation will have a significant equity interest, pursuant to a merger or other form of combination. *Leverage* involves the use of debt to increase the return on equity. The extent of leverage is measured by the ratio of (i) debt to (ii) debt plus equity. The higher the ratio, the greater the leverage (or, to put it differently, the more highly leveraged the corporation is). A *leveraged buyout* ("LBO") is an MBO that is highly leveraged—*i.e.*, in which the newly organized acquiring corporation has a very high amount of debt in relation to its equity. Characteristically, an LBO is arranged by a firm that specializes in such transactions; can find investors to participate (or will itself invest) along with senior management in the purchase of the new corporation's securities; and can arrange for (or help arrange for) placement of the massive amount of debt that the new corporation must issue to finance the acquisition of the old corporation's business.

m. Two-tier tender offer [§1219]

A "two-tier tender offer" is a takeover bid in which the bidder makes an offer for less than all the shares at one price (the "first-tier," or "front end" price), and announces that if the first-tier offer is successful, the bidder will acquire the remaining shares through a freeze-out transaction (the "second tier" or "back end"). In some cases, the bidder states that the back-end price will be less than the front-end price. This kind of tender offer is called a "front-loaded" two-tier offer. The effect is to pressure all shareholders to accept the first-tier offer, so as not to get stuck with the lower back-end price.

2. Tender Offer—In General [§1220]

A tender offer is an offer by a bidder to shareholders of a target corporation, asking the shareholders to tender their shares in exchange for either cash or securities. A tender offer almost invariably invites the tender of at least a majority of the target's shares, and frequently invites the tender of all of the target's shares.

a. Conditions [§1221]

Typically, the terms of a tender offer provide that the bidder will acquire the shares that are tendered only if certain conditions are met. The most important of these conditions is that some specified minimum of shares be tendered.

b. Toehold stock acquisitions [§1222]

A tender offer is often preceded by a preliminary "toehold acquisition" of shares in the target on the open market.

c. Second-step transactions [§1223]

If a tender offer by a corporate bidder is successful, the target initially becomes a subsidiary of the bidder. However, a successful tender offer is frequently followed by a "second-step" or "second-tier" transaction, such as a merger, in which the target is merged into or otherwise combined with the bidder. Shares held by nontendering shareholders are often cashed out as part of the second step, through a freeze-out transaction. (*See supra*, §§1185-1194.)

d. Friendly vs. hostile tender offers [§1224]

Tender offers are classified as friendly or hostile. A friendly tender offer is an offer that is supported by the target's board. A hostile tender offer is an offer that is opposed by the target's board.

e. Approval required [§1225]

Strictly speaking, neither type of tender offer is a corporate transaction from the target's perspective. Rather, the transaction is an offer to the target's shareholders in their individual capacities. Accordingly, in the absence of a special statute (*see infra*, §§1275-1281) a tender offer does not require a vote by the target's shareholders and does not give rise to appraisal rights in those shareholders. A tender offer also normally does not require the approval of, or give rise to appraisal rights in, the bidder's shareholders, unless it constitutes a de facto merger (*see supra*, §§1119-1132).

f. Defensive tactics [§1226]

Often, the board of a target company takes some defensive action to ward off a takeover. For example, the board may seek to combine with an alternative

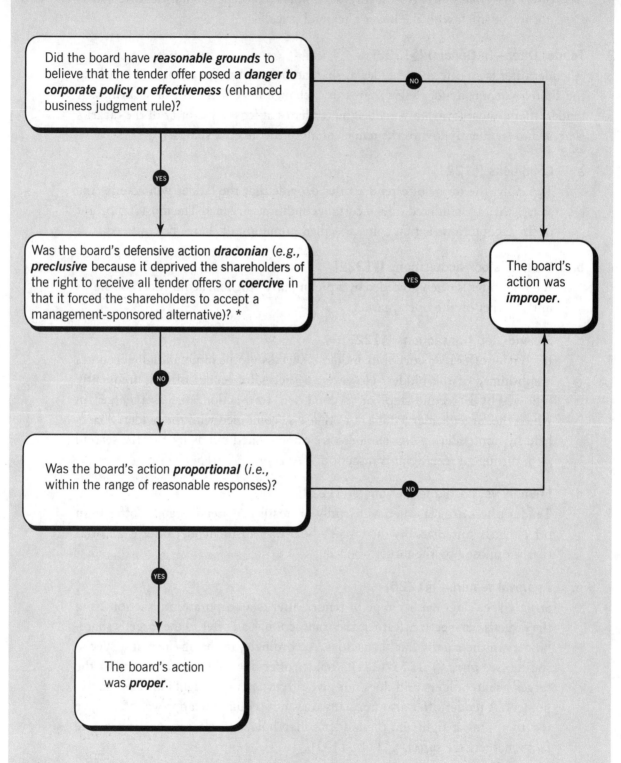

* If the board's defensive action involved selling the corporation, its duty is to do whatever it can to obtain the highest price for its shareholders, and its actions will be judged by that standard.

corporation (a white knight), or may agree to sell the business to management (a management buyout), or may give a third party or management an option (lock-up) on a key division of the corporation (the crown jewel). The major source of the rules governing defensive measures is a series of Delaware cases. Certain generalizations can be drawn from these cases, but because they are all important and highly fact-specific, a full understanding of the relevant legal rules requires consideration of the facts and holdings of each case.

(1) The *Unocal* test [§1227]

In **Unocal Corp. v. Mesa Petroleum Co.**, 493 A.2d 946 (Del. 1985), Mesa made a two-tier front-loaded tender offer for 37% of Unocal's stock at $54. Mesa was controlled by Pickens, who had a reputation as a greenmailer. The back end of the two-tier offer was to involve an exchange of securities that were also nominally worth $54. However, the securities were junk bonds and, therefore, the value at the back end might have been much lower than $54, so that the offer was coercive. Unocal's board defended against the tender offer by making a self-tender for Unocal stock at $72, but excluding stock owned by Mesa from the self-tender. Mesa sued to enjoin Unocal's defensive measure. In deciding the case, the Delaware court laid down the basic rules to be applied in Delaware to defensive measures:

(a) Enhanced business judgment rule applies [§1228]

When a board addresses a pending takeover bid, it has an obligation to determine whether the offer is in the best interests of the corporation and its shareholders. However, because of the "omnipresent specter" that a board may be acting primarily in its own interests, rather than those of the corporation and its shareholders, there is an "enhanced duty," which calls for judicial examination at the threshold, before the protections of the business judgment rule may be conferred. In the face of this inherent conflict, directors must show that they had *reasonable grounds for believing that a danger to corporate policy and effectiveness* existed because of the bid. They satisfy that burden by showing good faith and reasonable investigation, and such proof is materially enhanced by the approval of a board comprised of a majority of outside independent directors who have acted in accordance with the foregoing standards.

(b) Proportionality required [§1229]

A further aspect of the *Unocal* test is the element of balance. A defensive measure must be reasonable in relation to the threat posed. This entails an analysis by the directors of the nature of the takeover bid and its effect on the corporate enterprise. Examples of such concerns may include: inadequacy of the price offered, nature and timing of the offer, questions of illegality, the impact on "constituencies" other than shareholders (*e.g.*, creditors, customers, employees, and perhaps even the community generally), the risk of nonconsummation, and the quality of securities being offered in the exchange. A board may reasonably consider the basic stockholder interests at stake, including those of the short-term speculators whose actions may further the coercive aspect of the offer at the expense of the long-term investors. In *Unocal* itself, the court held that a threat was posed by a grossly inadequate two-tier coercive tender offer, coupled with a threat of greenmail, and that the board's response to the threat was reasonable.

1) Note

The specific outcome in *Unocal,* allowing an exclusionary (discriminatory) tender offer, has been superseded and reversed by the "all-holders" rule under the Williams Act (*see infra,* §1259), which requires equal treatment of shareholders in a tender offer.

(c) An intermediate standard [§1230]

Although the *Unocal* test has been somewhat elaborated (and a different test, known as the *Revlon* test, *see infra,* is applied in certain cases), the core of the *Unocal* test has been largely preserved. The key elements of the test are "enhanced scrutiny" by the courts, on the one hand (*i.e.,* enhanced as compared with the ordinary scrutiny given to board action under the business judgment rule), and determining whether the defensive measure is "reasonable in relation to the threat posed," on the other. In effect, the *Unocal* test is an intermediate standard of review, which is somewhat harder for a board to satisfy than the business judgment rule, but somewhat easier for the board to satisfy than a full fairness review.

(d) *Unitrin* refinements [§1231]

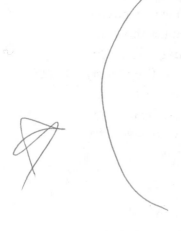

In **Unitrin, Inc. v. American General Corp.,** 651 A.2d 1361 (Del. 1995), the Delaware court refined the *Unocal* test. Under the refined test, a court should **first** direct its enhanced scrutiny first to whether the defensive action was "draconian" by being either preclusive or coercive. A defensive action is "preclusive" if it deprives stockholders of the right to receive all tender offers, or precludes a bidder from seeking control by fundamentally restricting proxy contests or otherwise. A defensive action is "coercive" if it is aimed at forcing upon stockholders a management-sponsored alternative to a hostile offer. If the court finds that the defensive action was **not** draconian, it should then look to whether it was within a range of reasonable responses to the threat posed by the tender offer.

(e) *Paramount v. Time*

1) Facts [§1232]

In **Paramount Communications, Inc. v. Time, Inc.,** 571 A.2d 1140 (Del. 1989), Paramount made an all-cash offer for all of the shares of Time, Inc. Time then entered into a business combination with Warner Brothers. Although the merger was in part a response to Paramount's takeover bid, it also executed a preexisting strategic plan of Time. Paramount challenged the combination.

2) Holdings

a) Reasonable to believe takeover posed danger [§1233]

The Delaware court held that even an all-cash, all-shares tender offer could constitute a "danger" within the meaning of the *Unocal* test. *Unocal* involved a two-tier, highly coercive tender offer. In such a case, the threat is obvious: shareholders may be compelled to tender to avoid being treated adversely in the second stage of the transaction. However, the court said, Time's board reasonably determined that inadequate value was not the only legally cognizable danger that a tender offer could present. One concern was that Time's shareholders might elect to tender into Paramount's cash offer in ignorance or a mistaken belief of the strategic benefit that a business combination with Warner might produce. Moreover, Time viewed the conditions attached to Paramount's offer as introducing a degree of uncertainty that skewed a comparative analysis. Accordingly, the court said, it could not conclude that the Time board's decision, that Paramount's offer posed a threat to corporate policy and effectiveness, was lacking in good faith or dominated by motives of either entrenchment or self-interest.

b) Response reasonable and proportionate [§1234]

The court also concluded that Time's defensive action to Paramount's tender offer was reasonable and proportionate under *Unocal*. It was not aimed at cramming down on its shareholders a management-sponsored alternative, but rather had as its goal the carrying forward of a preexisting transaction. Thus, the response was reasonably related to the threat. Furthermore, the business combination with Warner did not preclude Paramount from making an offer for the combined Time-Warner offer. Thus, the response was proportionate.

(2) The *Revlon* test

(a) Facts [§1235]

In **Revlon, Inc. v. MacAndrews & Forbes Holdings, Inc.,** 506 A.2d 173 (Del. 1986), Pantry Pride made a tender offer for the stock of

Revlon. In response, Revlon's board adopted a variety of defensive measures, including authorizing management to negotiate with other parties interested in acquiring Revlon, which management did. Competing offers for Revlon went back and forth from Pantry Pride and Forstmann, a white knight. Finally, Revlon gave Forstmann a lock-up on key Revlon assets, and agreed to a no-shop provision.

(b) Holdings

1) Duty changed [§1236]

The Delaware Supreme Court found that the Revlon board's authorization permitting management to negotiate a merger or buyout with a third party was a recognition that the company was for sale. Once the board made the decision to sell the corporation, its duty changed from the duty to preserve Revlon as a corporation to the duty to maximize the price that a bidder would pay for the corporation's stock. Thus, once it is clear that a corporation will be sold, defensive measures are moot and should not be judged under the *Unocal* test. Instead the court will look to see whether the board's actions were geared toward obtaining the best price for the stockholders' benefit. (This has since become known as the *Revlon* standard.)

2) Lock-up provision [§1237]

The court said that a lock-up is not per se illegal under Delaware law, because it can entice a new bidder to enter a contest for control of the corporation, creating an auction for the company and thereby maximizing shareholder profit. However, while a lock-up that draws bidders into the battle benefits shareholders, a lock-up like the one here that ends an active auction and forecloses further bidding operates to the shareholders' detriment and is improper.

3) No-shop provision [§1238]

The court also held that, like a lock-up, a no-shop provision is not per se illegal, but is impermissible when a board's primary duty becomes that of an auctioneer responsible for selling the company to the highest bidder.

(c) When directors must seek best value for shareholders [§1239]

In **Arnold v. Society for Savings Bancorp, Inc.**, 650 A.2d 1270 (Del. 1994), the Delaware Supreme Court stated that the directors of a corporation have the obligation to act reasonably to seek the transaction offering the best value reasonably available to the stockholders when:

1) A corporation *initiates an active bidding process* seeking to sell itself or to effect a business reorganization involving a clear break-up of the company;

2) In response to a bidder's offer, a *target abandons its long-term strategy and seeks* an alternative transaction involving *the break-up of the company*; or

3) Approval of a transaction results in a *sale or change in control.* However, there is no sale or change in control when control of both companies continues to be held by a large, fluid, changeable, and changing market.

(d) Paramount v. QVC

1) Facts [§1240]

In **Paramount Communications, Inc. v. QVC Network,** 637 A.2d 34 (Del. 1994), Paramount (the spurned suitor in the *Time* case, *supra,* §1232) entered into a merger agreement with Viacom. If the merger went through, control of Paramount would be vested in a new controlling shareholder. The merger agreement contained a no-shop provision, as well as a stock option agreement that gave Viacom an option to purchase almost 20% of Paramount's stock on extremely favorable terms—a variant of a lock-up. QVC then made a takeover bid for Paramount. Although a bidding contest developed, Paramount's board gave favored treatment to Viacom.

2) Holdings [§1241]

Paramount's board decided to sell the corporation. Thus, the directors' obligation was to seek the best value reasonably available to the stockholders. The no-shop and lock-up provisions were invalid under these circumstances because they interfered with the duty of Paramount's board to get the highest price for Paramount once it decided to sell the company.

(3) Poison pill [§1242]

In **Moran v. Household International, Inc.,** 500 A.2d 1346 (Del. 1985), the Delaware Supreme Court held that adoption of a poison pill was not per se improper, on the ground that a poison pill might deter coercive or other questionable tender offers, and there are various ways to launch a tender offer even in the face of a poison pill—such as attempting to replace the board and "redeem" the pill (*i.e.,* causing the new board to effectively revoke the pill). The court also stated that in reviewing a preplanned defensive measure, it was even more appropriate to apply the business judgment rule than in reviewing a defensive measure adopted in response to an actual takeover bid.

(a) Fiduciary duties [§1243]

Although *Moran* held that the mere adoption of a pill was not necessarily improper, it did not say that the board had a free hand to leave a pill in place in the face of a tender offer. In the *Unitrin* case, *supra*, §1231, the court said that although *adopting* a poison pill in given circumstances might be appropriate, keeping a poison pill *in place* may be inappropriate when the circumstances dramatically change. Accordingly, even if a poison pill has been properly adopted, a decision by the board *not to redeem* the pill is subject to judicially enforceable fiduciary standards. However, courts have been extremely reluctant to order the redemption of poison pills on fiduciary grounds. The reason is a judicial belief that poison pills are in the shareholder's interest, because they often result in a bidding contest for the corporation that culminates in an acquisition of the corporation on better terms than the initial hostile offer.

1) Tender offer coupled with proxy contest [§1244]

Once it became clear as a practical matter that the courts were unlikely to require boards to redeem poison pills, there was a further step in the evolution of takeover strategy. A bidder would couple (i) a tender offer with (ii) a proxy solicitation to remove directors and replace them with the bidder's nominees. The idea is that if the bidder's nominees are elected to the board, on assuming office they will redeem the poison pill.

2) Dead-hand pills [§1245]

In response to the above technique, corporations began employing "dead-hand" poison pills. A dead-hand pill is a pill that can be redeemed only by the directors who adopted the pill, or their designated successors. If only the incumbent directors or their designated successors can redeem a pill, it would make little sense for a bidder to wage a proxy contest to replace the incumbent directors. Doing that would eliminate the only persons who had the power to redeem the pill. In **Carmody v. Toll Brothers, Inc.,** 723 A.2d 1180 (Del. 1998), the court held that a dead-hand pill is invalid on several grounds: First, a dead-hand pill violates the Delaware statute by (i) impermissibly creating voting-power distinctions among directors, without authorization in the certificate of incorporation; and (ii) interfering with the directors' statutory power to manage the business and affairs of the corporation. Second, a dead-hand pill purposefully interferes with the shareholder voting franchise, without any compelling justification. Third, a dead-hand pill is a disproportionate defensive measure, under *Unocal/Unitrin*, because it either precludes or materially abridges the shareholders' rights to receive tender offers and to wage a proxy contest to replace the board.

3) No-hand pills [§1246]

The next step in the evolution of the poison pill was a "no-hand pill." A no-hand pill provides that a newly elected director cannot redeem a pill for six months after taking office, if the purpose or effect of the redemption is to facilitate a transaction with a person who proposed, nominated, or financially supported the election of the new director to the board. In **Quickturn Design Systems, Inc. v. Shapiro,** 721 A.2d 1281 (Del. 1998), the Delaware Supreme Court implicitly approved the decision in *Carmody*, and held that a no-hand pill was also invalid.

(4) Fiduciary outs [§1247]

Often merger agreements contain "deal-protection" devices. A deal-protection device is any measure that is intended to protect the consummation of a negotiated merger transaction by restricting the discretion of the board of the corporation that is to be acquired in the merger. Among the kinds of deal-protection devices are no-talk clauses, which prohibit the board from discussing a merger of the corporation into a third party, and provisions that require the board to submit the merger to the shareholders for their approval. Merger agreements that contain deal-protection devices may also contain a "fiduciary out." A fiduciary out is a term in a merger agreement that provides that a deal-protection term does not apply if the restriction on the board's discretion would result in a breach of the board's fiduciary duties. In **Omnicare, Inc. v. NCS Healthcare, Inc.,** 818 A.2d 914 (Del. 2003), the Delaware Supreme Court held that a board has a continuing obligation to discharge its fiduciary responsibilities after a merger agreement is announced. Thus if a merger agreement contains deal-protection devices, it must normally also include a fiduciary out provision, to protect the stockholders if the protected transaction became an inferior offer. The court said that "Any board has authority to give the proponent of a recommended merger agreement reasonable structural and economic defenses, incentives, and fair compensation if the transaction is not completed . . . . Just as defensive measures cannot be draconian, however, they cannot limit or circumscribe the directors' fiduciary duties. Accordingly, a board has no authority to execute a merger agreement that subsequently prevented it from effectively discharging its ongoing fiduciary responsibilities."

3. Federal Securities Law—The Williams Act [§1248]

Tender offers, and the toehold share acquisitions that often precede them, are regulated in a great number of respects by the Williams Act (and its amendments), which added sections 13(d), 14(d), and 14(e) to the Securities Exchange Act of 1934. A discussion of the obligations imposed by these sections follows.

TENDER OFFER REPORTING—AN OVERVIEW　　gilbert

CHECKLIST OF REPORTING PROVISIONS:

☑ Anyone acquiring **5% or more** of an equity security registered under SEA section 12 **must report** the acquisition, sources of funds used for the purchase, plans with respect to the corporation, etc.

☑ Anyone who **makes a tender offer** for a class of equity securities registered under section 12 **that would result in that person owning more than 5%** of the class must file a **disclosure statement** setting forth, among other things, the bidder's financial statements, contracts regarding the matter, and plans.

☑ The target's management generally must **disclose its recommendation** with respect to the bid.

☑ It is unlawful for anyone to make **material untrue statements or omissions**, or otherwise commit fraud, with respect to a tender offer.

---

a. Notice of five-percent beneficial ownership [§1249]

A person who has acquired beneficial ownership of more than 5% of any class of equity securities registered under section 12 of the 1934 Act must file a schedule 13D within 10 days of the acquisition. [Exchange Act §13(d)]

(1) Contents [§1250]

The schedule 13D must include the purchaser's identity and background; the amount and sources of the funds for the purchase; the purpose of the purchase; any plans with respect to extraordinary corporate transactions involving the corporation whose stock has been acquired; and any contracts, arrangements, or understandings with other persons regarding the corporation's securities.

(2) Formation of a group [§1251]

For this purpose, the term "person" includes a group. Furthermore, merely combining existing shareholdings for the purpose of control, without more, is sufficient to constitute a "group," and trigger the filing requirements, if the members of the newly constituted group own more than 5% of the corporation's stock. [Exchange Act Rule 13-5(b); **GAF Corp. v. Milstein**, 453 F.2d 709 (2d Cir. 1971)]

(3) Remedy [§1252]

A target corporation has an implied right of action for a violation of section

13(d). The appropriate remedy for such violation is an injunction to require a corrective amendment to the filing and to prohibit additional purchases until the filing is corrected. Normally, an injunction that prohibits the purchaser from voting the acquired shares, or requires that previously acquired shares be divested, is not an appropriate remedy, at least where the failure is cured by a subsequent filing. [**Rondeau v. Mosinee Paper Corp.,** 422 U.S. 49 (1975); **General Aircraft Corp. v. Lampert,** 556 F.2d 90 (1st Cir. 1977)]

b. Tender offers under Williams Act [§1253]

The Williams Act also regulates tender offers. What constitutes a "tender offer" within the meaning of the Williams Act is not completely settled.

(1) Eight-factor test [§1254]

Some courts have adopted the following eight-factor test to determine whether an offer to buy stock is a tender offer under the Act:

(i) Did the purchaser engage in *active and widespread solicitation* of public shareholders?

(ii) Is the solicitation made for a *substantial percentage* of the issuer's stock?

(iii) Is the offer to purchase made at a *premium* over the prevailing market price?

(iv) Are the terms of the offer *firm* rather than negotiable?

(v) Is the offer *contingent* on the tender of a fixed number of shares?

(vi) Is the offer open only for a *limited period of time*?

(vii) Are the offerees under *pressure* to sell their stock?

(viii) Do *public announcements* of a purchasing program precede or accompany a rapid accumulation of large amounts of the target's securities?

[**Wellman v. Dickinson,** 475 F. Supp. 783 (S.D.N.Y. 1979), *aff'd on other grounds,* 682 F.2d 355 (2d Cir. 1982), *cert. denied,* 460 U.S. 1069 (1983); **SEC v. Carter Hawley Hale Stores, Inc.,** 750 F.2d 945 (9th Cir. 1985)]

(2) Alternative test—substantial risk of insufficient information [§1255]

The Second Circuit has rejected the eight-factor test. It has held instead that the question of whether an offer to buy stock constitutes a tender offer under the Williams Act turns on whether there appears to be a likelihood that unless the Act's rules are followed, there will be a substantial risk that solicitees will lack information needed to make a carefully considered appraisal of the proposal put before them. [**Hanson Trust PLC v. SCM Corp.,** 774 F.2d 47 (2d Cir. 1985)] In practice, the Second Circuit test might not be very different from the eight-factor test, because in determining whether there is a substantial risk that solicitees will lack the needed information, a court is likely to consider many of the factors in the eight-factor test.

---

e.g. **Example:** Applying the above standard, the Second Circuit held in *Hanson* that the transaction before it was not a tender offer because:

(i) The target had 22,800 shareholders and offers were made to only six of the shareholders. This number was deemed *minuscule* compared with the number of shareholders usually involved in public solicitations of the type against which the Williams Act was directed.

(ii) At least five of the six selling shareholders were *highly sophisticated professionals*, knowledgeable in the marketplace and well aware of the essential facts needed to exercise their professional skills and to appraise the offer.

(iii) The sellers were *not pressured to sell* their shares by any conduct that the Williams Act was designed to alleviate, but only by the forces of the marketplace.

(iv) There was *no active or widespread advance publicity* or public solicitation.

(v) The price received by the six sellers was *not at a premium* over the then-market price.

(vi) The purchases were *not made contingent* upon acquiring a fixed minimum number or percentage of the target's outstanding shares.

(vii) There was *no time limit* within which the buyer would purchase the target's stock.

[**Hanson Trust PLC v. SCM Corp.,** *supra*]

---

(3) Open-market purchases [§1256]

Purchases made anonymously on the open market almost certainly do not constitute a tender offer within the meaning of the Act. [**Kennecott Copper Corp. v. Curtiss-Wright Corp.,** 584 F.2d 1195 (2d Cir. 1978); **Calumet Industries, Inc. v. MacClure,** Fed. Sec. Reg. Rep. (CCH) ¶96,434 (N.D. Ill. 1978)] However, the SEC has not entirely acquiesced in this position.

c. **Information statement by person who makes tender offer [§1257]**

Section 14(d) requires any person who makes a tender offer for a class of registered equity securities that would result in that person owning more than 5% of the class to file a schedule TO containing specific information.

(1) Contents [§1258]

The schedule TO must contain extensive disclosure of such matters as the offer; the identity of the bidder; past dealings between the bidder and the corporation; the bidder's source of funds; the bidder's purposes and plans concerning the corporation; the bidder's contracts and understandings or relationships with respect to securities of the corporation; financial statements of the bidder, if they are material and the bidder is not an individual; and arrangements between the bidder and those holding important positions with the corporation.

d. **Regulation of terms of tender offers [§1259]**

Section 14(d) of the Securities Exchange Act, and rules 14d and 14e, regulate the *terms* of tender offers. Under these provisions:

(1) A tender offer *must be held open for at least 20 days.*

(2) A tender offer must be *open to all security holders of the class* of securities subject to the tender offer (the "all holders rule").

(3) Shareholders *must be permitted to withdraw tendered shares* during the first 15 days of an offer, or after 60 days if the shares have not been purchased by then.

(4) If the tender offer is *oversubscribed*, the *offeror must purchase on a pro rata basis* from among the shares deposited during the first 10 days, or such longer period as the bidder may designate.

(5) If the tender-offer price is *increased*, the higher price must be paid to *all* tendering shareholders—even those who tendered in response to the lower price—and the offer must remain open at least 10 days after notice of the increase is first published.

e. **Obligations of target's management [§1260]**

Rule 14e-2 requires the target company, no later than 10 business days from the date the tender offer is first published, to give its shareholders a statement disclosing that the target either: (i) *recommends acceptance or rejection* of the tender offer; (ii) *expresses no opinion* and is remaining neutral toward the tender offer; or (iii) is *unable to take a position* with respect to the tender offer. The statement must also include the reason for the position or for the inability to take a position.

f. Tender offers by issuers [§1261]

Corporations that tender for their own stock ("issuer" or "self" tenders) are subject to obligations similar to those imposed on outside bidders under rules 14d and 14e. [Exchange Act Rules 13(e), 13e]

g. Anti-fraud provision [§1262]

Section 14(e) prohibits material misstatements, misleading omissions, and fraudulent or manipulative acts, in connection with a tender offer or any solicitation in favor of or in opposition to a tender offer. Section 14(e) is closely comparable to rule 10b-5, except that it does not contain the limiting language, "in connection with the purchase or sale" of securities, found in rule 10b-5. It is not yet completely clear who may bring an action under section 14(e). A major Supreme Court decision, **Piper v. Chris-Craft Industries, Inc.,** 430 U.S. 1 (1977), lays down some important rules, but leaves a number of gaps.

(1) Suit by offeror

(a) Damages [§1263]

Under *Piper,* the bidder does not have standing to sue for damages under section 14(e), particularly in a suit against the target corporation's management for false statements made in opposition to the tender offer.

1) Rationale

The Williams Act was designed to protect shareholders of the target. It is not consistent with the underlying legislative purpose to imply a damages remedy for the bidder, particularly because the target's shareholders might end up bearing the burden of an award based on misrepresentations by the target's management.

EXAM TIP   gilbert

Be on the lookout for an exam fact pattern where the bidder is defeated in an attempted tender offer because the target has disseminated false information about the bidder or the offer. While the target's action may be unlawful—and the government may prosecute or sue the target for its wrongful conduct—the *bidder has no private cause of action for damages*, as unfair as this might seem. *Rationale:* In *Piper,* the Court held that Congress's intent in passing the Williams Act was to protect the *target's shareholders*; there is no evidence of any congressional intent to protect the bidder.

(b) Injunctive relief [§1264]

Piper left open the question of suits by the bidder under section 14(e) for injunctive relief against the target or its management. Lower courts have held that the target corporation can sue for an injunction against the bidder for violation of section 14(e), because such an injunction will protect the interests of the target's shareholders. [**Gearhart Industries, Inc. v. Smith International, Inc.,** 741 F.2d 707 (5th Cir. 1984); **Weeks Dredging & Contracting, Inc. v. American Dredging Co.,** Fed. Sec. Reg. Rep. (CCH) ¶96,414 (E.D. Pa. 1978)] The bidder can also bring a suit for injunctive relief against competing bidders. [**Humana, Inc. v. American Medicorp, Inc.,** Fed. Sec. L. Rep. (CCH) ¶96,298 (S.D.N.Y. 1978)]

1) Rationale

Unlike damages, an injunction does not impose any burden on the target's shareholders. Furthermore, an injunction prior to the time when the target's shareholders must decide whether to accept the tender offer allows them to make their decision in an environment purged of false and misleading information. [**Weeks Dredging & Contracting, Inc. v. American Dredging Co.,** *supra*]

(2) Suit by target corporation

(a) Damages [§1265]

Because *Piper* was based on the conclusion that the Williams Act was designed to protect the target's shareholders, the target corporation itself would not have standing to sue the bidder for damages under rule 14e.

(b) Injunction [§1266]

The target corporation can sue for an injunction against the bidder for violation of section 14(e), because such an injunction will protect the interests of the target's shareholders. [**Gearhart Industries, Inc. v. Smith International, Inc.,** *supra*]

(3) Suit by target's shareholders

(a) Suit by tendering shareholders [§1267]

Based on the Court's interpretation of the Williams Act in *Piper*, shareholders of the target have standing to sue for both damages and injunctive relief if they tender their shares on the basis of false and misleading information. (Under these circumstances, tendering shareholders could also sue under rule 10b-5.)

(b) Suit by nontendering shareholders [§1268]

The Court in *Piper* did not express a view on suits by nontendering shareholders, but because the statute does not contain the purchaser-seller limitation associated with rule 10b-5, nontendering shareholders can probably sue under section 14(e), provided they can show damage resulting from a violation of that section. [*See* **Electronic**

Specialty Co. v. International Controls Corp., 409 F.2d 937 (2d Cir. 1969)]

4. **State Statutes Regulating Tender Offers [§1269]**
Many states now have statutes regulating takeover bids.

a. **First-generation statutes [§1270]**
The so-called first-generation statutes imposed very stringent requirements on takeover bids. In **Edgar v. MITE Corp.,** 457 U.S. 624 (1982), the Supreme Court held one such statute, the Illinois Takeover Act, unconstitutional. Only six justices ruled on the merits of the case. The Court considered the following theories:

(1) **Supremacy Clause [§1271]**
Three of the six justices who passed on the merits of the case held that the Illinois statute was unconstitutional under the Supremacy Clause, on the ground that a major objective of the Williams Act was maintaining a neutral balance between management and the bidder, and the Illinois Act violated this balance. (*See infra*, §§1277-1280.)

(2) **Commerce Clause [§1272]**
All six justices who addressed the merits held that the Illinois Act violated the Commerce Clause by:

(a) *Directly regulating commerce taking place across state lines*, because the Act applied to prevent an offeror from making an offer even to non-Illinois shareholders; and

(b) *Imposing an excessive burden on interstate commerce*, by permitting the Illinois secretary of state to block a nationwide tender offer.

b. **Second-generation statutes [§1273]**
After the decision in **Edgar v. MITE Corp.,** a number of states adopted "second-generation" takeover statutes. These statutes fall into two major categories: "fair price" statutes and "control share acquisition" statutes.

(1) **Fair price statutes [§1274]**
Under the fair price statutes, an acquiror must pay all shareholders the "best price" paid to any one shareholder.

(2) **Control share acquisition statutes [§1275]**
Under control share acquisition statutes, if a designated stock-ownership threshold is crossed by an acquiring shareholder, he cannot vote the acquired shares without the approval of a majority of the disinterested shareholders.

(3) *CTS* case [§1276]

In **CTS Corp. v. Dynamics Corp. of America,** 481 U.S. 69 (1987), the Supreme Court upheld a control share acquisition statute adopted by Indiana. The Indiana statute is limited to targets incorporated in Indiana. The statute applies whenever a person acquires "control shares," *i.e.*, whenever a person acquires shares that (but for the operation of the statute) would bring the person's voting power in the corporation to or above any of three thresholds: 20%, 33^1/3%, or 50%. An acquiror that crosses such a threshold cannot vote the acquired stock unless voting rights are approved by a majority of all disinterested shareholders voting at the next regularly scheduled meeting of the shareholders or at a specially scheduled meeting. The acquiror can require the management of the corporation to hold such a special meeting within 50 days.

(a) Supremacy Clause [§1277]

The Court held that the Indiana statute was not preempted by the Williams Act. The Illinois statute in **Edgar v. MITE Corp.** had three offending features that the Indiana statute did not share.

1) Communicating with shareholders [§1278]

The Illinois statute provided for a 20-day precommencement period. During this time, management could disseminate its views on the upcoming tender offer to shareholders, but bidders could not publish their offers. This conflicted with the Williams Act, because Congress had deleted express precommencement notice provisions from the Williams Act. In contrast, the Indiana statute does not give either management or the bidder an advantage in communicating with shareholders about an impending tender offer.

2) Delay [§1279]

The Illinois statute provided for a hearing on a tender offer. Because no deadline was set for the hearing, management could indefinitely stymie a takeover. This conflicted with the Williams Act, because Congress anticipated that bidders would be free to go forward without unreasonable delay. In contrast, the Indiana statute does not impose an indefinite delay on tender offers. Nothing in the statute prohibits an offeror from consummating an offer on the 20th business day, the earliest day permitted under applicable federal regulations, and full voting rights will be vested or denied within 50 days after commencement of the tender offer.

3) Fairness evaluation [§1280]

The Illinois statute provided for review of the fairness of tender offers by the Illinois Secretary of State. This conflicted with the Williams Act, because Congress intended investors to be free to make their own decisions. In contrast, the Indiana statute does not allow the state government to interpose its views of fairness between willing buyers and sellers of shares of the target company. Rather, the statute allows shareholders to collectively evaluate the fairness of the offer.

(b) Commerce Clause [§1281]

The Court in *CTS* also concluded that the Indiana statute does not violate the Commerce Clause, because it does not discriminate against interstate commerce and does not subject activities to inconsistent regulation. The statute applies only to Indiana corporations, and a state has authority to regulate domestic corporations, including the authority to define the voting rights of shareholders.

c. Third-generation statutes [§1282]

"Third-generation statutes" fall into various patterns. Many of the third-generation statutes are aimed at preventing a successful bidder from merging with the target, or engaging in certain other transactions with the target, for a designated period of time unless certain conditions are satisfied. (The idea here is that in many cases the bidder expects to finance the bid partly by using assets of the target as collateral. If the bidder cannot merge with the target, that kind of financing is difficult or impossible. In addition, the bidder may have various business and tax reasons for wanting to merge with the target in a freeze-out merger that eliminates the target's minority shareholders, rather than running the target as a partly owned subsidiary. These purposes are also frustrated by third-generation statutes.) The following illustrate the approaches of third-generation statutes:

(1) New York [§1283]

The New York statute provides for a five-year waiting period between the time a tender offer occurs and the time the target can be merged or otherwise combined with the bidder, unless the transaction was approved by the target's board of directors prior to the date control was acquired. [N.Y. Bus. Corp. Law §912]

(2) Wisconsin [§1284]

The Wisconsin statute provides that, unless the target's board agrees to the transaction in advance of a successful tender offer, a successful bidder must wait three years after buying the target's shares to merge with the target or acquire more than 5% of its assets.

(3) Delaware [§1285]

Delaware imposes a three-year waiting period, but allows a merger to occur before the end of the waiting period if the merger is approved by

85% of the shares other than shares held by the bidder, on the one hand, or by management and employee stock plans, on the other. [Del. Gen. Corp. Law §103]

(4) Constitutionality [§1286]

In **Amanda Acquisition Corp. v. Universal Foods Corp.**, 877 F.2d 496, *cert. denied*, 493 U.S. 955 (1989), the Seventh Circuit held that the Wisconsin third-generation statute (*supra*)—a strong third-generation statute—was constitutional. The court held that the statute was not preempted by the Williams Act, because it did not prevent takeover bids or alter any of the procedures governed by the Act, but only made such bids less attractive to engage in. The court also held that the statute was not invalid under the Commerce Clause, because it applied only to the internal affairs of corporations domiciled in Wisconsin, allowed purchasers of stock in Wisconsin corporations to take immediate control of the corporation, and did not regulate or forbid any interstate transaction.

(5) Other third-generation statutes [§1287]

Amanda, and perhaps other factors, emboldened some states to adopt other, extremely exotic, and in some cases extremely draconian, third-generation statutes. For example, the Pennsylvania statute provides, among other things, that persons who own, offer to acquire, or publicly announce an intention to acquire, 20% of the stock of a publicly traded Pennsylvania corporation must disgorge any profits they realize from the disposition of that corporation's stock within a defined period. The Massachusetts statute requires every publicly held Massachusetts corporation to have a classified board.

(6) Constituency statutes [§1288]

A number of states have also adopted constituency statutes that allow a board to consider the interests of groups ("constituencies") other than shareholders in making decisions, including decisions to resist takeovers. These statutes give the board increased leeway to resist a takeover because often these other constituencies—*e.g.*, labor and the local community—are opposed to takeovers.

Chapter Eleven: Conflict of Laws Principles

CONTENTS

Chapter Approach

Chapter Approach

Conflict of laws issues rarely arise on Corporations exams. However, you should remember that all questions concerning the internal affairs of the corporation are decided according to the law of the *state of incorporation*. Also keep in mind that a state may refuse to apply that law if it violates local public policy.

A. General Rule

1. Law of State of Incorporation Applies [§1289]

No matter where the litigation occurs, the general choice of law rule is that all questions concerning the *organization or internal affairs* of a corporation are decided according to the law of the state in which it was *incorporated*. [RMBCA §15.05(c)]

> **Example:** A corporation organized in state A has its principal office and place of business in state B. In litigation in state B (or elsewhere) involving the corporation's internal affairs, the court will generally refer to and apply the law of state A.

a. Effect

This is the reason that many businesses choose to incorporate in Delaware, Nevada, or other states having laws historically considered to be favorable to corporate management. For example, Delaware is one of the (many) states that does away with mandatory cumulative voting (*supra,* §548) and eases the limitations against a corporation indemnifying its officers and directors for liabilities incurred in office (*supra,* §§837-843). However, a number of more recent judicial (and legislative) developments point in the opposite direction. [*See, e.g.,* **Smith v. Van Gorkom,** *supra,* §247; **Zapata Corp. v. Maldonado,** *supra,* §762; **Unocal Corp. v. Mesa Petroleum Co.,** *supra,* §1227]

B. Limitations

1. Local Public Policy [§1290]

Nevertheless, local courts may refuse to apply the law of another state if this would validate some act strongly offensive to local public policy.

> **Example:** A California court has refused to permit a Delaware corporation to solicit shareholder approval for an amendment to its articles of incorporation

that would have eliminated cumulative voting for directors. Even though such an amendment would have been permitted under Delaware law, the California court held that California had a legitimate interest in the matter because the corporation's principal business was in California and many of its shareholders resided there. Hence, the court insisted upon applying its own local laws prohibiting the amendment. [**Western Air Lines v. Sobieski,** 191 Cal. App. 2d 399 (1961)]

2. Local Statutes [§1291]

A few states now have statutes that subject foreign corporations having substantial local "contacts" to various local regulations intended to protect shareholders and creditors. [Cal. Corp. Code §2115; N.Y. Bus. Corp. Law §§1306, 1317-1320]

a. "Pseudo-foreign" corporations [§1292]

Under the California statute, if more than *half* of the corporation's business (average of its property, payroll, and sales) is done within the state and more than half of its shareholders have California addresses, it is treated as a "pseudo-foreign" corporation. Such corporations are subject to California law with respect to such matters as election and removal of directors, directors' standard of care and liability for unlawful distributions, shareholder rights to cumulative voting and inspection of records, shareholder approval and dissenters' rights in the case of reorganizations, and required corporate records and reports to shareholders. [Cal. Corp. Code §2115(a), (b)]

b. Constitutionality [§1293]

The validity of these statutes under the Full Faith and Credit and Commerce Clauses of the Constitution has been questioned, but not yet authoritatively resolved.

c. Exemptions [§1294]

The "pseudo-foreign" corporation statute does not apply to out-of-state corporations whose shares are listed on national securities exchanges or the Nasdaq Stock Market. These exchanges are deemed to have adequate "fairness" rules of their own, and their geographical shareholder-distribution requirements make it unlikely that more than half the shareholders would ever be residents of a single state. [Cal. Corp. Code §2115(e)]

Review Questions and Answers

Review Questions

CHARACTERISTICS OF CORPORATIONS

1. If Jim owns 10% of the outstanding shares of Family Co., a small family owned corporation, is Jim responsible for 10% of Family Co.'s debts?

     _____

2. Do shareholders in a corporation generally have management power and direct control of its affairs?

     _____

3. Allie, Britney, and Cindy are the sole shareholders of ABC Corporation. Allie dies; Britney and Cindy sell their shares to Debbie and Ellie, respectively. Does ABC Corporation still exist?

     _____

4. Are both corporations and partnerships "legal entities"?

     _____

5. In a limited partnership, does a limited partner have the same right to management and control as a partner in an ordinary partnership?

     _____

ORGANIZING THE CORPORATION

6. Under typical statutes governing incorporation, must the articles of incorporation state:

   a. The specific business purpose for which the corporation is formed?

        _____

   b. The number of shares it proposes to issue?

        _____

7. Under typical statutes governing incorporation, is it required that the incorporators also be permanent directors?

     _____

8. Under typical statutes governing incorporation, must *both* the articles of incorporation and the bylaws be filed with an appropriate state official in order to create corporate status?

     _____

9. The incorporators of White Corporation inadvertently filed defective articles of incorporation but thereafter contracted and acted as a corporation. Which, if any, of the following parties can attack White's status as a corporation?

     _____

   (A) Its own shareholders.

   (B) Its creditors.

   (C) The state.

10. The "corporation by estoppel" doctrine operates only against a third party who has dealt with the corporation and only as to the particular dealing. True or false? _____

11. Where statutes provide that corporate status is conclusively presumed from a proper filing of articles of incorporation, may shareholders rely on the "de facto incorporation" doctrine if the articles are *not* properly filed? _____

12. Able and Baker formed Acme Corp., a widget manufacturing business. Corporate formalities were observed when Acme Corp. was formed, but since then Able and Baker have neither held any meetings nor maintained any corporate records. Lately, Baker has been paying his household bills from Acme's account, and Able bought his wife a car with an Acme check. May C Corp., an Acme creditor who has not been paid for months, reach Able and Baker's personal assets to satisfy its claim? _____

13. Don, Ed, and Frank formed DEF Trucking Corporation, with investments of $250 each. They are the sole shareholders. They have observed all corporate formalities and have kept DEF's assets separate from their own. They have allowed DEF to run up debts of $100,000 in excess of its assets. Can the creditors "pierce the corporate veil" to reach the assets of Don, Ed, and/or Frank? _____

14. Does the "Deep Rock" doctrine permit the creditors of an insolvent corporation to collect their debts directly from the shareholders? _____

15. Beulah is a major shareholder of the XYZ Corporation. XYZ owes Creditor $10,000. Can XYZ assert, as an offset against its debt, a claim that Beulah has against Creditor? Can XYZ sue in its own name on Beulah's claim? _____

16. During the promotion stage of Central Corporation, Promoter Perry enters into a contract on behalf of the corporation for the purchase of equipment from Manufacturer. After formation, Central rejects the contract and refuses to proceed with the purchase. Can Manufacturer enforce the contract against Central? _____

17. Same facts as above except that Central, after formation, ratified the promoter's contract. _____

    a.   If it subsequently changes its mind, can it be held liable on the contract? _____

    b.   Can Central enforce the contract against Manufacturer? _____

    c.   If Central rejects the contract, is Perry liable individually? _____

POWERS AND LIABILITIES OF A CORPORATION

18. Can a corporation exercise powers other than those explicitly enumerated in its articles of incorporation? _____

19. Does a corporation have the *implied* power to enter into a partnership? _____

20. May a corporation validly make an educational or charitable gift that serves *no* direct corporate business purpose? _____

21. Can a *lawful* act ever be an "ultra vires" act? _____

22. If a corporate employee, in the course of employment, commits a tortious act that was within the scope of employment, but was unauthorized, can the corporation use ultra vires as a defense? _____

23. Brown Corporation enters a contract with Bob the builder. The contract is of a kind that is ultra vires for Brown.

    a.   If neither side has performed, can Bob enforce the contract if the corporation raises an ultra vires defense? _____

    b.   If both sides have performed, can Brown rescind? _____

    c.   If Bob has performed, but Brown has not, can Bob enforce the contract? _____

MANAGEMENT AND CONTROL

24. At their annual meeting, the shareholders of XYZ Corp., a publicly held corporation, voted to fire President and hire Jones as new general manager at $1 million per annum. Are these resolutions effective? _____

25. Does "statutory close corporation" status depend entirely on the existence of a specified number of shareholders? _____

26. Small Corporation is a statutory close corporation with five shareholders, who are also the five directors.

    a.   May the five shareholders make a written agreement concerning distribution of dividends and election of officers? _____

    b.   One of the shareholders makes a permissible sale of one-half of his shares to an outsider. The share certificate indicates the existence of a written agreement concerning management. Is the transferee bound by the agreement? _____

27. Is it ever permissible for a corporation to have only one director? _____

28. May the board of directors remove a director? _____

29. In most states, a director must own at least one share in a corporation of which he is a director. True or false? _____

30. Under modern statutes, can the shareholders ever, *without cause*, remove a director before the expiration of her term? _____

31. XYZ Corp. has seven directors, elected annually for one-year terms.

    a.   May the board of directors enter into a five-year employment contract with the general manager, thus binding future boards?   _____

    b.   May the XYZ board delegate interim management decisionmaking authority to an executive committee comprised of three of the directors?   _____

    c.   May five of the seven directors properly agree in advance as to how they will vote at board meetings?   _____

    d.   At an unscheduled meeting, four members are present and make a decision by a three-to-one vote. The three absent directors subsequently waive notice and approve the minutes of the meeting. Is the board action valid under most statutes?   _____

32. Even without prior agreement, a director is always entitled to reasonable compensation for ordinary services as a director. True or false?   _____

33. By majority vote, the directors of Shield Corp., acting in good faith, reduce existing fire insurance coverage without investigating the value of the property insured, even though Shield was not in a position to self-insure. As a result, Shield sustains a major financial loss when the property is destroyed by fire.

    a.   Does the "business judgment rule" absolve the directors of liability for the losses?   _____

    b.   Is each director who voted with the majority personally liable for the losses to Shield?   _____

    c.   Are those who voted against the decision also liable?   _____

    d.   If two of the directors were serving without pay, are they nevertheless personally liable?   _____

    e.   If the directors relied on apparently sound reports by corporate officers (or on the advice of professional experts) that the property was "fireproof," are the directors relieved of liability?   _____

34. Under most statutes, corporate officers are elected by the shareholders. True or false?   _____

35. The president of Green Corp. hired three new employees as division managers without consulting the board of directors. On finding out, can the board cancel the employment contracts as unauthorized?   _____

CONFLICT OF INTEREST IN CORPORATE TRANSACTIONS

36. Acme Corp. has nine directors, but four are absent from a meeting of the board. Director Donald, making full disclosure of all pertinent facts, offers to sell an

office building to Acme. Donald's offer is accepted by a three-to-two vote, with Donald voting in favor. Under modern statutes—

a.   Was Donald properly counted toward a quorum? _____

b.   Was Donald's vote properly counted on the sale? _____

37.   Same facts as above. Assume Acme buys the building from Donald, after full disclosure to the board, a proper quorum, and a disinterested majority vote of the board.

a.   At a later date, can the corporation rescind simply on the ground that the contract was made with an interested director? _____

b.   If the contract is later challenged as unfair in a shareholders' derivative suit, is the burden of proof on Donald to prove that it was fair to the corporation? _____

c.   If the shareholders *unanimously* ratify the contract, can Acme sue to rescind for unfairness? _____

d.   If the contract is ratified by a *majority* of the shareholders, can Acme avoid it? _____

38.   On the same facts as above, *if* the contract had been unfair, and Acme sought damages, could Donald be held liable for more than the difference between the price paid by Acme and the fair market value of the building? _____

39.   Red Corp. and Blue Corp. have a majority of directors in common. Is it ever proper for the two corporations to contract with each other? _____

40.   Winnie is a director of Textile Corp. The inventor of a new weaving machine, having offered it to Textile, also offers to sell it to Winnie.

a.   May Winnie buy the invention for her own business use while Textile is still considering the offer? _____

b.   If Winnie knows that Textile is financially unable to meet Inventor's price, may she buy the machine? _____

c.   If Textile makes a firm decision to reject the offer, may Winnie buy? _____

d.   If Winnie purchases from Inventor while Textile is still considering the offer, may Textile force Winnie to transfer the machine to Textile *at her cost*? _____

41.   Herbert is a director of Blank Corp. and has also served as Blank's secretary for five years.

a.   May Herbert properly vote on the amount of his own salary as secretary? _____

b. If Herbert's salary is set by the disinterested directors, can it later be challenged in a derivative suit simply on the grounds that it is more than the average salary paid for similar positions in other corporations? _____

c. If Herbert's salary is based on a percentage of corporate profits, is it automatically subject to challenge as a waste of corporate assets? _____

d. If a disinterested board votes a substantial, but reasonable, increase in Herbert's salary, retroactive to the beginning of his service as secretary, can the corporation (*e.g.*, under a new board or as a result of a shareholder suit) recover the amount of the retroactive increase? _____

INSIDER TRADING

42. At common law, do directors and officers owe fiduciary obligations to individual shareholders to disclose inside information about the corporation when trading in its stock? _____

43. Do section 10(b) and rule 10b-5 of the 1934 Act apply to securities that are *exempt* from the registration and reporting requirements of the Act? _____

44. Virginia, a promoter of Round Corp., sold to Round, without full disclosure, property worth $20,000 in exchange for its issuance of shares having a par value of $35,000.

a. Can Round sue Virginia under rule 10b-5? _____

b. Can a shareholder of Round maintain a derivative suit against Virginia under rule 10b-5? _____

c. If Round had paid Virginia $35,000 in *cash* instead of stock, could Round sue under rule 10b-5? _____

45. Can a plaintiff suing in state court on a state law claim join with it a 10b-5 claim arising from the same transaction? _____

46. Edgar, a shareholder of Circle Corp., brings an action seeking rescission of a just-completed merger of Circle into Square Corp., on the ground that Square made a false statement of a material fact in order to induce the shareholders' consent to the merger. Does rule 10b-5 apply? _____

47. Old Corp. issues a very optimistic press release that intentionally misstates material facts about its earnings. In reliance on the press release, Davis buys stock. Also in reliance on the press release, Edward, a shareholder, decides *not* to sell his stock. When the true facts are known, the stock falls sharply.

a. Can Davis sue Old under rule 10b-5, even though he purchased his shares on the open market and not from Old? _____

b.   Can Davis seek either rescission *or* damages?   _____

c.   Can Edward sue Old?   _____

48.   John is a director of New Corp. and knows that New has a new invention that will make its stock rise. Before any public announcement, John buys 1,000 shares directly from Thomas and also advises his neighbor, in confidence, to invest heavily in New Corp. stock because of the invention. The neighbor promptly follows John's advice.

a.   Can Thomas rescind?   _____

b.   Is the neighbor liable under rule 10b-5?   _____

49.   Nondisclosure of a mere *possibility* may give rise to an action under rule l0b-5. True or false?   _____

50.   Is a corporate officer liable under rule 10b-5 for a merely negligent omission of a material fact in a corporate report, if a purchaser relies on the report to his detriment?   _____

51.   Franklin is vice president of Grand Corp., which is listed on the New York Stock Exchange and has 1 million shares outstanding. In March, Franklin bought 1,000 shares of Grand from Greg at $30. In June of the same year, he sold the shares at $45.

a.   Is Franklin liable under section 16(b) of the 1934 Act to disgorge the profit he made?   _____

b.   Can Greg rescind or recover $15,000 from Franklin under section 16(b)?   _____

c.   If Franklin's trading was *not* based on any inside information, does this affect his liability?   _____

52.   Regina is a director of Home Corp. In February, she sold 100 shares of Home at $12; in March, she bought 200 shares at $10; in August, she sold 200 shares at $10. Is Regina liable under section 16(b)?   _____

53.   Stone Corp. has 100,000 shares outstanding. Alice, who is neither an officer nor a director of Stone, sold all of her 25,000 shares in July at $10. In August, she purchased 5,000 shares at $8. Is she liable under section 16(b)?   _____

54.   Robert, the secretary of Wood Corp., is designated by Wood to represent its stock interest (less than 10%) in Rock Corp. by serving as a director of Rock. Can Wood Corp. be held liable for short-swing profits it derives from Rock stock under section 16(b)?   _____

55. If an insider uses confidential information in *purchasing* stock of his corporation, but does *not* sell any stock in the corporation within six months of the purchase, can he be held liable either by the corporation or by the persons from whom he purchased?   _____

VOTING BY PROXY

56. If shares are sold between the "record date" and the time of a shareholders' meeting, is the new owner entitled to vote the shares at the meeting?   _____

57. If 100 shares are eligible to vote and four directors are to be elected by cumulative voting, a shareholder must have one-fourth of the shares (*i.e.*, 25 shares) to be able to elect one director. True or false?   _____

58. In a corporation with cumulative voting, will reducing the size of the board or providing for staggered terms reduce the effective voting strength of a minority bloc of shares?   _____

59. Is proxy voting permitted after a shareholder's death?   _____

60. Shareholder Simon, owner of 10,000 shares, pledges 5,000 to Theodore as security for a loan, and gives Theodore an irrevocable proxy. Simon then gives Alvin a proxy for his other 5,000 shares. Simon, Theodore, and Alvin all appear at the meeting to vote.

   a.   May Theodore vote 5,000 shares?   _____

   b.   May Alvin vote 5,000 shares?   _____

61. The management of Ace Corp., whose shares are traded on a national exchange, solicits proxies for its annual meeting. Under the federal proxy solicitation rules, which, if any, of the following shareholder proposals is management required to include in the proxy solicitation materials?   _____

   (A)   Nomination of directors with supporting statements.

   (B)   A demand that the corporation take a public stand on foreign policy issues.

   (C)   A proposal that would bind the board to replace a corporate vice president.

62. The management of Black Corp. solicited proxies for a vote on a proposed merger. The solicitation included several misstatements of material facts. The merger was approved.

   a.   In a shareholder suit to rescind the merger, must the plaintiff-shareholder prove the *materiality* of the misstatements?   _____

b.   Must the shareholder prove that the merger approval *resulted* from the misstatements?   _____

c.   If the terms of the merger were fair to the corporation and the shareholders, can the plaintiff still obtain relief?   _____

63.   Following a proxy contest involving basic policy decisions of Alpha Corp., management loses in the voting.

a.   Can the corporation reimburse management for its expenses in the proxy contest?   _____

b.   Can the corporation reimburse the victorious insurgents?   _____

SHAREHOLDER AGREEMENTS

64.   Is a pooling agreement among fewer than all shareholders in a close corporation valid?   _____

65.   Will most courts enforce an agreement among shareholders that binds them in their actions as *directors*, if all shareholders are not parties to the agreement?   _____

66.   Alex, Becky, and Chloe, three shareholders in a close corporation, create a voting trust, transferring legal title in their shares to Thomas as trustee.

a.   Can Alex revoke before expiration of the term of the trust?   _____

b.   Does the trust last as long as Alex, Becky, and Chloe are shareholders?   _____

c.   Can Thomas vote the shares in *every* shareholder vote?   _____

TRANSFER Of SHARES

67.   Small Corp., a close corporation, has a provision in its articles that no shareholder may sell or transfer her shares without first giving the corporation, and then the other shareholders, a right of first refusal for 30 days.

a.   Is this restriction valid under most modern statutes?   _____

b.   If Small Corp. is in a state following the traditional par value rules, may Small Corp. exercise the option if the repurchase would impair its stated capital?   _____

c.   If a shareholder dies, may Small Corp. insist on the right to repurchase from her legatee?   _____

d.   If a shareholder, in violation of the restriction, sells her shares to a transferee with notice of the restriction, may Small Corp. refuse to recognize the transfer?   _____

68.	Under modern statutes, if a corporation has a lien on shares, is a transferee without notice liable for the amount owed?	_____

SHAREHOLDER'S INFORMATIONAL RIGHTS

69.	At common law, did a shareholder have an *absolute* right to inspect corporate books and records?	_____

70.	Under modern statutes, can the shareholders' right to inspect corporate books and records be eliminated by specific provision in the articles of incorporation?	_____

71.	Is the objective of gaining control of a corporation through a proxy fight a "proper" purpose that justifies obtaining access to the shareholder list by insurgent shareholders?	_____

CONTROLLING SHARES

72.	The majority shareholder of Beta Corp. causes the board of directors to declare an excessive—but lawful—dividend. Does a minority shareholder have standing to object, even though he too will receive the dividend?	_____

73.	Minority shareholders in a close corporation actually owe a stricter fiduciary duty to other shareholders than do controlling shareholders of a publicly held corporation. True or false?	_____

74.	Owen, the owner of 60% of the shares of Omega Corp., sells his Omega stock to Olive at a premium, *i.e.*, a price above market value. Must Owen share the premium with the other shareholders?	_____

75.	If a majority shareholder is selling his stock, may he, as part of the sale transaction, arrange for the incumbent directors to resign so that the purchaser can take immediate control?	_____

76.	Sally, a majority shareholder in Epsilon Corp., sells her Epsilon shares to Louis at a price far above their fair value. Louis subsequently loots the corporate treasury.

	a.	Can Sally be held liable to the minority shareholders?	_____

	b.	If Sally is liable, is her liability limited to the minority's "share" of the premium that she received?	_____

DERIVATIVE SUITS

77.	The test of whether an action should be brought as a direct suit or as a derivative suit is the number of shareholders who claim to have been injured. True or false?	_____

78.	The board of directors of Red Corp. has failed to sue for damages on a Red Corp. contract with another corporation, which the latter has breached. Jane, a Red

Corp. shareholder, wishes to bring a derivative suit to enforce Red Corp.'s cause of action.

   a.   Must Jane first make a demand on the Red Corp. board of directors?   _____

   b.   If a disinterested Red Corp. board rejects Jane's demand, can she still maintain her suit?   _____

   c.   Must Jane also make a demand on the Red Corp. shareholders?   _____

   d.   If a demand on the Red Corp. shareholders was required and the shareholders refuse to sue, may Jane maintain her suit?   _____

79.   Must a derivative suit plaintiff always have been a shareholder at the time of the alleged wrongdoing?   _____

80.   If a sole shareholder cannot file a derivative suit against former managers because he owned no stock when the wrongful acts occurred, may he instead instigate a suit by the corporation?   _____

81.   If a corporate director is a defendant in a derivative suit, may the corporation's attorney represent the director?   _____

82.   Is a corporation a necessary party to a derivative suit brought on its behalf?   _____

83.   Is a jury trial ever available in a shareholder derivative suit in federal court?   _____

84.   If a losing derivative suit plaintiff was required to post security for expenses, is the corporation automatically entitled to recover the amount posted?   _____

85.   If a plaintiff-shareholder proves her derivative suit claim, will the court normally enter judgment in favor of the *corporation*?   _____

86.   If a plaintiff-shareholder loses in a derivative suit against a third party, may the corporation later sue in its own name on the same claim?   _____

87.   Plaintiff in a derivative suit recovers a judgment against defendant directors.

   a.   Is the plaintiff entitled to reimbursement from the corporation for his expenses?   _____

   b.   Are the losing directors entitled to indemnification by the corporation for damages assessed against them?   _____

   c.   If the plaintiff had lost, could the corporation reimburse the defendants for their expenses?   _____

88.   May a corporation properly provide insurance coverage for its officers and directors to protect them against personal liability or expenses in derivative suits?   _____

CLASSES OF STOCK

89. If a corporation's articles authorize "preferred" stock, but fail to state what preferences the stock is entitled to, is it entitled to at least dividend and liquidation preferences? _____

90. The articles of Corporation Y provide for preferred stock with a "5%, cumulative, dividend preference."

    a. Must the directors pay the 5% dividend in a year in which funds are available? _____

    b. If no dividends were paid on the preferred stock in a given year, do the arrearages have preference over dividends on the common stock in a subsequent year? _____

AUTHORIZATION AND ISSUANCE OF SHARES

91. Once all of the authorized shares have been issued, may the board of directors authorize the issuance of more shares? _____

92. If a corporation repurchases shares and holds them as "treasury stock," does this affect the corporation's authorized or issued capital? _____

STOCK SUBSCRIPTIONS

93. Prior to the formation of Star Corp., Arthur, Beatriz, and Calvin each agree to subscribe to 100 shares of stock when issued at an agreed price. If Arthur revokes before Star's incorporation is completed, can Star enforce the agreement against Arthur? _____

CONSIDERATION FOR SHARES

94. Which of the following shares have been lawfully issued by ABC Corp.? _____

    (A) 1,000 shares issued to Politician Paul as a gift.

    (B) 1,000 shares issued to Promoter Pat in exchange for her preincorporation services.

    (C) 1,000 shares issued to Promoter Pamela in exchange for her management services to be performed during the following two years.

95. May par value shares be sold by a corporation—

    a. For *less* than par value? _____

    b. For *more* than par value? _____

96. In April, Union Corp. issued to Arthur 100 shares of $10 par stock—marked "fully paid"—in exchange for property worth only $300. In March, one month before

the transaction between Union and Arthur, Creditor Cal extended $1,000 credit to Union. In June, following the transaction between Union and Arthur, Creditor Cora extended $1,000 credit to Union. Union has now become insolvent.

    a.   Can Cal sue Arthur for $700? _____

    b.   Can Cora? _____

97.   Same facts as above. If both Arthur and the directors of Union believed in good faith that Arthur's property *was* worth $1,000 when it was exchanged for stock, is Arthur's liability changed? _____

PROMOTERS

98.   Promoters Peter and Paul of Acme Corp. sell a warehouse to Acme that they bought for $30,000 and that has a fair market value of $40,000. In exchange for the property, they receive 5,000 shares of stock. The corporation contemporaneously issued stock to other subscribers for $10 per share. If Peter and Paul have not made full disclosure as to the amount of their profit, may Acme rescind? _____

99.   Assume the same facts except that Peter and Paul were the *sole shareholders* at the time of the transaction.

    a.   If only 5,000 shares have been authorized, does the corporation have a cause of action at common law? _____

    b.   If the corporation has an authorized capital of 10,000 shares, and the issuance of the remaining 5,000 shares is planned as part of the original capitalization, will the corporation have a cause of action after the other shares are issued? _____

PREEMPTIVE RIGHTS

100.   Did common law preemptive rights protect a stockholder against the dilution of her control by *any* new share issuances? _____

101.   When a shareholder's preemptive rights have been violated by an issuance of shares, his only remedy is to seek damages from the corporation. True or false? _____

UNDERWRITING

102.   Can underwriters be held subject to the same liabilities as issuers for fraud in the sale of securities under federal law? _____

STATUTES REGULATING ISSUANCE OF SHARES

103.   Can state blue sky laws validly require disclosure of information in connection with the issuance and sale of securities that is *not* required under applicable federal securities laws? _____

104. Can the Securities and Exchange Commission, under the 1933 Act, veto a proposed stock issuance if it is economically unsound?

_____

105. Which of the following issuances or transfers, if any, are exempt from the registration requirements of the Securities Act of 1933?

_____

(A) Mr. Smith inherits 100 shares of X stock and sells them to his neighbor.

(B) Y Corp. offers a new issue to only 20 persons, all of whom live in the same state and have financial experience and access to full information about Y.

(C) Same facts as (B), but the 20 persons live in four different states.

(D) Same facts as (B), but two of the offerees are brokers who intend to resell the stock to the public.

106. Can the purchaser of shares issued under a "private offering" exemption ever sell these shares *without registration?*

_____

107. Orange Corp. knowingly files a false registration statement containing material misstatements. Ralph, without knowledge of the misstatements, buys 1,000 shares from Orange at the issuing price of $10. The stock goes down to $7 per share. Ralph promptly files suit.

a. Is Ralph entitled to judgment against Orange, its directors, its underwriter, and the accountant who certified the financial portion of the registration statement?

_____

b. Must Ralph prove the elements of common law fraud?

_____

c. Must Ralph prove reliance on the misstatements?

_____

108. Same facts as above except that Ralph, immediately after purchasing the shares, sold them to Cynthia at $10 per share. The price then went down to $7.

a. Does Cynthia have a cause of action against Orange under section 11?

_____

b. Is Cynthia entitled to either rescission *or* damages from Orange?

_____

109. Same facts as above, but assume that Orange had sold its stock by use of a material misstatement *other than* in its registration statement. Under section 12 of the 1933 Act—

a. Does Ralph have a cause of action against Orange?

_____

b. Does Cynthia?

_____

110. The purchaser of securities that were exempt from the registration requirements of the 1933 Act may nevertheless recover under the Act for material misstatements or omissions in connection with the purchase of such securities. True or false?

_____

DIVIDENDS

111. Can common stockholders, by majority vote, compel payment of dividends, *if* sufficient funds are available? _____

112. In states following the traditional approach, may dividends generally be paid out of stated capital if there are current net profits? _____

113. Corporation A sold 100,000 shares of its $20 par stock for $23 per share. Can the $300,000 later be available for dividends? _____

114. In a state following the traditional par value approach Corporation B reduced the par value of its 100,000 shares of common stock from $12 to $10. Can it distribute the $200,000 as dividends? _____

115. Corporation C owned real property with a book value of $200,000 based on its acquisition cost. The property is now worth $500,000. Can Corporation C pay dividends from the $300,000 increased value? _____

116. Can a director who votes for an illegal dividend be held *personally* liable for the amount distributed? _____

117. The directors of Acme Corporation all voted for an unlawful dividend, rendering Acme insolvent. Are the shareholder-recipients liable? _____

REDEMPTION AND REPURCHASES

118. If funds are available, does a corporation always have inherent power to redeem its shares? _____

119. May a corporation *repurchase* its shares on a selective basis (from certain shareholders and not from others)? _____

120. If a corporation contracts to repurchase its shares on an installment payment basis, is it enough that it has adequate funds available from a legal source on the date the contract is made (as distinguished from the dates each installment comes due)? _____

121. The directors of Gold Corp., knowing that shareholder Hunt was planning a fight to unseat them, authorized the repurchase of Hunt's shares at a premium. As long as a lawful source of funds was available, was their action proper? _____

FUNDAMENTAL CHANGES

122. The boards of directors of Red Corp. and Blue Corp. adopt a plan to merge Red into Blue. Neither corporation had any prior relationship with the other. Which, if any, of the following statements is correct under most statutes? _____

    (A)   The merger must be approved by shareholder votes of *both* Red and Blue.

(B)   The debts and contract obligations of Red are automatically assumed by Blue upon completion of the merger.

(C)   Red is automatically dissolved upon completion of the merger.

123.   Same facts as above. Assume that both Red Corp. and Blue Corp. had dissenting shareholders who complied with all the statutorily required procedures.

   a.   Do the dissenting shareholders of both Red and Blue have appraisal rights? _____

   b.   Can a shareholder who voted for the merger nevertheless exercise appraisal rights? _____

   c.   Is the "fair value" for a dissenter's shares always the recognized market price at the effective date of the merger? _____

124.   Green Corp. owns 90% of the stock of Brown Corp.; two individual shareholders each own 5% of Brown.

   a.   If both boards of directors approve a "short-form" merger of Brown into Green, must both corporations' shareholders also approve? _____

   b.   Do dissenting shareholders of Green have appraisal rights? _____

   c.   Can Green eliminate the two minority shareholders by giving them cash instead of Green stock? _____

125.   The board of directors of Gray Corp. contemplates a sale of "substantially all of its assets" to Black Corp. for cash. Which of the following statements, if any, is correct under most statutes? _____

(A)   The shareholders of Gray usually must approve.

(B)   The shareholders of Black must approve.

(C)   In defining "substantially all" of Gray's assets, the determining factor is the percentage of gross assets to be sold.

126.   The board of directors of Day Corp. wishes to acquire Night Corp., but fears opposition from a strong minority of its own shareholders. Day offers to buy Night's assets in exchange for Day stock with the proviso that Night will then vote on a plan of dissolution.

   a.   Can the minority shareholders of Day object that they had no opportunity to vote on the transaction? _____

   b.   If the sale has been consummated, can it be set aside? _____

127. If a board of directors unanimously approves a change in the articles of incorporation, is shareholder approval ordinarily also required? _____

128. May the state bring an action for involuntary dissolution of a corporation for abuse of its corporate authority? _____

129. Is a bankrupt corporation automatically dissolved? _____

130. If, after dissolution, directors conduct further business not reasonably incident to liquidation, can they be held personally liable for corporate debts? _____

131. If the assets of a dissolved corporation have been distributed while a creditor's timely claims are unsatisfied, the creditor can recover from the shareholder-distributees. True or false? _____

132. If controlling shareholders materially misrepresented the facts of a proposed merger so as to advantage themselves, can a dissenting shareholder exercise her appraisal rights under state law *and also* bring an action under federal securities acts? _____

133. Acme Corp. makes a tender offer to buy 60% of the shares of Star Corp. for cash.

    a.   Must the shareholders of both corporations approve? _____

    b.   After acquiring the Star shares, may Acme dissolve Star? _____

    c.   Must Acme disclose its plans for Star at the time it makes the tender offer? _____

Answers to Review Questions

1. **NO**   Shareholder liability is usually limited to the amount of the investment, and only the corporation is liable on its debts. [§2]

2. **NO**   Except in extraordinary circumstances, shareholders have *no* power to manage and control; these powers are vested in the board of directors and the officers acting under the board's authority. This is a major difference between corporations and partnerships, because partners do have the right to participate in management. [§§4, 38]

3. **YES**   A corporation is a separate entity, whose existence can be perpetual and is unaffected by changes in the owners of its shares. This is another major difference between a corporation and a partnership. In a partnership governed by the UPA, the death, withdrawal, or insolvency of any partner normally terminates the partnership. [§§5, 24-26] However, under the RUPA, dissociation (*i.e.,* withdrawal) of a partner does not necessarily cause dissolution of the partnership. [§33]

4. **DEPENDS**   A corporation is a legal entity, but under the UPA, a partnership is not, even though the law sometimes treats partnerships as if they were legal entities. [§§12-13] In contrast, the RUPA confers entity status on partnerships. [§14]

5. **NO**   A limited partner, whose financial liability is limited to the amount of his investment, *may not* participate in the management of the business in most jurisdictions. [§§52, 54-57]

6.a. **GENERALLY NO**   Although a few states require a specific statement, most do not, and some statutes (*e.g.,* Delaware) permit a purpose as general as to engage in any lawful activity for which a corporation may be organized. [§§81-84]

 b. **NO**   Statutes commonly require the articles of incorporation to indicate the number of shares *authorized*. The number of shares to be issued is usually decided at a post-incorporation meeting of the board of directors. [§§82, 86-87]

7. **NO**   Incorporators file the articles and, if the statute does not provide that the initial directors be named in the articles, the incorporators hold an organizational meeting at which bylaws are adopted and directors are elected to serve until the first shareholders' meeting. [§§85-86]

8. **NO**   The filing of the articles in proper form is required to create the corporation, but bylaws are usually adopted at a post-incorporation organizational meeting. Bylaw provisions may be regulated by statute, however. [§§81, 86-87]

9.	**(C)**	On the facts, it appears that White Corp., lacking sufficient compliance for "de jure" status, has met the conditions for "de facto" status—good faith, a colorable attempt to comply with a statute under which the corporation could have been formed, and actual use of corporate powers. Under modern law, the status of a "de facto" corporation can usually be challenged *only* by the state. In contrast, complete compliance with statutory requirements creates a "de jure" corporation, whose corporate status cannot be challenged by anyone. [§§91-96]
10.	**FALSE**	Both the shareholders of a nominal corporation, having claimed corporate status in a transaction with a third party, and a third party who has dealt with the enterprise as if it were a corporation may be estopped from denying corporateness. [§§97-100]
11.	**DEPENDS**	Jurisdictions with statutes based on the old Model Act have abolished the de facto doctrine. However, under the Revised Model Act, only persons who *knew* there was no incorporation are barred from asserting de facto status. [§§106-107]
12.	**YES**	In determining whether to "pierce the corporate veil" (*i.e.*, disregard the corporate entity and impose liability on shareholders for corporate obligations), the commingling of assets (treating corporate assets as if they were the shareholders' own assets) and lack of corporate formalities (no directors' or shareholders' meetings, and no corporate records) are major factors considered by the court. Both suggest the corporation is merely the "alter ego" of the shareholders and should be disregarded. [§§111-114, 117]
13.	**DEPENDS**	Although DEF *was* maintained as a separate entity, some courts would permit creditors to disregard corporateness and reach the shareholders because DEF was undercapitalized; *i.e.*, Don, Ed, and Frank should have reasonably anticipated that $750 was inadequate capitalization to meet the obligations of DEF. [§§115, 119]
14.	**NO**	When this doctrine is applicable, the corporation's debts to shareholders are *subordinated* to its debts to outside creditors, but no additional personal liability is imposed on shareholders. (In effect, the debt owed to the shareholders is treated as additional investment capital.) [§§124-127]
15.	**NO (both questions)**	The rule that the corporate form may be disregarded to avoid injustice is for the benefit of third parties, not the corporation; therefore, a corporation generally may not assert in its own name a claim or defense that belongs to a shareholder. (Note, however, that Beulah could *assign* her claim to XYZ Corp., in which case it could assert the claim.) [§123]
16.	**NO**	Even under the American rule, the corporation is not liable on promoters' contracts, unless the corporation adopts the contract. [§§131-136]
17.a.	**SPLIT**	Under the English rule, even corporate ratification will not create contractual liability (but the corporation may be liable in quasi-contract for any benefits

obtained). Under the American rule, contractual liability *is* created by either express or implied ratification. [§§131-132, 134, 137]

b. **YES** Under both the English and American rules, Central may choose to enforce the contract. [§138]

c. **DEPENDS** If Perry had expressly disclaimed individual liability, he cannot be held. Otherwise, most courts will allow Manufacturer to enforce the contract against Perry, who may then have a right to indemnification by Central. [§§139-143]

18. **YES** Under modern law, courts broadly construe a corporation's implied power to do what is *reasonably necessary to achieve its express purposes*, unless otherwise prohibited. Moreover, modern statutes confer many powers on corporations. [§§152-153]

19. **NO** Because participation in a partnership involves an impermissible delegation of managerial responsibility, in the past most courts held that a corporation could not enter into a partnership, absent specific authorization. (Modern statutes now specifically authorize this.) [§156]

20. **YES** Under the modern view, such gifts, if *reasonable*, are permitted even without any showing of a direct benefit to the corporation. [§§157-163]

21. **YES** Any action outside corporate purposes and powers may be "ultra vires," regardless of its legality. [§§164-166]

22. **NO** The corporation cannot rely on a disclaimer of its legal power to commit the particular act to avoid liability. [§§167-168]

23.a. **YES (modern law)** At common law, neither party could enforce an ultra vires executory contract. Under modern statutes, ultra vires is not a defense to an executory *or* executed contract. Under some circumstances, however, a shareholder may seek to *enjoin* performance. [§§170, 175-176]

b. **NO** The rule is the same at common law and under modern statutes. A fully performed contract, although ultra vires, is not subject to rescission. [§§171, 176]

c. **NO (modern law)** Under modern law, the ultra vires defense is *disfavored* even when one party has performed, but most statutes permit recovery in quasi-contract from the nonperforming party. At common law, the majority view denied the ultra vires defense to the nonperforming party in such a case. [§§172-173, 176]

24. **NO** Such management decisions are within the powers of the directors; shareholders have no *direct* control over the management of ordinary corporate affairs, including the hiring and firing of corporate officers. (Some statutes, however, permit powers of management and control to be exercised by shareholders in a *close corporation*.) [§§183, 189, 193-194, 198-200]

25.	**NO**	Most close corporation statutes impose additional requirements, such as identification as a close corporation in the articles of incorporation and restrictions on the transfer of shares. [§§191, 195-197]
26.a.	**YES**	At common law, such an agreement would be deemed an improper infringement of the powers of the directors, but under modern statutes for general corporations and under close corporation statutes written shareholder management agreements are generally permitted. [§199]
b.	**YES**	Statutes frequently require a "conspicuous" notation of the existence of the agreement on a share certificate of a close corporation. If such a notation is present, a transferee takes subject to the agreement. [§§202-206]
27.	**YES**	Modern statutes commonly authorize single-member boards, especially—although not exclusively—when there is only one shareholder. [§208]
28.	**DEPENDS**	Under common law and the majority view, the board cannot remove a director, with or without cause. However, some modern statutes permit removal for cause. [§218]
29.	**FALSE**	However, unless prohibited by statute, the articles of incorporation or the bylaws may prescribe any reasonable qualifications for directors—including share ownership. [§209]
30.	**YES**	Unlike common law, which permitted removal only for cause, many modern statutes generally permit removal, without cause, by a vote of shareholders. [§§215, 217]
31.a.	**YES**	Absent a prohibition in the articles of incorporation, a board may make a contract that extends beyond the directors' term of office. A future XYZ board could remove the general manager, but he would then have a cause of action for breach of contract. [§§214, 267]
b.	**YES**	It is common for a board to authorize day-to-day management by such a committee, although there are limitations on the committee's power to make certain decisions of a fundamental nature (*e.g.*, dividends, mergers, etc.). [§§228-231]
c.	**NO**	Fiduciary duties of directors require that directors be able to exercise free discretion in making corporate decisions. (Exceptions have been created for close corporations.) [§235]
d.	**YES**	Modern statutes reduce required formalities and permit waiver of notice before *or* after an unscheduled meeting. Furthermore, an action taken by a majority of the directors present is binding, *if* there was a quorum. A quorum is ordinarily a majority of the authorized number of directors. [§§221-224]

32.	**FALSE**	Generally, a director is not entitled to compensation for ordinary services as a director, unless compensation is provided for by the articles or by board resolution passed *before* services were rendered. However, a director may be entitled to compensation for authorized *extraordinary* services and for services as an officer or employee. [§§236-240]
33.a.	**PROBABLY NOT**	The business judgment rule protects a director who has made an erroneous policy decision in good faith *and* in the exercise of diligence. In the majority view, it does not protect a director who has not acted diligently. [§§244-247]
b.	**YES**	Because the directors' action *caused* the loss, they are personally liable, and the liability is joint and several. Note that some statutes permit limitation or elimination of director liability absent bad faith, intentional misconduct, or illegal acts. [§§251-255]
c.	**NO**	If the director has recorded her dissent, then she is not liable. [§§253-254]
d.	**YES**	Lack of compensation is ordinarily no defense. The director's fiduciary duty is not diminished by the fact that service is without pay. [§256]
e.	**YES**	If the reliance was reasonable *and if* the report or advice was within the competence of the person providing it, the directors have a defense to liability. [§§258-259]
34.	**FALSE**	Under most statutes, the major officers of a corporation are elected by the board, although some statutes permit election of officers by shareholders. [§§267, 304]
35.	**PROBABLY NOT**	The president of a corporation, by majority view, has *apparent authority* to make decisions and bind the corporation in transactions that are part of the ordinary course of the corporation's business. Hiring division managers is probably within that category. [§§273-277]
36.a.	**YES**	Most states permit an interested director to be counted toward a quorum (although a contrary result would have been reached at common law). [§§281-282, 304]
b.	**NO**	Neither at common law nor under most statutes may an "interested" director's vote be counted on the transaction in which he has a personal interest. [§§281-282, 296]
37.a.	**NO**	Because there was full disclosure, most courts would require a showing of fundamental unfairness to the corporation. However, at common law such a contract was automatically voidable by the corporation. [§§283-289]
b.	**YES**	The burden of proof is generally on the interested director, who must prove the fairness of the transaction. However, the burden may be shifted to the plaintiff in cases where the shareholders have ratified the contract. [§§290, 294-295]

c. **NO**   Assuming full disclosure, unanimous shareholder ratification will preclude a suit by the corporation. However, if the corporation is insolvent, a creditor's suit may be possible. [§292]

d. **DEPENDS**   Ratification by a disinterested majority may estop the corporation or at least shift the burden of proof to the plaintiff. Courts are split as to the effectiveness of an attempted ratification by an interested majority of the shareholders. [§§293-300]

38. **POSSIBLY** The difference between price and fair market value would be the *usual* measure of damages. However, if Donald had purchased the building in order to resell it to Acme at an excessive price, some courts would penalize him by fixing damages at the difference between Donald's acquisition cost and the amount paid to him by Acme. Some courts may also order the interested director to repay his salary earned during the breach period, and others may assess punitive damages. [§§308-312]

39. **YES**   Modern statutes generally permit transactions between two corporations with interlocking directorates, *if* the transactions are fair and there is full disclosure. At common law, however, a transaction between Red and Blue was voidable at the option of either. [§§314-317]

40.a. **NO**   Because Textile was already considering the offer, this would be a clear usurpation of corporate opportunity and a breach of Winnie's fiduciary duty of loyalty. [§§321, 323]

b. **DEPENDS**   Some courts hold that Textile's inability frees Winnie to take advantage of the opportunity. However, some courts would bar Winnie, on the rationale that her duty is to attempt to find the necessary financing for Textile. [§§327-328]

c. **YES**   If Textile, fully informed, refuses the opportunity, there is no conflict of interest to prevent Winnie from proceeding. [§330]

d. **YES**   Textile may compel a transfer of the machine and an accounting for any interim income or profits. If Winnie buys while the offer is a corporate opportunity and then sells the machine to Textile, Textile may recover Winnie's entire profit. [§§332-333]

41.a. **SPLIT**   Most states would not permit Herbert's vote to be counted to make up a majority vote, although some statutes provide otherwise. The effect of shareholder ratification would be the same as in any other case of an "interested director" transaction. [§§336-339]

b. **NO**   As long as the salary is reasonable, the fact that it is above market value for the services will not preclude application of the business judgment rule to protect both Herbert and the board of directors. The directors may, in good faith, believe that Herbert is worth more than an average secretary. Note that the business judgment rule nearly always precludes finding executive compensation excessive in a publicly held corporation. [§§340-344]

c. **NO** As long as the total compensation bears a reasonable relationship to the value of Herbert's services, there is no "waste." And, note that under such an arrangement, Herbert's interests would be more likely to coincide with Blank's interests than to conflict with them. [§§347-349]

d. **PROBABLY** On general contract principles, past services are not ordinarily a legally sufficient consideration for the payment by Blank. A contrary result might be reached, however, if there was consideration (*e.g.*, the retroactive increase was expressly conditioned upon Herbert's remaining in the position for a specified period); or if it could be shown that the increase fell within the business judgment rule. [§§350-353]

42. **NO** The common law majority view was that no duty was owed. However, exceptions were recognized in many cases where "special facts" compelled disclosure (*e.g.*, in cases involving face-to-face dealing). [§§360-363]

43. **YES** Section 10(b) and rule 10b-5 apply to the purchase and sale of *all* securities. The only jurisdictional limitation to section 10(b) is the requirement that the "purchase or sale" must be effected by an instrumentality of interstate commerce. [§369]

44.a. **YES** Section 10(b) extends to any purchase or sale. "Sale" is construed broadly so as to include an original issuance by a corporation. [§§368-369, 430, 437-438]

b. **YES** If the corporation-seller does not act, a shareholder who meets the relevant procedural requirements can bring a derivative suit under rule 10b-5. [§430]

c. **NO** If there is neither a purchase nor sale of any *security*, the Act does not apply. [§§369, 436-441]

45. **NO** Federal courts have *exclusive* jurisdiction over rule 10b-5 actions. *Compare:* If the plaintiff sues in federal court, he may, under the doctrine of supplemental jurisdiction, join his state law claim in the federal action. [§§476-477]

46. **YES** "Purchase or sale" is broadly defined. The term includes the exchange of shares that occurs in connection with a merger. [§439]

47.a. **YES** Davis was a purchaser. It is not necessary that the defendant be either a purchaser or a seller. Nor is privity between defendant and the injured purchaser required. [§§371, 412-413, 436, 467-468]

b. **NO** Davis is limited to damages, because the defendant corporation was not the seller. *If* Davis had bought from Old, rescission would be available. [§§412, 461-466]

c.	**NO**	Edward was neither a purchaser nor a seller within the meaning of the Act. "Aborted" sales are not sufficient. [§436]
48.a.	**DEPENDS**	If New Corp. is publicly held, Thomas can recover damages, but probably cannot rescind, because he can replace his stock. However, rescission is permissible if New Corp. is a close corporation. [§§461-466]
b.	**YES**	A tippee who knows or should know that the tipper breached his fiduciary duty to the corporation is liable under rule 10b-5. A tipper breaches that fiduciary duty by communicating inside information for personal gain. Tips to friends are treated as benefiting the tipper because they are the same as trades by the insider followed by gifts of the profits. [§§419-423]
49.	**TRUE**	A possibility may be *material* if the likelihood of the occurrence of the event and its anticipated effect on the corporate business are such that a prospective buyer or seller would attach importance to the information. [§372]
50.	**NO**	Scienter is an element in a rule 10b-5 action. Mere negligence is an inadequate basis for liability. [§§373-374]
51.a.	**YES**	If a corporation's securities are covered by section 16, an officer is liable for short-swing profits, no matter how few shares he owns. [§§487-488, 496]
b.	**NO**	Greg may do neither under section 16(b), as the liability runs only in favor of the corporation. However, Greg would have an action under rule 10b-5 if Franklin traded on the basis of material inside information. [§§492, 519-521]
c.	**NO**	The language of section 16(b) appears to be absolute and courts hold the defendant liable whether or not he used inside information. [§§488, 519]
52.	**YES**	To find short-swing profits, a court looks at the six-month period after *or before* any purchase or sale. The highest sale price is matched with the lowest purchase price; thus, Regina's liability is $200. [§§489-491]
53.	**NO**	Section 16(b) covers only persons who were more-than-10% beneficial owners at both the time of purchase and the time of sale. However, one who is an officer or a director at *either* purchase *or* sale is liable. [§§487-488, 500]
54.	**YES**	Robert has been *deputized* to act as a director for Wood Corp. However, if Robert had been requested to be a director *by Rock* and was not selected to represent Wood's interest, Wood Corp. would not necessarily be considered an insider of Rock. Even so, Wood might be considered an insider if Robert in fact represents Wood's interest or gives inside information to Wood. [§§497-498]
55.	**YES**	He may be liable to the sellers under rule 10b-5, as to which there is no six-month limit. In addition, he also incurs a common law liability to the corporation for his profits, on the ground that he breached a fiduciary duty by converting

a corporate asset (inside information) to his own use. However, if the sellers recover a judgment against him, the amount could probably be deducted from any corporate recovery. [§§521-529]

56. **DEPENDS**   On whether the record owner gives the new owner a proxy. The new owner can *compel* the record owner to give a proxy, but until he does, the record owner alone is entitled to vote. [§§532-533]

57. **FALSE**   Twenty-one shares will be enough to elect one director. $x > \dfrac{1 \times 100}{1 + 4}$ [§546]

58. **YES**   Any device that reduces the number of directors to be elected at one time results in a higher percentage of outstanding shares being needed to elect a director—and thus, ordinarily reduces minority power. [§§550-552, 557]

59. **YES**   Unless written notice is given to the corporation before the vote is counted. [§561]

60.a. **YES**   Assuming that Theodore's proxy was expressly made irrevocable, Simon's appearance is of no effect, because the proxy was coupled with an interest. When Simon repays the loan, the proxy will become revocable. [§§562-563, 565]

b. **NO**   Simon may revoke Alvin's proxy by express notification, by executing a new proxy, or as here, by voting the shares himself. [§560]

61. **NONE**   (A) is incorrect because the rule requiring inclusion of shareholder proposals with management proxy solicitations does not apply to elections of directors. [§600]

(B) is incorrect because management may exclude proposals that are beyond the corporation's power to effect or are not significantly related to the corporation's business. [§§599-600]

(C) is incorrect because a proposal need not be included if it purports to bind the board on a matter that is within their discretion, and not that of the shareholders. A purely advisory proposal, however, would probably be upheld. Note that the burden of proof is on management whenever it excludes a shareholder proposal. [§§595, 600]

62.a. **YES**   If misstatements or omissions are not material, there is no violation. A statement is material if the omitted fact would have assumed actual significance in the deliberations of the reasonable shareholder. [§§604-608]

b. **NO**   If the plaintiff proves that the misstatements were material, courts will assume that they may have affected the voting process and outcome, *i.e.*, causation. [§§609-611]

c. **YES**   Fairness is no defense when shareholders have been misled. Fully informed shareholders might have rejected even a "fair" proposal. [§614]

63.a.	**YES**	Management has the right to recover its reasonable expenses, whether or not it wins, as long as the controversy is over corporate policy, not personnel. [§620]
b.	**PROBABLY**	*If* the insurgents win, some courts have upheld voluntary reimbursement on the ground that a benefit has been conferred on the corporation. [§621]
64.	**YES**	Most statutes and cases normally allow such agreements. [§§625, 632]
65.	**NO**	When the agreement is not unanimous, the majority view is that it is unenforceable as an infringement on the discretion of the board. However, recent statutes and case law liberalize this rule for close corporations. [§§636-641]
66.a.	**NO**	A voting trust is usually irrevocable for its life, unless there is unanimous agreement to terminate it. [§§642, 645]
b.	**NO**	Statutes generally limit the duration of voting trusts. Most statutes provide for extensions. [§§645-646]
c.	**NO**	Unless there is explicit authorization in the trust agreement, most courts will not allow the trustee to vote on extraordinary matters, such as dissolution of the corporation. [§647]
67.a.	**YES**	Most statutes authorize restrictions on the transfer of shares *if* they are reasonable and are not total restraints on alienability. [§§652, 659, 662-664]
b.	**NO**	A corporate right of first refusal in connection with a restriction on transfer of shares does not ordinarily alter the limitations on proper sources for repurchase of shares. [§665]
c.	**NO**	Absent a specific provision, restrictions may not be held to apply to involuntary transfers. Generally, stock transfer restrictions are narrowly construed. [§669]
d.	**YES**	A corporation may continue to recognize the transferor as the owner, *if the transferee had notice* (as here). [§§670-672]
68.	**NO**	Under the U.C.C., unless a lien is shown on the face of a share certificate, the corporation cannot enforce it against a bona fide purchaser who lacks notice of any restriction. The corporation must transfer the shares and recognize the new owner. [§§670-673]
69.	**NO**	The right was not absolute. The burden of proof was on the shareholder to show that the inspection was for a proper purpose. (Under most modern statutes, the burden is on the corporation to show an improper purpose.) [§§675-676]
70.	**NO**	Today, shareholder inspection rights are in most cases statutory. Considered fundamental, they cannot be eliminated by the articles. [§676]
71.	**YES**	The purpose is proper because it is related to the shareholder's legitimate interests in the corporation. [§§678-679, 681-682]

72.	**YES**	If the dividend distribution was designed to serve the interests of the majority shareholder and is harmful to the corporation, the controlling shareholder has breached his fiduciary duty to the minority shareholder. [§693]
73.	**TRUE**	*All* shareholders of closely held corporations owe each other the same duty of utmost good faith and loyalty that is owed by partners to each other. [§705]
74.	**NO**	Absent fraud, knowledge of purchaser's plan to loot, or other unfairness in the transaction, the majority view is that sale of control at a premium is not in itself a breach of a fiduciary duty. The seller need not account to the minority for the premium he has received. [§§712-717, 723-727]
75.	**YES**	This practice is permitted as long as the stock interest is large enough to give the purchaser effective control, so that he could have effected the changes immediately himself. However, the "sale" of directorships would be invalid if not connected with the sale of a stock interest large enough to carry effective voting control. [§§719-722]
76.a.	**PROBABLY**	If the seller of controlling shares knows or has reason to know that the transferee plans to deal unfairly with the corporation, the seller has breached her fiduciary duty. A price far above fair value should probably have put Sally on notice of Louis's intent. [§§726-729]
b.	**NO**	A seller who has breached her duty is liable to the minority shareholders either for their portion of the premium *or* for the actual damages caused to the corporation by the buyer, whichever is larger. [§730]
77.	**FALSE**	The critical questions are *who* suffered the injury—*i.e.*, the corporation or the shareholders—and to whom the breached duty ran. [§738]
78.a.	**YES**	A potential derivative suit plaintiff must first exhaust corporate remedies and a demand on the board of directors is an essential element of the cause of action, unless, in some states, the shareholder can show that such a demand would have been futile. [§§747-751]
b.	**NO**	If a disinterested board has, in good faith, refused to act, courts will protect its exercise of business judgment and bar the derivative suit. [§§753-754]
c.	**SPLIT**	Some states require demand only on the board of directors. Others require a demand on the shareholders if the act in question was within their power to ratify, but excuse the demand if such ratification were not possible. [§§768-769]
d.	**PROBABLY NOT**	If disinterested shareholders have refused to sue, they have, in effect, ratified the board's decision. If such ratification was within the shareholders' power, and was reasonable, the derivative suit is barred. [§§776-777]

79.	**NO**	Contemporaneous share ownership is the *usual* requirement in most states. However, even in these states exceptions exist for a plaintiff who subsequently acquired his shares by operation of law (*e.g.*, inheritance), and some statutes waive the requirement when serious injustice would otherwise result. [§§783-788]
80.	**PROBABLY NOT**	If the sole shareholder is disqualified, equity may also bar suit by the corporation itself. [§§789-790]
81.	**NO**	The director's interest is adverse to that of the corporation, so each must ordinarily have separate counsel. [§794]
82.	**YES**	The corporation *must* be joined as a party. The corporation is a defendant, even though its interests are ordinarily adverse to those of the other defendants. [§794]
83.	**YES**	Even though such suits are equitable in nature, the Seventh Amendment right to trial by jury applies to those issues upon which the corporation, as a plaintiff, would have been entitled to a jury. [§§796-797]
84.	**NO**	Even if statutes provide that the defendant corporation, if it wins, may automatically move against the posted security, the court determines the amount of the award (usually limited to its reasonable costs and attorneys' fees). In some states, the security is available for the defendant's costs only if the court finds that the plaintiff acted unreasonably in bringing suit. [§§804, 806]
85.	**YES**	Recovery usually goes to the corporation. However, if the corporation has been dissolved or if a corporate recovery would benefit shareholders not entitled to participate in it, the court may award payment directly to the innocent shareholders. [§§814, 820-822]
86.	**NO**	A judgment on the merits in a derivative suit is res judicata as to both the corporation and other shareholders. [§813]
87.a.	**YES**	The corporation must ordinarily reimburse the plaintiff because he has obtained either a "common fund" or some other "substantial benefit" for the corporation. He is entitled to his expenses, including attorneys' fees. [§§823-826]
b.	**NO**	A director who has lost on the merits is not entitled to indemnification for the liability imposed. Otherwise, the recovery by the corporation would merely go right back to the defendant. [§§839-843]
c.	**YES**	In most states, reimbursement of a winning defendant is discretionary with the board, but some statutes require the corporation to reimburse a defendant who wins on the merits in a derivative suit. [§§832-836]

88. **YES**   Many statutes permit such insurance, but they differ as to whether the coverage may extend to *any* liability or expenses. [§§846-847]

89. **NO**   Any preferences must be *expressly set forth* in the articles. Otherwise, all classes of shares will be treated alike. [§§851, 857]

90.a. **NO**   Unless the payment of dividends is expressly made mandatory, payment is within the discretion of the directors. If no dividend is declared on the preferred stock, however, no dividend may be paid on the common stock. [§§858-859]

   b. **YES**   Because the preferred shares are cumulative, both the current preferred dividend *and* all arrears take precedence over the common stock in any year. [§§858-859]

91. **NO**   No further shares can be issued unless there is an amendment to the articles of incorporation authorizing a larger number of shares. The board of directors alone cannot amend the articles of incorporation; a shareholder vote is required. [§§866, 1146]

92. **NO**   Treasury stock is considered as "issued" while in the hands of the corporation. The repurchase by the corporation does not affect the number of shares the corporation is authorized to issue. [§870]

93. **YES**   By statute, in most states today pre-incorporation subscriptions are irrevocable for a designated period of time in the absence of a contrary agreement. [§876]

94. **(B) AND PERHAPS (C)**   (A) is not lawful consideration. Some statutes require that shares be issued in exchange only for money paid, property acquired, or labor done. Others allow stock to be issued for promises to pay or work in the future, or in exchange for any benefit to the corporation. But even under the most liberal of policies, an outright gift would not suffice. [§878]

(B) is lawful in most states, although some courts require that the "labor done" be done *after* the corporation is in existence (most, however, do not). [§878]

(C) Under some statutes, (C) is not lawful because executory promises—whether for money, property, or future services—are not legal consideration for the issuance of shares. However, a promise of future payment or services in exchange for issuing shares is permitted under modern statutes. [§§879, 881]

95.a. **GENERALLY NO**   Except in special situations, a corporation may generally not sell its shares for less than par value, although the par value price may include underwriting commissions. Shares sold for less than par are "watered." [§§883-885]

   b. **YES**   Corporations frequently issue "low par" stock to provide financial flexibility, to create "paid-in" surplus, and to avoid watered stock problems. [§883]

96.a. **NO**   At least under the majority view, based on a "misrepresentation" theory, a prior creditor (Cal) could not have been misled by the issuance of watered stock and therefore cannot compel the issuee to make up the difference. Under the minority "trust fund" theory, Arthur is liable to Cal. [§§886-890]

b. **YES**   Under both the misrepresentation theory and the trust fund theory, Arthur is liable to Cora, who was a subsequent creditor. (Some courts that follow the misrepresentation theory would require Cora to show reliance when she extended the credit.) [§§886-890]

97. **YES**   Most courts apply a "good faith rule" to preclude watered stock liability when there is no intentional overvaluation of property being exchanged for stock. [§891]

98. **YES**   Promoters owe a fiduciary duty to the corporation. Hence, if the promoters did not make full disclosure (either to an independent board of directors, *or* to all existing shareholders and to persons known to be planning to become shareholders), rescission is a proper remedy. [§§897, 902-903]

99.a. **NO**   Where the promoters were the sole shareholders, the common law view was that the corporation had no cause of action, because full "disclosure" had been made to all shareholders. [§898]

b. **YES**   Most courts allow suit by the corporation on the rationale that the later, but planned-for, subscribers are among the stockholders to whom disclosure must be made. [§§899-901]

100. **NO**   Preemptive rights at common law generally do not extend to the issuance of shares for property or services, the reissue of treasury shares, or the issue of previously authorized shares. [§§910, 912, 914]

101. **FALSE**   The shareholder may also seek to compel issuance of additional shares to himself. [§916]

102. **YES**   Although underwriters, like issuers, have a "due diligence" defense. [§§989-990] Additionally, full disclosure of arrangements between issuers and underwriters is required by federal and some state laws. [§924]

103. **YES**   Although section 18 of the Securities Act of 1933 exempts securities from blue sky substantive regulation, the exemption applies only to securities traded on stock exchanges approved by the SEC. [§933]

104. **NO**   The thrust of the 1933 Act is informational—*i.e.*, to compel disclosure, usually through the registration requirements. The SEC neither approves nor disapproves of proposed issuances. [§934]

105. **(A), (B), and (C)**   (A) is exempt under the "casual sale" exemption. [§951]

(B) is exempt under the "private placement" exemption, assuming that each purchaser acquires the stock as an investment and signs a letter of intent to that effect; and possibly under the "intrastate offering" exemption as well. [§§956-963, 971]

(C) is still exempt. The "private placement" exemption and the "intrastate offering" exemption are separate. Failure to qualify for one does not prevent qualification for the other. [§§956-970]

(D) is not exempt. The "private placement" exemption requires an intent by purchasers to acquire the securities *as an investment* (not for resale). [§961]

106. **YES**

Rule 144 exempts limited resales under specified conditions. [§§963-970] Also, the purchaser may resell without registration if he has held the shares for a significant length of time and is a noncontrol person. [§§964, 967]

107.a. **DEPENDS**

Only Orange is absolutely liable. The others may avoid liability if they exercised due diligence with respect to those portions of the registration statement for which Ralph seeks to hold them liable. Note that the burden of proof of due diligence is *on the defendants*. [§§988-993]

b. **NO**

Section 11 of the 1933 Act requires only a showing of the materiality of the misstatement; *i.e.*, that it concerned a matter that would influence the decision of an average prudent investor. [§§981-982]

c. **NO**

Ralph need not prove his reliance on the misrepresentation nor that the misrepresentation caused the decline in price of the stock. [§§984-985]

108.a. **YES**

Under section 11, *anyone* who acquired the securities without knowledge of the misstatement may sue; privity is not required. [§§978-980]

b. **NO**

Cynthia is entitled only to damages. [§§983, 994-995]

109.a. **YES**

Issuers and dealers are liable for the use of any material misstatements or omissions, assuming the use of the mails or any means of interstate commerce. [§§996-997, 999]

b. **NO**

Section 12 liability runs only in favor of the original purchaser, not a transferee. [§998]

110. **TRUE**

Sections 12 and 17 apply to the offer or sale of *any* securities, whether or not subject to the registration requirements. [§1004]

111. **NO**

Declaration of dividends is within the discretion of the board of directors. Absent an abuse of discretion, the shareholders have no power to compel declaration of a dividend. [§§1013-1015]

112.	NO	In states following the traditional par value approach, if there is no earned surplus (*i.e.*, current net profits are offset by prior losses) and no other available surplus account, payment of a dividend would "impair capital." The current profit must be used to "repair" capital. Otherwise, the payment of a dividend might jeopardize creditors and preferred shareholders. [§§1017-1039]
113.	YES	In states following the traditional par value approach, the excess over par value is paid-in surplus, which is a lawful source of dividends. Some statutes require that the shareholders be notified if the source of a dividend is anything other than earned surplus. [§§1019, 1028-1029] In states following the modern approach, dividends may be paid from any source, as long as the corporation's total assets are at least equal to its total liabilities. [§1039]
114.	YES	Assuming that it is not needed to repair the capital account, most states following the traditional par value approach would permit dividend payments from capital reduction surplus. [§§1018-1019, 1030-1034]
115.	DEPENDS	Most states following the traditional par value approach do *not* permit unrealized appreciation in value of assets as a source of dividends. A few such states do permit such use of revaluation surplus, especially if the asset is readily marketable (*e.g.*, listed securities). [§§1035-1037] In states following the modern approach, dividends may be paid from any source, as long as the corporation's total assets are at least equal to its total liabilities. [§1039]
116.	YES	Unless absolved by good faith reliance on corporate financial statements, the directors are liable—at least up to the amount of injury to shareholders and debts owed to creditors. Liability is joint and several. [§§1044-1048]
117.	YES	When the corporation is insolvent, each shareholder is absolutely liable for the return of the amount of the dividend. *If* the corporation were not insolvent, shareholder liability would depend on notice. [§§1049-1051]
118.	NO	Redemption must always be expressly provided for in the articles of incorporation. In contrast, a corporation generally *does* have an inherent right to repurchase its own shares. [§§1053-1054, 1056]
119.	YES	Unlike a redemption, which usually must be by lot or pro rata, a repurchase can be made selectively, subject only to limitations of fiduciary duty. [§§1054-1056, 1067-1070]
120.	NO	The availability of funds is tested by most courts **when the payment** (or each installment) **is due**. Most states permit repurchase out of only those sources of funds then available for a cash or property dividend. [§§1063, 1067]
121.	NO	A redemption or repurchase must serve some **bona fide corporate purpose**. Self-perpetuation in office, alone, would not satisfy this requirement. [§§1067, 1070]

122.	**GENERALLY ALL**	(A) is correct because most states require approval by shareholders of both corporations, and often there are special voting requirements for such a fundamental change. [§§1101-1103] It should be noted, however, that if Blue Corp. will issue only a small amount of stock as a result of the merger and will not change its articles, under some statutes the shareholders of the survivor will not have the right to vote. Such mergers are sometimes referred to as "small-scale mergers" from the survivor's perspective. But note that the shareholders of the disappearing corporation will have the right to vote on such a merger even if the shareholders of the survivor do not. [§1109]
		(B) is correct because the surviving corporation succeeds to the rights and obligations of the transferor by operation of law. No agreement is necessary. [§§1097-1098]
		(C) is correct because no further action is required to dissolve the transferor; it ceases to exist upon the filing of the merger certificate with the state. [§§1095, 1118]
123.a.	**GENERALLY YES**	A merger makes such fundamental changes in both corporations that, under most statutes, shareholders who reject the changes are entitled to force the corporation to buy them out. [§§1073, 1104] However, if the merger qualifies as a small-scale merger, some states would not grant appraisal rights to shareholders of the survivor. [§1110]
b.	**NO**	A shareholder must have voted *against* the merger and also have met other procedural requirements in order to qualify for appraisal rights. He cannot vote in favor, assess the effects, and then change his mind. [§§1088-1091]
c.	**NO**	Other factors such as asset value and investment value will be weighed, as will temporary market-price distortions. Furthermore, adjustments will be made for the effect of the merger on the market price. [§§1074-1087]
124.a.	**NO**	Approval is not required from *either* corporation's shareholders. In a "short-form merger" of a subsidiary into a qualifying parent, statutes generally permit simplified procedures. [§§1106-1108]
b.	**NO**	In a short-form merger, the shareholders of the parent do not have appraisal rights. However, the shareholders of Brown Corp., the subsidiary, would have such rights. [§§1109, 1114]
c.	**YES**	Under most statutes, the surviving corporation may issue cash, securities, or other property to the subsidiary's minority shareholders, even if it results in a freezeout. [§1187]
125.	**(A) ONLY**	(A) is correct; approval is everywhere required, although statutes vary as to the percentage vote needed. There are a few exceptions, however (*e.g.*, sales made

in the regular course of business, however, do not require shareholder approval). [§§1137-1141]

(B) is wrong because no fundamental change in Black occurs, and hence approval by its shareholders is not required. [§1137]

(C) is wrong because the test is whether the transaction will essentially terminate the transferor's business. Thus, the controlling factor is the percentage of *operating* assets sold. [§§1143-1144]

126.a. **YES**   This is a classic de facto merger. The use of Day's stock for the purchase and the projected dissolution of Night suggests that the ultimate effects are those of a merger. A court may require the same shareholder vote as for a merger. (But note that some courts—principally Delaware—do not recognize the de facto merger doctrine). [§§1119-1120, 1122-1124, 1128]

b. **YES**   The boards of directors may be required to submit the plan as a merger to both sets of shareholders and to recognize appraisal rights of dissenters. [§§1122-1132]

127. **YES**   Under most statutes, amendments to the articles must be approved by holders of a majority or two-thirds of the corporation's shares *and* by the board. [§§1146-1149]

128. **YES**   However, dissolution is discretionary with the court, which may—depending on the seriousness and persistence of the misconduct—instead either suspend the corporation's powers or enjoin future misconduct. [§§1164, 1174]

129. **NO**   Dissolution requires affirmative action by the corporation itself or by the court. [§1162]

130. **YES**   However, liquidation can be a long and complex process, so that courts may be hesitant to conclude that the business transacted was not incident to the liquidation. [§1176]

131. **TRUE**   A creditor's claim is superior to that of shareholders. Each shareholder is liable up to the amount of assets he received in liquidation. [§§1177, 1180, 1183]

132. **YES**   In this situation, the appraisal rights are not an exclusive remedy. Depending on the nature of the transaction, the 1933 Act and/or the 1934 Act might apply. [§1195]

133.a. **NO**   The Acme Board must authorize the transaction, but its shareholders do not vote unless Acme's articles must be amended. No offer is made to Star, *as a corporation*, and there is therefore no vote. Each Star shareholder, as an individual, may accept or reject the offer. [§1225]

b. **YES**   As controlling shareholder, Acme may vote to dissolve Star. [§1223]

c. **PROBABLY** Various federal and state statutes now require the filing of information statements disclosing contemplated changes in the target corporation should the tender offer be successful. The federal statute (Williams Act) requires filing of such information with the SEC if the target corporation is subject to the reporting requirements of the 1934 Act or its securities are traded on a national securities exchange. [§§1257-1258, 1273-1286]

Exam Questions
and Answers

QUESTION I

About a year ago, Daniel Dollar, an accountant, and Peter Prop, a salesman, agreed to form a corporation, Wingtip, Inc., to engage in the business of selling private airplanes. The planes would be purchased from a major private airplane manufacturer under credit arrangements whereby Wingtip would pay only a small amount down, and the manufacturer would retain a security interest in the plane. The business would operate out of rented hangar and office space located at a local airport. It would have only one salaried employee, a bookkeeper-secretary. In lieu of salary, Wingtip's salespeople would work on a commission basis. Prop would generally oversee Wingtip's business, would hire the personnel, and would be Wingtip's president, but would not be compensated (except by way of dividends); he would devote only about 20% of his time to Wingtip's affairs. The parties estimated that to operate the business on this basis, Wingtip would need $4,000 in capital. Of this amount, $3,000 would be put up by Dollar and $1,000 by Prop. However, Dollar would take 60% of Wingtip's shares and Prop would take 40%, since Prop was to oversee Wingtip's business while Dollar was to be involved only in important policy decisions.

Wingtip was incorporated a few months ago. Prop and Dollar put up the agreed amounts of cash, and 60 shares were issued to Dollar and 40 to Prop. Dollar then transferred five of his shares to his married daughter, Joan Green. Prop rented the hangar and office space, engaged the necessary personnel, made arrangements with a major private airplane manufacturer, and began Wingtip's business in the contemplated manner. Because Prop and Dollar were able to make major decisions between them, and because they were old friends, no formal board was ever designated, nor were formal officer elections ever held. Over the first six months of business, Wingtip broke even.

Recently, Prop learned that Flyout Corporation, a competitor of Wingtip, was going out of business, and was offering the 15 used planes in its inventory at a very low cash package price. Prop felt that this was too good an opportunity to pass up, and signed a contract with Flyout, on Wingtip's behalf, as its president, to purchase the 15 planes for $150,000. Prop realized that Wingtip could not pay this amount, but he was sure he could make the necessary credit arrangements. However, when Dollar learned what Prop had done, he refused to go along with the deal, and informed Flyout that Wingtip would not buy the planes. Flyout then brought an action for breach of contract, naming Wingtip, Prop, Dollar, and Green as defendants.

Assume that Flyout's suit is meritorious and that the judgment will be in the $20,000 range. Discuss the liability of Wingtip, Prop, Dollar, and Green.

QUESTION II

About five years ago, Oliva purchased a new highway ice cream stand for $15,000, the list price of the building and equipment. In the same year, Allen opened a new hot dog stand, at a cost of $15,000, on adjoining property. After four years, Oliva and Allen decided to combine, and to continue personally operating the stands. Without the aid of an attorney, Oliva formed the Cream Dog Corporation with an authorized capital of 50 shares of $1,000 par common stock. Pursuant to statute, she filed articles of incorporation with the secretary of state, but due to inexperience, failed to comply with the statutory requirements of local filing and proper publicity of the incorporation. Oliva told Rollins, one of her suppliers, of everything that she had done. Rollins offered Oliva $30,000 for the ice cream stand. Despite the fact that a number of independent appraisers had just valued Oliva's business at a maximum of $27,000, Oliva refused.

Oliva transferred the ice cream stand to the corporation in exchange for 30 shares of stock marked "fully paid." On behalf of the corporation, she offered Allen 15 shares for the hot dog stand. Oliva stated only that she was entitled to the greater share because her ice cream business had been making the greater profit. On the other hand, Oliva argued, Allen's business was worth no more than its original cost. Allen agreed with Oliva on the value of his business, but disagreed as to the valuation of Oliva's business. As a compromise, Oliva agreed to have the corporation issue 20 shares to Allen, marked "fully paid," in exchange for his hot dog stand. Allen agreed that these shares be recorded on the corporation's books as having been issued in exchange for $15,000 worth of property, and that Oliva handle all of the legal and accounting details. Oliva and Allen both became directors of Cream Dog.

Shortly thereafter, having examined the corporate financial statements, Rollins began to sell supplies to both of the Cream Dog stands. Subsequently, Cream Dog became insolvent, and Rollins obtained a judgment against it for $10,000. He is the sole creditor who remains unsatisfied.

Advise Rollins of his rights against Oliva and Allen.

QUESTION III

Machine, Inc. was organized about eight years ago, in a state following the traditional par value approach, by Bilker to manufacture small tools. Its authorized stock was as follows: 6% Nonvoting Preferred—1,000 shares at $100 par value; Common—200,000 shares at $1 par value. Bilker then owned some machinery that he had purchased from Abel and Cane in the year before for $40,000. It had a present market value of about $30,000. Bilker transferred this to Machine in exchange for 40,000 shares of common stock. Several days thereafter, Machine issued 30,000 shares of common stock each to Abel and Cane, who each paid $35,000 cash. A few days later, a half dozen investors bought all of the preferred stock for $100 per share.

At the first shareholders' meeting, Bilker, Abel, and Cane were elected as Machine's three directors. They continued to be elected annually as such until last month, when Abel died. The next shareholders' meeting is scheduled for the 15th of next month.

Machine's business has not done well from the outset. For several years, Bilker unsuccessfully attempted to interest some outsiders in buying some of Machine's unissued common stock. Early last year, the board became interested in diversifying Machine's business by acquiring control of the Crafts Company, a lawn furniture manufacturer. Crafts had just recently been purchased for $50,000 by Kanine Corporation, all of whose stock was owned jointly by Cane and his wife, Nina. Bilker and Abel were unaware of the identity of Kanine's shareholders.

At a Machine's directors' meeting in April last year, at which Abel was unable to be present due to illness, the directors voted unanimously to buy Crafts from Kanine in exchange for the 100,000 shares of unissued Machine common stock.

When Abel died, he bequeathed his Machine common stock to his nephew, Doltless. Doltless also owns 100 shares of Machine preferred stock, which he purchased in January of last year from an original owner.

Doltless wishes to be elected to Machine's board and to redress any legal wrongs done to the corporation. He seeks advice as to what, if anything, can be done toward these ends, and how he should go about doing it. Discuss fully.

QUESTION IV

Consolidated Orange Products, Inc. ("CO") is a corporation engaged in freezing and canning orange juice and other fruit juices and food products. It has eight plants located nationwide. CO's stock is listed on the New York Stock Exchange. Article IV(3) of CO's certificate provides for cumulative voting.

In connection with CO's forthcoming annual meeting, Donald Deem, a CO shareholder, has submitted the following proposals for inclusion in CO's proxy materials:

1. To amend CO's bylaws to provide that any director may be removed by the shareholders without cause.

2. To amend CO's bylaws to provide that whenever CO proposes to construct a new plant, it shall first prepare an impact statement showing the effects of the proposed plant on the environment (including details on air, water, and thermal pollution, if any), a copy of which statement shall be sent to each of CO's shareholders.

3. To amend CO's bylaws to provide that no new plant shall be constructed without shareholder approval.

Discuss which of these proposals, if any, must be included in CO's proxy materials.

QUESTION V

Hardback Corporation is engaged in the book publishing business. Hardback has 2,000 shares of common stock issued and outstanding; of these, 1,000 shares are owned by Denise Dure, and 1,000 by Stanley Stray. Dure oversees marketing strategy, and the development and maintenance of author relations; Stray oversees the administrative, financial, and editorial side of the business. Dure and Stray had operated Hardback as a partnership for 15 years before they incorporated for tax reasons. Hardback's board consists of Dure, Stray, and Wright, a senior employee.

Dure has learned that Stray proposes to sell his stock in Hardback to Lawrence Light. Light is a wealthy playboy who has always wanted to have an interest in a publishing house. Dure knows him, does not particularly like him, and thinks very little of his business ability. Although Dure and Stray never entered into a formal shareholders' agreement, Dure feels that a sale of stock by Stray would be contrary to what was understood, even if not made explicit, in the Dure-Stray relationship.

Dure now seeks advice on whether she can prevent Stray from selling to Light, and if not, whether there are any arrangements she can make, or steps she can take, to protect her economic interests against Light's lack of skill and judgment.

(Assume that Dure cannot afford to buy Stray's shares at the price Light is willing to pay.)

QUESTION VI

Jax, Inc. was incorporated in 2004 with 2,500 shares of common stock having a par value of $100 per share authorized. Of those, 2,200 shares of Jax stock have been issued and are outstanding. From 1998 through 2003, Jax incurred net operating losses totaling $80,000. At the end of 2004, the corporation had net earnings of $25,000 for that year. The Jax board of directors, consisting of Avondale, Barton, and Carlisle, met on February 16, 2005, and unanimously voted to declare a cash dividend of $10 per share on outstanding stock.

Pursuant to a bylaw authorizing the board to appoint officers and committees, at the February meeting Avondale, Barton, and Carlisle also unanimously voted to create an Executive and Finance Committee composed of Barton, Carlisle, and Walters. Walters was not a director or officer of Jax, but was a shareholder. The bylaw permitted, and the board resolution provided, that the Committee would have all of the powers of the board of directors.

On June 15, 2005, the board authorized the purchase by Jax of 200 shares of Jax stock, held by Dalton, at a price of $95 per share. Dalton had indicated that he was ready to sell them at that price to a competitor of Jax.

On July 18, 2005, the Executive and Finance Committee directed Jax to issue 100 shares of previously unissued stock to Ellington, as "fully paid" shares in return for Ellington's promissory note to Jax in the sum of $7,500. Such stock was issued to Ellington for his note as described.

On August 31, 2005, as president of Jax, Avondale wrote to Foster, a shop superintendent employed by the company who was retiring on his 65th birthday, as follows:

> In light of your years of faithful service to this company since it was established, I have decided that upon your retirement today, Jax will pay you a monthly pension of $300 for the rest of your life, so long as our financial condition warrants it.

Gavin, a Jax shareholder, seeks advice as to the legality of:

1. The declaration of the cash dividend.

2. The appointment of the Executive and Finance Committee.

3. The purchase of shares from Dalton.

4. The issuance of the 100 shares to Ellington.

5. The promise to Foster to pay him a monthly pension.

Discuss.

ANSWER TO QUESTION I

1. **Liability of Wingtip:** Wingtip's liability depends on whether Prop had authority to make the contract with Flyout on its behalf. There is nothing to indicate that Prop had *actual* authority. Wingtip's business plan called for the planes to be "purchased from a major private airplane manufacturer under credit arrangements whereby Wingtip would pay only a small amount down . . . ." Prop was to oversee Wingtip's business, but Dollar was to be involved in "important policy decisions." Certainly, a major deviation as to financing, source of supply, and quality of aircraft seems to be an important policy decision, which Prop had no actual authority to make. The issue then is whether Prop had *apparent* authority, or *power of position.*

An initial question in considering apparent authority is whether Prop was president of Wingtip. Although it had been agreed between Prop and Dollar that Prop would be Wingtip's president, he was never formally elected to that office. Nevertheless, Prop should be deemed Wingtip's president, at least as to third parties, and probably even within the corporation. It is characteristic of a close corporation that formalities are not rigorously followed. Prop and Dollar, who owned all but five shares of Wingtip's stock, explicitly agreed to Prop's being a president, and in all probability Green either acquiesced, or was represented in corporate affairs by Dollar.

Assuming that Prop was Wingtip's president as to third persons, he would have a president's *apparent authority* (power of position) as to those persons. There are several competing rules as to a president's apparent authority. An older rule, now discarded for all practical purposes, is that a president has no more authority than any other director, but the two rules that continue to have support are (i) that the president has power to bind the corporation to contracts within the ordinary course of its business; and (ii) that the president has power to bind the corporation even to contracts of an "extraordinary" nature, provided, at least, that the contract is one the board could authorize or ratify. Under the second rule, which is less widely accepted, Wingtip would be bound. Under the first rule, Wingtip's liability is less certain.

Because this situation concerns apparent authority, presumably the issue is whether the transaction would appear to be in the ordinary course of Wingtip's business when viewed from the perspective of the third party—here, Flyout. The amount involved may very well have indicated to Flyout that the transaction was not in the ordinary course, particularly because Flyout, as a competitor, may have been familiar with Wingtip's business.

On the other hand, Wingtip was engaged in the business of selling airplanes, and it seems reasonable for Flyout to assume that the president of such a corporation would have authority to buy airplanes for resale. Therefore, Wingtip should be held liable on the contract.

2. **Liability of Prop, Dollar, and Green:** Even if Wingtip is liable on the contract, Flyout would also seek to hold Wingtip's shareholders liable (because Flyout will recover a judgment of $20,000, and Wingtip has assets of only $4,000). Normally, of course, a

shareholder's liability is limited to his or her investment in the corporation (a shareholder has no individual liability for the corporation's debts).

However, two factors in this case might justify "piercing the corporate veil" and holding the shareholders individually liable. One is the failure to follow normal corporate formalities. Shareholders' and board meetings were not held, and officers were not elected. However, while lack of such formalities is often pointed to in piercing the veil cases, it normally would not suffice to justify individual liability in itself, especially in a close corporation (if only because it is seldom connected with the plaintiff's loss).

A very important factor is the possibility that Wingtip was undercapitalized. It is true that Wingtip was able to break even for six months. Nevertheless, $4,000 does not seem like sufficient capital for engaging in the kind of business Wingtip set up (particularly considering the kind of personal injury liability that might be involved in such a business). Few cases have rested individual liability solely on the ground of undercapitalization, but in this case a lack of formality is present as well.

It is also arguable that a contract creditor is in a weaker position than a tort claimant to base recovery on this theory, because he goes into the situation knowing that he is dealing with a limited liability enterprise and had a prior opportunity to investigate the enterprise's resources. However, the better view is that even a contract creditor is justified in expecting that the entity with which he deals will be capitalized to absorb the consequences of predictable business events.

Assuming individual liability would be imposed in this case, the next question is which shareholders should be liable? Again, there are conflicting rules. Under one rule, all of the shareholders would be liable as partners. Under a second, only the individual who actually conducted the transaction—Prop—would be liable. Under a third rule, which is probably the soundest rule, only the corporation's *active managers* would be liable—Prop and Dollar.

ANSWER TO QUESTION II

1. **Defective Incorporation**

The first issue is whether Oliva and Allen are insulated against personal liability despite the defects in the incorporation process (failure to file locally and properly publicize filing). Three questions must be asked:

(a) Was a *de jure corporation* formed despite these failures? The answer to this question is almost certainly no. For a de jure corporation, there must be substantial compliance with the statute. These are more than insignificant defects.

(b) Was a *de facto corporation* formed? Some modern statutes appear to eliminate the de facto doctrine. Assuming that Cream Dog's state of incorporation does not have such a statute, it is a close question whether Cream Dog is a de facto corporation. Clearly there was a good faith actual use of the corporate existence. The issue then is whether there was a good faith, colorable attempt to comply with the statutory requirements for incorporation. Since the defects were due to inexperience, the good faith test is met. Moreover, the most essential step, proper filing of the original articles, was taken.

(c)   If, however, the omitted steps are found to be too important for the enterprise to be a de facto corporation, the next question is whether it constitutes a *corporation by estoppel* as against Rollins? (That is, will Cream Dog be treated as a corporation for purposes of transactions with Rollins?) Statutes that put an end to the de facto doctrine may or may not have a comparable effect on the estoppel doctrine.

Assuming the applicable statute does not have such an effect, there is a strong case for applying the doctrine. Rollins dealt with Cream Dog as if it were a corporation. Because he had actual notice of the attempted incorporation, there was no causal relationship between the failure to file and properly publish (both of which may be seen as provisions directed toward giving notice) and the loss resulting to Rollins. All parties were proceeding on the premise that the liability of the owners was limited by due incorporation. Therefore, the doctrine may be applied, and Oliva and Allen may be insulated from personal liability.

(Note that even if Oliva is liable, Allen might argue that he should not be held personally liable, on the ground that he did not participate in organizing the corporation, and the court should hold liable only the person responsible. It seems doubtful that this is a good defense because Allen was also a director and, therefore, responsible for corporate activity. Some courts even impose liability on shareholders where a corporation is defectively formed.)

2.   Watered Stock

The second issue concerns watered stock. States following the traditional approach require that par value shares be sold for at least par. If they are not, creditors can require, upon bankruptcy, a stockholder who has not paid par (at least on an original issue, such as is involved here) to pay the difference between what he originally paid and par. The theory behind the par value rule is that creditors have a right to rely upon the corporation's receiving capital equivalent to the par value. The only creditor (Rollins) examined the balance sheet, and undoubtedly saw that the corporation did not receive par. Thus, in those states that require reliance to be proved by a creditor before he can recover, it seems doubtful that Rollins can prove reliance. (Some states, however, presume creditor reliance, and would put the burden on the defendant to prove that Rollins did not rely.) Other states do not require reliance. They treat the corporation's stated capital as a "trust fund" for creditors, and permit all creditors to recover irrespective of reliance.

Assuming that Rollins can recover if the stock was issued for less than par, was there such an issuance here? From the facts, Allen received $20,000 par value stock for property worth no more than $15,000 (under any theory of value), so Allen owes $5,000. Thus, Rollins may recover the $5,000 from Allen.

Rollins will have a more difficult time arguing that Oliva's stock was watered (*i.e.*, that her property was overvalued), because Rollins himself offered her $30,000 for it. Under the majority rule, watered stock liability exists only for **intentional** overvaluation of assets received by the corporation. If, as appears to be the case here, the parties believed in good faith that the property was equal to par value, the stock is not watered.

Therefore, in a state following the traditional approach Rollins will be limited to any corporate assets still available and Allen's $5,000 to satisfy the claim.

In a state following the Model Act, shares may be sold for whatever price the board of directors determines in good faith to be their value. Here, Oliva and Allen agreed to issue Allen his 20 shares in exchange for his hot dog stand. Absent a showing of bad faith, that determination would negate any claim of water that Rollins could present. Thus, Rollins would not be able to recover anything in a Model Act state.

ANSWER TO QUESTION III

1.   Doltless's ability to be elected to Machine's board will greatly depend on whether there is cumulative voting. In some states cumulative voting is mandatory; it is permissive in the rest, usually existing only if so provided in the articles or bylaws. Assuming that it exists in this case, with 200,000 voting common shares outstanding, Doltless would need 50,001 shares to elect one director:

$$X > \frac{200,000}{3 + 1} \qquad \frac{200,000}{3 + 1} = 50,000 \qquad X > 50,000$$

As things presently stand, Doltless will be unsuccessful because he owns only 30,000 shares. However, there are several routes he might pursue to improve his situation.

Doltless could attempt to assert preemptive rights in the 100,000 shares issued to Crafts. Because Abel (Doltless's predecessor in interest) held 30% of the common stock at the time, if Doltless is successful, he would get an additional 30,000 shares. This would give him enough to elect a director. This assumes preemptive rights exist (in some states they exist unless negated by the articles; in other states, the opposite is true).

These 100,000 shares were authorized and issued, and the general rule is that there are no preemptive rights in such shares (the rationale being that all shareholders knew that 200,000 shares were previously authorized and they had no right to rely on more than their percentage of that). But, in this case, five years have passed with the original percentage existing. It might well be argued that after this period of time the original issue had terminated. In fact, in some states, statutes provide a limited time, *e.g.*, six months, for the original issue after which preemptive rights again attach. Furthermore, there is the doctrine that if originally authorized stock is subsequently sold for expansion purposes, rather than just raising additional working capital to be used in the original business, preemptive rights attach. That would seem to be the case here. However, Doltless will fail in this preemptive rights approach because preemptive rights do not apply if the stock is issued for property rather than cash. It should also be clear that preferred stock has no preemptive rights.

Alternatively, Doltless could seek to get the issuance of the 100,000 shares to Crafts rescinded. If he were successful, it would take only 25,001 shares to get a director elected, and his 30,000 shares would be more than sufficient.

At the April meeting last year, only two directors were present, Bilker and Cane. Cane was clearly an interested director vis-a-vis the Crafts transaction, due to his holdings in Kanine. As a director, he was necessary for a quorum. This alone might make the transaction voidable at common law, as would the fact that he voted for the deal. However, in most states today, the quorum issue is not determinative, nor is Cane's vote, despite the fact that it was a determinative vote. The transaction would not be voidable under modern statutes unless it is unfair.

If the action to rescind is held to be a derivative suit because it alleges injury to the corporation, most jurisdictions would require Doltless to be a contemporaneous owner. As an owner of preferred stock (who would have a general interest in the integrity of the corporation's assets), he would meet this requirement. Even as an owner of common stock, it would seem that he could qualify under the exception for shares devolving by operation of law (here, inheritance). Historically the contemporaneous ownership requirement existed to prevent the buying of lawsuits by strikers (the reason for the rule has no application here).

A few states have statutes that require the plaintiff-shareholder to post security to indemnify the corporation for expenses. If there is a minimum percentage requirement (*e.g.*, 5% in New York), Doltless would be excused. In other states (*e.g.*, California), security rests within the discretion of the court. Doltless's action will benefit the corporation, so here too he would be excused.

Demand on directors, generally required in all states, might be excused here because it would be futile. Cane is interested and that leaves only Bilker. Demand on shareholders (a prerequisite in a number of states "if necessary") might be required, especially because it would be simple and inexpensive and might result in Bilker's joining the suit and making it more effective. The wrong (voidable board action) might also be considered subject to shareholder ratification. Cane would clearly cast his 130,000 votes against the suit, but because this is an ***interested*** vote, it clearly should not bar suit.

If Bilker casts his 40,000 votes against suit, this arguably could be a decision of a majority of the disinterested shareholders, having full disclosure, that the suit was not in the corporation's best interests. This might be held to be a reasonable judgment given Machine's alleged need for diversification by purchase of Crafts. (But some courts might hold the transaction void and thus incapable of shareholder ratification. *Note:* This might excuse shareholder demand altogether.) Or, some courts might find that there just are not enough disinterested shareholders, because Cane owns 65%; or, because Bilker might be a defendant in another suit by Doltless (*see* below), his vote might be considered interested; or there is the possibility that Bilker can be divested of 10,000 of his shares (*see* below), thus removing his edge over Doltless.

There are other possibilities in respect to the Crafts transaction that would provide redress to the corporation, but would not enhance Doltless's voting position.

It appears clear that Crafts's value was much less than the $100,000 worth of par value stock paid for it. Perhaps it could be argued that it was a reasonable business judgment for the board to believe that the value to Machine was $100,000, but this is unlikely due to Cane's interest in the matter and the recent market valuation of $50,000.

Usually, only creditors can recover for watered stock. However, an occasional case has permitted enforcement by the corporation, when it needs the money (such as the case here). Since this is the corporation's cause of action, the suit would be derivative, thus presenting the issues discussed above.

Apart from the par value rule, Cane's failure to disclose his interest in the transaction would be considered a breach of his fiduciary duty resulting in damages for the corporation (if not rescission, as discussed above). The corporation would at least be entitled to the difference between the value of the stock issued and the value of the assets received. It might even be possible to force Cane to disgorge his entire profit as a penalty and deterrent, for breach of fiduciary duty. This, again, would be a derivative suit.

The nondisclosure by Cane in connection with his "purchase" of stock from Machine, and his consequent breach of fiduciary duty would also appear to give Machine a cause of action under rule 10b-5, assuming some use of the mails or interstate commerce. Doltless could bring a derivative action for this, and this federal action would excuse him from any state security for expense requirements.

There is a possible argument that Cane appropriated Machine's corporate opportunity when he caused Kanine to purchase Crafts. This argument depends on facts not available—was Machine actively seeking diversification at the time? In what capacity did Cane learn about Crafts's availability? To the contrary, the facts appear to indicate that Kanine bought Crafts before Machine decided to diversify. Because Crafts was therefore not even in Machine's "line of business," the argument would seem to fail. But if an action lies, it is derivative because it was the corporation's opportunity.

Finally, there is Bilker's sale of machinery to the corporation. Again, under either valuation test, Bilker's stock appears to be watered to the extent of $10,000. (The fact that Cane and Abel paid $10,000 over par value would not appear to cure the defect. This would be a premium over par value and was probably so recorded. As such, it would not be so permanently "locked in" for the benefit of the corporation and its creditors.) But, again, most states would hold the corporation estopped from bringing suit since it was a party to the contract. Doltless was not a contemporaneous owner for purposes of a derivative suit, and he might well be barred by a statute of limitations. But if Doltless could counter all these hurdles, he probably would be more benefited by a suit to rescind the issuance of 10,000 shares to Bilker. The corporation, however, clearly would be better off if damages were recovered, and, after all, it is the corporation's cause of action.

Bilker was a promoter in 1991. As such, he was obliged to disclose his profits on the transaction. Although he was the sole party in interest at the time, it was clearly contemplated that other shareholders were to be brought in immediately. Under the better rule, disclosure should have been made to them. It may well be that Cane and Abel will be held to have had disclosure because of their prior dealings with Bilker in respect to this very machinery. Thus, Bilker's duty as to them was satisfied. But there is no evidence that the 1991 purchasers of preferred stock had any knowledge or disclosure of Bilker's profits— and they had a real interest in the integrity of the "cushion" or assets that Machine had.

Thus, as to them, it would appear that Bilker violated his duty of disclosure, thereby affording a common law cause of action to the corporation for his gain (also under rule 10b-5), which was at least $10,000: the difference between what he got, and what he gave up. But the suit is derivative, Doltless is not a contemporaneous owner, and what about the statute of limitations? Even if there is no contemporaneous ownership requirement, Doltless may be barred because he is Able's successor, who may have been estopped because of knowledge.

ANSWER TO QUESTION IV

Proposal 1: CO is governed by the proxy rules, because its stock is listed on the New York Stock Exchange. Proxy rule 14a-8 provides that management must include a timely filed shareholder proposal in the corporate proxy materials, unless the proposal falls within an exclusion in rule 14a-8. The only exclusion that might be applicable to Proposal 1 is rule 14a-8(c)(1), which allows management to omit a shareholder proposal if "under the laws of the issuer's domicile [it is] not a proper subject for action by security holders."

The issue is whether the proposed bylaw conflicts with CO's certificate. If it does, Proposal 1 would not be a proper subject for shareholder action, because in case of conflict between certificate and bylaw, the certificate prevails. Article IV(3) of CO's certificate provides for cumulative voting. This provision would be undercut by removal without cause, because the majority shareholders could eliminate minority-elected directors seriatim, by removing each one without cause. Then each vacancy could be filled by an election, for a single director, in which the minority could not effectively cumulate its votes.

It is true that under the cases the mere fact that a certificate or bylaw amendment weakens cumulative voting does not render it invalid, but Proposal 1 seems to cross the line—not only weakening cumulative voting, but effectively destroying it. Many statutes bar removal of a director if the votes against removal would be sufficient to elect the director through cumulative voting. On this basis, the proposed bylaw would be invalid if adopted, and the proposal to adopt it would, therefore, not be a proper subject for CO's shareholders.

Proposal 2: Proposal 2 raises several problems under rule 14a-8. First, it can be argued that Proposal 2 is not a proper subject under state law because it infringes on the powers of the board to manage the corporation's business. But Proposal 2 only requires a report. The decision whether or not to build a plant would still be in management's hands. (However, it could be argued that the *manner* in which decisions are made is itself a management function.)

Second, rule 14a-8(c)(7) permits management to omit a proposal if it deals with a matter relating to the conduct of the ordinary business operations of the issuer. Certainly, Proposal 2 deals with the conduct of business operations. Because the addition of a plant would be a major undertaking, it is not clear that it relates to the conduct of "ordinary" business operations, but for this purpose any decision within the general framework of CO's business would probably be regarded as "ordinary." However, the relation of Proposal 2 to business operations is only indirect.

The bylaw would not regulate how management operates the corporation's business; it would not even set parameters for management's decisions; all it would do is direct that when a certain type of decision is proposed, management must send the shareholders information concerning the proposal. While the decision could go either way (because the proposed bylaw would increase the flow of information to shareholders, which is the object of the proxy rules, and because it gives no direction or recommendation concerning how CO's business should be conducted), it should not be deemed to fall within the rule 14a-8(c)(7) exception.

Finally, the proxy rules allow management to omit a proposal if it deals with a matter that is not significantly related to the issuer's business or is beyond the issuer's power to effectuate. However, Proposal 2 is within the power of CO to effectuate, and it seems to be significantly related to CO's business (because it deals with closely relevant externalities of CO's operations). Therefore, Proposal 2 must be included in CO's proxy materials.

Proposal 3: Unlike Proposal 2, Proposal 3 directly regulates the allocation of powers over CO's business, by shifting the power to approve new plants from management, where it would normally be located, to the shareholders. Statutes sometimes provide that the business of a corporation shall be managed by the board, unless the certificate otherwise provides. However, Proposal 3 does not call for amendment of the certificate, and the statutory provision vesting management in the board cannot normally be varied (at least outside the context of a close corporation), except insofar as the statute explicitly permits. Therefore, Proposal 3 may be omitted from CO's proxy materials.

ANSWER TO QUESTION V

1. **Prevention of Sale:** Corporate stock is normally freely transferable, absent an agreement to the contrary. Dure's major argument for preventing Stray from selling his shares would be based on the fact that such a sale "would be contrary to what was understood,

even if not made explicit, in the Dure-Stray relationship." More specifically, Dure would claim that Hardback is really a joint venture, in which the prior "understanding" was preserved, notwithstanding adoption of the corporate form. There is some support in the facts for this position, since Hardback was operated as a partnership for 15 years, and was incorporated only for tax reasons. Certainly such an implicit understanding would probably be reasonable in almost any close corporation.

However, it is doubtful that a court would view this kind of implicit understanding as sufficient to override the well-entrenched rule that corporate stock is freely transferable, particularly when the circumstances do not indicate that the sale violates any fiduciary obligation that Stray might owe Dure. Thus, Dure probably could not restrain Stray from selling his stock to Light.

2.   **Protection of Dure's Interest:** The first point in a discussion of whether there are any arrangements Dure can make, or steps she can take, to protect her economic interests against Light's lack of skill and judgment, is to note that Dure's position is not as bad as she might think. The mere fact that Light holds stock will not, in itself, give Light any voice in corporate management, because the power to manage the corporation's business is in the board, not the shareholders. Light's holding would, of course, give him a voice in *shareholder* matters, but that would probably not be very significant as to the corporation's day-to-day affairs. In any event, with only a 50% interest Light would not be able to take any effective action as a shareholder, unless Dure concurs.

The immediate question, then, is whether Light could get a seat on the board. Because the directors are elected by the shareholders, and because Dure holds 50% of the stock, again the answer seems to be no (at least for the short term). Assuming Light could not cumulate his votes, the most votes he could give any one candidate, including himself, is 1,000. Dure could also cast 1,000 votes for any one candidate, and therefore if Dure does not vote her shares for Light, the result of any election would be a tie. In that case, a new (also futile) election would have to be called, and the old directors would hold over. The old directors, of course, are Dure and Wright. Assuming that Wright stayed on the board and did not side with Light, Dure would have a quorum for board action and probably could get the board to vote as she wished. Thus, at least for the short term, Dure probably has no great reason for alarm.

In the long run, however, such a posture might not be viable. Several statutes provide for the appointment of a provisional director if the directors are divided, but these would be inapplicable because Hardback's *directors* would not be divided. However, under the hypothesized facts, Light might be able to obtain involuntary dissolution on the ground of deadlock at the shareholder level (although some courts are unwilling or reluctant to grant this remedy in the case of a prosperous corporation, particularly when the deadlock does not threaten the prosperity). But while dissolution might be undesirable to Dure, it would probably be even more undesirable to Light, who could not carry on a similar business, as could Dure. (Alternatively, Dure might seek dissolution herself, on the theory that she could effectively take over Hardback's business on the dissolution sale, because Light would be in no position to do so. However, if Dure sought dissolution herself, she would be accountable to Light for Light's share of the prospective business opportunity, if she purchased the business, and probably this would also be true in a custodial dissolution as well.)

Taking into account the bargaining power of each party, Dure is probably in a position to strike a bargain with Light under which Light would get some, but limited, participation in business decisions of Hardback. Such limited participation might satisfy Light, because he is, after all, only a dilettante. Because Hardback is a close corporation, such an agreement would probably be valid at common law and under many states' statutes. If Hardback is incorporated in a state with special close corporation legislation, the articles could be amended to qualify it as a statutory close corporation, and ensure the enforceability of such an agreement.

ANSWER TO QUESTION VI

1.   **Cash Dividend:** In some states, Jax would not be legally permitted to declare a cash dividend. As of the end of 2003, Jax's capital was impaired in an amount of $80,000 (its accumulated operating losses). In states following the traditional par value rules, the $25,000 net earnings in 2004 is ordinarily not available for dividends, but must instead be used to repair the impairment of capital. As of the end of 2004, Jax has no surplus (assets in excess of liabilities and stated capital), which is usually required for the payment of dividends in states following the traditional approach. Rather, it still has a deficit of $55,000.

However, some states following the traditional approach permit the payment of "nimble dividends." Under this rule, dividends may be paid to the extent of current net profits (profits during the preceding year or two), even though capital is impaired (*i.e.,* even if there is no surplus). Under this rule, Jax could pay its declared $22,000 dividend.

In California, Jax could pay the dividend as long as after such payment its total assets were at least 1.25 times its total liabilities, and its current assets were at least equal to its current liabilities. Because the figures are not available in respect to these matters, one cannot say whether Jax's dividend would be permissible in California.

In any event, even in California or a nimble dividend state, Jax could not legally pay the dividend if it were insolvent or would thereby become insolvent. Moreover, this is the only test for payment of dividends in states following the modern approach. Jax is obviously not insolvent in the bankruptcy sense, *i.e.,* its liabilities do not exceed its assets, since it has capital of $165,000. However, insolvency includes inability to meet debts as they mature, and as to this the facts are incomplete.

2.   **Appointment of Committee:** Virtually every statute contains provisions allowing the board to create committees, and delegate to them certain of the board's powers. However, the composition and powers of the Jax Executive and Finance Committee conflict with those statutory provisions in two respects. First, the statutes typically limit committee

membership to directors, and Walters is not a director. Second, the statutes typically carve out certain powers that cannot be delegated, and here the Jax board delegated all of its powers. It can therefore be argued that the Jax Executive and Finance Committee was not validly created and constituted, and its actions are void.

As to the first point, however, unless the relevant statute provided that executive or finance committees consist of at least three directors, the Jax committee could have been constituted of only Barton and Carlisle. Therefore, any action (such as the issuance of stock in this case) in which Barton and Carlisle concurred might be deemed valid notwithstanding Walters's participation. Similarly, as to the second point, the fact that the Jax committee was vested with more powers than was legally permissible should not necessarily make invalid the exercise of a power that could be legally delegated, and the issuance of stock is a power that can be delegated to an executive committee under most statutes.

3.   **Purchase of Shares:** Under both common law and statute, corporations are empowered to repurchase their own shares. However, the general rule is that the same conditions that are prerequisite to the payment of dividends must also be met before a corporation may repurchase its own shares (*i.e.,* the corporation must have a surplus at least equal to the amount of the repurchase, in states following the traditional approach; and in all states the corporation must not be insolvent or rendered insolvent by the payment). Here, the repurchase amount is $19,000. Jax has no surplus whatever. Even in a "nimble dividend" jurisdiction, there is only $3,000 of current net profits remaining after the February 16 dividend declaration. As for the "California rule" and in states following the modern approach, the facts are not known, as indicated above. Thus, it would seem that Jax cannot legally repurchase from Dalton.

Many states do make certain exceptions to this rule and permit a corporation to repurchase its shares out of capital, under designated circumstances. Here, Dalton will sell to a competitor if not to Jax, but this is not within the exceptions to the general rule.

4.   **Issuance of Shares:** The issuance may be illegal on two separate grounds. First, states following the traditional par value approach require that par value shares be originally issued by the corporation for at least par value. Here, Jax issued previously authorized, but unissued stock, at $75 per share, despite the fact that it was $100 par. Unless the jurisdiction has special procedures for such issuance at less than par, this issuance is illegal. In states following the modern approach, shares may be issued for consideration deemed adequate by the directors, but it is possible the directors could be found liable for breach of fiduciary duty for issuing shares for less than the par value stated in the articles.

Even though the shares may have been improperly issued for less than par, the general rule is that neither the corporation, nor a shareholder in a derivative suit, can sue the shareholder for the balance up to par. Jax, having issued the shares as "fully paid" in an arm's length transaction, is ordinarily estopped to claim otherwise. However, in a state following the traditional approach, if Jax were to become insolvent, certain of its creditors may be able to sue Ellington for the difference between par and what Ellington paid for the stock.

Second, some states have constitutional or statutory provisions that a corporation may issue its shares only for "money paid, labor done, or property actually acquired." Ellington's promissory note (assuming it is not secured by adequate collateral), is *not* lawful consideration for these purposes. Unless this is a jurisdiction that follows the modern view permitting a corporation to issue its shares in exchange for a promise to pay in the future, the issuance to Ellington may be considered void and subject to cancellation by Jax.

5.   **Pension for Foster:** It would appear that Avondale, as president of Jax, has authority to compensate corporate employees, like Foster, in the usual and regular course of the business. Furthermore, because there is no indication that there is any conflict of interest in respect to this transaction, Avondale cannot be held liable for this promised pension, as long as the payment involves a matter of reasonable business judgment. Nonetheless, neither officers nor directors may "give away" or "waste" corporate assets, absent unanimous shareholder approval. Pursuant to this doctrine, it has often been held that agreements by the corporation to pay for past services is a waste of corporate assets on the ground that the corporation has received nothing in exchange. Furthermore, because Foster has given no consideration for the pension, Foster cannot enforce this promise against Jax.

On the other hand, some courts have held that a corporation may pay reasonable bonuses or pensions to employees for past services, if approved by a majority of the shareholders. (But there is no evidence of shareholder approval here.) In addition, some states have statutes that specifically authorize the board to provide pensions in recognition of past services. (But the pension here was promised by Jax's president and not by the board. Thus, unless this is a jurisdiction that grants the president authority to do any act that the board could authorize, the pension cannot be sustained on this approach.)

Table of Cases

Jacksonville Mayport, Pablo Railway & Navigation Co. v. Hooper - §165

Janas v. McCracken - *see* Silicon Graphics Inc. Securities Litigation

Janigan v. Taylor - §459

Jeppi v. Brockman Holding Co. - §1138

Johnston v. Greene - §§322, 325

Jones v. H.F. Ahmanson & Co. - §§704, 717

Jordan v. Duff & Phelps, Inc. - §662

Joseph Greenspon's Sons Iron & Steel Co. v. Pecos Valley Gas Co. - §276

Joseph Schlitz Brewing Co. v. Missouri Poultry & Game Co. - §173

Joy v. North - §245

K

Kamen v. Kemper Financial Services, Inc. - §§749, 751

Kaplan v. Wyatt - §762

Kardo Co. v. Adams - §101

Kardon v. National Gypsum Co. - §§369, 371

Katcher v. Ohsman - §635

Katz v. Bregman - §1143

Katzowitz v. Sidler - §918

Keller v. Wilson & Co. - §1160

Kelly v. Bell - §160

Kelner v. Baxter - §131

Kemp & Beatley Inc., *In re* - §1168

Kennecott Copper Corp. v. Curtiss-Wright Corp. - §1256

Kennerson v. Burbank Amusement Co. - §231

Kerbs v. California Eastern Airways - §355

Kern County Land Co. v. Occidental Petroleum Corp. - §515

Kerrigan v. Unity Savings Association - §330

Kidwell *ex rel.* Penfield v. Meikle - §433

King Manufacturing Co. v. Clay - §363

Kinney Shoe Corp. v. Polan - §117

Kirk v. First National Bank - §782

Kirwan v. Parkway Distillery, Inc. - §299

Klang v. Smith's Food & Drug Centers, Inc. - §1037

Klinicki v. Lundgren - §328

Knapp v. Bankers Securities Corp. - §740

Kridelbaugh v. Aldrehn Theatres Co. - §136

Kullgren v. Navy Gas & Supply Co. - §812

L

Lampf, Pleva, Lipkind, Prupis & Petrogrow v. Gilbertson - §479

Landreth Timber Co. v. Landreth - §944

Landford, SEC v. - §367

Leader v. Hycor, Inc. - §1081

Leventhal v. Atlantic Finance Co. - §§1165, 1172

Levine v. Smith - §754

Levisa Oil Corp. v. Quigley - §540

Levitt v. Johnson - §775

Levy v. American Beverage Corp. - §729

Lewis v. Anderson - §767

Lewis v. Curtis - §752

Lewis v. Graves - §749

Lewis v. Mellon Bank - §500

Lewis v. Powell - §665

Lewis v. Varnes - §500

Lichens Co. v. Standard Commercial Tobacco Co. -§1165

Lincoln Stores, Inc. v. Grant - §334

Lindy Bros. Builders v. American Radiator & Standard Sanitary Corp. - §827

Ling & Co. v. Trinity Savings & Loan Association - §672

Long v. Georgia Pacific Railway - §171

Long Park, Inc. v. Trenton-New Brunswick Theatres Co. - §§193, 638

Lovenheim v. Iroquois Brands, Inc. - §599

Lynch v. Vickers Energy Corp. - §§567, 711

M

MacDonald, SEC v. - §465

McCarthy v. Litton Industries, Inc. - §150

McClure v. Borne Chemical Co. - §808

McConnell v. Estate of Butler - §1064

McCrory v. Chambers - §159

McDonald v. Williams - §1051

McDonnell v. American Leduc Petroleums, Ltd. - §257

McNulty v. W. & J. Sloan - §1160

McQuade v. Stoneham & McGraw - §§193, 235, 637

Maddock v. Vorclone Corp. - §548

Marciano v. Nakash - §302

Maryland Metals, Inc. v. Metzner - §335

Marx v. Akers - §748

Matteson v. Ziebarth - §1186

Mayer v. Adams - §770

Meiselman v. Meiselman - §1168

Memorial Hospital Association v. Pacific Grape Products Co. - §276

Michigan Wolverine Student Cooperative v. William Goodyear & Co. - §1139

Miller v. American Telephone & Telegraph Co. - §248

Miller v. Magline, Inc. - §1015

Miller v. Miller - §327

Miller v. Register & Tribune Syndicate - §765

Mills v. Electric Auto-Lite Co. - §§605, 609, 614, 617, 825

Milwaukee Refrigerated Transit Co., United States v. - §122

Miner v. Belle Isle Ice Co. - §1165

Minton v. Cavaney - §115

Mitchell v. Texas Gulf Sulphur Co. - §§464, 468

Montecito Water Co., People v. - §92

Moran v. Household International Inc. - §§1242, 1243

Mountain State Steel Foundries Inc. v. Commissioner - §1066

N

Namerdy v. Generalcar - §108

Schwartz v. United Merchants & Manufacturers, Inc. - §275

Sea-Land Services Inc. v. Pepper Source - §112

SEC v. - *see* name of party

Shapiro v. Merrill Lynch, Pierce, Fenner & Smith, Inc. - §470

Shidler v. All American Life & Financial Corp. - §613

Shlensky v. South Parkway Building Corp. - §§291, 309

Shlensky v. Wrigley - §§160, 246, 291

Shores v. Sklar - §393

Silicon Graphics Inc. Securities Litigation (Janas v. McCracken) - §§384, 386

Silva v. Coastal Plywood & Timber Co. - §667

Sinclair Oil Corp. v. Levien - §§320, 694, 695, 696

Sisco-Hamilton Co. v. Lennon - §121

Skouras v. Admiralty Enterprises, Inc. - §679

Smith v. Atlantic Properties, Inc. - §§710, 1016

Smith v. Brown-Borhek Co. - §772

Smith v. Van Gorkom - §§247, 1289

Smith, United States v. - §399

Smolowe v. Delendo Corp. - §514

Sohland v. Baker - §879

Solimine v. Hollander - §833

Speedway Realty Co. v. Grasshoff Realty Corp. - §144

Stahl v. Gibralter Financial Corp. - §612

Stanley J. How & Associates v. Boss - §141

State *ex rel.* - *see* name of party

State Teachers Retirement Board v. Fluor Corp. - §418

Steinberg v. Adams - §620

Sterling v. Mayflower Hotel Corp. - §§319, 1184

Stifel Financial Corp. v. Cochran - §836

Stokes v. Continental Trust Co. - §§905, 915

Strong v. Repide - §362

Studebaker v. Gittlin - §572

Suez Equity Investors v. Toronto-Dominion Bank - §390

Summers v. Dooley - §38

Sunstrand v. Sun Chemical Corp. - §374

Superintendent of Insurance v. Bankers Life & Casualty Co. - §371

Surowitz v. Hilton Hotels Corp. - §793

Sutton's Hospital Care - §165

Swinney v. Keebler Co. - §729

T

T. Rowe Price Recovery Fund, L.P. v. Rubin - §291

TSC Industries, Inc. v. Northway, Inc. - §605

Tandycrafts, Inc. v. Initio Partners - §826

Taylor v. Standard Gas & Electric Co. - §§124, 127

Taylor v. Wright - §362

Teicher, United States v. - §399

Teller v. W.A. Griswold Co. - §1139

Terry v. Penn Central Corp. - §1136

Teschner v. Chicago Title & Trust Co. - §1193

Texas Gulf Sulphur Co., SEC v. - §§367, 370, 372, 412, 414, 473

Theis v. Spokane Falls Gaslight Co. - §1186

Theodora Holding Corp. v. Henderson - §778

Thompson & Green Machinery Co. v. Music City Lumber Co. - §108

Tift v. Forage King Industries - §§146, 151

Timberline Equipment Co. v. Davenport - §§106, 108, 109

Tri-Continental Corp. v. Battye - §1078

Trustees of Dartmouth College v. Woodward - §§1151, 1158

Tucson Gas & Electric Co. v. Schantz - §676

Tu-Vu Drive-In Corp. v. Ashkins - §666

U

Union Pacific Railroad v. Trustees, Inc. - §160

United Copper Securities Co. v. Amalgamated Copper Co. - §753

United States v. - *see* name of party

Unitrin, Inc. v. American General Corp. - §§1231, 1245

Unocal Corp. v. Mesa Petroleum Co. - §§1227, 1229, 1230, 1231, 1233, 1234, 1236, 1245, 1289

Untermeyer v. Fidelity Daily Income Trust - §756

Upjohn Co. v. United States - §795

V

Valuation of Common Stock of Mcloon Oil Co., *In re* - §1086

Van Dorn Co. v. Future Chemical and Oil Corp - §111

Van Kampen v. Detroit Bank & Trust Co. - §665

Veco Corp. v. Babcock - §335

Village of - *see* name of village

Vincent Drug Co. v. Utah State Tax Commission - §106

Vine v. Beneficial Finance Co. - §439

Virginia Bankshares, Inc. v. Sandberg - §§606, 607, 608, 610, 611

Vogel v. Melish - §669

W X Y

W.J. Howey Co., SEC v. - §942

Walkovszky v. Carlton - §§115, 121

Waltuch v. ContiCommodity Services, Inc. - §§835, 842

Watson v. Button - §782

Webber v. Webber Oil Co. - §219

Weeks Dredging & Contracting, Inc. v. American Dredging Co. - §1264

Weil v. Berseth - §633

Weinberger v. UOP, Inc. - §§567, 1081, 1187, 1194, 1206, 1207

Weiss Medical Complex, Ltd. v. Kim - §281

Wellman v. Dickinson - §1254

West Milwaukee, Village of, v. Bergstrom Manufacturing Co. - §149

Index

when excused, §§776-777

direct suit distinguished, §§738-745

exhaustion of corporate remedies, §§746-777

former shareholders action, §782

indemnification of officers and directors, §§829-845.
  See also Indemnification

  defendant loses, §843

  defendant settles, §§840-842

    public policy limits, §842

  defendant wins, §§832-836

  statutory, §829

insurance against liability, §§846-847

liability for court costs, §§809-810

limited liability company, §72

multiple suits, §780

piercing corporate veil, §§789-790

plaintiff qualifications, §§778-791

  contemporaneous ownership, §§783-790

  fair and adequate representation, §791

  shareholder status, §§778-782

procedural issues, §§792-797

  jury trial, §§796-797

  verified pleadings, §§792-793

reimbursement for litigation costs, §§823-828

  common fund doctrine, §824

  fee amount, §§827-828

  "substantial benefit," §§825-826

res judicata, §813

security for expenses, §§798-810

  attorneys' fees, §810

  court costs, §809

  covered expenses, §805

  discretionary, §803

  mandatory, §§800-802

settlement and recovery, §§814-822

  court approved, §§815-819

  shareholder recovery, §§820-822

state statutes, effect of, §§807-808

suits by directors or officers compared, §848

DIRECT SUITS, §§733-734, 738-744

See also Derivative suits

class actions, §744

close corporations, §744

compel dividends, §740

derivative suits distinguished, §§738-745

indemnification, §§829-838, 844-845. *See also*
  Indemnification

shareholder recovery, §733

special duty cases, §743

DIRECTORS

See also Conflict of interest; Officers

appointment, §§207-211

  number, §208

  qualifications, §209

  vacancies, §§210-211

classified boards, §213

compensation. *See also* Conflict of interest

  as director, §§236-237

  as officer or employee, §§238-240

    conflict of interest, §239

    extraordinary services, §237

    waste limitation, §240

conflict of interest, §§249-258. *See also* Conflict of
  interest

duties, statutory, §§262-266

duty of care, §§244-260

  abolishment of, §255

  amount of care, §§245-250

  bank directors, §250

  business judgment rule, §§246-249

  defenses, §§254, 256

  liability, §§251-255

    reliance on others, §§258-259

  shareholder ratification, §§260, 768-777

  standard of care, §244

duty of loyalty, §261. *See also* Conflict of interest

election of, §§86, 186

  by incorporators, §86

  by shareholders, §186

executive committees, §§229-230

functioning of board, §§221-235

  delegation of authority, §§228-231

  meetings, §§221-227

  noncompliance, consequences, §§225-227

  provisional directors, §§232-234

  voting agreements, §235

illegal dividends, §§265, 1044-1048. *See also*
  Dividends

indemnity. *See* Indemnification

insider trading. *See* Insider trading

insurance against liability. *See* Derivative suits

interested. *See* Officers

meetings, §§87, 221-227

  noncompliance, §§225-227

  notice, §222

  organizational, §87

  quorum, §223

  voting, §§224-227

nominal, §256

power to bind beyond term, §214

provisional, §§232-234

removal, §§187, 215-220

  by board, §218

  by court, §§219-220

  by shareholders, §§187, 215-217

  for cause, §§187, 215, 218, 220

  without cause, §217

right to inspect records, §§241-243

statutory duties, §§262-266

  criminal liability, §266

  illegal dividends, §265

tracing assets, §1183

nature of, §1175

shareholders' rights, §§1177-1179

M

MANAGEMENT AND CONTROL

See also Conflict of Interest

centralized, §4

directors. *See* Directors

limited liability companies, §66

officers. *See* Officers

partnerships, §38

shareholders' rights, §§183-206. *See also* Fiduciary
duties; Shareholders

    close corporations. *See* Close corporations

    generally, §183

MASTER LIMITED PARTNERSHIP, §79

MEETINGS

directors'. *See also* Conflict of interest; Directors

    noncompliance, §§225-227

    notice, §222

    organizational, §§85-87

    quorum, §223

    voting, §224

shareholders', §§537-565

    informal action, §542

    notice, §539

    timing, §538

    voting, §§543-565

    withdrawal of quorum, §§540-541

MERGERS, §§1095-1136

See also Appraisal rights

appraisal rights, §§1073-1094, 1104-1105, 1111-
1117

    exceptions, §§1113-1117

    procedure, §§1088-1094

        costs, §1094

        notice, §§1089-1092

    valuation of shares, §§1074-1087

consolidations, §1096

de facto mergers, §§1119-1132. *See also* De Facto
mergers

statutory mergers, §§1095-1118

    board approval, §1099

    consolidation, §1096

    contracts, §1098

    effect, §§1097-1098

    filing requirement, §1118

    generally, §1095

    notice, §1100

    shareholder approval, §§1101-1117

        appraisal rights, §§1104-1105, 1109-1117

            exclusivity, §1105

            no rights, §§1113-1117

        approval not required, §§1106-1112

    short-form mergers, §§1107-1109

    small scale mergers, §§1110-1112

    class voting, §1103

    percentage required, §1102-1103

triangular mergers, §§1133-1136

    conventional, §1134

    reverse triangular merger, §1135

    voting and appraisal rights, §1136

MINORITY RIGHTS

See Close corporations, Fiduciary duties; Voting rights

N

NIMBLE DIVIDENDS, §1022

See also Dividends

NO-PAR VALUE STOCK

See Par value

NOTICE

appraisal rights, §§1089-1090

creditors, §§1180-1182

directors' meetings, §222

mergers, §§1089-1092, 1100

private offerings, §969

source of dividends, §1038

transfer of shares, §§670-673

O

OFFICERS

See also Control persons; Directors

authority, §§268-278

    power to bind corporation, §§276-277

    president, §§273-278

    ratification, §272

    types of authority, §§269-272

casual sales, §§951-954

conflict of interest. *See* Conflict of interest

duties, §278

election, §§86-87, 267

insider trading. *See* Insider trading

suits by, §848

ORGANIZATIONAL MEETINGS, §§85-87, 222

notice, §222

ORGANIZING THE CORPORATION, §§80-109

articles of incorporation, §§81-84. *See also* Articles of
incorporation

corporations by estoppel, §§97-102, 105

de facto corporations, §§94-96, 106-107

de jure corporations, §§91-93

defective, liability, §§89, 100-109

organizational meetings, §§85-87. *See also* Organizational meetings

P

PAR VALUE, §§883-891

defined, §128

fiduciary duties, §§129, 896-903

    to corporation, §§896-901

        additional shares, §§899-901

        disclosure, §897

        sole shareholders, §898

    to each other, §129

    watered stock, §§885-891

        creditors' remedies, §§886-891

securities laws, §§902-903

PROXY SOLICITATION, §§566-621

See also Voting rights

expenses of proxy contests, §§619-621

federal proxy rules, §§568-618

    communications safe harbor, §573

    continuous plan, §572

    form of, §592

    jurisdiction, §618

    material facts, §§605-606

        "proxy" and "solicitation" defined, §571

        scope of rules, §§578-591

            annual disclosure, §§579-580

            proxy contests, §589

            proxy statement, §§581-588

            shareholder communications, §590

            transactional disclosure, §578

        shareholder lists, §602

    shareholder proposals, §§593-601

    violation of, §§603-617

        administrative remedies, §603

        causation, §§609-611

        "fairness," §§608, 614

        private suits, §§604-618

        remedies, §§615-617

        scienter, §613

        standing, §612

generally, §§566-570

securities covered, §§569-570

state regulation, §567

PURPOSE

corporate, §84

Q

QUASI-CONTRACT, §§132, 137

QUO WARRANTO ACTIONS, §§90, 96

QUORUM, §223

R

RATIFICATION

directors' failure to exercise due care, §260

directors' misconduct, §§768-777

interested director transactions, §§292-300

officers' acts, §272

promoters' contracts, §§131-144

REDEMPTION AND REPURCHASE, §§1052-1071

limitations on, §1061

    bona fide purposes, §§1067-1070

    insolvency, §§1062-1066

    rule 10b-5 distinguished, §1070

redemption, §§1052-1053

    source of funds, §1053

remedies for unlawful, §1071

repurchase, §§1054-1060

    effect of, §1055

    power to repurchase, §1056

    source of funds, §§1057-1060

        any source approach, §1060

        stated capital, §1059

REGISTRATION STATEMENT, §§934-1011

See also Securities Act of 1933

false, §§976-1011

REPURCHASE, §§1054-1060

See also Redemption and repurchase

REVERSE STOCK SPLITS, §1188. *See also* Freeze-outs

RULE 10b-5, §§365-481, 517-521

See also Insider trading

common law liability, compare, §§482-484

elements, §§371-395

    causation, §§387-390

    materiality, §372

    Private Securities Litigation Reform Act, §§376, 379-386

    recklessness, §§374, 386

    reliance, §§387, 391-395

    scienter, §§374-386

        motive and opportunity, §§380-385

insider trading. *See* Insider trading

jurisdiction, §§476-477

    state class actions preempted, §477

nondisclosure, §§366, 396-412

persons liable, §§368, 487-516

    aiders and abettors, §428

    insiders, §§366, 402-407, 429-442

    temporary insiders, §427

    tippees, tippers, §§419-426

section 16, compared, §§517-521

securities covered, §369

statement of rule, §365

standing, §§370-371, 436-442

statute of limitations, §§479-481

S

SALE OF SUBSTANTIALLY ALL ASSETS, §§1137-1144

appraisal rights, §1142

defined, §§1143-1144

shareholder approval, §§1137-1141

    failing circumstances, §1139

mortgages, pledges, **§1140**

"ordinary course of business" sales, **§1138**

SECTION 16

See Insider trading

SECURITIES ACT OF 1933, §§902-905, 934-1011

anti-fraud provisions, **§§976-1011**

basic provisions, **§§934-939**

integrated disclosure, **§§938-939**

registration statement, **§§935-937**

criminal liability, **§§1002-1003**

exempt securities, **§1004**

false registration statement, **§§977-995**

corporation absolutely liable, **§988**

damages, **§§983, 994-995, 1001**

defenses, **§§988-993**

elements, **§§981-985**

experts, **§§992-993**

materiality, **§982**

standing, **§§978-980**

who may be liable, **§§986-987**

general civil liability, **§§996-1001**

indemnification, **§§1005-1006**

rule 10b-5 distinguished, **§§1007-1011**

disclosure, integrated, **§§938-939**

effective date, **§948**

exempt securities, **§949**

exempt transactions, **§§950-975**

casual sales, **§§951-954**

control persons, **§§953-954**

secondary distributions, **§952**

dealer sales, **§955**

exempt securities distinguished, **§950**

intrastate offerings, **§971**

private placements, **§§956-970**. *See also* Private

placements

regulation A, **§973**

rule 145, **§974**

small businesses, **§975**

generally, **§934**

"offer to sell," **§940**

promoters' fiduciary duties, **§§902-903**

registration statement, **§§935-937, 946, 977-995**

contents, **§946**

false, **§§977-995**

waiting period, **§§936-937**

remedies, **§§976-1011**

security defined, **§§941-945**

shelf registration, **§939**

statutory prospectus, **§947**

SECURITIES EXCHANGE ACT OF 1934

See Insider trading; Proxy solicitation; Rule 10b-5

SHAREHOLDERS

alter ego theory, **§§111, 117**. *See also* Piercing

corporate veil

appointment of directors. *See* Directors

bylaws, **§190**

close corporations, **§§191-194, 199-201**

Deep Rock doctrine, **§§124-127**

derivative suits. *See* Derivative suits

dividends. *See* Dividends

election of directors, **§§86, 186**

fiduciary obligations. *See* Fiduciary duties

liability

corporation by estoppel, **§§98, 100-101, 108**

no corporation, **§§102-107**

statutes, **§§105-108**

management and control, **§§185-197**. *See also*

Management and control

meetings, **§§537-542**

organic changes, **§185**. *See also* Fundamental changes

preemptive rights. *See* Preemptive rights

ratification, **§188**. *See also* Ratification

redemption and repurchase. *See* Redemption and

repurchase

removal of directors, **§§187, 215-217**

right to inspect records, **§§674-692**. *See also* Inspection

of records

common law, **§675**

political and social interests, **§684**

proper purpose, **§§678-683**

proxy fights, **§682**

Securities Exchange Act of 1934, **§§686-689**

state disclosure statutes, **§§690-692**

statutes, **§§676-677**

types of records, **§674**

subordination of debts, **§§124-127**. *See also* Piercing

corporate veil

suits by, **§§732-848**

class action, **§674**

close corporations, **§744**

derivative, **§§735-848**. *See also* Derivative suits

direct, **§§733-734, 739-744**

generally, **§732**

suits by creditors vs., **§§111-119**. *See also* Piercing

corporate veil

voting rights, **§§531-649**. *See also* Voting rights

SHARES

authorization, **§§865-866**

classes, **§§851-863**

common, **§§852-853**

preferred, **§§854-862**

convertibles, **§862**

cumulative, **§859**

noncumulative, **§860**

participation, **§861**

redemption, **§856**. *See also* Redemption and

repurchase

consideration. *See* Consideration for shares

defined, **§849**

derivatives, **§863**

generally, **§§849-850**

issuance, §§86-87, 867-870. *See also* Issuance of
shares

redemption. *See* Redemption and repurchase

transfer. *See* Transfer of shares restrictions

SHORT-FORM MERGERS, §§1105-1108, 1113, 1208
appraisal rights, §§1108, 1208

SHORT-SWING PROFITS, §§482-516
See also Insider trading

SMALL-SCALE MERGERS, §§1109-1111, 1113

STATUTORY MERGERS, §§1095-1118. *See also*
Mergers

STOCK
See Shares

STOCK DIVIDENDS
See Dividends

STOCK SUBSCRIPTIONS, §§871-876
defined, §871
offer and acceptance, §§872-876
pre-incorporation, §§873-876
continuing offer, §874
irrevocable contract, §875
statutes, §876
post-incorporation, §872

STOCK TRANSFERS
See Transfer of shares

STOCKHOLDERS
See Shareholders

SUBORDINATION OF DEBTS, §§124-127
See also Deep Rock doctrine

SUBSCRIPTIONS
See Stock subscriptions

SUBSTANTIAL COMPLIANCE, §92. *See also* De jure
corporations

SURPLUS
See Dividends

T

TAXATION, §§6-8, 79
corporations, §§6-8
"eligible entity," §79
firm taxation, §6
flow-through taxation, §6
master limited partnership, §79
noncorporate entities, §79
Subchapter S corporations, §8

TENDER OFFERS, §§1207-1288
definitions, §§1207-1219
crown jewels, §1211
fair-price provision, §1216
greenmail, §1215
junk bonds, §1213

leveraged buyout, §1218
lock-up, §1210
no-shop clauses, §1214
poison pill, §1217
raider, §1207
standstill, §1212
target, §1208
two-tier tender offer, §1219
white knight, §1209
federal securities law, §§1248-1268. *See also* Williams
Act
generally, §§1209-1247
approval, §1225
conditions, §1221
defensive tactics, §§1226-1247
fiduciary outs, §1247
poison pill, §§1242-1246
dead-hand pills, §1245
fiduciary duties, §1243
no-hand pills, §1246
offer coupled with proxy contest, §1244
Revlon standard, §§1235-1239
best price for shareholders, §§1236, 1239
lock-up provision, §1237
no-shop provision, §1236
Unocal test, §§1227-1234
enhanced business judgment rule, §1228
intermediate standard of review, §1230
proportionality required, §1229
definitions, §§1207-1219
friendly vs. hostile, §1224
second-step transactions, §1223
toehold acquisitions, §1222
state law, §§1269-1288
constituency statute, §1288
first generation—unconstitutional, §§1270-1272
second generation, §§1273-1281
third generation, §§1282-1287
Williams Act, §§1248-1268, 1271, 1277-1280, 1286
antifraud provision, §§1262-1268
offeror's suit, §§1263-1264
target shareholders' suit, §§1267-1268
target's suit, §§1265-1268
first generation statutes, §§1270-1272
information statement, §§1257-1258
issuers' tender offers, §1261
management's obligations, §1260
notice of ownership, §§1249-1252
second generation statutes, §§1273-1287
Supremacy Clause, §§1277-1280
tender offer determination, §§1253-1256
eight-factor test, §1254
open market purchases, §1256
substantial risk of insufficient information, §1255
terms regulated, §1259
third generation statutes, §1286

toehold acquisitions, **§1248**

TORTS

no corporation, **§101**

ultra vires acts, **§167**

TRANSFER OF SHARES RESTRICTIONS, §§3, 650-
                                            673

common law, **§§654-661**

    consent restrictions, **§§655-657**

      options to buy, **§§660-661**

      reasonableness requirement, **§654**

      right of first refusal, **§659**

      transferee restriction, **§658**

generally, **§3**

notice required, **§§670-673**

"proper fund" limitation, **§665**

shares restricted, **§§666-668**

statutes, **§§662-665**

transactions restricted, **§669**

types, **§§651-653**

    mandatory buy-sell, **§653**

    right of first refusal, **§652**

validity, **§§654-661**

TRANSFER RESTRICTIONS

See Transfer of shares restrictions

U

ULTRA VIRES ACTS, §§164-182

contract actions, **§§169-174**

    common law, **§§169-174**

    executory contracts, **§170**

    federal rule, **§174**

    fully performed contracts, **§171**

    partly performed, **§§172-174**

    statutes, **§§175-182**

criminal actions, **§168**

defined, **§164**

erosion of, **§164**

shareholder ratification, **§166**

torts, **§167**

UNDERWRITING

"best efforts," **§923**

defined, **§921**

exempt transactions, **§955**

"firm commitment," **§922**

indemnification agreement, **§§1005-1006**

insider trading, **§427**

liability for registration statement, **§986**

regulation of, **§924**

V

VOTING AGREEMENTS

See also Voting rights

close corporations, **§§623-640**

directors, **§235**

shareholders. *See* Voting rights

voting trusts, **§§642-649**

VOTING RIGHTS, §§531-649

close corporations, **§§622-649**

    voting agreements, **§§623-641**

    voting trusts, **§§642-649**

cumulative voting, **§§545-557**

    avoidance devices, **§549**

      reducing board size, **§557**

      removal of minority directors, **§§554-556**

      staggered terms, **§§550-553**

    mandatory, **§547**

    permissive, **§548**

generally, **§§531-536**

proxy, **§§558-621**

    defined, **§558**

    expenses of proxy contests, **§§619-621**

    formalities, **§559**

    revocability, **§§560-565**

    solicitation, **§§566-618**. *See also* Proxy solicitation

shareholders' meetings, **§§537-542**

straight voting, **§§543-544**

VOTING TRUSTS, §§642-649

WXYZ

WASTE, §§347-358

See also Conflict of Interest

WATERED STOCK, §§885-891, 893-894

creditors' remedies, **§§886-891**

    misrepresentation theory, **§888**

    trust fund theory, **§889**

    value of consideration, **§891**

effect of statutes, **§§893-894**

    no-par shares, **§893**

types, **§§814-816**

WILLIAMS ACT, §§1248-1268

See also Tender offers

NOTES

NOTES

NOTES

NOTES

NOTES

NOTES